# Nothing but Love in God's Water

Volume

2

# Nothing but Love in God's Water

## BLACK SACRED MUSIC FROM SIT-INS TO RESURRECTION CITY

ROBERT DARDEN

The Pennsylvania State University Press, University Park, Pennsylvania

A grant from the Andrew W. Mellon Foundation supported the creation of an online resource companion to this book, which includes additional archival and multimedia materials. The companion can be accessed at http://pennstate.fulcrumscholar.org.

Some of the material in this volume has appeared, in an earlier form, in the *Huffington Post*.

Library of Congress Cataloging-in-Publication Data
Darden, Bob, 1954– , author.
Nothing but love in God's water / Robert Darden.
    volumes    cm
Summary: "The second of two volumes chronicling the history and role of music in the African-American experience. Explains the historical significance of song and illustrates how music influenced the Civil Rights Movement"—Provided by publisher, Volume 2.
Includes bibliographical references and index.
Contents: Volume 2. Black sacred music from sit-ins to the Resurrection City.
ISBN 978-0-271-07576-1 (Volume 2, cloth : alk. paper)
1. African Americans—Music—History and criticism.
2. Spirituals (Songs)—History and criticism.
3. Gospel music—History and criticism.
4. African Americans—Civil rights—History.
I. Title.

ML3556.d33 2014
780.89'96073—dc23
2014018652

The Pennsylvania State University Press is a member of the Association of American University Presses.

It is the policy of The Pennsylvania State University Press to use acid-free paper. Publications on uncoated stock satisfy the minimum requirements of American National Standard for Information Sciences—Permanence of Paper for Printed Library Material, ANSI Z39.48–1992.

This book is printed on paper that contains 30% post-consumer waste.

Typeset by CLICK! PUBLISHING SERVICES
Printed and bound by SHERIDAN BOOKS
Composed in MINION PRO, TRADE GOTHIC, CG EGIZIANO, LEAGUE GOTHIC
Printed on NATURES NATURAL
Bound in ARRESTOX

*Dedicated to the people who sang and marched and danced during the darkest hours of the civil rights movement and then wrote about it in such a way that the movement's days and music remain magically real and powerful even now:*

**Guy and Candie Carawan**
**Fannie Lou Hamer**
**Bernice Johnson Reagon**
**Pete and Toshi Seeger**

**"The preservers of history are as heroic as its makers."**

PRESIDENT PAT M. NEFF,
*Baylor University*

# Contents

# Special Thanks

As with the first volume of *Nothing but Love in God's Water,* this book would not have been possible without the generous support of many people, departments, and institutions. That's not hyperbole. Nobody (knowingly) takes on something this big without the encouragement, expertise, and generosity of a small army behind them. I hope you all know how grateful I am for your help.

More than two hundred thousand words later, I must again thank historians David Garrow and Taylor Branch for their encouragement before I embarked on this journey. David, in particular, provided invaluable tips, contacts, suggestions, advice, and support as I pursued this path.

Thank you to the following:

> Dr. Elizabeth Davis, Provost, Baylor University, and Dr. David Garland
> Dr. Lee Nordt, Dean of Arts and Sciences, and Dr. Robyn Driskell, Divisional Dean, Baylor University
> Dr. Sara Stone, Chair of the Department of Journalism, Public Relations and New Media, Baylor University
> My colleagues in the Department of Journalism, Public Relations and New Media
> The staff of Moody Library and Pattie Orr, Vice President for Information Technologies and Dean of University Libraries
> Interlibrary Loan, Moody Library, Baylor University
> Institute for Oral History, Baylor University
> Birmingham Public Library, Department of Archives and Manuscripts
> Birmingham Civil Rights Institute
> University of Memphis Library, Special Collections/Mississippi Valley Collection
> Center for Black Music Research, Columbia College, Chicago
> American Gospel Quartet Convention
> Black Gospel Music Restoration Project, Baylor University

Thanks to James Abbington, Eric Ames, James Barcus, Stephen Bolech, Gardner Campbell, Brendan Coyne, Doug Ferdon, Bob Friedman, Casey Graham, Steve

Gardner, Lance Grigsby, Terry Gross, Bill Hair, Barry Hankins, Hannah Hebert, Carol Hobbs, Carl Hoover, Kelly Hughes, Janet Jasek, Stanley Keeble, Margaret Kramer, Tim Logan, Bob Marovich, Harry Marsh, David McHam, Patty Mitchell, Alan Nelson, Patricia Nolan, Jennifer Norton, Mark Osler, Billie Lugo-Peterson, Emmett G. Price, Ella Wall Prichard, Laura Reed-Morrisson, Denyse Rodgers, Charles Royce, Becky Shulda, George W. Stewart, Darryl Stuhr, Tony Tadey, Talj Tatum, Alex Vose, David Wallace, and Michael O. West.

Thanks to those who paved the way: Horace Boyer, Ray Funk, Anthony Heilbut, John Lovell, Jr., and Jerry Zolten; to John Kutsko and Robert A. Ratcliff for the initial idea and early support; to Patrick Alexander, director of the Pennsylvania State University Press, for his continued, unflagging support and editorial expertise; and to Lindsay Denton, Rachel Payne, Jon Platt, Katie Buchanan Spitaletto, Ryan Pierce, Zhang Fangfang, Brittany Shaver, Yan Shi, Yueqin Yang, Lian Qiu, and Kelsey Prenger.

To my late parents, Col. Robert F. Darden, Jr. (USAF Ret.) and JoAnn Darden, who were always so supportive of me and of this project; and to my family, Dan, Ashley, and Rhett Barkley; Mark, Rachel, Asa, and Eilan Menjivar; and Van Darden.

Special thanks to my wife, Dr. Mary Landon Darden, the best traveling companion, co-interviewer, faithful supporter, eagle-eyed editor, and dearest, most cherished friend.

# INTRODUCTION

## *What Came Before*

PLAYBOY: *We Shall Overcome* has become the unofficial song and slogan of the civil rights movement. Do you consider inspirational anthems important to morale?

KING: In a sense, songs are the soul of a movement. Consider, in World War II, *Praise the Lord and Pass the Ammunition*, and in World War I, *Over There* and *Tipperary,* and during the Civil War, *Battle Hymn of the Republic* and *John Brown's Body.* A Negro song anthology would include sorrow songs, shouts for joy, battle hymns, anthems. Since slavery, the Negro has sung through his struggle in America. *Steal Away* and *Go Down, Moses* were the songs of faith and inspiration which were sung on the plantations. For the same reasons the slaves sang, Negroes today sing freedom songs, for we, too, are in bondage. We sing out our determination that "We shall overcome, black and white together, we shall overcome someday."

—MARTIN LUTHER KING, JR.

### What Came Before

The goal of these two volumes is to show the continued use and impact of the protest spiritual from the era before the American Civil War through Reconstruction, the Great Migration, the civil rights movement of the 1950s and 1960s, and beyond. Further, I seek to show both how the protest spirituals and freedom songs were used and why they were vitally important to the movement.

In volume 1, I wanted to glean as much as possible from the documents and oral histories from a century when the African-American experience was poorly documented, and to establish the unbroken transmission of these songs, usually (but not always) by word of mouth from the unknown "slave poets" to the lips of freedom marchers in Birmingham and Memphis. I hoped to show that the protest spirituals sustained and nurtured African-Americans through times when—to the white population of America, at least—they were virtually invisible, such as during the 1930s and '40s, when blacks were grudgingly included in the labor movement.

But more than just establishing this continuity, I aim with these two volumes to emphasize the vitality and importance of that music in the African-American's ongoing fight for justice and equality in the United States. To me, the fact that these protest spirituals endured and were preserved in an almost apostolic succession from the Civil War to the civil rights movement strongly suggests that they were *more* than just marching songs. Because of their direct connection to the African-American church and because of the black church's leadership during the civil rights movement, these songs bore the weight of a mandate from God. The protest spirituals affirmed and reinforced the profound statement that the God who delivered Moses from Egypt and the American slaves from bondage in the South was the same God who would free African-Americans in modern-day Dixie. For those who truly believed, this movement was more than a simple political movement. It was a religious crusade—one that could have only one outcome.

In their autobiographies and biographies, virtually all of the participants of the civil rights movement cite the importance of the freedom songs, martial hymns, protest spirituals, gospel songs, and occasional revised R & B song to the success of the movement. And with individuals like Bayard Rustin—a singer who performed with African-American artists who knew former slaves and who later became both a union activist *and* confidant of Dr. Martin Luther King, Jr.—it is a relatively straight line from the Civil War to the civil rights movement.[1] But to quantify the power and importance of that music, of those words, of that heritage, is the more difficult task for the scholar. That the participants agree, no matter how strongly, that the songs were important, even crucial, to the civil rights movement may not be enough. Men and women, young and old, faced death with these songs on their lips, *believing* the divine power behind these words. Some died while singing these songs, whether on a protest march in St. Augustine, in a crowded jail cell in Parchman, or on a lonely Mississippi back road as a hooded hangman prepared a noose. That makes these songs different, by a very real degree, from a marching song sung in cadence to make a long trek bearable.

Modern scholarship has shown that the spirituals of the nineteenth century were not just about longing for physical freedom in the world to come, but were direct challenges to the slave-owning states, albeit challenges usually couched in a hidden language that the overseers did not understand. The protest spirituals of the twentieth century took that challenge directly to the oppressors in an "explicit message of collective resistance." No more would the identity of the enemy be hidden behind the masks of "Pharaoh" or "Satan." Beginning in Albany, Georgia, specific obstacles (such as Sheriff Laurie Pritchard) would be named—and challenged.[2] In short, as Bernice Johnson Reagon, who began her long career of activism in Albany, would say of the combination of spiritual and protest song, the overt message of the songs became "where I am is not where I'm staying."[3] And lest we think that this process begins in the middle of the twentieth century, the influential protest spiritual "Oh, Freedom" ("And before I'll be a slave / I'll be buried in my grave") is recorded as having been sung during the Atlanta riots of 1906.[4] Likewise, a number of gospel songs—the heir to the spiritual—in the 1940s and '50s have been cited as commentaries against the existing order: "Oh Yes, He Set Me Free" (1951), "Jesus Is a Friend Until the End" (1952), "I Had a Talk with Jesus (1954), "Soldiers in the Army" (1956), and "When the Lord Gets Ready" (1960), among others.[5]

Volume 1 ends with the use and importance of protest spirituals in the successful resolution of the Montgomery bus boycott in late 1956. The newspaper accounts, diaries, and biographies emphatically record the widespread use of carefully chosen hymns, protest spirituals, and other forms of African-American sacred music, particularly in the regular church services that sustained the walkers and their supporters.

The presence and support of black churches intensified and, in the parlance of some participants, "sanctified" the power of the songs. Subsequent scholarship has shown that the "church's culture content played a crucial role in transforming individual discontent into collective interests and action." Political activists were usually church activists as well. The deep and well-disciplined organization of the African-American church had a "direct and independent role in facilitating collective action."[6]

One question that arises from that assertion is whether the "cultural symbols" of the black church—"gospel music, spirituals, prayer and social justice sermons"— are part of the process that births and promotes community action. The belief that those "symbols" did (and do) engender activism was shared by every interviewee in this book. Belief is a difficult concept to prove or disprove from an academic standpoint. But the studies that have undertaken to prove (or, again, disprove) that hypothesis have indicated their agreement, including convincing work by Sandra L. Barnes, who found "clear linkages between gospel music as a cultural symbol and community action regardless of church and pastoral dynamics."[7]

J. W. Alexander of the Soul Stirrers recalled that during the group's March 1956 tour, the group would request prayers for Autherine Lucy, the first African-American to attempt to integrate the University of Alabama, and for the bus boycott in Montgomery. The requests "electrified" their audiences.[8] Said Joseph Williams, Jr., of the Dixie Hummingbirds, "I believe gospel music, Negro spirituals, and gospel songs [were] the fuel that made the buses run, the trains run, kept the airplanes in the air, and kept us walking on foot when we were so tired with the Montgomery boycott situation. . . . The people would sing."[9] Robert Shelton, a music writer for the *New York Times* who covered the Albany Movement protests of 1961–62, interviewed a number of participants at the time. He reported that the "current phase of protest in song gained impetus" during the Montgomery bus boycotts, "gained momentum" during the sit-in demonstrations of 1960, and eventually spread to Nashville and beyond the following year.[10] It was also in Montgomery that singing became an essential part of the services during the regular mass meetings that were first held in sympathetic African-American churches. As T. V. Reed and others have noted, the singing of protest spirituals, carefully chosen hymns, and (later) freedom songs helped prevent angry and hurt participants from becoming a mob, "conveyed messages of quiet defiance," and clarified values. The singing was both a "rehearsal for collective activity and a direct part of the action." Singing is a nonviolent activity and the songs consistently and emphatically reinforced the "core value" of the movement: "nonviolence." In time, the songs sung at mass meetings would be used for tactical purposes as well.[11]

Part of the lack of visibility of religious-based protest music in the early years of the civil rights movement may derive from the scarcity of direct mentions of this music in the white media's coverage of King, the most visible and most widely covered of the movement's leaders. But King, who was steeped in the lore and music of the African-American church, peppered his sermons and speeches with lines from spirituals, gospel songs, and hymns. The white reporters of the day were rarely versed in the literature and music of the black church. Even if they caught the references, the reporters rarely remarked on those inclusions. "We do not understand the persuasiveness of Martin Luther King, Jr., our most important twentieth-century rhetor," writes Keith D. Miller in an article on King's epistemology, "because we do not understand his relationship to the black folk pulpit." For instance, in his widely reported "Drum Major Instinct" sermon, King incorporates lyrics from "Never Alone," "If I Can Help Somebody," and at least two other gospel songs.[12] If his white audiences could not recognize the words and their origins and context, his black, mostly church-going audiences most certainly would.

The presence of those undertones, of those coded messages, has meant that people, black and white, who were not part of the movement may underestimate the power of the protest spirituals. It has also meant that observers have misunderstood the urgency implied in the lyric, "We shall overcome someday." A word like "shall" sounds, to the untrained ear, passive and gentle. But there is an impetus to "shall," particularly when it is sung at a sit-in, on a freedom ride, during a mass meeting, or on a protest march, that *propels* listeners to action.

King often ended mass meetings with a call-and-response dialogue: "What do you want?" "Freedom!" the crowd would roar back. "When do you want it?" "Now!" would come the response. King would then lead the audience out of the church singing a protest spiritual, such as "Ain't Gonna Let Nobody Turn Me Around."[13] Conversely, "We Shall Overcome" would often be used to close meetings that did not require immediate action of the listeners. Instead, it was often employed as a reminder for listeners to continue to strive actively, to endure steadfastly, and—if necessary—to sacrifice again and again.

King was well aware of the continuity of the spirituals. In one published sermon, he talked movingly of the worst times of slaves—of the beatings, of the auction blocks, of families torn asunder. And in those times, just as in the middle of the twentieth century, the advice was, "Go on somewhere and just start singing." During the slaves' darkest hour, King said, they sang "Nobody knows de trouble I've seen" and, just a little while later, they were able to sing, "I'm so glad trouble don't last always."[14] As discussed in volume 1, different spirituals and gospel songs came to be used in specific circumstances and thus, by repetition, their power was reinforced. Even today, "Take My Hand, Precious Lord," is heard at virtually every African-American funeral in the United States. Its majesty and solace has been handed down from generation to generation since its creation.

Reagon is one of those rare academics who lived, participated in, and influenced the era she writes about as a historian and musicologist. While she is one of the great proponents of the power of protest spirituals and freedom songs, she reminds us that it was more than just the singing alone that transformed and galvanized the movement. It is imperative to remember, she states, that the singing had to be conducted within a sphere of community. "If you cannot sing a congregational song at full power, you cannot fight in any struggle," she writes. "It is something you learn." It takes commitment, passion, and courage:

> In congregational singing you don't sing a song—you raise it. By offering the first line, the song leader just offers the possibility, and it is up to you, individually, whether you pick it up or not. . . . It is a big personal risk because you will put everything into the song. It is like stepping off into space. A mini-revolution takes place inside you. Your body gets flushed, you tremble, you're tempted to turn off the circuits. But that's when you have to turn up the burner and commit yourself to follow that song wherever it leads. This transformation in yourself that you create is exactly what happens when you join a movement. You are taking a risk—you are committing yourself and there is no turning back.[15]

According to activist Willie Bolden, those in attendance at mass meetings were often "just so high from freedom singing, they didn't need any preaching, they were ready to go, and we just marched them right out the church."[16]

## After Montgomery

Though the actions of the movement in the years immediately following the bus boycott are not as well known (or as well chronicled) as Montgomery, a host of civil rights–related activities took place across the United States, all of which continued to churn segregation's waters. As Morris and others have noted, it was during this period that the movement experienced the actions of a new "cadre of social change-oriented ministers and their congregations" and the emergence of the weekly mass meetings, where strategies were hashed out and crucial information (including nonviolence) was disseminated, as well as the "adaptation of a rich church culture to political purposes" where "spirituals, sermons and prayers were used to deepen the participant's commitment to the struggle." In short, the period provided "pivotal resources for the emerging civil rights movement."[17] For the purposes of this study, of course, I will examine the impact of those spirituals (and the other forms of black sacred music).

When popular accounts of the movement in recent years mention the music, it is usually in the context of the Albany, Georgia, boycotts and jailings, which began in late 1961. Some books skim over the post-Montgomery years altogether, touching only briefly on the restaurant sit-ins and freedom rides. However, the protest spirituals endured and flourished during this era as African-Americans continued their systematic efforts to secure their civil rights.

Despite the Supreme Court's decision in late 1956 against segregation and other practices on Montgomery's public buses, various appeals delayed implementation, forcing the Montgomery Improvement Association (MIA) to continue raising money. Ruth Bunche and Aminda Wilkins cochaired a fund-raiser, titled the Montgomery Anniversary Concert, on December 5, 1956, in New York's Manhattan Center. The concert, which featured Coretta King, Harry Belafonte, Duke Ellington, and others, raised money for the drivers, to defray gasoline costs and for the continuously mounting legal expenses. Coretta King sang both classical selections and spirituals at the concert, including "Honor, Honor," said to be her husband's favorite.[18]

The eventual success of the Montgomery bus boycott spawned similar boycotts in Tallahassee, Atlanta, Miami, Mobile, New Orleans, Birmingham, and other cities, even as NAACP-sponsored legal cases slowly wound their way through the state and federal courts. On January 9, 1957, King joined a number of pastors, including the Reverend Ralph Abernathy, in Atlanta to found what would eventually be named the Southern Christian Leadership Conference (SCLC). King's connection with organized labor, through E. D. Nixon in Montgomery, A. Philip Randolph, Bayard Rustin, and others, meant that much of the SCLC's original budget would be provided by the integrated United Packinghouse Workers of America, just as Randolph's Brotherhood of Sleeping Car Porters had supported the MIA's efforts in Montgomery.[19]

While in Atlanta, King and Abernathy received late-night calls from Montgomery, where Ralph Abernathy's home and several churches had been bombed.[20] Violence, in fact, escalated in the South after the *Brown v. Board of Education* decision and the boycott's success in Montgomery. One study reported 530 known cases of violence, reprisal, and intimidation in the aftermath of the boycott and *Brown* decision between 1955 and 1958.[21] Following a trip to Ghana for that country's independence ceremonies, the Kings made a brief European tour, eventually returning to New York where, along with Randolph and Wilkins, King joined in the planning of a proposed May 17 prayer pilgrimage in Washington, DC.[22]

One of the earliest recorded uses of a protest spiritual in King's sermons would become one of his most enduring. At a Freedom Rally on April 10 in St. Louis,

Missouri, King closed his address with a final line that Clayborne Carson writes was "likely borrowed"[23] from a fellow pastor:

> From every mountain side, let freedom ring. Yes, let us go out and be determined that freedom will ring from every mole hill in Mississippi. Let it ring from Stone Mountain of Georgia. Let it ring from Lookout Mountain of Tennessee. Let it ring from every mountain and hill of Alabama. From every mountain side, let freedom ring. And when that happens we will be able to go out and sing a new song: "Free at last, free at last, great God almighty I'm free at last."[24]

After months of planning, and long, tough negotiations with the Eisenhower administration, King participated in the May 17 Prayer Pilgrimage for Freedom demonstration at the Lincoln Memorial. Though organizers, including musician-turned-strategist Rustin, NAACP executive secretary Roy Wilkins, and union legend Randolph, had hoped for more than 50,000 people, about 25,000 showed up (though figures vary). They included a large contingent from Montgomery. The pilgrimage was arranged, in part, to prompt the Eisenhower administration to begin forcefully implementing the now three-year-old *Brown* decision. For three hours, the peaceful assemblage drew national media attention, though much of it concerned King's closing Give Us the Ballot speech.[25] Also speaking were Wilkins, Representative Adam Clayton Powell, the Reverend Fred Shuttlesworth, Sammy Davis, Jr., Ruby Dee, Sidney Poitier, and Belafonte. The one musical soloist, Mahalia Jackson, sang the patriotic hymn "My Country 'Tis of Thee," which Marian Anderson had "politicized" at the Lincoln Memorial years earlier, and the emotional protest spiritual "I've Been 'Buked and I've Been Scorned."[26]

By the spring of 1957, following resolution of the bus boycott and the Prayer Pilgrimage, King had become the undisputed face of the civil rights movement in the United States, meriting feature-length (and sympathetic) profiles in *Time* magazine, the *New York Times*, and an appearance on *Meet the Press*. While there were many efforts by African-Americans across the United States to integrate the schools that year, the eyes of the nation turned to Little Rock, Arkansas, from September through November, with the attempt by nine students to integrate the local high school, the defiance of Governor Orval Faubus, and Eisenhower's subsequent decision to send the National Guard to protect the young students. In the aftermath of Little Rock, the administration oversaw passage of the virtually toothless Civil Rights Act of 1957.[27]

Throughout this period, the Highlander Folk School in East Tennessee continued operation, teaching leadership courses on integration, voting rights, and nonviolence, as well as the use of music as an educational and organizing tool. The school survived despite ferocious opposition from conservative Tennessee authorities. One early attendee had been Rosa Parks, and it was at Highlander that cofounder Myles Horton's wife, Zilphia, had learned how striking North Carolina tobacco workers had transformed the old gospel song "I'll Overcome Someday" into "We Will Overcome" and, along with Pete Seeger, had changed it to "We Shall Overcome." Seeger, Horton, and young activist Guy Carawan taught an early version of the song at the near-weekly Highlander workshops to civil rights activists from across the South.[28] Among the early participants was a young John Lewis, who witnessed a performance of "We Shall Overcome" by Seeger and a passionate closing message by Horton, and then returned to Nashville "on fire" for justice.[29] Carawan, like Seeger and the Hortons, had learned from the labor movement that "group singing could be a strong unifying force in struggle," especially the more familiar songs. Since many of the African-Americans came from predominantly religious backgrounds, those "familiar songs" were the protest spirituals. At one such workshop, activist C. T. Vivian recalled that Carawan would offer a detailed background on a spiritual, then teach it to attendees: "And little by little, spiritual after spiritual began to appear—with new sets of words, new changes, 'Keep Your Eyes on the Prize, Hold On' or 'I'm Gonna Sit at the Welcome Table.' Once we had seen it done, we could begin to do it."[30]

One of the first times King is recorded as hearing the new rendition of "We Shall Overcome" occurred during a workshop honoring Highlander's twenty-fifth anniversary, Labor Day 1957. Afterward, King kept humming the song's melody. On the way home, he told Abernathy and activist Anne Braden, "There's something about that song that haunts you."[31]

In July 1959, Carawan, now musical director of Highlander, sent a letter to each of the communities where Highlander had helped establish citizenship schools, offering his services as a song leader. The letter also outlined the organization's intention to publish a book of integration-related songs, to hold song-leader workshops, to release vinyl recordings of antisegregation songs, and to sponsor integrated music festivals. All of these ambitious goals became a reality within five years.[32]

Long antagonistic to the integrated setting, Tennessee state troopers and sheriff's deputies finally raided the Highlander campus, including several private homes, during a desegregation workshop on July 31, 1959, and arrested a number of people, including Carawan.[33] As authorities rampaged through the buildings, ostensibly looking for illegal alcohol, one participant was arrested for merely strumming the chords to "We Shall Overcome." Blockaded into one darkened room while the search continued, educator and activist Septima Clark suggested that the staff sing, which they did. Moments later, a policeman barked at those present, "All right, you can sing. But don't sing so loud!" The group sang "We Shall Overcome" and other hymns until the nightmarish evening ended.[34] State pressure eventually forced the closing of Highlander's Monteagle campus, though the school reopened with a slightly different name in Knoxville in 1961 and continued its workshops.[35]

Elsewhere, Mahalia Jackson's visibility among both white and black audiences continued to soar. On Sunday, July 7, 1957, she became the first gospel artist to perform at the Newport Jazz Festival, accompanied by a choir that included Clara

Ward and Marion Williams.[36] The performance was broadcast over both the Voice of America and NBC Radio. At one point, while Jackson was singing, jazz legend Mary Lou Williams told promoter Joe Bostic, "That goddam woman makes cold chills run up and down my spine." Press and magazine reviews were "rapturous." The following year at Newport, Jackson sang "Keep Your Hand on the Plow" and was accompanied by Ellington's band for a suite he had composed especially for her, "Come Sunday Morning."[37] Director Bert Stern's documentary, *Jazz on a Summer's Day*, chronicles the 1958 festival and spotlights Jackson as the artist "identified as the star of the festival." Stern closed his well-received film with Jackson and Ellington's performance.[38] While she was always identified with the Democratic Party, Jackson sang four selections at a surprise sixty-eighth birthday party for Eisenhower in October 1959.[39]

As for King himself, during the fall of 1958 he would be arrested, freed, see the publication of his book *Stride Toward Freedom,* and stabbed by a mentally disturbed woman in New York. In February and March of 1959, King fulfilled a longtime dream to visit India and various sites and people related to Mahatma Gandhi. Joined by Coretta and author Lawrence Reddick, King toured the country, making pilgrimages, meeting prominent Indian politicians and religious figures, and speaking widely, usually accompanied by Coretta, who sang spirituals (which, he writes, Indian audiences "loved").[40] The music critic for the influential *Times of India* praised the "grace and beauty of expression" of Coretta's spirituals, writing that her performance of "Nobody Knows the Trouble I've Seen" featured "sweet and plaintive strains" as she "invested her songs with a rare glow and intensity of feeling."[41]

The year 1960, building on the slow but important work of previous years, saw a marked rise in antisegregation actions across the United States. In retrospect, we know that some of the protest spirituals and freedom songs honed in the mass meetings of Albany, Selma, and Birmingham would eventually transcend the African-American community. Within a few years, they would become part of the national dialogue, used by presidents and protesters alike. Appalachian miners at the Pittston Coal Company sang "We Shall Overcome" on protest lines in 1989. Chinese pro-democracy demonstrators that same year wrote "We Shall Overcome" on their headbands and T-shirts.[42] During the breakup of the Soviet Union and the dissolution of Yugoslavia, televised clips of the events showed workers singing "We Shall Overcome."[43] And the song was sung by pro-democracy protesters in Egypt during the Arab Spring of 2010–11, where comic books featuring King's words and beliefs were widely circulated in Egypt and throughout the Middle East.[44]

According to Reagon, it is the singing of songs that creates the "revolution of courage" in the singers. It is in that act, she says, that "you raise a freedom song."[45] In 1960, the freedom song was raised in such a way that forever changed America— and the world.

# 1

## THE SIT-INS

Without music, and I mean this, without music, the Civil Rights Movement would have been like a bird without wings.

—REPRESENTATIVE JOHN LEWIS

*I long to see that great day come,*
*When everybody will be as one,*
*When there will be no separating,*
*When there will be no discriminating.*

—"MY PRAYER FOR TOMORROW,"
THE DIXIE HUMMINGBIRDS

Between 1957 and 1960, the NAACP Youth Councils and the Congress on Racial Equality (CORE) sponsored a series of sixteen sit-ins, protests where primarily African-American demonstrators sat quietly and asked for service at segregated diners and restaurants. The two organizations had built extensive communication and support systems, with the youthful participants carefully selected and trained. One of the sixteen cities was Oklahoma City, where the Youth Council took part in a series of sit-ins in August 1958. Among advisor Clara Luper's (who herself had studied King's writings on nonviolence) protégées was 14-year-old Barbara Ann Posey, who led the sit-ins. Eventually, sixty-one restaurants opened their doors to African-Americans in Oklahoma City.[1]

But when four North Carolina Agricultural & Technical State University students occupied seats at a Woolworth's lunch counter in Greensboro on February 1, 1960, few observers would have guessed that this particular sit-in would serve as a catalyst for what followed. The state at the time had a number of courageous NAACP branches, many with a history of activism.[2] But the four young men in

**FIGURE 1**

A sit-in at the Woolworth's lunch counter in
Tallahassee, Florida on March 13, 1960. Photo
courtesy of State Archives of Florida.

Greensboro "just got tired talking . . . and decided to do something" about discrimination at the lunch counter, as Joseph McNeill told the *Pittsburgh Courier*.[3] Not surprisingly, one of the four, Ezell Blair, Jr., had heard King speak in Greensboro two years earlier.[4] Within days, other A&T students joined them. Within a week, similar sit-ins were under way in Charlotte and Durham. More sit-ins soon spread across the South from Portsmouth, Virginia, to Tallahassee, Florida.[5]

Subsequent sit-ins were staged by (mostly) students with a wide variety of backgrounds and training, including some with nonviolent direct action training from CORE. Nearly all were physically harassed during their sit-ins by managers and staff, white patrons, local police, and "hoodlums." Participants were encouraged to dress well, speak respectfully, and ignore verbal and physical violence. The 1960 sit-in model was ultimately so successful that it would continue to be adopted by protesters for decades to come.[6] The sit-ins themselves were almost always silent, since protesters did not want to provoke already hostile crowds nor give store or restaurant owners or the police an excuse to arrest them for "disturbing the peace." The purpose was to expose segregation—that blacks were being denied service and were subsequently arrested solely on the basis of their race.[7]

Less than two weeks after Greensboro, forty students staged a sit-in at the Woolworth's in Nashville, ignoring a snowstorm, cigarette burns from hecklers, and the bloody beating of a supportive white student from Vanderbilt. Among the participants in Nashville were John Lewis, Bernard Lafayette, Diane Nash, James Bevel, and John Lawson, some of whom had also first heard and responded to King in the previous years. Seventy-six students were imprisoned.[8] The protests continued as still more students were arrested and spent varying amounts of time in Nashville jails until the first wave of boycotts was finally called off in May. Based in part on the Montgomery model, regular mass meetings in the city's African-American churches were immediately organized to support the students. Once again, singing was an integral part of those services.[9] According to singer and teacher Guy Carawan, the sit-ins themselves had an almost immediate effect on the singing. Once dominated by "stiff" hymns, the church-based mass meetings now led by the Nashville students featured the "new freedom songs that were sung with hand clapping and in a rural free-swinging style." This made Nashville, he writes, "the first city to develop a diversified repertoire of freedom songs."[10]

As the public demonstrations in support of the sit-ins and jailed protesters grew, students sang in the streets. And when they were arrested, they sang in Nashville's jails. Among the songs sung in jail was a new version of the old International Workers of the World parody, "They Go Wild Over Me," first performed by Candie Anderson (later Carawan), which continued the legacy of protest labor songs.[11] For Lewis, the thrill of the sit-ins was tempered by the fear of violence at the hands of local thugs and arrest by police. Once, during a snowstorm on February 29, both happened: "We went to jail by the hundreds, singing 'We Shall Overcome,' and it was fantastic, just a moving thing," he said. "You had the fear, but you had to go on in spite of that, because you felt that you were doing something that *had* to be

**FIGURE 2**

Led by James Bevel (second from right), demonstrators protest the segregated Post House Restaurant inside the Greyhound Bus Station in Nashville, March 3, 1960. Photo: *Nashville Banner* Archives, Nashville Public Library Digital Collection (Vic Cooley).

done, and in the process maybe you could make a contribution toward ending the system of segregation."[12] The earliest spiritual that Lewis remembered from Nashville was "Amen," a single-word African-American "spiritual chant": "This song represented the coming together. You really felt it—it was like you were part of the crusade, a holy crusade. You felt uplifted and involved in the great battle and a great struggle. We had hundreds and thousands of students from the different colleges and universities around Nashville gathering downtown in a Black Baptist church. That particular song . . . became the heart of the Nashville movement." "The power of this traditional song came from the richness of Afro-American harmonic techniques and improvisation in choral singing," adds Bernice Johnson Reagon. "Within the Nashville setting, it gained a new force by being wedded to a dynamic social upheaval. A simple word change from 'Amen' to 'Freedom' made it a musical statement of the ultimate national goal of the student activists."[13]

Toward the end of the protests, King had been scheduled to speak in Nashville's War Memorial Auditorium, but the city broke the contract at the last minute, forcing a relocation to the Fisk campus. As the crowd filed in to the venue, someone, perhaps James Bevel, suddenly sang out, cutting through the noise, "Oh, tell me how did you feel when you / Come out the wilderness." Immediately, the audience joined in, rocking and clapping on the beat: "Oh, tell me will you fight for freedom / When you / Come out the wilderness." King "eloquently proclaimed his appreciation for the spirited young people who packed the hall."[14]

In the spring of 1960, the number of the sit-in protests slowed. Several national chain stores had desegregated, but the bulk of locally owned restaurants and department stores still resisted. Sit-ins, stand-ins, wade-ins, and other such protests were instituted, and continued, particularly in the South, for several more years. During April 1960, two hundred students, many of whom had been involved with the various sit-ins, converged on the campus of Shaw University in Raleigh, North Carolina. The students met at the urging of Ella Baker, a longtime civil rights veteran, then employed by the SCLC. The keynote speaker was Lawson, a divinity student at American Baptist Theological Seminary in Nashville. It was at this meeting that the Student Nonviolent Coordinating Committee (SNCC, quickly dubbed "Snick" by its members and friends) was formed.[15] Among those invited to Raleigh was Carawan, who performed and taught the participants the civil rights songs he had been collecting. When Carawan closed the first evening with "We Shall Overcome," the audience spontaneously stood, joined hands, and sang along.[16] Jane Stembridge, the SNCC's first staff member, remembered being electrified by hearing "We Shall Overcome" that evening: "There was no SNCC, no ad hoc committees, no funds, just people who didn't know what to expect who came and released the common vision of that song."[17] Another attendee, Cordell Reagon, recalled that it was on that night that the tradition began of linking hands and crossing arms right over left while singing "We Shall Overcome." "It became the theme song of the movement, closing all mass meetings and raised on all the battlefields when needed."[18]

Once the conference ended, the attendees took "We Shall Overcome" and the other protest spirituals—the term "freedom songs" was not yet in the movement's vocabulary—home with them. In time, "We Shall Overcome" became so pervasive that singers used it in a variety of settings, for a variety of reasons. Julius Lester recalls an occasion where protesters returning from a demonstration in Nashville were forced to wade through the middle of an angry mob of whites throwing rocks and bottles. As they walked, the protesters sang "We Shall Overcome." "This was not a pretentious display of non-violence," writes Lester. "The song was simply their only recourse at a time when nothing else would have helped."[19]

Carawan participated in the sit-ins as well, writing about his experiences for the folk music publication *Sing Out,* chronicling what he heard being sung by the demonstrators: "They adapt everything. Blues, rock-and-roll songs, pop ballads, hillbilly songs, gospels and spirituals were all used and freely adapted. I began to realize that folk music was more than a matter of musical forms. I wish that some of our 'experts' on folk song could hear these Negro 'sit-in' veterans as they sang their songs." Carawan also noted the popularity of "You Better Leave Segregation Alone," "I Shall Not Be Moved," "This Little Light of Mine," and "Keep Your Eyes on the Prize." His article included the words and music to "Sit Down, Children," as adapted by Betty Sanders, and "inspired by the lunch counter sit-ins": "Sit down children / Sit down in every Jim Crow state and town / Bear your cross and wear your crown / Sit down children, sit down / Walk right in and take your seat / Sit down children, sit down / Sit right down and rest your feet / Sit down children, sit down."[20]

The sheer numbers of protesters severely taxed the Nashville jail, just as they would in Birmingham and elsewhere in the years to come. Candie Carawan writes that whites and blacks were separated, then male and female protesters, even though that meant the African-American cells were badly overcrowded. The groups passed the time by singing to each other: "The contact became more real when it was vocal," she notes. "Never had I heard such singing. Spirituals, pop tunes, hymns, and even slurpy old love songs all became so powerful. The men sang to the women and the girls down the hall answered them. . . . Some songs that the kids had written or revised came out—notably some rock-and-roll protests composed by four young Baptist preachers. Calypso songs and Ray Charles numbers made us dance in our roomy quarters and then all of us were singing spirituals—'Amen-Freedom.'" (Sometimes called "Everybody Sing Freedom," "Amen-Freedom" is an adaptation of the single-word spiritual, "Amen," mentioned above.) Carawan said that their jailers "seemed to enjoy" the singing and even requested a few tunes. When many of the same group were jailed again a few days later, she writes, the "wardens actually welcomed us back."[21]

The trials of the Nashville sit-in participants drew crowds of thousands of African-Americans who thronged outside the city courthouse. While the group waited, "Amen-Freedom" spontaneously emerged once again. With the completion of each verse, a new word or words would be inserted for "amen." At one point,

Carawan noticed a "burly cop leaning back against his car, singing 'civil rights'" with the crowd. When he saw Carawan's interest, he stopped singing and walked to the other side of the squad car.[22]

During the early hours of April 19, a bomb ripped through the Nashville home of one of the attorneys representing the students. This prompted a march of several thousand students on city hall, where they encountered Mayor Ben West, still smarting over an ongoing economic boycott by African-Americans and the adverse national publicity that had grown daily since February. Guy Carawan led the singing of "We Shall Overcome." Multiple verses, some improvised on the spot, swelled across the courthouse square. In the opinion of David Halberstam, "the young seminarians knew that it was perfect for the Movement; its words, its chords, above all its faith seemed to reflect their determination and resonate their purpose perfectly." This is a crucial moment, as Halberstam writes: "The students now had their anthem." When West appeared, he was confronted by C. T. Vivian and Diane Nash. Eventually, moved by their arguments and the music, West publicly agreed that segregation of the lunch counters was immoral and the city began taking steps to end the practice. "It was a modern spiritual which seemed to have roots in the ages, the perfect song for this particular moment," Halberstam added.[23]

Taylor Branch has called the Nashville students the "largest, most disciplined, and most persistent of the nonviolent action groups in the South."[24] The city also produced what would become one of the most popular of the protest song–oriented singing groups, the Nashville Quartet, the "four Baptist preachers" mentioned by Carawan above. Led by Bevel, with Joseph Carter, Samuel Collier, and Lafayette, all four attended American Baptist Theological Seminary in Nashville and participated in the Freedom Rides of the following year.

In the summer following the opening of Nashville's lunch counters on May 10, Guy Carawan approached the leaders of the Nashville sit-in about creating a documentary recording of the music of the movement. The *Nashville Sit-In Story* (Folkways FH 5590) was released later that year. The LP was a mix of narration, a sermon by Vivian, audio recreations of pivotal moments in the movement, and sit-in songs by the Nashville quartet and others. The quartet recorded "You Better Leave Segregation Alone" (a parody of the Little Willie John song, "You Better Leave My Little Kitten Alone"), "Moving On" (a parody of the Hank Snow hit), and two originals, "Your Dog Loves My Dog" and "I Hope We'll Meet Again." All participants sang "I'm Gonna Sit at the Welcome Table," "Keep Your Eyes on the Prize, Hold On" and "We Shall Not Be Moved" (referred to in the liner notes by Carawan as being three "old spirituals but are used as theme songs in Nashville") and, of course, "We Shall Overcome." ("It is the theme song of the Nashville Sit-Ins," he noted.)[25]

Besides providing later generations with the opportunity to hear what the protest spirituals sounded like within months of their actual use, *The Nashville Sit-In Story* offered listeners several intriguing moments. For one, the recording included Bevel and Lafayette's quirky "My Dog Loves Your Dog," which would become a

**FIGURE 3**

Guy Carawan leads the singing of freedom
songs at a mass meeting at Fisk University in
Nashville on April 21, 1960. The meeting was
held to protest the bombing of the home of
African-American attorney Z. Alexander Looby.
The photographer also identifies Matthew
Walker (far left), Peggy Alexander, and John
Lewis (far right). Photo: *Nashville Banner*
Archives, Nashville Public Library Digital Col-
lection (Jack Gunter).

**FIGURE 4**

The Reverend Martin Luther King, Jr., and
the Reverend Kelly Miller Smith confer as an
unknown singer performs at Fisk University on
April 21, 1960, following the bombing of Z. Alexander Looby's home. It is during this speech that
King said, "We will say, 'Do what you will to
us, but we will wear you down by our capacity
to suffer.'" Photo: *Nashville Banner* Archives,
Nashville Public Library Digital Collection (Jack
Gunter).

staple in the movement. Growing up next to a white family, also with numerous children and a friendly dog, Bevel wrote that while the children could not play together, the dogs would play daily—and wrote lyrics to reflect that observation.[26] Also interesting is the sound and feel of "We Shall Overcome." In 1960, the song was still decidedly formal, more akin to a church choir anthem. The more familiar swaying version, with the emphasis on the beat, was still a year or more away.

A year later, Folkways also released *The Sit-In Story: The Story of the Lunch Room Sit-Ins*, a spoken-word account of the movement, narrated by Edwin T. Randall, a radio announcer working for Friendly World Broadcasting. The LP contained interviews, sermons, and speeches from a host of civil rights activists, including King, Abernathy, publisher Ralph McGill from the *Atlanta Constitution,* activist Peggy Alexander, and others. While there is no music, Abernathy quotes from "Walk Together Children" as part of his sermon on side 2 of the LP.[27]

The sit-in protests continued and their songs spread, changed, and evolved and new ones emerged. In August 1960, Highlander Folk School cofounder Myles Horton and Septima Clark organized the first "Sing for Freedom" workshop. Participants included both veterans of the bus boycott and various sit-in movements, as well as a number of well-known folk singers. Organizers printed and distributed a mimeographed songbook during the workshop. The student leaders clearly thought that singing protest spirituals was an essential part of the movement. Carawan was invited to sing at both the first three large SNCC conferences in 1960 and 1961 and at the first three SCLC meetings.[28]

The practice of singing during the protests and in jail soon became ubiquitous. In Virginia, protesters adapted the now familiar spiritual, "Sit Down, Children."[29] In Atlanta, "The City Too Busy to Hate," thousands of African-Americans marched on the downtown business district in early December in an attempt to speed the desegregation of lunch counters there. Led by baseball great Jackie Robinson and the Reverend William Holmes Borders, the group sang "We Shall Overcome" as it surged toward Plaza Park "in waves, each time pausing to sing and pray before dispersing."[30] Among those who continued the long protests in Atlanta were rhythm and blues singer Clyde McPhatter and the Reverend Martin Luther King, Sr.[31]

Another protest of lunch counters in Tallahassee resulted in students from both Florida State University and the historically black Florida Agricultural & Mechanical University spending months in the city's jails in early 1961. Virginia Delavan, an editor with the FSU student newspaper, wrote of black students who had been jailed for 143 days. When her white contingent from FSU arrived, the FAMU students were already singing. At night, the students sang "Rock of Ages," "A Mighty Fortress Is Our God," "You'll Never Walk Alone," "Swing Low, Sweet Chariot," "My Country 'Tis of Thee," "The Battle Hymn of the Republic," and others. The white students were released the following day. And when they were, Delavan wrote, "The Negro students were still singing."[32] At the University of Texas in Austin, a hundred students marched and sang "We Shall Not Be Moved" following arrests resulting from a sit-in protesting segregated dormitories on campus.[33]

In Atlanta, SNCC member Gwendolyn Zoharah Simmons and her friends sang "Ain't Gonna Let Nobody Turn Me 'Round" while they picketed Shoney's Big Boy and future Georgia governor Lester Maddox's Pickrick restaurant. Outside the Pickrick, they were arrested and the "paddy wagon literally shook with our singing, clapping, stomping and shouting, 'Oh freedom, Oh freedom, and before I'll be a slave, I'll be buried in my grave!'"[34]

In New Orleans, future Freedom Rider Jean Denton Thompson and a friend were jailed after a sit-in. The pair sang "throughout the night," she recalls. "The jailers didn't like it, but we continued to sing and that . . . gave us the strength to continue on." She likened the effect to that of having "somebody else with you" and said the songs gave the singers the reassurance that they were doing "the right thing." The singing of the protest spirituals in jail "gave you the impetus to just keep going on. Whatever was happening around you, it wasn't going to stop you. And you need to put that into words—your actions and your words were in sync. And there were other times, when you were in jail singing songs like 'We Are Climbing Jacob's Ladder' that just inspired you. Just knowing that every little thing you did was going to bring you closer and closer to justice in this country. The other one was, 'Walk Together Children, Don't Be Weary.'" Thompson said the singing was like a "saving grace" that gave her "inspiration" and a "connectiveness" with her fellow protesters. "If you were by yourself, you can sing and that just gave you the courage to go on . . . at times you can have an out-of-body experience and a communication with a higher power." At mass meetings, Thompson said the singing of the movement songs, while holding hands, "just makes you feel there are possibilities that things will change."[35]

While this was happening across the United States, the historic presidential campaign between John F. Kennedy and Richard M. Nixon often pushed the sit-in protests—and the sometimes violent responses to them—off the front pages. Both Kennedy and his running mate, Senator Lyndon B. Johnson of Texas, were supported at different times on their campaign whistle stops by Clara Ward and the Ward Singers, particularly in the North.[36] In the days before the election, Mahalia Jackson publicly endorsed Kennedy in an advertisement in an influential African-American newspaper, the *Chicago Defender*.[37] When King was arrested during an October 1960 protest and sentenced to four months of hard labor in the Georgia penitentiary, Kennedy made a supportive telephone call to Coretta King. The same day, his brother, Robert Kennedy, telephoned the judge directly. King was released the following day. The Reverend Martin Luther King, Sr.'s response was, "This man was willing to wipe the tears from my daughter-in-law's eyes. I've got a suitcase full of votes and I'm going to take them to Mr. Kennedy and dump them in his lap."[38]

Following the election, Mahalia Jackson was invited to perform at an inauguration gala produced by Frank Sinatra and featuring a host of Hollywood stars, including Belafonte, Poitier, and Nat King Cole. The tribute to the president raised more than $1.5 million to defray the party's campaign debt and was widely covered in the black press.[39] Jackson was introduced to both Vice President Lyndon

Johnson and President-elect Kennedy, who told her he had "admired" her singing since Newport. In all, the Kennedys hosted five inauguration balls. In addition to Jackson, Cole, and Belafonte, other African-American artists who performed included Count Basie (Basie's wife, Kate, had been active for the Kennedys during the campaign) and Ella Fitzgerald.[40] On January 27, 1961, Jackson joined many of the same actors and performers in a fund-raiser for SCLC at Carnegie Hall that raised another $50,000. After the Carnegie Hall benefit, King flew to Chicago, where he was a guest at the Jackson home.[41]

As for SNCC, the new organization kept a low profile in its early days, other than joining a sit-in at Rock Hill, South Carolina, along with members of CORE. The participants were arrested and spent thirty days on a brutal chain gang. Those arrested, including Charles Sherrod and Charles Jones, sang freedom songs "so fervent and affecting" that they were each placed in solitary confinement.[42] It was not until May 1961, when an integrated group of CORE leaders undertook an interstate bus ride from Washington, DC, to New Orleans that SNCC actively began working in its first major civil rights offensive, the integration of interstate buses and terminals.[43] The harrowing, heroic story of the Freedom Riders would offer still another glimpse into the importance—and vitality—of the emerging music of the movement.

# 2

## THE FREEDOM RIDES

I remember one night at the jail a voice called up from the cell block beneath us, where other Negro prisoners were housed. "Upstairs!" the anonymous prisoner shouted. We replied, "Downstairs!" "Upstairs!" replied the voice, "sing your freedom song." And the Freedom Riders sang. We sang old folk songs and gospel songs to which new words had been written, telling of the Freedom Ride and its purpose. Then the downstairs prisoners, who the jailers had said were our enemies, sang for us. The girl Freedom Riders in another wing of the jail joined in the Freedom Ride songs.

—JAMES FARMER

Like the sit-in movement, the concept of Freedom Rides actually began some years earlier.[1] Following the release of the first of two Supreme Court decisions (*Irene Morgan v. Commonwealth of Virginia*, 1946) outlawing segregation on carriers involved in interstate travel, the Congress of Racial Equality (CORE) organized one of the first rides in 1947. Called the Journey of Reconciliation, a small group of interracial riders rode segregated buses and stopped at segregated terminals in Virginia, North Carolina, Tennessee, and Kentucky. It was on that trip that Bayard Rustin introduced the protest spiritual "You Don't Have to Ride Jim Crow" to his fellow riders.[2] Among the riders were James Peck and African-American musicians Dennis Banks and Dorothy Maynor. Members of the group were arrested and treated roughly at several stops, including Durham and Chapel Hill, and Rustin and two others served thirty days doing hard labor on a road gang for their "crimes." While the trip confirmed that segregation was widespread in southern terminals and on southern buses, it drew little national attention.[3]

However, buoyed by the success of the ongoing sit-ins, a second Supreme Court decision (*Boynton v. Virginia* in 1960), and with a new director in James Farmer, himself a sit-in veteran, the CORE leadership planned a second set of rides for May 4, 1961, leaving from Washington DC and planning to end in New Orleans. Farmer, who is credited with coining the term the "Freedom Rides," contacted the offices of the president and the attorney general, as well as the Interstate Commerce Commission, and the presidents of the Greyhound and Trailways bus corporations, providing them with itineraries.

The fourteen riders included Farmer, Peck, college students Hank Thomas and John Lewis, and folk singer Jimmy McDonald. As had become the norm during the sit-ins, riders were first drilled on nonviolent responses to violent situations.[4] Seventeen-year-old McDonald, already known for his "vast repertoire of labor and freedom songs," had previously participated in a number of CORE's direct actions in New York, and had campaigned for Progressive Party candidate Henry Wallace. According to McDonald, he was chosen for the initial trip, despite his age, because CORE officials wanted him "to lead the singing."[5]

The group passed uneventfully through Virginia and North Carolina, only to run into trouble in South Carolina, where several riders were attacked in Rock Hill. Earlier, in February 1961, ten African-American students in Rock Hill, including eight members of the Friendship Junior College CORE chapter and Peck, had been arrested while staging a sit-in at a McCrory's lunch counter. Arrested for trespass, the ten "entered jail singing hymns and patriotic songs."[6] Others would be arrested in support of the original ten, who employed the newly popular "jail, no bail" tactics that marked the movement in Nashville and, later, in Alabama.[7] During their stay in the York County road-gang stockade, Peck and the other participants continued to sing the freedom songs during their morning "devotionals." By the end of their stay, some of the white prisoners were requesting the songs. Eventually, Peck and the others were placed in solitary confinement for singing the protest spiritual "Before I'll be a slave / I'll be buried in my grave."[8] Upon arrival in Rock Hill, several Freedom Riders, including Lewis, were injured by an angry mob and worse injuries were only avoided by the appearance of the Reverend C. A. Ivory, the wheelchair-bound leader of the Rock Hill movement. Ivory whisked the riders to a mass meeting, where they were joined by the original Rock Hill students, who had only recently been released. McDonald led the singing "with a joyous round of freedom songs."[9]

The small band continued its journey the following day. During the periods of relative calm, the Freedom Riders fought a rising sense of unease that was only relieved at one point when Hank Thomas continued a tradition established by Rustin by singing the spiritual-like "Hallelujah, I'm a Travelin'": "Hallelujah, I'm a travelin', hallelujah, ain't it fine / Hallelujah, I'm a travelin', down freedom's main line / In 1954 our Supreme Court has said / "Looka Mr. Jim Crow / It's time you

**FIGURE 5**

Unidentified NAACP Freedom Riders, photographed in 1961 by Opie Evans. Photo courtesy of the State Archives of Florida.

were dead." The group improvised numerous verses on the song and, no doubt led by McDonald, sang other protest spirituals as well.[10]

The ride through Georgia was calm. The riders had dinner with Martin Luther King, Jr., in Atlanta on May 13 and, following the nightly briefing, the group retired after singing "We Shall Overcome." In Alabama, however, the small band was attacked at the state line and college professor Walter Bergman was beaten so severely that he became permanently wheelchair-bound. Peck was also beaten savagely by a mob of whites in the Birmingham terminal. While in Anniston, one of the buses was firebombed and the riders were attacked once again by a mob that included several uniformed policemen. The events were reported by the *New York Times*, which published photographs of Peck's beating.[11] The Mother's Day (May 14) beatings and assaults prompted surviving riders to write new words to long-time movement supporter Harry Belafonte's hit, "The Banana Boat Song." The new song, titled "Freedom's Coming and It Won't Be Long," featured the lines, "We took a trip down Alabama way / We saw much violence on Mother's Day" and soon became an established freedom song, with lyrics changing to match events.[12] It was after the carnage in Anniston that members of the SNCC in Nashville volunteered to continue the rides.[13]

Back in Birmingham, the original riders endured more violent attacks, this time administered by known Klansmen, while the city's police, under the direction of Eugene "Bull" Connor, refused to intervene. Newsmen filming the scene, along with a host of innocent bystanders, were assaulted as well. (In Anniston, even injured riders convalescing at the local hospital were besieged.[14]) In Birmingham, Connor tormented the jailed young people, who bravely continued to sing what were now widely known as "freedom songs."[15] At one point, Connor took the African-American riders from "protective custody" in jail and deposited them unprotected in the countryside in the middle of the night. When Connor was later questioned as to why he dumped the battered Freedom Riders, he responded, "Because I couldn't stand their singing."[16] A few of the riders found a telephone and called Diane Nash and other SNCC members in Nashville, who quickly drove them back to the Birmingham station to continue their journey, but no drivers would let them board their buses. Exhausted, Lucretia Collins said that the riders eventually began to sing. "I don't think that song—'We Shall Overcome'—ever had so much meaning as it did that morning. It was really felt that morning, after we had waited so long and been refused so much."[17]

Some of the original Freedom Riders eventually completed the trip to New Orleans by plane, but only after long hours of sitting outside the airport, surrounded by hostile whites with only a thin line of police protection. Their flight was delayed twice, once because of a bomb threat. A reporter and a photographer from *Jet* magazine who had accompanied the group the entire way, documenting the horrific assaults, were also on the plane. But only eight of the original Freedom Riders arrived in New Orleans on May 17 for a planned Freedom Rally.[18] One poignant scene was burned in the mind of a reporter for the *New York Herald Tribune*.

Following still more assaults, some of the riders sat for eighteen hours waiting for a bus to take them to Montgomery. Among them, according to Stuart H. Loory, was a white college student, James M. Zwerg. Two hours before the bus finally departed Birmingham, Zwerg, still bleeding, sat with the others on the platform, and sang spirituals. It was Zwerg, Looney noted, who sang the solo on "Keep Your Eyes on the Prize."[19]

The replacement Freedom Riders from Nashville were escorted by heavy police protection en route to Montgomery on May 20. But once in Montgomery, all traces of authority vanished and the new students (this time male and female), bystanders, and newsmen were ambushed and brutally assaulted yet again in the terminal. While rider John Lewis lay bleeding in the street, the Alabama state attorney general served him an injunction against future rides.[20]

On the evening of Sunday May 21, when King, Nash, Farmer, and others arrived for a previously scheduled 8 p.m. mass meeting at Abernathy's church, they found hundreds of people already in attendance, some of whom had gathered three hours early, singing and praying without benefit of an organist or a minister, "a sign of the old spirit of Montgomery." A group of angry whites stood outside, kept at bay by a dozen or so U.S. marshals, armed only with nightsticks. As the evening progressed, the battered riders were introduced to "emotional waves of tribute" as they sang "We Shall Overcome."[21]

Suddenly, those in the church found themselves once again surrounded by a swelling crowd of hundreds of what one observer called "homicidally racist Alabamans" howling for blood and repeatedly charging the church. Inside the un-air-conditioned church, with the fumes of tear gas, improvised Molotov cocktails, and stink bombs seeping in, King, Abernathy, Shuttlesworth, and others took turns preaching, consulting on strategy, contacting representatives of the Kennedy administration, and leading the estimated 1,600 people in attendance in song. At one point, the mob kicked open the front doors and surged in, only to be beaten back by the thin line of marshals.[22] At times, the shouted threats and sirens outside "rivaled the sound of the singing inside." Preacher after preacher exhorted the frightened captives to sing. "I want to hear everybody singing," one shouted, "and mean every word of it." When Montgomery police ordered everyone—including those sheltered inside the church—to disperse, the congregants sang "There'll Be Freedom in That Land Where I'm Bound."[23] In the early hours of the evening, those inside the church sang the Montgomery bus boycott staples "Love Lifted Me" and "Leaning on the Everlasting Arms." When the tear gas fumes became unbearable, Abernathy stubbornly shouted, "Open the windows! Let fresh air in! Let those outside hear us sing a little louder!"[24]

As the evening turned toward morning and the prospects for safety appeared to dim, the music turned from Protestant hymns to defiant movement songs, such as "Ain't Gonna Let Nobody Turn Me 'Round" and "We Shall Overcome." Some of the songs were led by the various Freedom Riders, many of whom had been smuggled into the church disguised as choir members. In the basement, King and the others continued their frantic calls to Attorney General Robert Kennedy. Throughout the long hours, those inside the sanctuary continued to sing, pray, or even try to sleep until dawn, when marshals and late-arriving members of the Alabama National Guard smuggled them out in small groups.[25]

On May 24, two buses with twenty-seven Freedom Riders left Montgomery for Jackson, Mississippi, four hours apart, determined to continue their ride. In Jackson, those inside the terminal were arrested for "disturbing the peace, inciting a riot, and disobeying an officer." Farmer and the others were led to a waiting patrol wagon. Once inside, amid the shouting and sirens, one of the riders, Lucretia Collins said, "Let's sing." Moments later, she added, "Louder, louder." "Suddenly, the air was rent with another sound exploding through the barred windows of the paddy wagon," Farmer recalled. "'We Shall Overcome' came first, and we sang at the top of our lungs, as though shouting to straining ears in cotton fields and shacks on plantations in the far reaches of the state. . . . The greatest fervor was reserved for the stanza 'We are not afraid. We are not afraid. Oh, deep in my heart, I do believe, we shall overcome, someday.'" In his memoirs, Farmer admitted that the group sang so loudly to drown out their fears of what was to come and "rouse" their courage. "There is no armor more impenetrable than song," he writes.[26] Among those booked and jailed with Abernathy and Walker was William Sloan Coffin, Jr., chaplain at Yale University. Coffin writes that Abernathy and Walker spent their time in prison leading "prayer services" for the other inmates, and that Abernathy spent most of the evening "counseling an alcoholic around the corner in the next cell."[27]

What followed was a nightmarish series of stays in the Jackson City and Hinds County jails as more than three hundred riders were eventually incarcerated. Upon arrival in Hinds, James Bevel immediately began preaching and singing, much to the displeasure of the jailers. When he would not stop, they confiscated the cigarettes from the smokers in the group and then eliminated their afternoon snacks.[28] In the decrepit Hinds County jail, riders were separated by race and gender. At 2 A.M. on the first morning, Bevel led the male African-American inmates in singing the freedom song, "If You Can't Find Me in the Back of the Bus." Soon, other Freedom Riders responded until the entire cell block rang with music. Eventually, regular prisoners also began singing, and the women riders in a distant part of the sprawling facility joined as well, despite threats from the guards. After a long, sometimes abusive week in Hinds, a surprise visit by the NCAA's Roy Wilkins set off "an explosion of song" that prompted the "regular" African-American inmates, who were housed on a different floor and who had been charged with a number of violent crimes, including murder and rape, to call out, "Freedom Riders, if you teach us your songs, we'll teach you ours." The riders taught the other inmates freedom songs and learned, in return, "work songs, protest songs, unfamiliar gospel songs."[29] From then on, the riders continued to sing the "hated" songs, despite threats from the guards: "You gotta stop that singing." You know, "O-o-h, freedom, o-o-o-o-h freedom, before I'd be a slave, I'd be buried in my grave and go home to the Lord and be free." . . . "Stop that singing!" The other prisoners upstairs began to sing. The guards intensified the process of denying the Freedom Riders various privileges because of their singing. But Farmer said that the other prisoners smuggled treats and "knickknacks" to the singers. Eventually, the punishment for singing the protest spirituals included the manipulation of the heating and cooling units and salting their food so heavily that it was inedible.[30]

A few riders, such as Alphonso Petway, spent time in both the Jackson City and County jails. He recalled that the halls rang with song, even among those riders who were only jailed briefly. Petway, who had attended song training seminars at Highlander, said his "theme" song during the days he was incarcerated was set to the tune of "Which Side Are You On?": "My father was a freedom fighter, I am his grateful son / I'll stick to the freedom fight until the battle is won / Oh, tell me if you can, Will you be an Uncle Tom / Or will you be a man?" Another popular song was set to the tune of "Brother John" and referenced Mississippi Governor Ross Barnett: "Are you sleeping, Brother Ross, Brother Ross?" / The Freedom Rides are coming / The Freedom Rides are coming." Petway said he also sang "Ain't Gonna Let Nobody Turn Me 'Round," "Fired Up, I Ain't Gonna Take No More," and "If I Had a Hammer." The music, he declared, was a "rallying cry, a fighting song; it was a pep rally—it kept you up."[31] It was in the Hinds County jail that Farmer rewrote Florence Reece's "Which Side Are You On," in part to encourage the African-American jail trustees: "They say in Hinds County no neutrals have they met / You're either for the Freedom Ride or you 'tom' for Ross Barnett."[32]

Freedom Rider Pauline Knight-Ofosu remembered one special Sunday morning in Hinds. The female prisoners had finished singing when they heard "the melodious tones of male voices." The legendary Blind Boys of Alabama were serenading the prisoners. While she did not remember if they were outside the jail walls or had been incarcerated themselves, she said the singing "took us up higher."[33] Ruby Doris Smith originally shared her four-bunk cell with thirteen other women, then seventeen others, then finally twenty-three inmates, all crowded in the tiny room. Smith said that her two-month sentence in Hinds was "a nice set up": "When the windows were open we could talk to the fellows. We sang. We wrote freedom songs. A Negro minister from Chicago sang: 'Woke Up in the Mornin' with My Mind Stayed on Freedom' so everyone began singing it. It started there. . . . Other songs were composed—'I Know We'll Meet Again' was written by a fellow I knew from Nashville and Rock Hill." When the women riders were not singing, they were conducting ballet lessons or teaching Spanish to other prisoners. But all that changed, she said, when the riders were shipped to Mississippi's infamous state penitentiary, Parchman Plantation.[34]

In mid-June, the continued arrival of Freedom Riders and the subsequent overcrowding of the city and county jails prompted authorities to bus current and future riders straight to Parchman, an eighteen-hundred-acre maximum security prison farm. Once there, they were again divided by sex and race. By September, more than three hundred Freedom Riders were in various Mississippi jails, but none as brutal as Parchman. The first arrivals included Bernard LaFayette, Jr.,

James Lawson, Jean Thompson, Vivian, Farmer, Bevel, Lewis, and others. White student and rider Peter Ackerberg recalled the singing on the bus from Montgomery to Jackson and said that his experience with the riders was "a highlight" of his life.[35] The group sang the entire trip to Parchman, but that came to an abrupt end as they were herded from the buses. "Sing your freedom song inside," one guard snarled. "We have niggers here who are bad enough to eat you up. Sing your song inside."[36]

Since the riders were not allowed to work in the cotton fields with other prisoners, allegedly for their own protection, and were quickly separated, they faced long periods of isolation. Lewis, Lawson, and Farmer organized their days and nights with prayer sessions, educational sessions, nonviolence training and, according to Jesse Harris, extensive periods of singing: "The songs of freedom, that's what would help morale. 'All right, come on. Somebody come out with a song,' and that would cheer everybody up. Basically, that's what kept us going, the songs. I was learning new songs. The old spiritual songs—the music's the same but the words have been changed."[37]

Among the songs that Lewis remembered from Parchman were "Amazing Grace," the many forms of "Amen," "Will the Circle Be Unbroken," "I'll Fly Away," "I Woke Up This Morning with My Mind Stayed on Freedom," "The Battle Hymn of the Republic," "Steal Away," "Keep Your Eyes on the Prize," and "I've Been in the Storm So Long." Each song, he said, was sung for a different purpose: "Music created a sense of solidarity, that sense of togetherness. When you felt there's something troublesome around you, when you were about to be arrested or jailed or beaten, someone would just start singing a song or just humming. It just had a soothing effect. But I think at times it helped disarm the opposition and it gave us the strength to go on in spite of some of the concerns that we might have had. We were able, because of music, to conquer some of our fears; it gave us this sense that we were involved in almost a holy cause."[38]

Nineteen-year-old David Fankhauser was the rare white student at Central State College (Wilberforce, Ohio) when the call came from SNCC's Nash for more Freedom Riders. His parents, members of the Fellowship of Reconciliation, supported his activities. Fankhauser arrived at Parchman within a week of Lewis and remembered many of the same songs, including "I Woke Up This Morning with My Mind Stayed on Freedom," "I'm Going to Sit at the Welcome Table," "We Shall Overcome," "Keep Your Eyes on the Prize," and "We Are Soldiers in the Army." At one point, the guards told the riders to quit singing because the songs were "disturbing" the cooks—who, as Fankhauser pointed out, were all African-American trustees. While Fankhauser said he did not consider himself a "highly religious person," he noted that the performance of the protest spirituals "brought me into that realm where they were very, very powerful."[39]

Another inmate at Parchman was eighteen-year-old Bob Filner, who, like Lewis, would later serve in the U.S. House of Representatives. Filner's father had been active in the labor movement and the young man knew many of the movement's songs when he was arrested in June. As a white man, Filner was kept apart from the other Freedom Riders, though he could hear them when they sang. The singing, he said, helped him deal with the arbitrary tyrannies of life at Parchman, along with the loneliness. Filner recalled making up verses to "Keep Your Eyes on the Prize," and singing "We Shall Overcome." As for the singing in Parchman, "I think it saved my life, basically."[40]

As more riders streamed in, tempers frayed. Riders who continued to sing the freedom songs were slapped with the extremely uncomfortable "wrist-breaker" handcuffs by guards, dragged by their hands, and thrown into the six-foot by six-foot solitary confinement boxes. In response, the Freedom Riders, led by Stokely Carmichael, sang, "I'm Gonna Tell God How You Treat Me."[41] SNCC field secretary MacArthur Cotton was hung by his thumbs as a particularly painful punishment for his refusal to stop leading the Freedom Riders in freedom songs.[42]

Women riders were housed in the Parchman infirmary. Their constant singing, even "The Star-Spangled Banner," also cost them their mattresses and sheets, then their towels and toothbrushes. It did not deter the women: "The singing kept getting louder all the time. They slept on steel for three nights, without coverings, with cold air deliberately blown into their cells all night long."[43] Freedom Rider Marilyn Eisenberg carefully collected many of the songs the women riders sang. Some, like the rewrite of "Hully Gully" and songs set to popular dances like the twist and Watusi, were both for singing *and* dancing. Other songs collected by Eisenberg included rewritten versions of "Yankee Doodle," "On Top of Old Smokey," "Battle Hymn of the Republic" (two versions), "Frere Jacques," "Careless Love," "Streets of Laredo," and even "Dixie." ("No more racist rule by Anglo-Saxon / Black and white, we ride to Jackson / Look ahead! Look ahead! Look ahead, Dixieland!") Some of the songs were light-hearted; others, such as her own rewrite of "Careless Love," reflected the riders' sense of loss and loneliness. The singing created at least one convert: the infirmary's "matron," who was initially hostile to the women. By the end of their sentence, Eisenberg notes, "she was singing for us on our make-believe radio programs and was often heard humming our freedom songs."[44]

Jean Denton Thompson, who had been jailed during the sit-ins and was also with the first group of Freedom Riders arrested on May 24, said the singing was the "glue" that held the Parchman inmates together. When she was not singing "We Shall Not Be Moved," "Over My Head, There's Freedom in the Air," or the many incarnations of "Amen/Freedom" with the other prisoners, Thompson said she sang "Walk Together Children" (also known as "There's a Camp Meeting Tonight") to herself as a "mantra." She said she believed that the reason the guards hated the singing so much was not just because the music showed them that jail had not broken the spirit of the Freedom Riders, but also because the jailers feared the songs might "convert" the other prisoners. "The main thing was that they didn't like the idea that you weren't following their rules," she said, "and they could not stop you, regardless of what they did."[45] Another Freedom Rider at Parchman, Reginald Green, agreed that it was the loss of control that the guards most feared and hated about the singing. "Music became your strength," he noted. "That's what you had. Because you didn't have ownership to much, but you had ownership to your music."[46] As Lafayette mused some years later, "They could take away everything else except our songs, which meant we kept our souls."[47]

As the weeks dragged on, the Freedom Riders were featured in a host of newspaper and magazine articles and television profiles. The costs incurred by the riders, CORE, SNCC, SCLC, and other civil rights-related organizations grew as well. A fund-raiser in Los Angeles, featuring Mahalia Jackson, Sammy Davis, Jr., rising young African-American comic Dick Gregory, and others attracted 20,000 people.[48] Jackson personally visited the major radio stations in the city to promote the concert. By now, her Chicago home was the unofficial headquarters of King, Abernathy, and other SCLC activists and she began performing at and sometimes organizing regular fund-raisers on their behalf. At one point during her portion of the mid-June program in Los Angeles, Jackson took to the aisles, singing "On My Way to Freedomland" and personally collecting additional donations from concertgoers. After the show, she remained to oversee the tallying of the evening's take: "And Mahalia *stayed,* baby, and counted that money. I told 'em before, and I'll tell 'em again—I'll come to any benefit if I *see* SCLC get all the money."[49] Between June 1961 and May 1962, numerous benefit concerts were staged in support of the riders. Performers included Louis Armstrong, Nina Simone, Lena Horne, Max Roach and Abbey Lincoln (who performed their *Freedom Now Suite* at the NAACP annual convention in Philadelphia on July 14, 1961), Count Basie, Harry Belafonte, Miles Davis, Dizzy Gillespie, and dozens of others.[50]

The isolation that many of the Freedom Riders experienced while being spread across the sprawling Parchman complex was vastly different from the family-like atmosphere that had marked their sit-ins, bus trips, and even previous jail experiences, and eventually began to wear on the male riders in particular. The young people fought monotony. They were provided with no reading materials, save a small copy of the New Testament, and were permitted one letter and two showers per week. "With a few exceptions," writes Raymond Arsenault, "interaction beyond adjoining cells was limited to singing, which became a treasured lifeline for many of the riders." Still, they persevered. When one California Freedom Rider with operatic training was placed in the dreaded isolation box, he chose to use the resonance of the tiny metal cell to serenade the other inmates with "a beautiful spiritual" as they began their nightly ritual of sing-along protest songs. Rider Steve Green recorded this impression of that night in the memoirs of his Parchman days: "The volume was incredible—his deep baritone could be clearly heard in every room of the building, by prisoners and guards alike. In silence, with tears of joy in some eyes and rage in others, we listened to the most moving concert I have ever heard."[51]

Eventually, their captors again threatened to remove their mattresses if they resumed singing. When it continued, the mattresses, their lone conveniences in the stark cells, were confiscated. Some of the Freedom Riders were speechless with anger or hopelessness. But Bevel again began preaching, equating the removal of the mattresses to a ploy by Satan to weaken the resolve of the riders and convince them to bail out of Parchman. Another rider, Hank Thomas, spontaneously broke into another protest spiritual, "Come get my mattress, I'll keep my soul." This was followed by "Ain't Gonna Let Nobody Turn Me 'Round": "Ain't gonna let no jail house, Lordy, turn me 'round / I'm gonna keep on a-walkin', Lord, keep on a-talkin' / Lord, marching up to freedom land." The mattresses were returned the following day, but with the warning that they would be removed permanently, should the singing resume. Thomas and the others began singing again, "louder than ever," and this time their mattresses were removed for good. Later, when one of the deputies threatened the riders, Thomas sang new lines to "Which Side Are You On?": "Ole *big* man Deputy Tyson said, I *don'* wanna cause you pain / But *if* you don't stop that singin' now, you'll be singin' in the rain." At this point, Tyson ordered the guards to flood the cells with high-pressure water hoses, then ordered the windows opened and the exhaust fans left on high all night.[52]

Because of the widespread publicity the rides generated, Mississippi Governor Barnett instructed the Parchman guards to be "careful" with the riders, avoiding the kinds of beatings and direct physical abuse they had suffered earlier. This prompted one guard to complain, "Guv'nor, how we goin' stop their singing if we cain't go upside their heads?"[53] Still the riders endured. "Jails are not a new experience for the riders," Farmer said later, "but the Freedom Riders were definitely a new experience for Mississippi jails."[54] In the end, the forty days that the riders spent in the notorious Mississippi jail had an outcome that Barnett would have doubtless prevented, had he known—"Parchman Farm became a Highlander-style song swap as members of SNCC and CORE taught each other their separate repertories."[55]

While the Freedom Riders heroically endured the thousand and one petty tortures at Parchman and other southern penitentiaries, neither CORE nor the SNCC nor the hundreds of volunteers could sustain the financial costs indefinitely. Finally, on July 7, most of the riders were bailed out by CORE with $500 appeal bonds, since forty days was the longest a prisoner could be incarcerated under Mississippi law and file an appeal. Once the majority had left the state, Mississippi officials decreed that all would have to return in August to be tried in the state appeals court, or forfeit the bonds.[56] The last major arrests in Mississippi took place on July 30 when a group of Freedom Riders from Los Angeles were taken into custody at the Jackson railroad terminal. But the movement, which had been foundering at this point, was reinvigorated by the return of the far-flung Freedom Riders to Mississippi, especially following a mass meeting in the Masonic Temple in Jackson on the night before the mass arraignments, Sunday August 13. Amid the speeches, sermons, and freedom songs, Walker sang a revised version of the ancient minstrel song, "Old Black Joe": "I'm coming, I'm coming, And my head ain't bending low / I'm coming, I'm coming, I'm America's new Black Joe" to a strong response.[57]

The August mass meetings in Jackson marked the end of Guy Carawan's role in disseminating the protest spirituals and freedom songs. Convinced that others, including Cordell Reagon and Charles Sherrod, were "better equipped" to take the music to the next stages of the movement, he began to focus more on recording the songs and organizing larger musical seminar retreats on the music.[58]

Ultimately, the focus of the movement shifted from the Freedom Rides to continued "direct action" in the form of voter registration. Many of the riders were able to work for SNCC full-time at this point, their salaries paid in part by money raised by Belafonte.[59] The "diffusion" of the battle-tested riders into the rest of Mississippi and, soon after the rides, into Albany, Georgia, was a significant turning point in the civil rights movement.[60]

The music of the Freedom Riders was captured, in part, on *We Shall Overcome: Songs of the Freedom Riders and the Sit-Ins*, released in 1961. Produced by Carawan and Folkways founder Moe Asch, the LP contained only a few songs already featured on the two previous Folkways releases. New tracks included a number of what were, by then, well-established rewrites of older, mostly religious, material: "This Little Light of Mine," "There's a Meeting Here Tonight," "Rock My Soul," "Hold On," "Let Us Break Bread Together," "We Are Soldiers in the Army," "We Shall Not Be Moved," "Your Dog," "Michael Row the Boat Ashore," "I'm So Glad," "Oh, Freedom," and a five-and-a-half minute version of "We Shall Overcome." The vocals were provided by the Nashville Quartet (Joseph Carter, Bernard Lafayette, James Bevel, and Samuel Collier) and the Montgomery Trio (Minnie Hendrick, Mary Ethel Dozier, and Gladys Burnette Carter), with guitar accompaniment by Carawan. The extensive liner notes and photographs summarized both the sit-ins and Freedom Rides. The songs were performed "live" in an "impromptu" session, recorded by Asch. Save for the unobtrusive guitar accompaniment, these recordings mirror what the freedom songs sounded like in smaller, more intimate settings, such as in prison cells or on buses. Obviously, a song like "We Shall Overcome," sung by thousands in an open venue, would have sounded much different, much more commanding. The differences between the performance of "We Shall Overcome" from *The Nashville Sit-In Story* (1960) and *We Shall Overcome: Songs of the Freedom Riders and the Sit-Ins* (1961) reflect the emerging changes in the movement. The earlier version is slower, more magisterial. The *Freedom Riders* version has a more pronounced pulse, almost a beat. As one of the singers calls out the next verse, the emphasis in the words becomes more urgent, with less of the prayer-like delivery of the older version.[61] The singers, some of whom have now survived the Montgomery bus boycotts, the Nashville sit-ins, and Parchman, are proud, hopeful veterans and their singing reflects that transformation. There is also a seriousness in the voices, an admission that what was once a series of skirmishes appears to be evolving into a conflict where resolution may be years away. "These are songs of protest," says Julian Bond. "These are songs of rebellion."[62]

A second set of recordings from this era, *Sit-In Songs: Songs of the Freedom Riders*, produced by CORE in late 1961, remains out of print and difficult to find.

The LP was advertised regularly in *CORE-LATOR*, the bimonthly publication of the Congress of Racial Equality, for $3.95: "Most of the singers here had just been released from jail on CORE's 'Freedom Highway' project," but only Hank Thomas is identified among the singers. The liner notes say that Tom Wilson, then Audio-Fidelity's artists and repertoire man, responded to Thomas's rendition of "Do You Want Your Freedom?" by holding up his hand and exclaiming, "One take is enough; a man can't pour out his soul like that more than once!" The song list included: "Certainly, Lord," "Which Side Are You On," "Hallelujah, I'm Traveling," "Hold On," "I Woke Up This Morning," "Do You Want Your Freedom," "Get Your Rights, Jack," "I Know We'll Meet Again," "We Went Down to Mississippi," "How Did You Feel?," "Michael Row the Boat Ashore," and a five-minute version of "We Shall Overcome."[63]

Even popular singers of the day responded to the message and example of the Freedom Riders. Both Chuck Berry and folk singer Phil Ochs included tributes to the Freedom Riders in songs. Ochs's song "Freedom Riders" includes the lines "Jim Farmer was a hard-fightin' man / Decided one day that he had to make a stand / He led them down to slavery town / And they threw Jim Farmer in the can."[64]

The music continued to spread in other ways. A few months later, on November 16, 1961, King spoke to the annual meeting of the Fellowship of the Concerned in Atlanta. As might be expected, the Freedom Rides were a singular focus of the address. King cited in particular "We Shall Overcome," which he called a "theme song" for the movement, as a crucial element in the decision to continue the rides to Jackson after the bloody night in Montgomery. After discussing whether to resume the rides throughout the evening, the group held hands and sang "We Shall Overcome." King said the singing of the gently defiant words by the riders was a revelation to him—that through their faith, these riders and others would, indeed, "overcome."[65]

But throughout the South, that "overcoming" was still years away. Even in Nashville, various establishments continued to mistreat African-Americans or even prohibit them from entering. As late as Christmas 1963, students picketing segregated hamburger restaurants and singing "God Rest Ye Merry Gentlemen" were physically and verbally assaulted by whites, as the police watched impassively. "But we kept singing," one of the student demonstrators said, "like we were going to hold them off with this one song about brotherhood, and they didn't come and get us." This, writes Jon Michael Spencer, is another example of singing as "both a defensive weapon of mitigation as well as an offensive banner of courageous self-assertion" for civil rights movement participants.[66]

The long periods in Mississippi jails had done much for the Freedom Riders as well, creating strong bonds of friendship and expanding the freedom song repertoire. "This was probably one of the more important events in the development of movement singing," write the Carawans. The songs of the Montgomery bus boycott mingled with songs from Highlander, CORE, and the Nashville SNCC, and new songs were created or adapted in Parchman. Some riders, like Cordell Reagon, would take those songs to Albany, Georgia.[67]

**FIGURE 6**

John Lewis (left), Archie E. Allen, and other
students representing the Nashville Christian
Leadership Council protest on Jefferson Street in
Nashville during the Freedom March, March 23,
1963. Photo: *Nashville Banner* Archives, Nashville Public Library Digital Collection (Bill
Goodman).

In the end, the Supreme Court ruled that Mississippi had to refund the outrageously excessive bond money and, at Attorney General Robert Kennedy's urging, the Interstate Commerce Commission issued directives ordering the official end to segregation in southern buses and bus terminals, though compliance was slow and grudging.[68] The Freedom Rides and prison sentences had been the "crucial beginning" that the civil rights movement had needed, according to one writer. The sit-in and Freedom Ride survivors were now more "committed" than ever before.[69] They now knew the devious intricacies of segregation, what to expect in the kangaroo courts and Star Chambers of the legal systems, the unregulated brutality of the penal system, and the levels of violence they could expect in pursuit of basic human rights. They also knew the songs of the movement.

"Music was just as important as learning about nonviolence," Ernest "Rip" Patton, one of the original Freedom Riders, said later. "Music brought us together— we can't all talk at the same time, but we can all sing at the same time. It gives you that spiritual feeling. It was like our glue."[70]

# 3

## ALBANY, GEORGIA

I don't know where that feeling came from or what was different then, but our spirit was strong and it could be heard in our songs. You sing the same songs now, and it won't move you the same way it did then. It was time. It was ripe. It was harvest time. And when it's ripe, you had better pick it. There was fire in our singing; those songs touched you way down inside until you shook. It was more than singing. It has got to be that it was harvest time. Those were harvest songs and we were ripe for the picking.

—ALBANY NATIVE JANIE (CULBRETH) RAMBEAU

After the sit-ins and Freedom Rides, the SNCC leadership split between those wanting more direct action, such as demonstrations and sit-ins, and those who wanted to focus the group's activities on southern voter registration. Eventually, the SNCC divided into two "wings," with the registration wing headed by James and Dina Bevel, Bernard Lafayette, Marion Barry, and a charismatic newcomer, Bob Moses. In the fall of 1961, the direct action wing chose Albany, Georgia for a citywide series of demonstrations.[1] Albany was a strategic choice, with students from the historically black Albany State College supported by an active branch of the NAACP, the Federated Women's Clubs, the Negro Voter's League, and the Baptist Ministerial Alliance. White Albany also had a long history of mistreatment of black soldiers from the nearby military base.[2] SNCC field secretaries Charles Sherrod and Cordell Reagon were sent to Albany where they met with existing organizations, as well as pastors, high school students, and students at Albany State, eventually becoming part of an umbrella organization, the Albany

Movement. The group quickly laid plans for demonstrations against a host of seg-regated restaurants, transportation facilities (including buses and bus terminals), public facilities (including the library and swimming pool) and entertainment ven-ues.[3] In October, Sherrod and Reagon arranged the first meeting of interested citi-zens in the basement of Bethel African Methodist Episcopal Church. Among those in attendance was Annette Jones White, Miss Albany State College, who recalled the two men's "beautiful tenor voices," and that they taught attendees freedom songs even as they gathered information about the oppressive conditions in the city.[4]

The Albany Movement enjoyed widespread support among African-Americans, as Sherrod and Reagon soon become "folk heroes" among the long-oppressed young people of Albany. The movement designated the Albany Trail-ways terminal, where black students were heading home for Thanksgiving 1961, as the site of its first public demonstration. African-American students entered the "whites only" sections of the terminal restaurant and waiting rooms. Nine members of the local coordinating board, along with two Albany natives, were immediately arrested by Albany Police Chief Laurie Pritchett.[5] On November 26, a spontaneous march composed of students from Albany State, some of whom had gone from dorm to dorm gathering supporters, protested the arrests. The march circled City Hall and demonstrators sang freedom songs, then marched back to Union Baptist Church, where they discussed the events of the day.[6] The follow-ing day, an estimated six hundred African-Americans demonstrated in Albany's downtown to protest the arrests. That evening, the city's first mass meeting was called at Shiloh Baptist Church, which was packed long before the scheduled 8 p.m. start. Among those present was Bertha Gober of the SNCC, who herself had spent time in jail. Sherrod was also among those in attendance: "And when we rose to sing 'We Shall Overcome,' nobody could imagine what kept the church on four corners," Sherrod said. "I threw my head back and closed my eyes as I sang with my whole body."[7] The initial mass meeting was electrifying. Goldie Jackson, the Albany Movement's secretary, also remembered the first time the congregation heard "We Shall Overcome" and the spirit was such that those who heard it "stayed there all night that first night, singing and praying." From that moment on, all Albany mass meetings began with freedom songs. Soon, the largest portion of the Albany services was given over to singing. "Songs were the bed of everything," one participant said, "and I'd never seen or felt songs do that before."[8]

For the first time since the Montgomery bus boycott, as many adults as stu-dents participated in the protests. This necessitated a change in some of the free-dom songs. Because the mass meetings were held in churches, the songs based on secular sources were rarely sung and the protest spirituals, which older church members were more likely to be familiar with, again took center stage. According to one movement veteran, "every song that went through Albany took a change," including "This Little Light of Mine," "We Shall Not Be Moved," and "Oh Freedom."[9]

On December 10, the Albany Movement was joined by Bob Zellner and James Forman of SNCC, Tom Hayden of the Students for a Democratic Society, Bernard

Lee of SCLC, and others, who sat together on the train from Atlanta as an integrated group. When the train arrived in Albany, Pritchett and his men were waiting. All of the movement supporters were arrested, along with Gober and Jones, who were in the crowd watching, and charged with obstructing traffic, disorderly conduct, and failure to obey an officer, though all had followed Pritchett's orders. Albany's mayor would later call the arrests, which drew national attention, "a mistake."[10]

As before, the nightly mass meetings in churches served multiple essential purposes for the movement. Volunteer Prathia Hall called the meetings "the central rallying points of the Movement." Following a prayer service, the "raised voices and the rhythmic stomping of feet" could be heard long before visitors actually arrived at the churches. Hall said it was "impossible to stand as a spectator outside the circle of this communion." And while she had heard many of these songs before in the rural Virginia churches of her grandparents, in Albany they were now "worship that contained within the reality of its expression a power affirming life and defying death." For Hall, the "power" in the songs and prayers "transcended" the reality of the situation in Albany, refashioning "fear into faith, cringing into courage, suffering into survival, despair into defiance, and pain into protest."[11] Penny Patch, one of the few white riders, called the mass meetings at Mount Zion Baptist Church "exhilarating," and remembered the music "above all," including "Ain't Gonna Let Nobody Turn Me 'Round," "Over My Head I See Freedom in the Air," and "We Shall Overcome." The song that Patch described as becoming "embedded" in her heart, the one she continued to sing through a host of difficult times, was "Oh Freedom," with the line, "Before I'll be a slave / I'll be buried in my grave."[12]

Margaret Long, who covered the movement for *The Progressive,* wrote emphatically about how the "old spirituals and Protestant hymns channeled into the town's sacrificial uprising." She recounted how in the early days in Albany, different movement leaders would recruit volunteers for jail time by singing "Just a Closer Walk with Thee" at various mass meetings:

> They'd sing the yearning, erotic melody first in a sweet, and nearly jazzy tempo, and then slow down to hum before a slow, soprano wail of love and pleading, "O, sweet *Jesus,* let it *be-e-e* . . . I am *weak,* but thou art *strong, sa-ave* and *shield* me from all *ha-*arm," a solo bit in which she might inject a plea about a child in jail, a brother fired for demonstrating. And then, booming bassos, lively tenors, and brave contraltos would reach up and bear the soprano along in a great flood of love. Or, in "Jesus Lover of My Soul," or a Freedom song, the domestics, business and professional people, the dogged Snicks, and the rousing preachers seemed to sing down God's promise to walk close with them through demonstrations, arrest, and jail.

Long also cited the power of "Woke Up This Morning with My Mind Stayed on Freedom" and "Keep Your Eyes on the Prize," which featured the defiant couplet,

"Singing and shouting is mighty well / But get up off your seat and go to jail" even as, she writes, "the hand-clapping crashed like cymbals."[13] Andrew Young marveled at the singing and clapping as well, calling the music the "backbone" of the movement and adding that the freedom songs "have done as much for inspiring our students as all the teaching and preaching. There is a liberating effect that comes from shouting and clapping to songs which express the long suppressed desire for freedom within the Negro."[14]

When the trials for the eleven Freedom Riders who had been arrested began on December 13, two hundred and sixty-seven African-Americans, "praying and singing" in support, paraded three abreast downtown. Pritchett's response was to quickly arrest the entire group. He then told the national media, "We can't tolerate the N.A.A.C.P. or the Student Nonviolent Committee or any other 'nigger' organization to take over this town with mass demonstrations."[15] Among the songs sung that morning, according to the unnamed *New York Times* reporter, were "We Want Freedom" and "We Are Not Afraid." The singing continued long after incarceration, including "Keep Your Eye on the Goal."[16] During the proceedings, Judge Abner Israel found activist Slater King in contempt of court for leading a group of African-Americans in song and prayer while his court was in session. A few days later, Israel had King's wife jailed, leaving their children at home with a housekeeper.[17]

As the days progressed, hundreds more activists were arrested during peaceful demonstrations, filling not just Albany's city jails, but Terrell County's jail, as well as the jails of surrounding counties. With each new wave of arrests, additional mass meetings were called. In each prison, at each protest, at each mass meeting, the singing of the new freedom songs and protest spirituals continued unabated. At a morning mass meeting at Shiloh, one participant declared, "Children, I woke up this morning with freedom on my mind."[18] The evening mass meetings often continued long into the night. The danger from roving bands of whites and capricious policemen was equally real, if not more so, after dark. Eventually, someone would urge the singers to form lines and depart the church, still singing: ". . . and that music kept us together, and kept us less afraid. It's like an angel watching over you. You know you are in trouble, you know you are going to get your butt beaten, you know you are probably going to jail, you know you might even get killed, but the sound, the power of the community was watching over you and keeping you safe."[19]

When the initial talks between the Albany Movement and city officials, led by Mayor Asa D. Kelley, broke down over allegations of abuse of the protesters, Martin Luther King, Jr., and Ralph D. Abernathy, representing the SCLC, came to the city at the request of the Albany Movement. At Shiloh on the evening of December 15, King and others addressed an overflow audience of nearly a thousand people. Three people led the singing: Rutha Harris, Cordell Reagon, and Albany College student Bernice Johnson. Johnson, who would become one of the fiercest, most talented proponents of the freedom song, was from nearby Dawson, where

African-Americans made up 75 percent of the population, yet they were continually tormented and abused by the local authorities. She writes that she experienced firsthand the freedom songs and thus heard them "pull together sections of the Black community" when other forms of communication failed. The moment Johnson writes that she knew of the "full power of song as an instrument for the articulation of our community concerns" came during an early stage of the civil rights struggle, when the local sheriff and his deputies stormed into her small country church in the middle of a service, glaring at the startled congregants: "Then a song began. And the song made sure that the sheriff and his deputies knew we were there. We became visible, our image of ourselves was enlarged when the sounds of the freedom songs filled all the space in that church."[20] Johnson first saw and heard freedom songs from television news coverage of the sit-ins, particularly those in Nashville, where she heard both "This Little Light of Mine" and "We Shall Overcome." At the initial Albany meeting attended by Sherrod and Reagon, they asked Johnson if she knew any freedom songs. But when she began "We Shall Overcome," they stopped her in mid-song, saying it was the "theme" song of the movement, and was always sung standing, with arms crossed, holding hands.[21] At Shiloh, Johnson began the singing with "Over My Head, I See Trouble in the Air," which had been a hit song twenty years earlier for Sister Rosetta Tharpe. But Johnson substituted "freedom" for "trouble" and experienced an epiphany: "That was the first time that I had an awareness that these songs were mine and I could use them for what I needed."[22] Though the church had both an organ and piano, all music was sung a cappella, including "tragic, sweet songs" such as "Oh Freedom" and "rollicking" freedom songs, such as "This Little Light of Mine." In the words of Taylor Branch, "The spirit of the songs could sweep up the crowd, and the young leaders realized that through song they could induce humble people to say and feel things that otherwise were beyond them." When the song leaders called out the "defiant" spiritual "Ain't Gonna Let Nobody Turn Me Around," they say, "Ain't gonna let Chief Pritchett turn me around." "It amazed them," Branch writes, "to see people who had inched tentatively into the church take up the verse in full voice, setting themselves against feared authority."[23]

Also present that evening was journalist Pat Watters, who recorded in detail the church service, the singing, the "Freedom!" chant, the deep-throated "Yeah!" that accompanied King as he entered the church, and the moment that the "Freedom" chant became a song: "The sound of such music, the fervor in all that packed crowd of people in the church were like nothing I had ever known." "Freedom" blended effortlessly, without an apparent signal from the song leaders into "I Woke Up This Morning with My Mind Set on Freedom."[24]

At sundown on December 16, King and Abernathy were among the nearly three hundred people who left Shiloh singing "We Shall Overcome," which grew louder as they neared City Hall, where the sidewalks were suddenly lined with onlookers. Once at City Hall, they were met by Pritchett and a hundred policemen, who arrested them on charges ranging from obstructing traffic to marching without a city-issued parade permit.[25] On December 18, a tentative agreement with Albany was reached where demonstrators would be released, a biracial committee to discuss issues would be established, and segregation would end at the bus and train terminals. King was among those released on bond and he returned to his church in Atlanta. A few weeks later, however, "white" and "colored" signs went up again in the terminals and Albany officials refused to meet with any African-Americans. King called the alleged agreement a "hoax," and some media outlets called Albany a "stunning defeat" for King and the civil rights movement. Refusing to give up, the Albany Movement resumed its protests.[26]

## 1962

City officials brought King and Abernathy back to trial in February 1962, when the court found the two men guilty of marching without a permit in December, but delayed sentencing until July.[27] Protests in Albany continued and the movement entered a difficult period as still more demonstrators were arrested and placed in area jails for lengthy stays. Their advocates faced unyielding, implacable opposition, extraordinarily large bail requirements, and stiff fines. The SNCC, the NCAAP, CORE, and other supportive groups again experienced financial issues in Albany and sought help. Harry Belafonte and his protégée Miriam Makeba sang at a benefit for King and the SCLC on June 6 in Atlanta[28] and Mahalia Jackson and African-American comic Dick Gregory performed at the sixth annual Fighting Fund for Freedom fund-raiser on June 17 in Chicago. Organized labor pledged $25,000 for the Chicago event, which the *Chicago Defender* wrote was designed to "supplement funds lost because of harassment by southern state officials."[29] The Dixie Hummingbirds, one of the most popular gospel quartets in the country, scheduled a benefit concert for Albany's civic auditorium during this period. But when they arrived, no one would unlock the building for the group and they reluctantly cancelled.[30]

On July 10, Abernathy and King returned to Albany for sentencing and were given the choice of either forty-five days in prison or a $178 fine. The two men chose the jail time. A large march was quickly organized to protest their incarceration. The prominent African-American weekly, the *Chicago Defender*, published a photograph of demonstrators, flanked by policemen, marching toward the jail singing "We Shall Overcome." They were arrested.[31] While King and Abernathy remained in jail, a group of young children stood outside their windows and sang "We Shall Overcome." They too were arrested—for singing.[32] On July 12, someone anonymously paid King and Abernathy's fines and they were released, much to their surprise. As Abernathy puckishly admitted at the mass meeting the evening after their release, "I've been thrown out of a lot of places in my day but I've never been thrown out of jail."[33] In a diary for *Jet* magazine, begun after his arrest on July 27, King wrote on Saturday July 28 that fifteen more demonstrators had been arrested in front of City Hall. They arrived "singing loudly," which was a "big lift" for King and Abernathy, but they too were arrested immediately and sent to another county jail.[34]

Though the two men vowed to return to Albany in August, they were thwarted when a federal district judge issued a temporary restraining order, prohibiting demonstrations for eight months. The injunction specifically mentioned King, Abernathy, and a number of the Albany Movement leaders.[35] That evening, following the robust singing of freedom songs, the Reverend Samuel Wells took the pulpit at Shiloh and shouted that he had seen the injunction and that his name was not on it: "I've heard a few names but my name hasn't been called. But I do know where my name is being called. My name is being called on the road to freedom. I can hear the blood of Emmett Till as it calls from the ground. . . . When shall we go? Not tomorrow! Not at high noon! Now!" Wells led nearly two hundred marchers singing "Ain't Gonna Let Nobody Turn Me 'Round" from Shiloh toward the courthouse, where Pritchett and his men promptly confronted them. When the entire group dropped to their knees to pray, Pritchett arrested more than a hundred people.[36] Following the mass meeting, the Albany leadership, meeting at William G. Anderson's house, received a report that armed white men were hunting for King. After long minutes, King rose, walked to the family piano, and asked, "Would anyone care to sing?" Those present, including attorney William M. Kunstler, began singing, "This Little Light of Mine." As they sang, Kunstler writes, "the fears and discouragements of the long day disappeared, to be replaced by a transcendental feeling of love and hope for all humanity." The small group continued singing into the night:

> As we sang, I wished that there was some way to remove the roof above us so that the whole world could witness what I was witnessing and feel what I was feeling. I wanted everyone everywhere to listen to five Negroes and one white man singing freedom songs by the light of a single candle in a darkened house on a dirt road somewhere in southwestern Georgia.
>
> An hour after we began singing, we ended with "We Shall Overcome." We linked hands together as we raised our voices. We ended with a prayer. While we hummed the melody, Dr. King asked for our protection from those who would do us harm. When he said Amen, we joyously finished the refrain. "Oh, deep in my heart, I do believe, we shall overcome some day."[37]

*New York Times* reporter Claude Sitton spent months in Albany and, in his efforts to cover the story, often found himself in harm's way. In a report filed on July 26, Sitton traveled to Sasser, Georgia, where thirty-eight African-Americans and two whites had held a voter registration rally the night before at Mount Olive Baptist Church. The group had been confronted by Sheriff Z. T. Matthews

("We want our colored people to go on living like they have for the last hundred years.") and armed deputies "badgering" and warning participants against registration efforts even as they sang "Pass Me Not, Oh Gentle Savior" and "We Are Climbing Jacob's Ladder." At least thirteen law officers interrupted the meeting and collected the names of participants as an angry group of whites assembled outside the church. The lawmen appeared "taken aback" by the presence of Sitton, who observed no violence that night. At 10 p.m., he writes, the group joined hands in a circle and sang "We Shall Overcome" while swaying together. "Their voices had a strident note as though they were building up their courage to go out into the night, where the whites waited." Upon leaving, they discovered that one of their cars had been badly damaged.[38] One observer recalled that between "singing and moaning," the sheriff was "confused" and perhaps "afraid to tell the people to shut up." "Those beautiful people sang that sheriff right out of their church!" writes Sherrod. "That was some powerful music."[39] Meanwhile, Sitton's article infuriated the Kennedy administration, which at long last filed a voting rights complaint against Matthews.[40] A few nights after the meeting, someone burned the small church, along with two other African-American churches, to the ground.[41] However, just as Eisenhower once refused to meet with Harry Belafonte in October 1958, Kennedy was unable or unwilling to meet with a delegation of more than a hundred ministers who converged on the White House on August 6 to urge the White House to "speak out" and act on civil rights violations in Albany, including King's incarceration on July 27.[42]

The summer of 1962 wound on, with no compromises from Albany officials. Protests continued and those who were jailed saw increased violence by the jailers. Albany Movement members who were not in jail tried to keep the local office open, organizing protests, mass meetings, education, and registration. As had happened in Nashville, the music permeated even the office, writes Reagon: "There was music in everything we did. If you had a staff meeting, or if we were just around the office, somebody would just come out with a song. Or if there were bad feelings, a painful discussion, tension, anybody, not a singer or anything, just anybody at the meeting or in the office, would open up with a line of a song, and somebody else would take it over, and somebody else would add a verse, and by the end, everybody would be hugging each other. You can't have a movement without that."[43]

The Albany Movement and its mass meetings continued, filling both Mount Zion and Shiloh Baptist churches with song, their voices, which "blended so forcefully, vibrantly, joyfully, told the blending of their wills; the music spoke as one person formed of all the many people, saying that it was more than all of the many people combined." Historian Howard Zinn, who was in Albany that summer, writes that a song that had not been sung earlier in the movement was now being widely sung, "Come By Here, My Lord," based on the old spiritual "Kum Bi Yah." On one of those summer evenings, Zinn notes that a congregation sang, without apparent direction by a song leader, "Oh, Freedom," "We're on Our Way to Freedom Land," "This Little Light of Mine," "Over My Head, I See Freedom in the Air,"

"Keep Your Eyes on the Prize," "Ain't Gonna Let Nobody Turn Me 'Round," and "Marching on the Freedom Highway," ending with the "Freedom" chant, accompanied only by powerful, rhythmic clapping . . . only to repeat the entire process over again. "Such music cannot be described," he recalls, "or recaptured. I was there. I heard it, was privileged to hear it night after night in the packed-in heat." The mass meetings closed with "We Shall Overcome," the congregation continuing to hum the melody under the closing benediction.[44]

While in jail, King continued writing in his diary for *Jet*. He recorded that he read, answered mail, worked on his forthcoming book of sermons (titled *Strength to Love*), held devotional services, and sang with prisoners in nearby cells, none of whom either King or Abernathy could see. After court hearings on August 7 and 8, King and Abernathy were released on August 10 with suspended sentences. Both agreed to leave Albany for the Albany Movement's promised meetings with city officials.[45] When no meetings took place, King returned again on August 13, 1962, addressing more than a thousand people at Mount Zion Baptist, urging them not to give up their "fight for freedom." City officials estimated more than twelve hundred people had been arrested since the protests began in November, and arrests were continuing daily.[46] This included fifteen young women who were arrested in mid-August solely for singing.[47] There were other difficulties for the more visible members of the Albany Movement. Many lost their jobs. Most of the Albany State students were summarily expelled, though Atlanta-area colleges Spelman, Morehouse, and Morris Brown quickly offered scholarships to those students who met admission requirements.[48]

The mayor finally agreed to meet with Albany Movement officials in the days that followed, but again offered no concessions. Over the Labor Day weekend, more protesters arrived, including a host of religious leaders. Pritchett promptly arrested and jailed them. Among the visitors were Ralph Lord Roy, a retired United Methodist minister, and Rabbi Israel Dresner of New York, who had received permission to visit King and Abernathy in jail earlier that month. As they walked the jail hallways, students jammed in a neighboring cell loudly sang "Oh Freedom" to prevent the guards from hearing the conversation between King and Dresner. After the meeting, the two visitors remained in Albany, were harassed by officials, met with Movement leaders, spoke at registration drives, and eventually were among the seventy-five religious leaders who were arrested.[49] During and after the third imprisonment of King and Abernathy, small groups continued their sit-ins, prayer marches and kneel-ins. The nightly mass meetings also continued, where a *Jet* magazine reporter noted the singing of "Ain't Gonna Let Chief Pritchett Turn Me Around," "Give Me Freedom," and "Woke Up This Morning with My Mind Set on Freedom."[50]

By the summer of 1962, the importance of the music to the Albany Movement was significant enough that the *New York Times* sent music writer Robert Shelton to the city. A sympathetic observer with a fine ear for music, Shelton would write widely on freedom music in years to come. In a lengthy article published on August 20, 1962, Shelton noted that the movement leadership was "in agreement that music sets the tempo" for the freedom struggle. The freedom songs helped "bolster the morale of integrationists and disarm the hostility of segregationists." The songs sung at mass demonstrations, in jail, at sit-ins, prayer vigils, and Freedom Rides, made the "deep river of Negro protest in song run faster." Shelton interviewed a number of participants about the importance of the songs. He quotes Charles Jones as saying, "There could have been no Albany Movement without music." King is no less emphatic: "The freedom songs are playing a strong and vital role in our struggle. They give the people new courage and a sense of unity. I think they keep alive a faith, a radiant hope, in the future, particularly in our most trying hours."[51] As a journalist, Shelton also addressed the conflicts among the disparate groups of the Albany Movement—the original organizers, SNCC, NAACP, SCLC, and CORE—but quotes King as saying, "We all share the same songs." Among the songs quoted in the article is an arrangement of "Go Down, Moses," with the lines: "Go down Kennedy / Way down in Georgia land / Tell old Pritchett / To let my people go." Even Pritchett was interviewed. While he states that he believes the freedom songs "incite" the protesters, he admits: "These people got a lot of feeling and rhythm. I enjoy hearing them sing. The songs are catchy." The article detailed how the singing had been banned in many of the area jails and how protesters had been punished for singing them. Also intriguing is an account of how a student-led group (called the Freedomtones) sang freedom songs at a Durham church on August 12, but that the singing did not motivate or engage the congregation. However, when the service moved to a segregated Howard Johnson's restaurant nearby, the "apathy of the singing in the church disappeared" as more than five hundred protesters "belted out in full chorus," "We Shall Overcome." For Jones, a field secretary for SNCC, the songs were, in the end, essential for the Albany Movement: "We could not have communicated with the masses of people without music. They could not have communicated with us without music. They are not articulate. But through songs, they expressed years of suppressed hope, suffering, even joy and love."[52] Forman, commenting after a cessation of the protests, agreed that the music was essential: "You see why this is a singing movement? The songs help. Without them, it would be ugly. Ugly."[53]

Journalist Watters was one of the first to write about another aspect of the Albany mass meetings besides the singing, preaching, and praying—the humor. Abernathy was well known for his sense of humor, and students who had survived jail also quickly incorporated humor into their songs. To illustrate this, Watters cites a performance of "This Little Light of Mine": "All on Chief Pritchett / I'm gonna let it shine / Ohhh . . . all on Chief Pritchett / I'm gonna let it shine." During one series of announcements about the next mass meetings, Abernathy interrupted his instructions to sing, to the tune of "If You Can't Find Me at the Back of the Bus," these words: "If you meet me down at city jail / And you can't find me nowhere / Then you come on up to Camilla / Because they will have transferred me there."[54] Throughout the long months of protests, Abernathy often led supporters in singing "Ain't Gonna Let Nobody Turn Me 'Round" at Mount Zion Baptist

Church, improvising as always with each successive verse: "Ain't gonna let Chief Pritchett turn me 'round," "Ain't gonna let no injunction turn me 'round," "Ain't gonna let Mayor Kelly turn me 'round" and others. A camera crew documenting the movement for CBS caught students singing the song and clapping rhythmically, even as policemen carried them, two at a time, to a waiting paddy wagon.[55]

Following the lessons learned from reading King's book, Pritchett had avoided overcrowding Albany's jail, which would have drawn negative coverage by the national media, by calling on prison authorities in nearby counties. Each agreed to take some of the protesters.[56] The neighboring county jails were soon filled as well and the protesters gave each one a name to match the conditions: "Terrible Terrell," "Dogging Douglas," "Unmitigated Mitchell," "Lamentable Lee," "Unbearable Baker," and "Unworthy Worth," the last prison being "a notorious pocket of exploitation and oppression with a history of violence."[57]

Authorities in these jails quickly realized the "value of this singing in keeping the courage and morale of students high" and responded to the music with threats and punishment. But the singing continued. One of the most famous freedom songs to come from the Albany Movement originated in Dougherty County jail and name-checked both the chief of police and the mayor. The protest spiritual "Oh Mary, Oh Martha, Ring Them Bells" was recast by Gober and Janie Culbreath as "Oh Pritchett, Oh Kelly." The lyrics implored the men to "open them cells," even as they lamented "Bail's gettin' higher" and "Bond's gettin' higher." As one student explained, the singing of these songs "helped to ease the knot in the pit of my stomach."[58] "Oh Pritchett, Oh Kelly" was composed after the second of Gober's four arrests and was featured in the popular folk song magazine, *Broadside,* along with "If You Miss Me at the Back of the Bus," with the music notated for both songs. Also included in the issue were two new civil rights–related songs by Bob Dylan, "Oxford Town" and "Paths of Victory."[59] Pritchett apparently enjoyed the notoriety. Once, when he encountered Rutha Harris in jail, he shouted, "Rutha, sing that song about me and Kelly." Surprised, Harris complied.[60] Most of the sheriffs were not as tolerant. Another female protester in Mitchell, jammed with eighty-seven other prisoners in a cell designed to hold twenty, was warned by the sheriff upon their arrival by bus, "We don't have no singin', no prayin', and no hand-clappin' here.'"[61]

The best known of the county jails was Terrell and unlike Pritchett, Sheriff Zeke Matthews had *not* read King's book on Montgomery and freely physically abused demonstrators. When Sherrod was taken to Terrell, Matthews personally escorted him and predictably shouted at him, "There'll be no damn singin' and no damn prayin' in *my* jail. I don't want to hear nothin' about freedom!" Sherrod, perhaps unwisely, responded, "We may be in jail, but we're still human beings, still Christians." Matthews hit Sherrod in the face, took him to his office (where he was struck by another officer), and then threw him into a private cell.[62]

Bernice Johnson spent time in both the Albany city jail and the nearby Lee County Stockade. In an article for *Sing Out!,* she writes that Albany was "already a singing movement and we took those songs to jail." The singing of the freedom songs by people of different races, ages, and socioeconomic strata somehow erased all boundaries: "After the song, the differences among us would not be as great. Somehow, making a song required an expression of that which was common to us all. The songs did not feel like the same songs I had sung in college. This music was like an instrument, like holding a tool in your hand."[63] In a later interview, she notes that "I Laid My Burden Down" (sometimes called "Since I Lay My Burden Down") was her "jail song" at a time when avoiding jail was paramount among African-Americans in the South. But Johnson writes that she believes the singing of freedom songs enabled her, and thousands of others, to express what was happening in Albany and elsewhere, where lives and philosophies were being transformed in jail. "And in our singing we nurtured this different way of being that we were determined to bring about in our lives." The constant efforts by the police and jail guards to silence the singing proved to the singers that they were being heard even while imprisoned, and that a transformation was taking place in their lives and priorities. Jail, Johnson says, made the singing of Albany residents "bigger, more powerful singing, because we were bigger, more powerful." The singing "echoed" that personal transformation: "If people are transformed, they create the sound that lets you know they are new people. It is a sound you've never heard before, and they have never had it before, because they never been in that place before."[64] Student activist Tom Hayden also spent time in Albany jails. Like Johnson, he saw jail time as a transformative event, "where new faith was fortified" because the "spirit of intense solidarity, concern for others, singing and storytelling, and deep reflection bonded people into a stronger community."[65]

Once understandably feared and avoided by African-Americans, jails and prisons had now taken on a new meaning in the civil rights movement. Since the entire southern power structure had virtually outlawed the movement, going to jail over unjust laws was a supreme act of disobedience. Songs were sung and composed in jail and served a multitude of purposes. Some songs endorsed the experience: "Well, have you been to jail? / Certainly, Lord / Certainly, certainly, certainly Lord." Singing both enhanced the jail experience and provided another nonviolent weapon in the movement's arsenal: "Freedom songs did some of their best work in jail where they made all the more palpable the feeling that freedom was in the air, air that could move freely, like the mind and the spirit, out of the confines of a prison cell or the prison house of a racist society."[66] NAACP official Vernon Jordan remembered a meeting he had organized in nearby Hart County: "The people were cold with fear until music did what prayer and speeches could not do in breaking the ice."[67]

### Preserving Albany's Music

The Albany Movement treasured the power of the freedom song and recognized the importance of preserving it. In the summer of 1962, Sherrod, White, Rutha and

Emory Harris, and Brenda Darden, along with Cordell Reagon, Bernice Johnson, and others, worked with Guy Carawan and Alan Lomax to produce *Freedom in the Air: A Documentary on Albany, Georgia, 1961–1962*.[68] In the *New York Times*, Shelton called it the "stand-out" of four albums chronicling the freedom movement, saying it was the "most effective documentary recording to grow out of the integration movement" and requested more recordings from Albany. Shelton quotes Andrew Young as saying that there was "a 'soul' in the singing in Albany congregations that was unlike anything he had heard elsewhere."[69]

The LP makes it possible to hear the continuing evolution in the performance of the now-familiar freedom songs. Watters noted at the time that the singers at the mass meetings in Albany brought something new to "We Shall Overcome": ". . . a flourish in the rendering of the refrain, an adding, thrusting into it of extra notes which, with hundreds singing loudly, confidently, exultantly, made it, far more than in most singing of it, strong and joyful and imperative, an impetus to action: an added 'Oh . . . oh . . . oh' in two lines of the refrain; the first time a long 'Oooooh' in the background of the 'Oh . . . oh . . . oh . . . .'"

Transcribed, the lyrics now look like:

> *We'll all go to jail*
> *Today . . .*
> *Oh-oh-oh, deep in my heart*
> *I know that I do believe*
> *Oh-oh-oh, we shall overcome*
> *Some day . . .*

Watters quoted Leon Hall as describing the "Ooooh" in the background as sounding "like pouring out a bucket of stars."[70]

Something else the singers in Albany realized was the sense of continuity of the protest spirituals and the freedom songs; that the power in the lyrics had always been there, waiting, until the singers and listeners were at a point in their lives to be able to comprehend them. "They were saying what I was feeling," Johnson wrote of the lyrics sung in Albany. "Somehow, it felt like all those words that black people had been praying and saying was a language for us, a language we could not understand unless we were involved in a practical, everyday struggle."[71] Others soon recognized the power of the movement's music as well. Johnson, after her suspension from college, had traveled to upstate New York. Her first unaccompanied solo performance was at the legendary Caffé Lena in Saratoga Springs; her second performance was in Carnegie Hall.[72]

Folksinger Pete Seeger visited Albany several times during the tumultuous summer of 1962, singing at rallies and collecting material. Once he heard the new words to "Which Side Are You On," he collected the lyrics, including "Have you heard about the laws / That Chief Pritchett made? / If you stand up for your rights / He'll put you in a cage." Seeger also performed at area churches, where he introduced an old Weavers song, "I'm on My Way," which was quickly adopted by protesters.[73] Seeger suggested to SNCC executive director James Forman that the organization should form a singing group along the lines of his own Almanac Singers in the 1930s and '40s. Forman agreed and asked Cordell Reagon to assemble what came to be called the Freedom Singers (sometimes called the SNCC Freedom Singers). The original members, Reagon, Rutha Mae Harris, Chuck Neblett, Dorothy Vale, and Bernice Johnson, traveled widely singing freedom songs, raising money for the SNCC, and heightening national awareness of the movement.[74] In a borrowed compact Buick, the Freedom Singers drove fifty thousand miles, stopping in dozens of states and performing nonstop.[75] The Freedom Singers provided an "institutional form" to an essential component of the ongoing efforts for social justice—that "music was a vital political force in the movement."[76]

As the protests and jailings dragged on into September, a "hootenanny" in New York City's Carnegie Hall featured Seeger, who hosted and performed the hit "The Hammer Song" ("If I Had a Hammer"), along with Bob Dylan and nineteen-year-old Johnson, who, the reporter noted, "sang freedom songs and traditional Negro folk music in a contralto of enormous size and power."[77] On October 21, 1962, SNCC sponsored the Gospel for Freedom at Chicago's Arie Crown Theater at McCormick Place, featuring well-known gospel singers James Cleveland, the Caravans, the Highway QC's, and others, as well as the Freedom Singers and Chorus.[78]

### The End of Albany

Mass meetings and protests continued in Albany for six more years, though the later demonstrations were rarely chronicled by the national media. During that time, progress was glacial and incremental: the schools remained segregated and the parks were closed. The library was integrated, but only after all chairs had been removed.[79] In one of many asides during his sermons in Albany, Abernathy noted, "Let 'em close up all the parks. We aren't used to any parks anyhow."[80] Pritchett remained for a time in Albany before eventually leaving to become sheriff in High Point, North Carolina. Some African-Americans believed he left because he came to enforce the law too "stringently" on whites.[81] Sherrod, who eventually settled in Albany, later recalled one last exchange with Pritchett: "You know Sherrod, it's just a matter of mind over matter," Pritchett had said. "I don't mind and you don't matter."[82]

While the Albany Movement may not have ended with the dramatic changes the civil rights movement had sometimes spurred elsewhere, change did ultimately come to Albany, but not easily. Peace activist Barbara Deming spent nearly two months in Albany's jails in 1963–64 for participating in a peace walk, surrounded by African-American protesters who sang freedom songs even as they suffered continual physical abuse in prison. Many of the prisoners staged a lengthy, life-threatening fast to protest the brutal conditions.[83] Hundreds more were arrested in the years that followed. Still, for many of those who actively participated, their recollections were not colored by any supposed "failures" of the movement there, but by what was accomplished and how. In addition to intensified voter registration efforts both in Albany and in many of the surrounding counties where protesters had previously been kept in jail, and the momentum to keep the boycotts and protests alive for years after the departure of the national media, Albany also produced the singing of Bernice Johnson (who later married fellow Freedom Singer member Cordell Reagon). Of Bernice, Forman wrote, "nothing had been more important in creating the spirit of Albany than the freedom songs and the voice of Bernice Johnson Reagon."[84]

For movement activist Bob Zellner, the "momentum" for the civil rights movement was the "music, music, music" that "came to full bloom" in Albany: "[T]he movement's music leveled us all to the same emotional spiritual plane. None of us have ever forgotten those songs, and in the shock-troops days, in dangerous situations, the music gave the people strength and courage—soul force. It also gave quite a bit of pause to the posses, state troopers, and police. For some people who were going to break up the demonstrations and do possible violence, they had to steel themselves to attack people while they were singing and while they were praying."[85]

The civil rights movement itself carried the important lessons of Albany with it to the ongoing voter registration battles in Mississippi and then to Birmingham. As movement organizers had learned in Nashville, the mass meetings were essential to educate the broader population about what was happening in the civil rights movement elsewhere, to train listeners in nonviolent protest, to create a sense of community, to build and sustain courage and perseverance, and to instruct people how to respond to arrest. The music, which dominated most of those meetings, supplemented and sometimes led that effort. For an audience trained in the African-American church singing tradition, this "collective musicking" was a familiar, comforting, sometimes scintillating ritual. The call-and-response format of songs that gained popularity in Albany, such as "Sing Till the Power of the Lord Comes Down" and "I'm on My Way to Freedom Land," also reinforced the unbreakable ties with the centuries-long quest by African-Americans for racial justice and equality. The Albany Movement musical experience was important as a model for the next stages of the civil rights movement.[86]

For the SNCC, the lessons were specific and concrete. When the SNCC asked Sherrod to create the outline for community organizing the following summer, the first point on his list was the imperative for the organization to teach freedom songs in each new town or community.[87] Wyatt Tee Walker remained convinced that despite the long war with entrenched segregationists, the battles of Albany were essential learning experiences for all involved: "The strength of the Albany Movement was that it was perhaps the first time in this period of struggle of black people that we had mobilized an entire community against segregation. And secondly, we learned that valid and crucial lesson, that you must pinpoint your targets so that you do not dilute the strength of your attack."[88]

In an article published shortly after his time spent in Albany, *New York Times* music writer Shelton commented that the events in Georgia convinced him of the power of sacred song: "Albany was the most dramatic evidence of a whole community being wielded into a common entity through music—new freedom songs, old spirituals, long-metered, chanting hymns in which the improvisational activity is busily inventive."[89]

"Albany," Andrew Young told Tom Dent, "was a *singing* movement. If song could make us free, we would have been free."[90]

# INTERLUDE

## *McComb, Mississippi*

We would sing about anything we felt.
We would sing about why we sing.
We would sing about the abuses we
suffered, like not being allowed to vote.
We would sing of sorrow and hope.

—DOROTHY COTTON

**B**eyond Albany and before and during the chaos that would become Birmingham, the civil rights movement continued to spread throughout the South. One of SNCC's two "wings" chose to focus its efforts on voter registration in Pike, Amite, and Walthall counties in rural Mississippi. On August 7, 1961, Cordell Reagon, Robert Moses, Marion Barry, and others joined the first wave of workers and opened a voter registration school in McComb. Moses was beaten on August 22 and later jailed while working on registration issues. On September 7, John Hardy, an instructor at SNCC's voting school, was beaten by the Walthall County clerk while attempting to register two African-Americans (though it was Hardy who was subsequently charged with breach of the peace).[1] As for Moses, the vehemence of the attacks against the registration effort soon had him questioning whether to continue the struggle. During the lonely drive to the courthouse, the song "We Are Climbing Jacob's Ladder" came to him. "I sang it in my mind again and again like a mantra. 'Every rung goes higher, higher. Every rung goes higher, higher.' On the one hand it was spiritual and on the other hand it had a wider political meaning, and it was all connected in this act of driving down to the courthouse." Moses elected to remain in Mississippi, at least for a while longer.[2]

Violence against blacks in the counties eventually drew the attention of the Federal Civil Rights Commission, whose investigations found widespread efforts to stop the registration of African-Americans. In the process, Moses, a soft-spoken Harvard graduate, became a folk hero to the embattled Mississippians. The McComb police chief called Moses "a pretty shrewd damn duck." The SNCC, which established a small headquarters in McComb, the only city of any size in the area, was joined by representatives from the NAACP.[3]

The attacks prompted African-Americans to begin the area's first sit-in protests. But following a particularly savage attack on SNCC's Travis Britt, many of the local farmers and pastors were afraid to continue to support the registration efforts. And in late September, Amite County resident and NAACP member Herbert Lee was gunned down on a public street by a Mississippi State Representative for his efforts in voter registration. No charges were filed against Lee's killer and the lone black man who witnessed the murder and had agreed to testify for the prosecution was murdered two years later. More SNCC volunteers arrived in McComb and many were arrested while praying on the courthouse steps following Lee's murder. From a cramped jail cell with Hollis Watkins, Robert Talbert, Charles McDew, and others, Moses smuggled an account of the events to SNCC headquarters in Atlanta: "This is Mississippi, the middle of the iceberg. Hollis is leading off with his tenor, 'Michael row the boat ashore, Alleluia; Christian brothers don't be slow, Alleluia; Mississippi's next to go, Allelulia.' This is a tremor in the middle of the iceberg—from a stone that the builders rejected."[4]

On October 3, the high school students who had been jailed for their parts in various sit-ins were released, but the school principal refused to readmit Brenda Travis, one of the leaders. More than a hundred students promptly walked out, eventually finding their way to the SNCC's McComb headquarters, "engulfing" the small office "like a sudden tidal surge": "At first we heard only the faint sound of singing in the distance, the sound of freedom songs that gradually became louder and then thunderous as the marching students, still singing, came up the stairs and entered our headquarters."[5]

On the afternoon of October 4, Bob Zellner and other SNCC staff members in the tiny headquarters "huddled together near a window" facing the high school. A group of students approached singing, "we'll walk hand in hand." But soon the words transitioned into "I woke up this morning with my mind stayed on freedom." In a few moments, the beleaguered staffers, still mourning the murder of Herbert Lee, could both hear the tramp of the students' feet and see the "proud but grim smiles" on their faces. When the students drew even with the building, the SNCC staff joined them in singing, "it ain't no harm to keep your mind stayed on freedom."[6]

On October 31, a judge convicted McDew, Moses, Zellner, and several older McComb high school students of "disturbing the peace" and sentenced them to four to six months in the Magnolia County jail, where they spent the time "playing chess, reading, singing, and writing letters."[7] When Harry Belafonte paid their bail in December, most joined the newly formed Nonviolent High School to teach the many suspended high school students.[8]

Lee's murder and the serious wounding of SNCC field secretary James Travis prompted more protest spirituals, including some that addressed the issue directly:

> *We have hung our heads and cried*
> *For those like Lee who died*
> *Died for you and died for me*
> *Died for the cause of equality*
> *But we'll never turn back*
> *Until we've all been freed.*[9]

Written directly in response to the death of Lee, "We'll Never Turn Back" was composed by Bertha Gober, a veteran of the Albany protests and jails, using lines from two familiar spirituals, including "We've been 'buked and we've been scorned."[10]

Other songs emerged from SNCC's first foray into Mississippi for voter registration as well. Sam Block and Willie Peacock rewrote "Get on Board, Little Children" to include this chilling rhyme: "Can't you see that mob a'comin' / Comin' 'round the bend / If you fight for freedom / They sure will do you in."[11] Also popularized during this tumultuous period was an adaptation of Ray Charles's hit song, "Lonely Avenue." Charles Neblett wrote the new lyrics as an "abused prisoner" in Charleston, Missouri. Like "Get on Board, Little Children," the words, based on painful experience, have a decidedly darker edge: "My father told me / On his dying bed / If my son don't get his freedom / I'd rather see him dead / That's why I'm fighting for my rights." Neblett's experiences in Charleston were much the same as those of others in Alabama and Mississippi, with random beatings, overcrowded cells with no mattresses, and limited or no contact with the outside world. "We knew we had to go through it," he later told the *Washington Post,* "that we had to be there awhile. So we would just sing."[12]

A booklet published by the Students for a Democratic Society (SDS) detailed the systematic threats, abuses, beatings, and jailings endured by both SNCC and NAACP members and anyone foolhardy enough to attempt to register to vote or even to attend a voter registration meeting.[13] When Zellner arrived at the Negro Masonic Lodge in McComb on October 4 for an SNCC staff meeting, he was met by Bernard Lafayette, Charles Sherrod, McDew, and others. To his general inquiry, "How are you this morning?" the group responded in chorus, "We woke up this morning with our minds stayed on Freedom!" The SNCC workers spontaneously joined a group of Burgland High students protesting the expulsion of a fellow student and singing "I woke up this morning with my mind stayed on freedom."[14]

But McComb authorities kept the pressure on SNCC operatives, students, and supporters to such an extent that the SNCC quietly moved out in the waning days of 1961. Moses and the others took valuable lessons from their experiences in McComb, along with a number of students who had left college to work full-time for SNCC.[15]

# BIRMINGHAM, ALABAMA

"We Shall Overcome" has become almost
as famous as the "Star-Spangled Banner"
and today's marching feet will be as important to historians as the hoof beats of Paul
Revere's ride.

—REV. FRED SHUTTLESWORTH, JUNE 5,
1964, BIRMINGHAM, ALABAMA

**M**artin Luther King's prestige had suffered in the eight relatively quiet months following the perceived failure of Albany. The SNCC, deeply involved in Mississippi voter registration amid frequent oppression and violence, saw little press coverage and what appeared to be even fewer results. Nor did the other groups working for the civil rights movement, including the NAACP and CORE, generate much publicity with their work. The financially strapped SCLC and SNCC continually tapped into their network of friends in the music industry for support. At one such event, "A Salute to Southern Students," Thelonius Monk, Charles Mingus, Herbie Mann, Tony Bennett, and their groups, along with the Freedom Singers, performed at a benefit for the SNCC in on February 1, 1963 at Carnegie Hall,[1] but without widespread public awareness of the ongoing violence and intimidation in the South, fund-raising was difficult as well.

After long discussions, King and the SCLC ultimately chose Birmingham as the site of their next campaign. While a number of factors played into the decision, the impassioned advocacy of Birmingham's fiery, charismatic Reverend Fred Shuttlesworth was a crucial element.[2] At a March 31, 1963 meeting with Harry Belafonte in New York with various supporters, including actors Ossie Davis, Ruby Dee, Fredric March, and Anthony Quinn, along with the editors of two New York newspapers, Shuttlesworth made an impassioned plea on behalf of action in his city that swayed the SCLC toward Birmingham.[3]

Shuttlesworth and the Alabama Christian Movement for Human Rights (ACMHR), a local civil rights organization he had cofounded with three other Baptist pastors in 1956 when the state had banned the NAACP, had been fighting a long and heroic battle against the entrenched white supremacist leadership in the city. The ACMHR met every Monday night and within days of the group's founding, Shuttlesworth's home was bombed for what would be the first time.[4]

Birmingham was called "the most segregated city this side of Johannesburg" and "Bombingham" by local African-Americans because of the frequent (and unsolved) bombings of black churches and homes.[5] In addition to avowed and very public opposition from Alabama Governor George Wallace and State Director of Public Safety Albert Lingo, the movement also faced the power of Birmingham's commissioner of public safety, Eugene "Bull" Connor, who could and did enlist the fire department, the police force, and even the Alabama state militia to enforce segregation. Connor and others also exerted influence over the White Citizens' councils and the Ku Klux Klan, whose membership permeated many of the other organizations.[6] Connor's controversial past included a period where, at the behest of the out-of-town owners, he fought the unionization of Birmingham's heavy industries using intimidation, violence, illegal incarcerations, and, it is reported, murder. And Birmingham's jail had such a fearsome record of brutality against African-Americans that it had even its own song, "Birmingham Jail."[7]

Following lengthy strategy sessions designed to avoid the problems that had arisen in Albany, and working from a loose, wide-ranging plan of marches, sit-ins, and confrontations devised by Wyatt T. Walker, the SCLC surfaced in Birmingham on April 3, 1963, the day after a bitter mayoral election between the avowed segregationist Connor and the superficially more moderate Albert Boutwell. Though Boutwell won the run-off election, Conner and his supporters went to the courts in an effort to remain in office. For a period of months, the city had two opposing governments. The movement's first activities consisted of well-organized sit-in protests at various downtown restaurants that lay the groundwork for what the SCLC believed would be a long campaign. The sit-ins followed an ACMHR boycott of segregated downtown Birmingham merchants some months earlier. The protests resulted in a handful of low-key arrests, but drew little attention. That night, however, a rally at St. James Baptist Church began the first of sixty-five consecutive mass meetings at various African-American churches throughout Birmingham.[8] As in Albany, the meetings began at 6 p.m. and concluded at 9 p.m. and generally closed with the singing of a protest spiritual or freedom song such as "We Shall Overcome," led by Carlton Reese and the dynamic Alabama Christian Movement

**FIGURE 7**

Commissioner of Public Safety Theophilus
Eugene "Bull" Connor was the most ardent—
and dangerous—foe of the civil rights movement in Birmingham in April and May of 1963.
*Birmingham Post-Herald* Civil Rights Photographs, Collection 827, Archives Department,
Birmingham Public Library. Photo: Birmingham, Alabama, Public Library Archives.

Choir (ACMC), an arm of the ACMHR. The meetings were also attended by and usually taped by white uniformed police officers and sometimes paid informants from the African-American community. The police reports left an invaluable record of the meetings for future scholars to peruse.[9]

According to one estimate, the ACMHR had about a thousand members, primarily Baptist, from a dozen churches in the Birmingham area. As was the case in Montgomery and Albany, the ACMHR's mass meetings emphasized song. As a reporter for the *Pittsburgh Courier* noted, "When one sits in their mass meetings and hears them sing and pray and lift their voices to their God, you get the feeling here is a boundless and ever growing faith in God that will not let these people lose their hope and their faith."[10]

*Why We Can't Wait,* King's account of the events in Birmingham, details the standard mass meeting: an inspirational sermon by various pastors, including Shuttlesworth, the Reverend Ralph Abernathy, and sometimes King himself, instructions for the following day's confrontations, and the singing:

> An important part of the mass meetings was the freedom songs. In a sense, the freedom songs are the soul of the movement. They are more than just incantations of clever phrases designed to invigorate a company; they are as old as the history of the Negro in America. They are adaptations of the songs the slaves sang—the sorrow songs, the shouts for joy, the battle hymns and the anthems of our movement. I have heard people talk of their beat and rhythm, but we in the movement are as inspired by their words. "Woke Up This Morning with My Mind Stayed on Freedom" is a sentence needs no music to makes its point. We sing the freedom songs today for the same reason the slaves sang them, because we too are in bondage and the songs add hope to our determination that "We shall overcome, Black and white together, We shall overcome someday."[11]

In a city where many middle-class African-American business leaders and the pastors of the largest churches largely did not support the protests, the ACMHR Choir (also referred to as the ACMC Choir) was among the Birmingham movement's greatest allies, stemming in part from the city's long history of unions, protest spirituals, and gospel music.[12] Reece's ACMHR Choir was already a force in Birmingham music and politics when King and the SCLC arrived. Initially, the group consisted of the blending of the Forty-Sixth Street Baptist Church and Bethel Baptist Church (Shuttlesworth's congregation) choirs. Founding members included Mamie Brown and Nims Gay, and Brown recalled that the group's meetings went from Monday nights to nightly during the protests of 1963. During the choir's first years, the music was designed to "motivate" people to attend the ACMHR meetings. "Gospel music is what draws the people," she recalled. "We've had many people tell us on Monday nights, 'I didn't go to church yesterday, but I didn't care, because I knew I was going to come and hear some good singing and preaching Monday night."[13] Very quickly, the highly trained organization featured exceptional soloists, such as Brown and Cleopatra Kennedy, and adopted complex, "charismatic" arrangements of freedom song and protest spirituals into its repertoire. *But for Birmingham* author Glenn T. Eskew's book describes the "transcendence" of the ACMHR Choir's "distinct quality" as members faced "vigilantes" and the ferocious attacks of the white Birmingham "power structure."[14]

Two of the Birmingham movement's best-known and best-loved songs were staples of the choir: "God Will Make a Way" and Reese's arrangement of "Ninety-Nine and a Half Won't Do."[15] The Reverend Edward Gardner, a regular at the mass meetings, always requested that the choir sing Reese and Brown's "I'm on My Way to Freedomland." Brown rewrote the old protest spiritual "I'm on My Way to Canaan Land" at a Highlander workshop conducted by Guy and Candie Carawan.[16] In his collection of the songs of the civil rights movement, Guy Carawan asserts that the sheer "variety of singing to be heard at mass meetings in Birmingham probably wasn't matched in any other movement in the South." And, according to Bernice Johnson Reagon, the singing often culminated with "Ninety-Nine and a Half Won't Do," a dramatic reworking of an old spiritual counting song: "'Five, ten, fifteen won't do. Twenty, twenty-five, thirty won't do.' With a quickening tempo the choir would continue to 'Ninety-nine and a half won't do.' Then came the crescendo, when the choir, and audience shouted, 'One hundred percent will do!' The song articulated commitment to completing a task—to total involvement."[17] The prominence afforded "Ninety-Nine and a Half Won't Do" by the choir is significant because even while it is "exhorting absolute commitment," Dennis Chong notes that it also provides "an overt method by which people could reassure each other of their continued commitment to the movement." That sense of "mass cohesion," was essential to the continued success of the Birmingham campaign, which was continually "fortified" by the songs, prayers, and sermons of the mass meetings.[18]

Fifty years later, the ACMHR Choir has assumed almost mythic status in Birmingham, both for its political impact on the movement and for the power of its live performances. Shuttlesworth handpicked Reese, who had been involved in justice issues in the 1950s while still in high school, to direct the choir. "Music was very important in the movement and people begin to respond a lot when they hear music," Reese said later. "You know, without a song, the day will never end." In addition to teaching the choir gospel songs, spirituals, and freedom songs, Reece began writing songs as well.[19] Another choir director, Eloise Gaffney, who had joined the ACMHR Choir in 1962, called the choir an "inspiration" and said that it gave both singers and listeners "courage that they didn't think they had" before and after the performances. "When we were talking about 'we ain't gonna let nobody turn me around,' it kind of just fired them up," she said. "And Martin King was the one that said this choir can sing them out of their seats and into the streets." Longtime choir member Annie B. Levison agreed, saying that the choir's singing set people "on fire." "And when the fire starts burning all over," she recalled, "they going to run. So, where you going to run to? You're going to go out to people and say, 'Let's get free. Let's get free!'"[20]

At age 13, Gaffney was the youngest member of the choir in 1963. She recalled specific songs chosen for mass meetings ("Do You Want Your Freedom?"), for marching in Birmingham's streets ("I'm on My Way to Freedom Land") and, occasionally, when she and other members were en route to jail, she said they sang, "I'm gonna walk, walk / I'm gonna talk, talk /I'm gonna sing, sing / With my mind stayed on freedom." Choir members also sang "To Me It's So Wonderful to Know That Freedom Is Mine" in jail. Gaffney ultimately sang and worked with virtually every civil rights movement leader, including King, Stokely Carmichael, and A. Philip Randolph. She has vivid memories of how songs such as "Ain't Gonna Let Nobody Turn Me 'Round" would inspire people. "Everybody would get up on your feet and sway from side to side and get really excited about what the movement was about." She recalled that "Take My Hand, Precious Lord" would invariably bring tears to King's eyes and, from time to time, he would stop in the midst of an important speech or sermon and say, "Let's have a little more of that choir."[21]

The ACMHR, which had met every Monday night for seven years, rotated churches regularly, though the unofficial "home" was Sixteenth Street Baptist, situated between the white and black sections of Birmingham. The mass meetings combined "worship services, social visit, teen hangouts, choir concerts, sing-alongs, fish fries, strategy sessions, political debates, news reports, educational assemblies, fundraisers, crowd-rousers, and calls for volunteers." Teenage participant Gwendolyn Sanders called it a "shouting, singing . . . hallelujah time." Virtually every meeting was standing room only and crowds sometimes "spontaneously overflowed" into nearby African-American churches. Young people often conducted their own simultaneous meetings at a separate church, featuring their own choirs.[22] As for Reese, he said he believed that the choir served a number of purposes during the heady, dangerous days of Birmingham, from "inspiring activism and sacrifice" for the movement, to keeping high the sometimes flagging morale of participants. "People would really sing in the movement—leave the church singing and move on out into the streets and just march, march, march," he later recalled.[23]

The Birmingham campaign began inauspiciously. Though the organizers had hundreds of commitments for the protests (and the expected subsequent stints in jail), far fewer demonstrators actually showed up for the initial sit-ins and protests at downtown restaurants and department stores, in part because of an unexpected strike by city bus drivers. Only twenty-one protesters were arrested on April 3, including Rev. Abraham Woods, Rev. Calvin Woods, and Reese. Also arrested was Carter Gaston, who said that if he "had not gone to jail that next day, I just would have died." En route to jail, the first protesters "rocked" the paddy wagon with "Shall We Gather at the River." Once booked and placed in cells, other inmates befriended the "King and Shuttlesworth men" and sang freedom songs with them.[24]

On April 4, another small handful of protesters were arrested. One protest was cancelled by organizers when several of the targeted restaurants remained closed. Most of those arrested were charged with "Trespass After Warning," fined $100 each, and sentenced to one hundred and eighty days in jail.[25] Within a few days, several more SCLC staffers, including Walker, James Lawson, Bernard Lee, Andrew Young, and Dorothy Cotton, arrived in Birmingham to assist efforts. On Saturday, April 6, Shuttlesworth was among another small handful of protesters arrested by Connor's men even as Shuttlesworth lined out the old hymn "The Lord Will Help Us" with protesters. As the twenty-nine were crammed into paddy wagons, they broke into "We Shall Overcome."[26]

The speakers on the first Saturday night meeting urged listeners to place themselves in a position to be arrested and to fill the city's jails. Among those arrested on Easter Sunday, April 7, while singing "Hold My Hand While I Run This Race" were several well-known Birmingham pastors, including King's younger brother, Rev. A. D. King, Rev. Nelson Smith, and Rev. John Thomas Porter, pastor of the Sixth Avenue Baptist Church, the largest African-American church in the city. A large crowd of black spectators viewed the impromptu parade and when Birmingham police began roughly accosting the preachers, who were on their knees praying and singing, members of the crowd vociferously expressed their objections. For the first time, Connor called in the police dogs, then directed his officers to wade into one group of bystanders, swinging their billy clubs.[27]

Connor carefully monitored every mass meeting using Birmingham police officers, sometimes in plain clothes, though occasionally in uniform. Their handwritten notes ironically provide some of the best specific detail of the mass meetings, as well as numerous occasions of unintentional humor. At the Monday April 8 mass meeting at First Baptist Church, Ensley, officers B. A. Allison and R. A. Watkins reported that the church was so full, with attendees in the aisles and windows, that the officers themselves called the fire department. The fire marshal arrived and ordered Reverend Edward Gardner to reduce the number of people in attendance or risk being shut down. According to the handwritten notes now in the Birmingham Public Library: "He [Gardner] suggested that everyone who was not seated to go approximately one block to Rev. Hayes [*sic*] church and that some of the preachers would go and hold a service and they would even send half of the choir down there because they were singing too loud and there wasn't enough of them in jail." Other notes from April 8 referred to blind African-American singer Al Hibbler (misspelled "Hibler") and noted that the choir sang "I'm on My Way to Freedom Land" both during the offering and as the closing number.[28]

In one of the more curious twists of the campaign, Hibbler, best known for his version of "Unchained Melody," was among those arrested at "integration corner"—Nineteenth Street and Third Avenue—on the following day, April 9. Police quickly claimed there had been a "mistake" and released Hibbler, who performed at a civil rights–related rally that evening. The *New York Times*' account of the day's events also included a quote from A. G. Gaston, the most powerful of Birmingham's black businessmen, who expressed the ambivalence felt by some African-Americans toward the movement.[29] Gaston further alienated movement supporters when, apparently through a misunderstanding of the hall's booking policy, one of his subordinates refused a permit for Hibbler to perform in Gaston's L. R. Hall

Auditorium, despite the presence of hundreds of supporters.[30] The following day, April 10, crowds grew larger at the protest sites, though relatively few were arrested despite a very public protest in the city library. Hibbler was again detained by police while he picketed, but was soon released. When Hibbler demanded to know why, Connor sneered, "You can't work and anyone goes to jail has to earn his food. You can't do anything, even entertain."[31] Hibbler stubbornly remained in Birmingham, appearing on protest lines and singing at meetings large and small, including renditions of his hit "I Forgive" and the protest spiritual "Nobody Knows the Trouble I've Seen."[32]

Despite the few arrests, Birmingham city officials found a sympathetic judge to issue an injunction against King, Shuttlesworth, Abernathy, Hibbler, and 134 others, prohibiting further demonstrations, including kneel-ins at white churches. On April 11, twelve picketers were arrested, though they were charged with loitering or parading without a permit, not with violating the terms of the injunction. King, stung by criticism of the small size of the protests to date, promised to lead the next round of protests and, and if arrested for defying the injunction, to stay in jail "as long as necessary."[33]

The Birmingham leadership was running out of options. In the ten days since the protests began, a few hundred people had been arrested and only three hundred remained in jail—fewer than in the early days in the much smaller city of Albany—and media attention was waning. Connor had also pressured their original bondsman to withdraw. To keep the organization's spirits up, Abernathy spoke to the Thursday night rally, while King and others met at Gaston's hotel and participated in a lively discussion about the joint ACMHR-SCLC operation in the city.[34] At the rally, Abernathy discovered a poorly hidden microphone in the pulpit. While the SCLC knew their meetings were being monitored by Connor's men (a similar "bug" had been found in Montgomery), Abernathy responded with typical wry humor, adapting yet another freedom song: "It seems they they've put one of those electronic doohickeys under this pulpit, so they can find out what we're going to do tomorrow. Well, I want you to know, Mr. Doohickey, that we'll be marching tomorrow by the hundreds. We're going to fill the jailhouses, Mr. Doohickey. We won't let anybody turn us around. We won't let the Ku Klux Klan turn us around. We won't let J. B. Stoner turn us around. What's more, Mr. Doohickey, we won't let Bull Connor turn us around!"[35]

One of the most significant questions being discussed in the hotel room nearby was whether or not the struggling movement could afford for King to spend a lengthy period of time in jail. At last, after listening to the various arguments, King stood and donned a rough denim jacket, signaling his decision to march and accept jail time. Cotton recalled that those present then silently stood, "made a circle in the room, and sang 'We Shall Overcome.'" King left and went upstairs to bed without another word.[36] From the windows of the hotel, the movement leaders could hear the lusty singing of hymns and freedom songs from the nearby mass meeting at Zion Hill Baptist.[37]

On April 13, before cameras and dressed in work clothes, King, Abernathy, and more than sixty other protesters, all singing "We Shall Overcome," left the Gaston. From Sixth Avenue Zion Hill Baptist Church they continued through streets lined with African-Americans, some of whom sang or applauded the procession. Facing them was "every Birmingham police officer" in the city.[38] The march, which only lasted four and a half blocks, was the largest of the Birmingham campaign and police officers again used dogs to drive back onlookers. Police continued to indiscriminately arrest onlookers and protesters alike, though Connor allowed a group singing in a small park at Seventeenth Street to remain. "Let them stay there and sing all they want to," he is quoted as saying.[39] As they neared downtown, King and the other remaining marchers were roughly herded into paddy wagons as nearby onlookers and the remaining protesters continued to sing "We Shall Overcome."[40] That night at the mass meeting, Cotton attempted to quell the growing anger of the protesters over the brutal treatment of King and the others with a heartfelt performance of "O Freedom."[41]

King's first week in the Birmingham jail was spent trying to sleep on a steel frame bed without a mattress and he endured long days in solitary confinement.[42] It was during this period, scribbled on scraps of paper and newspaper margins, smuggled out by visitors, and painstakingly typed by friends, that King composed what came to be called "A Letter from Birmingham Jail." The essay was written in response to a statement critical of the movement from eight white clergymen in Alabama published a few days earlier in a local newspaper. However, once published, King's treatise initially received little coverage.

During the relatively calm period that followed, Belafonte, at King's urgent request, rushed $60,000 to Birmingham to offset the tens of thousands of dollars expended by another sympathetic local bondsman in freeing two hundred prisoners.[43] King and Abernathy were released on April 20 after posting a $300 bond, and resumed strategic planning on the Birmingham movement. Both men sported eight-day beards, their shaving equipment having been confiscated earlier.[44] Conditions had improved, he reported, after his wife Coretta spoke with President Kennedy by telephone and expressed her concerns. On May 1, the cases of 284 demonstrators, including King, Shuttlesworth, and Abernathy, who had been charged with violating various city ordinances, including parading without a permit, were reset, with trials to begin May 8.[45]

## The Children's Crusade

Following his release, King and the Birmingham brain trust, which by now also included Bevel, Young, Lee, and Cotton, all of whom had been campaigning in area high schools and colleges, came to a difficult conclusion. Bevel had urged that to jump-start the faltering campaign, they needed to include young people in the protests. Walker agreed and the plan was immediately adopted, though not without subsequent controversy in the press and even within the movement's ranks. In the days that followed, children were encouraged to attend the mass meetings and training sessions.[46] That evening at the mass meeting, King was upstaged by the impassioned sermon of young William "Meatball" Dothard, who told the congregation that Thursday's march, led by the young people, would be a pivotal day in the movement. He cited a lyric from their singing of "I'm on My Way to Freedom Land": "If you don't go, don't you hinder me." Then, while singing, "I Woke Up This Morning with My Mind Stayed on Freedom," Dothard pulled on stage an eight-year-old who had already been jailed in the protests and was singing the same protest spiritual. "Do you know why [he decided to go to jail]?" Dothard asked. "He said he 'woke up that Saturday morning with freedom on my mind.' . . . Let them go get what you supposed to have gotten a long time ago. . . . Parents, don't hinder the kids in the morning, guardians, don't mess with the kids in the morning, teachers, don't take your roll books in the morning." The congregation erupted in cheers and applause.[47]

### Thursday, May 2

African-American disk jockeys had early been incorporated into the movement, despite working in white-owned stations. Between the popular rhythm and blues and soul 45s they played, DJs "Tall Paul" White, Shelley Stewart, and Erskine R. Faush, Sr., broadcast what sounded like slangy double-talk to white listeners. But in reality, just as with the hidden messages and double entendre of the spirituals, the DJs were relaying important movement information to their black listeners, including the cues to leave for the staging points.[48] Faush said that in addition to the coded messages, the announcers sometimes sonically augmented the number of people gathering at Kelly Ingram Park to make a few dozen protesters sound like many more. "Crowds draw crowds," he said. "We were a bit creative in our commentary as well."[49]

Among those who had been recruited in the schools was Nettie L. Flemmon, who said that once the singing began outside the schools, "there was nothing the teachers could do" to prevent the children from leaving. "The minute they heard the singing, they joined on in with the other students and they went to marching."[50] Despite the best efforts of some (but not all) of their teachers and administrators, children and young people left their schools, usually on foot, and arrived by the hundreds at Sixteenth Street. There they received detailed instructions from movement organizers, including Shuttlesworth, who dashed about delivering encouraging "sermonettes" to each new group. By 8 a.m., the church was packed with "hooky-playing" students who clapped their hands and sang freedom songs, including "Woke Up This Morning with My Mind Stayed on Freedom."[51]

Shortly after noon, DJ "Tall Paul" White's apparently off-handed comment, "Kids, there's gonna be a party at the park. Bring your toothbrushes because lunch will be served," was a coded signal for young African-Americans to meet at Kelly Ingram Park, just down the street from WENN's studios. The "toothbrush" reference, of course, meant that listeners could expect their "lunch" to be followed by jail time. Just after noon, the DJ at WENN played the gospel song "All Men Are Made by God" and the students left the church and marched into the bright sunlight in groups of ten or fifty, each with a specific destination in mind. Facing them were hundreds of armed policemen.[52] Up-tempo and with a martial beat, "All Men Are Made by God" had recently been released by the Highway QCs and was already a popular hit.[53] The rows of police scrambled to keep up with the surging youngsters. More than fifty years after the fact, announcer Erskine R. Faush said that particular song "stands out" of the many coded songs he played in support of the movement "because that was the one that started the massive march that . . . broke the back of the concentration of police forces to disrupt the march."[54]

"There was no resistance to arrest by the laughing, singing groups of youngsters," one reporter noted. A handful actually made it to the steps of City Hall before being caught. Most, however, dropped to their knees and prayed at the approach of police. One estimate had five hundred protesters arrested in the first few hours and hauled off to the already crowded jails by virtually every police vehicle in Birmingham. When those proved inadequate, school buses were pressed into service as makeshift paddy wagons.[55] Of the four major groups of protesters that split off upon leaving the church, one sang a set of old union songs aimed as much, perhaps, at African-American adults as at white onlookers: "Which Side Are You On?" and "Will You Join Us or Will You 'Tom' for the Big, Bad Bull?" As the police approached, the students "ran gleefully" toward the patrol wagons.[56]

Inside Sixteenth Street Baptist, the remaining students sang "Ain't Gonna Let Nobody Turn Me 'Round," "Oh, Freedom," and "Keep Your Eyes on the Prize" as they waited their turn. As conditions changed, movement volunteers using walky talkies gave detailed instructions, including new destinations, to the waiting students. Some were given protest signs; each group emerged singing freedom songs and clapping. Most were promptly arrested. Audrey Faye Hendrick and a small band of friends, singing "Ain't Gonna Let Nobody Turn Me 'Round," made it to the next block before they were placed in the waiting paddy wagons. "The singing was like jubilance," Hendrick recalled.[57]

Before it was all over, more than one estimate had placed the total number of children in Birmingham city custody at one thousand, with sometimes as many as seventy-five young people in a cell designed for eight. The mood was buoyant, celebratory. Even as the young people were still being hastily processed, worshippers that afternoon began filing into Shuttlesworth's church.[58] Speaker after speaker described the excitement of the day, culminating with the charismatic Bevel, who spontaneously broke into freedom songs. It appears from their notes that Connor's three assigned observers that night were clearly uneasy. After one solo, the notes read, "At this time Doctor Nixon (?) sang 'I'll Never Walk Alone' and the Negroes went to screaming." Following a Bevel-led freedom song, "the Negroes got all worked up while singing, stomping their feet and waving their arms and screaming." The officers also quoted Shuttlesworth, who urged the young people not to attend school on Monday. "They had another singing and that was the end."[59] That evening, King complimented the "magnificence" of the actions taken by the young protesters, and of being personally "deeply inspired and moved" by their courage: "They did it singing the great soul songs of the freedom movement. And one can never grasp the meaning of this movement until he understands the music, with all of its glad thunders and gentle sighs, expressing the deep longings and aspirations of an oppressed people."[60]

### Friday, May 3

Friday morning, called "Double D-Day," and buoyed by the previous day's excitement and the fiery sermons the night before, young people again began trooping to Sixteenth Street Baptist. Only a few hundred of Birmingham's 7,386 African-American students reported to their schools. Connor, keenly aware that all jails, including those in nearby communities, were dangerously overcrowded, had surrounded the church and adjacent park with police, police dogs, and fire trucks, their high-powered hoses pointed and at the ready. A sizeable crowd, including representatives of the national media, assembled as well.[61] The first group of students left the church at 1 p.m. singing "Amen/Freedom."[62] Connor's men had arrested about seventy when it quickly became apparent that there were many more to come, and Birmingham had no place to put them. It was then that he ordered the hoses turned on the protesters. Police captain Glenn V. Evans shouted, "Disperse or you'll get wet." When the students continued to walk, the firemen opened up. The powerful jets of water toppled children, bloodied noses, tore clothes, and stripped bark from trees.[63] From his window, Gaston, who had opposed the Birmingham movement from the beginning, saw a small girl "being turned end over end by hose spray" and said that his position changed at that moment.[64] One participant took note of a particular moment of defiance. Gwen Webb, then in junior high, was nearby when the initial blast of water dispersed the marchers. "But when the water had subsided, there were ten kids still standing and they were singing one word over and over—'Freedom.'"[65] The students who evaded the jets of water were confronted by snarling police dogs. The light-hearted tone of the previous day's events was immediately replaced by one of fear and anger. Even as photographers snapped the disturbing images, an angry crowd of mostly African-Americans on the outskirts of the protests tossed bottles and bricks at the firemen. Two firemen and a news reporter were injured by the debris and two students were treated for dog bites. A few students made it as far as City Hall before they too were arrested. Within hours, police sealed the doors to Sixteenth Street Baptist, trapping many more students inside.[66] After only two hours, a fire inspector went into Sixteenth Street and offered to allow the packed spectators the opportunity to leave if they would call off the demonstrations for the day. The protesters quietly filed out and none were arrested.[67]

## Saturday, May 4

Saturday morning, young Steve Taylor, one of the singing Taylor siblings who would form the core of the Birmingham Sunsets gospel group, was watching early morning cartoons. A national news bulletin interrupted the programming to show the previous day's events in Birmingham. Amid the unsettling images of children being attacked with high-pressure water hoses and young people singing as they were loaded onto paddy wagons, Taylor saw his sister Joyce in jail. Taylor ran to wake his mother and brothers and together they watched the unfolding story.[68] Also among those who had been arrested and were spending time in Birmingham's jammed jails that morning was young James W. Stewart, who had given the police a fake name and age when he was arrested three days earlier. Stewart, who was in a cell with "three or found hundred young men," along with the Reverend A. D. King, had been in jail since D-Day, and remembered that King would sing for fifteen minutes until someone joined him, often on "Everybody Loves Freedom." Shuttlesworth had told the students prior to their arrests, "when you're arrested, sing your hearts out!" Soon, young people in other cells would join in.[69]

Saturday's protesters left Sixteenth Street Baptist and Greater Apostolic Overcoming Trinity Holy Church at the same time and were again immediately met by powerful water blasts. Police rushed forward and locked the remaining young people into Sixteenth Street. Spurred once again by the sight of young people sent sprawling by the hoses, an angry crowd gathered on the sidewalks, throwing rocks, bricks, and bottles at police and firemen. Seeing the violence, Bevel called off the demonstration. Records show that 211 protesters were arrested, more than half under the age of eighteen.[70] By now, conditions were "deplorable" in the jails and prison yards. Cells were so crowded that students slept in shifts and just five toilets, often overflowing, served hundreds of prisoners. Food, when it was available, was inedible. Other students were exposed to the elements while being kept outside in the yards.[71]

Andrew Young, one of King's lieutenants, attended virtually every mass meeting and reveled in the power surge created by the influx of young people. Coupled with the singing of the ACMHR Choir, the "up-tempo music brought a new vitality and power" to the services: "These songs, so powerful in their ability to inspire the marchers with the courage to face Bull Connor and his men, were very important in helping us keep the movement strong, dignified and centered on our goal of nonviolent resistance, of maintaining the high road. It was a beautiful example of the power of music to fill people with God's strength." Connor's painfully obvious police spies also attended every meeting and Young said he would periodically "sneak a glance" to see if they joined in the spirited singing. Usually, the stone-faced men would slip away during the climactic singing of "We Shall Overcome."[72]

**Sunday, May 5**

Though Sunday had been declared a "truce" day, at the 4 p.m. service at New Pilgrim Baptist Church, Connor threatened to arrest any white who crossed Sixth Avenue South. Guy and Candie Carawan, the white movement veterans who had been responsible, in part, for the widespread dissemination of freedom songs (most notably "We Shall Overcome"), had been invited to sing at New Pilgrim Baptist that evening and had hoped to record a mass meeting. But as they neared the church, Connor had them arrested and taken to the jail.[73] Popular folk singer Joan Baez, just 22, who said she first embraced nonviolence as a teenager after hearing King speak on the radio,[74] also tried to enter, but was turned back by the police. Inspired by an angry Bevel, New Pilgrim's copastor, the Reverend Charles Billups, Jr., spontaneously led his thousand-strong (some estimates place the number at closer to three thousand) congregation on a "walk," singing "I Want Jesus to Walk with Me," toward the Southside Jail. There, still in their Sunday best, his parishioners were met by Connor and rows of policemen and firemen. When Connor ordered the church members to disperse, Billups, tears streaming, declared, "Turn on your water, turn loose your dogs, we will stand here till we die."[75]

What happened—or, more precisely, what did *not* happen—is one of the signal moments of the civil rights movement. The firemen refused Connor's order to blast the peaceful, kneeling marchers; the police parted to allow them through. King called it "one of the most fantastic events of the Birmingham story."[76] Some firemen broke into tears, others lowered their hoses. One was heard to mutter, "We're here to put out fires, not people." Diane McWhorter called it "a miracle." The assembled marchers rose from their knees singing "Up Above My Head, I Hear Freedom in the Air," walked to the jail and conducted a peaceful prayer service outside the walls.[77] Young recalled one elderly woman in particular who, as she marched "ecstatically" through the barricades, shouted, "Great God Almighty done parted the Red Sea one mo' time!"[78] That evening at the mass meeting at New Pilgrim Baptist Church, amid the other services and sermons, a clearly upset Young reported on the arrest of the Carawans. "It looks like the police are getting nervous now, so don't do anything to make them act foolishly."[79] Elsewhere, the Department of Justice's lawyer, Burke Marshall, continued meeting with representatives from the white and African-American communities, with little movement on the part of Birmingham's powerful business and political leaders, in hopes of brokering a deal.[80]

**Monday, May 6**

On Monday morning, May 6, young people again left their schools by the hundreds and walked toward Sixteenth Street Baptist Church and Kelly Ingram Park. Among those in the church was Baez, smuggled downtown in the back of a friend's car.

Baez joined those inside in the "clapping, singing, talking and laughing." Every few minutes, someone would begin "the most popular tune of the day," "Freedom /Amen." "Everybody needs freedom," "All the children need freedom," "Bull Connor needs freedom, freedom, freedom, free-dom, free-dom!"[81]

Also present was civil rights attorney Len Holt, who had just arrived in Birmingham and later wrote about his experiences for a national newsweekly. Holt describes in vivid detail the scenes at the church where the thousands of African-Americans, both inside and out, were quickly surrounded by a phalanx of policemen, Alabama State Troopers, and the red pumpers of fire trucks.[82] As they left the building, Shuttlesworth admonished the young protesters, "It's to be a silent demonstration. No songs, no slogans, no replies to obscenities. However, when you're arrested, sing your hearts out."[83] From inside the church came the "the loud songs of Freedom," including "We Shall Overcome" and "Ain't Gonna Let Nobody Turn Me 'Round." Emerging from the church on that 90-degree day were an estimated three hundred grammar and high school students, chanting "Freedom! Freedom!" despite Shuttlesworth's pleas. This time, the police converged on the church steps, sticks held high, arresting the unresisting demonstrators. For the next few hours, Holt recalled, "Bedlam broke loose." The young demonstrators shouted freedom songs and "broke into a fast step that seemed to be a hybrid of the turkey-trot and the twist" as they sang, "I ain't scared of your jail 'cause I want my freedom!" As the buses took the students away, they continued their freedom songs and chants, accompanied by banging on the floors and sides of the buses.[84]

Social commentator and comic Dick Gregory led the first wave of students, who were immediately arrested. Hundreds of children stood waiting in lines where they danced and "shimmied their legs and wagged their bottoms" as they were transported to jail, often singing the defiant lyric: "I ain't scared of your jail / 'Cause I want my freedom / 'Cause I want my freedom." When authorities deemed the city jail too full for the most recent arrivals—nearly one thousand young, and mostly female, protesters—they were placed in a courtyard between buildings at the Juvenile Center. "We started singing," Stewart recalled. "We sang and we sang— all the Movement songs, all the gospel songs." At one point, a young girl knelt and sang "The Lord's Prayer" with such a beautiful voice," Stewart said, that even nearby office workers paused to listen.[85] While the older children sang, Gregory recalled that he talked to a little boy, perhaps four years old, sucking his thumb. "What are you here for?" Gregory asked him. "Teedom," the child responded. Gregory marveled that the police would arrest someone too young to even say the word "freedom."[86]

Back downtown, the protests and arrests continued for two more hours, as the students "marched gaily toward the waiting police" and older bystanders joined them in singing "We Shall Overcome." When a single bottle was thrown at police from someone in a watching crowd, organizers hurriedly cancelled the remaining protests for the day.[87] Baez, her long straight hair hidden in a scarf, walked past the melee back to the Gaston Hotel, where she was to meet her ride for an integrated concert that evening at Miles College.[88] Along the way, she also passed rows of homes, their porches "jammed with women singing, 'Black and white together / We shall overcome someday.'" In the main Birmingham jail, the Carawans gathered material for new protest songs, with lyrics that boasted, "Pushed by the policemen, herded like hogs / Some got the fire hose, some got the dogs."[89] Jailers had separated the prisoners by gender and in the desperately overcrowded cells, Guy and Candie Carawan were each told separately that the other was being beaten (untrue, though they did not know it at the time). As more prisoners, including "drunks and pickpockets," continued to be "squeezed" into the cells throughout the night, Guy could not sleep. "Really late I heard this remarkable sound—from outside the jail window I could hear hundreds and hundreds of voices singing freedom songs. People had marched over from the mass meeting to the jailhouse, just to let all those in jail know that everyone was thinking of them."[90]

Also in jail during this period was one of the mainstays of the movement choir, Cleopatra Kennedy, whose rendition of "A City Called Heaven" was King's favorite. Kennedy was jailed on several occasions, once for two weeks, for participating in the marches and protests, often with her friend Louella Gibner. Kennedy usually led the singing in the female cells, including the by-now familiar strains of "I Ain't Scared of Nobody 'Cause I Want My Freedom," "Freedom," and "Oh, Freedom." On some occasions, the male inmates—who they could hear but not see—would respond with singing, sometimes long into the night. As elsewhere, other prisoners encouraged the civil rights activists to sing along and initiate their own songs. In Kennedy's cells, the other singers would accompany themselves by "stomping" on the mattresses. "We would sing songs to keep ourselves up," Kennedy said, "keep our energy up. To stop thinking about . . . how long we're going to be here, wondering when they're going to let us out."[91]

On the afternoon of Monday May 6, the Carawans were released and they rushed to St. James Baptist, host to one of the evening's four scheduled mass meetings, where they recorded, with a single microphone, what would become one of the great records of the movement, *Birmingham, Alabama, 1963: Mass Meeting*, a one-of-a-kind documentary of a "typical" mass meeting during those tumultuous days and nights.[92] If this is indicative of the caliber of fiery musicianship by the ACMHR Choir and the inspired preaching of the Reverend Ralph Abernathy and the Reverend Martin Luther King, then it is somewhat easier to grasp the determination of the participants during the weeks and months of protest in Birmingham.

The album, released later that year (and re-released on CD by Smithsonian Folkways Archival in 1990), begins with a stunning performance of "Swing Low, Sweet Chariot" by coloratura soprano Kennedy, with only muted organ accompaniment by Carlton Reese. Suddenly, at three and a half minutes, the entire choir roars in, transforming the old spiritual into a rocking suite of freedom songs, including "Rock Me, Lord," lasting another four minutes. On the disk, the second track is a 13-minute sermon by Abernathy, marked by his legendary humor and folk wisdom. Abernathy assures the congregation that their jailed children, many of whom are still being kept in open-air prison yards, will be taken care of and urges his listeners to join them in jail. He announces that the following day's mass meetings will be held at Sixteenth Street Baptist and at a second, secret location. He also quotes from two freedom songs, "I'm on My Way to Freedom Land" and "Ain't Nobody Gonna Turn Me 'Round." Track three is the choir, led by soloist Mamie Brown's up-tempo rendition of "I'm on My Way to Freedom Land."

Track four is one of several highlights on the disk, a towering tour-de-force by Kennedy, who sings "City Called Heaven," again accompanied only by Reece, for nine and a half minutes. This is classic gospel "surge singing," full of vocal embellishments and melisma, a multi-octave prayer that has those closest to the microphone crying out in wonder. Track five is a nearly 11-minute sermonette by King, who tells listeners that he and Abernathy have already spoken to two previous mass meetings that evening, both of which were at capacity, with large crowds standing outside. Following this presentation, the two of them will leave to address yet a fourth mass meeting at St. Paul United Methodist Church. Unlike Abernathy's, King's homily is low-keyed, urging listeners to remain strong in the face of adversity and admonishing them to remain nonviolent, recounting a now-familiar illustration—the words ancient Greeks used to describe the different kinds "love."

Track five, and it is unclear if this sequence follows the actual order of the May 6 mass meeting, features the choir performing what, by now, had become one of the themes of the Birmingham movement, "Ninety-Nine and a Half Won't Do," led by an unidentified soloist. The disk closes with a snippet of another message by Abernathy, gently poking fun at King's use of the Greek and his scholarly description of "eros." While the disk is an extraordinary snapshot of one of the mass meetings, it is clearly a truncated service, since many nights the services continued for three or more hours. Still, given the limitations of the long-play, 33 rpm format, *Birmingham, Alabama, 1963: Mass Meeting* is an invaluable aural documentation of the power of the music in the movement. The songs are designed to celebrate, motivate, placate, instruct, enthrall, and entertain. Kennedy's vocals (she would later tour with a number of well-known gospel and secular artists, including Michael Jackson) clearly inspire her listeners, even as they retain their thrilling urgency fifty years later.

Elsewhere that evening, Baez performed before an integrated audience at the historically black Miles College, singing an array of her folk music–inspired hit songs and closing with "We Shall Overcome." The audience rose, held hands, and swayed as they sang what had become a movement hymn.[93]

**Tuesday, May 7**

Tuesday morning, representatives from SNCC and CORE again met the students at their schools and hustled them to Sixteenth Street Baptist before police barricades were in place. At noon, picketing began at eight downtown department stores. As police scrambled to cover the various sites, the strains of "We Shall Overcome" rang from the church, even as the estimated six hundred students downtown began singing "We Shall Overcome" as well.[94] By this point, even the young participants had an inkling that what they were doing was not only of a historic nature, it was also part of an unbroken connection, some would say a *spiritual* connection, with the past. Participant Mary Gadsen, who had managed thus far to avoid the hoses and the dogs as well as arrest, considered the singing of "Ain't Nobody Going to Turn Me 'Round" in the mass meetings an "incentive." "We also sang a lot of the old spirituals like 'Go Down, Moses,'" she recalled. "We considered Birmingham was Egypt."[95] In his account of the movement in Birmingham, gospel singer Henry Burton, Jr., agreed, equating Connor to the pharaoh in "Go Down, Moses." In addition to "Ain't Nobody Going to Turn Me 'Round" and "We Shall Overcome," Burton remembered singing "Jesus Is All the World to Me" in the rallies and, during the marches, "Marching to Zion."[96]

Once the doors to the church opened, hundreds of singing young people again swarmed downtown, approaching lunch counters, touching merchandise, and dispersing as the harried police arrived. With the city, county, and surrounding county jails and juvenile centers filled, the police did little but destroy the students' protest signs. After more than an hour, the protesters eventually filtered back toward Sixteenth Street Baptist Church, still singing "We Shall Overcome."[97] The SCLC's James Forman made multiple stops at the various downtown locations, encouraging the young demonstrators as they sang freedom songs. ACMHR representatives paused in the middle of a sidewalk for an impromptu prayer meeting. And when a crowd surrounded two policemen who had "roughed up" an onlooker, movement leaders swooped in and "freed" the officers.[98]

The mood remained light among the protesters. Mamie Brown was paired with a young man from Miles College and told to attempt to eat at Britt's Cafeteria. King himself approached the small group and warned them that the food in the jail was inedible. When he discovered that Brown had not brought much money, he reached into his pocket and gave her the contents. "Put this with your money," King told her, "because you won't be able to eat the food. When the trustees come by, you can send them and they can get you cheese and crackers and milk or something." Brown and her partner were, predictably, refused service at the restaurant and promptly arrested by "a very nice policeman." According to Brown, they chatted courteously en route to the city jail. "It's a beautiful day, isn't it?" the policeman said. "It certainly is," she responded. "Well, this is my job," he said. "This is what I have to do." Brown said, "I understand." Brown spent five days in the jail and said she had a "good time." As King had predicted, the food was inedible food ("beans cooked in water") and she gave it to the "regular prisoners" and asked the trustees to buy her meals. Once in jail, Brown said prisoners not related to the movement requested that they sing gospel songs and freedom songs. At Sunday service in jail, Reese himself played the piano and the prisoners sang "We Shall Not Be Moved."

In true Birmingham movement style, Brown added verses: "Go and tell Bull Connor / We shall not be moved." The guards requested the song again and again.[99]

When police returned to Sixteenth Street Baptist to direct movement leaders to tell the students downtown to leave, the approximately two thousand people in the church rose and departed for downtown as well. Along the way, they were joined by another two thousand people, all singing "We Shall Overcome." However, as Holt watched in dismay, when the protesters reached adjoining Kelly Ingram Park, Connor ordered the high-powered fire hoses to once again blast the defenseless, mostly young demonstrators . . . a horrific spectacle captured by the cameras of national television network and newspapers.[100] As before, the large crowd of onlookers and bystanders responded angrily, showering the police and firemen with rocks and bottles. At one point, the firemen trained a monitor—a mounted, high-powered fire nozzle—directly on Shuttlesworth, who suffered two broken ribs and bruises and was taken to a hospital. When Connor, who was elsewhere in his armored car and had missed the action, was told by reporters that Shuttlesworth had been taken by ambulance, he responded, "I'm sorry I missed it. I wish they'd carried him away in a hearse." Police again used their dogs and chased and beat random African-Americans as they raced through the city's streets. The bottle and rock throwing continued for several more hours, though movement organizers had called off the protests almost immediately. That evening, Connor and Alabama Governor George Wallace called in the Alabama Highway Patrol and police departments from surrounding communities. All the while, Marshall privately redoubled his efforts to get Birmingham's business and political leaders to talk directly with representatives of the movement.[101]

Among those arrested in early May was teenager Barry Taylor. Taylor left Sixteenth Baptist holding a sign that read "We Shall Overcome." Like many of his contemporaries, he had been mistakenly told that jail food was tasty ("pancakes, bacon, and wings"), so he did not eat breakfast that day. Taylor was quickly arrested and taken to broil in the sun at historic Rickwood Field, where he received neither food nor shelter. The next morning, his group was taken to the city jail where he ate "the worst breakfast I ate in my life," kept with five hundred other protesters in a room designed for one hundred and fifty, and slept "hanging on bars." Taylor was kept for a week. At one point, he shared the cell with both King and Bevel. But tensions were such that he recalled no singing that week.[102]

Birmingham was not the only place where arrests were taking place. Gaffney, when not singing with the ACMHR Choir, went home to nearby Gadsden, preparing African-Americans to register to vote. The registration process at the time required black applicants to know both the Bill of Rights and the Constitution. Gaffney and Stokely Carmichael were arrested for protesting without a permit. Local police used a cattle prod to prompt Gaffney into the paddy wagon, and took the unlikely pair to Gadsden's jail.[103]

Negotiations continued through Wednesday May 8, with the ACMHR-SLCC Central Committee (sans Shuttlesworth) making most of the concessions from what the movement called its "Points of Progress" demands: at least "token" black hirings, the abolishment of desegregation ordinances, the dropping of charges against jailed participants, and the establishment of a biracial committee to discuss other objectives. When the Marshall-brokered deal was announced, King and others agreed to suspend the protests. Almost immediately, factions within both groups denounced or repudiated the agreement. The heavily bandaged Shuttlesworth angrily left the morning's press conference and white Birmingham soon repudiated the agreement. After the meeting, King, Abernathy, and twenty-five other protesters who had been arrested earlier arrived, as scheduled, at the recorder's court, only to hear the judge summarily find them all guilty of parading without a permit, ordering jail time and fines. King and Abernathy were required to pay $2,500 if they wanted to post bond. Both men, somewhat stunned, decided to return to jail, imperiling the shaky agreement. Gaston hastily posted their bond and negotiations resumed.[104] Both President Kennedy and King separately spun the agreement with positive statements, Kennedy saying that the two parties had made "substantial steps" toward "the justifiable needs of the Negro community."[105]

As had become a nightly ritual, an estimated two thousand people crammed into Sixth Avenue Baptist Church for the nightly mass meeting on May 8, ignoring the extreme heat. Among the speakers were a group of twenty rabbis who had flown to Birmingham in support of the ACMHR. One rabbi compared Connor's actions to those of the secret police in East Berlin. The rabbis taught the congregation a peace song in Hebrew and joined hands in the customary closing and singing of "We Shall Overcome."[106] At the close of the meeting, the rabbis asked those in attendance to embrace the people closest to them. Once again, among those in attendance were the two most regular of Connor's police observers, B. A. Allison and R. A. Watkins. "Of course, Officer Watkins and myself were sitting between two negroes and they really gave us the treatment," their notes from the meeting say.[107]

One interesting dynamic of Birmingham was that young people gave their seats to older listeners in the always packed mass meetings. For young Barry Taylor, that meant that he never spent time with any of the movement leaders. His most vivid memories are of singing the old protest spiritual "Steal Away to Jesus," as well as the almost mandatory "Ain't Gonna Let Nobody Turn Me 'Round" and "We Shall Overcome." Taylor also remembered Sam Cooke and the Soul Stirrer's "When I've Gone the Last Mile of the Way" being sung. When, as a solo artist, Cooke released "A Change Is Gonna Come" in late 1964, Taylor said it too was immediately recognized as a "movement song." These songs and others "resonated" with him, he said, in part because they were sung with "spirit-filled" emotions: "Those songs gave us the opportunity to release frustration and . . . energy that we would otherwise have channeled in a different direction. Because at my age, during that time, I was ready to fight . . . listening to the music and listening to the people and seeing how they were able to handle the same thing I was going through and how the music tended to ease that frustration and pain that they were going through, I said, 'Well, if it can do it for them, it can do it for me.' So I toned it down."[108]

N. B. Wooding, a gospel quartet member who sang with the ACMHR Choir, called the nightly church services "strategy sessions" and "a relief valve" to release pressure from the day's events. He often participated in all-night protective vigils outside the churches, as well as at the homes of Shuttlesworth, attorney Arthur Shores, and other movement notables, armed only with a flashlight. Wooding was also part of a group that picked up SCLC officials at the Birmingham airport and served as decoys on the dangerous return trip into town because "at the time, the policeman was our biggest enemy; we were more scared of police than we were the Ku Klux Klan." Wooding's children were among those who were arrested and jailed. He recalled them singing "Ain't Gonna Let Nobody Turn Me 'Round" and "We Shall Overcome" while handcuffed or in jail. To Wooding, freedom songs were an essential part of the movement: "Songs will strike a tension [with] the worst person in the world. If you sing enough, that melody will go to him. I think they tamed snakes to that music."[109]

Carlton Reese was also arrested several times, in part because of his public identification with the movement and its music was well known in the community. Like Wooding, he said that he believed that the singing in the dangerously crowded jails affected the jailers:

> We carried on a lot of singing and praying in the jails. The guards and people in charge of all the prisoners would get highly upset because when white people heard this kind of singing, it got to them. They really couldn't stand that kind of thing. There's something about the kind of singing that black folk do that stirs the hearts of people. I'm not saying that other ethnic groups cannot sing. I'm saying that our music represents trials and tribulations. We are used to anthems and hymns, and we're used to much folk music, but the down-home gospel and old Dr. Watts' songs represent trials and tribulations and those kinds of experiences. When people mistreat you, they can't stand to hear that kind of thing.[110]

## Thursday, May 9

While movement leaders grappled with the increasing intransigence of Connor and the city's business leaders, the message, and the music, of Birmingham generated extensive media coverage. As violence against peaceful demonstrators was featured in publications such as The *New York Times* and *Life* magazine, and on the CBS News, a host of well-known musicians and actors began making public statements in support of the movement. Artists Fats Domino and Chubby Checker joined Ray Charles and Clyde McPhatter, who had long insisted on integrated audiences in the South. Charlton Heston joined Belafonte on picket lines and fund-raising for the jailed students. Meanwhile, Mahalia Jackson publicly approached Nat King Cole, Ella Fitzgerald, Lena Horne, and other African-American artists to perform at a proposed Chicago-area benefit for the SCLC. "I'm having a hard time," she told *Jet*. "The stars keep telling me they've given one benefit. Well, they have to keep giving them because the people keep going to jail down there and the white people keep consuming the money as fast as we get it." Jackson reiterated her readiness to join the picket lines. "Not for Dr. King, but for me, because I have walked all over this country and this world singing songs and I'm not free enough to have a decent TV show."[111]

Back in Birmingham, King said ACMHR-SCLC leaders met with city officials throughout the night in order to avert continued demonstrations on Friday May 10. More than a thousand people "milled" around Sixteenth Street Baptist in an uneasy, day-long faceoff with an equal number of enforcement officials, even as Wallace and Connor rejected any proposed settlement out of hand.[112]

The two groups did eventually agree, once again, on a settlement that addressed at least some of the ACMHR-SCLC's "Points of Progress," in a statement the group released on Thursday. However, Birmingham officials, most notably Mayor Boutwell (who had finally overcome the legal obstacles from Connor to assume his newly elected position) carefully disavowed the city's part in any agreement. The massive law enforcement presence at Kelly Ingram Park did, in time, begin to draw down during the course of the day. African-American leaders publicly worried that even this much-compromised settlement was unenforceable and that once the media withdrew and protests ended, white Birmingham would resume its segregated ways—as had happened in Albany. By midday, more than half of the more than two thousand young protesters had been released.[113] Also released was Gregory, who had been jailed since Monday. Gregory charged that he had been brutalized in prison, beaten by five policemen wielding "billy clubs, hammers and sawed-off pool sticks."[114]

In the days that followed, the specifics of the accord were released, with the downtown department stores pledging to desegregate over the next ninety days, hire black employees within sixty days, and create a biracial panel over the following two weeks. More young protesters were released from the jails, though the remaining eight hundred adult prisoners were required to post bond. Even as the agreement was praised nationally, Birmingham city leaders continued to keep their distance.[115] One estimate placed the economic loss from the year-long boycott by African- Americans, also called "selective shopping," at more than $300,000.[116] To make the third part of the "moral agreement," the release of remaining prisoners on "low bail," both movement leaders and the Kennedy administration turned again to their friends in labor. The United Auto Workers, the United Steelworkers Union, and the AFL-CIO quickly raised the needed $237,000 to bail out the remaining 790 demonstrators.[117] Facilitating the request and transfer, which included a massive $100,000 gift from Governor Nelson Rockefeller, was Belafonte.[118] For a few days, Birmingham—black and white—enjoyed relative peace.

On the evening of May 10, an inflammatory cross-burning rally with twenty-five hundred participants culminated with an attack on the modest accord by the local chapter of the Ku Klux Klan and threatened reprisals to white merchants and politicians who supported it.[119] The rally and a savage denunciation of the pact by Connor were the prelude to two bombing attacks by disgruntled whites. The first was on the home of Rev. A. D. King, and the second, minutes later, badly damaged portions of the A. G. Gaston Hotel, where King and other movement leaders had been staying while in Birmingham. While no one was seriously injured in either blast, the bombs were followed by an angry response by African-Americans, who attacked police with rocks, bottles, and bricks. Despite the best efforts of Walker and others, the unrest boiled into the early hours of the morning. Heavily armed Alabama Highway patrol units rushed to the city. The rioting continued through the evening.[120] "Tall Paul" White, who lived in a small apartment across the street from the motel, dashed through the debris, climbed in through a shattered window at the radio station, and began broadcasting what he saw. According to radio historian Bob Friedman, White was promptly arrested for his trouble.[121]

The twin explosions could be heard across the city, in a town where bombs were not uncommon. One of the young protesters in jail at the time was Myrna Carter, who remembered morning, noon, and nighttime prayer sessions in jail, followed by freedom songs and hymns. The demonstrators were singing on the night of the bombing at the Gaston Hotel, though they had no way of knowing what had been bombed. When the wardens began singing "Dixie" over the intercom, the students responded by drowning them out with rousing renditions of freedom songs.[122]

### Sunday, May 12

The rioting, mostly confined to an area near the hotel and Kelly Ingram Park, continued into early Sunday morning before burning itself out. Police, aided by movement officials, eventually convinced the estimated twenty-five hundred rioters to return home. In their wake, they left "scores" of burned police and private automobiles; more than fifty people injured, including one policeman; and several small stores and houses in the neighborhood gutted. King returned immediately to Birmingham, where he found ten blocks of the city cordoned off and manned by "Col." Lingo of the Alabama Highway Patrol's "sheriff's posse" and "irregulars" armed with sawed-off shotguns and wearing "GI helmets." Some Birmingham law enforcement officials pled unsuccessfully with Lingo to withdraw his men.[123] Also represented amid the law enforcement presence was a detachment of Sheriff Jim Clark's mounted deputies from Selma, Alabama. As the simmering violence slowly abated, the "thonk" of clubs crashing against heads could be heard across the street.[124] Kennedy urged that the preliminary agreement be preserved, ordered the Alabama National Guard from two nearby military bases to be on standby, and took "preliminary steps" to press them into federal service.[125]

In the pre-dawn hours of Monday May 13, movement leaders continued to try to quell the violence. Following the bombing of his home, A. D. King had called his brother, then in Atlanta, and described the horror and the "erupting tumult" still ongoing in the African-American community. But, as his brother talked, Martin later wrote that in the background of the telephone conversation: "I heard a swelling burst of beautiful song. Feet planted in the rubble of debris, threatened by criminal violence and hatred, followers of the movement were singing 'We Shall Overcome.' I marveled that in a moment of such tragedy the Negro could still express himself with hope and with faith."[126] A. D. King, his home still smoldering from the bomb, had driven to Kelly Ingram Park with a megaphone and again urged rioters to return to their homes. He had gathered three hundred protesters for an impromptu prayer meeting, which had culminated with the shaky singing of "We Shall Overcome" that his brother heard on the telephone.[127]

In an effort to help calm the situation, Martin King and Abernathy undertook the unusual step the next day of visiting several downtown African-American pool halls, where they collected weapons and donations, played pool, preached nonviolence, and led the startled pool players in freedom songs[128] before police ushered them back to the Gaston. The following two days were marked by claims and counterclaims from the two sides, but only sporadic, low-key violence, along with the regular nightly mass meetings and continued inflammatory rhetoric by Connor, former Mayor Art Haynes, and others. Still, there were no riots or demonstrations and few federal troops were stationed in the city itself. While Birmingham's city business leaders refused to embrace the agreement, and most would not allow themselves to be identified, few actively opposed it. As for King, he resumed his out-of-state fund-raising efforts.[129]

On Wednesday May 15, sixty of the nearly eighty members of the Senior Citizens Committee, the most powerful business leaders in Birmingham, gave their "implied support" for the "token desegregation." The list of business leaders, however, did not include any of the downtown merchants, who represented the only businesses directly involved in the agreement.[130] Details, implementation, and even enforcement, of the pact remained sketchy, and African-Americans repeatedly requested more information. More than seven hundred outside law enforcement officers and irregulars remained in Birmingham, and were involved in most of the complaints of violence by movement officials. As the weekend approached, one reporter noted than an "uneasy quiet" had descended on the city, though participants in the pact noted the usual anonymous telephone crank calls and threats.[131] Claiming to fear the power of the mass meetings, Lingo and Connor erected barricades around Sixteenth Street Baptist to discourage attendance at the nightly gatherings.[132]

The next major milestone involving Birmingham occurred in Washington, DC, on May 20 when the Supreme Court ruled that cities that enforced segregation through either ordinance or "public statement" could not prosecute African-Americans who sought service in stores or restaurants. The ruling set aside convictions of protesters in several southern states, including Alabama. Among those named in the argument were Shuttlesworth and Billups, who had been convicted of "aiding and abetting" a violation of the city trespass law, for "encouraging" students to conduct sit-ins. The judges ruled that the two men could not be arrested for something that was not a crime.[133] But before movement activists could celebrate, the Birmingham Board of Education ordered the expulsion or suspension of eleven hundred students, some of whom were still in jail, who had been arrested during the desegregation protests. King again rushed back to Birmingham from Atlanta in an effort to defuse what quickly became a volatile situation. The NAACP immediately requested an emergency hearing before a federal judge to seek reinstatement of the students. On Wednesday May 22, Chief Judge Elbert P. Tuttle of the Fifth Circuit Court of Appeals issued a restraining order against the school officials, overturning an earlier district judge's decision. Tuttle noted that there "could be no genuine dispute" that the students had been arrested because of their efforts to end discrimination. Movement officials breathed another sigh of relief on Thursday when Alabama's state Supreme Court unanimously upheld Birmingham's city elections, finally confirming the ouster of avowed segregationalists Connor and former Mayor Hanes. While King called Connor an "influence for evil," incoming Mayor Boutwell told reporters he would refuse to meet with King.[134]

Rather than respond to Boutwell's snub, King used to the relative calm to begin a series of speeches and fund-raising events throughout the United States. On May 26, he attended a fund-raiser at Wrigley Field in Los Angeles. The more than thirty-five thousand people in attendance made this the largest integrated civil rights rally to date and it raised more than $35,000. King closed the ecstatic meeting with a thundering recitation of "The Battle Hymn of the Republic." After, at a lavish reception hosted by Burt and Norma Lancaster, more money was raised for the SCLC. Actors, athletes, and musicians, such as Paul Newman, Polly Bergen, John Forsythe, Lloyd Bridges, and Elgin Baylor, each donated $1,000—the daily cost of operating the SCLC. Marlon Brando donated another $5,000, and Sammy Davis, Jr., pledged $20,000. At the end of the evening, all gathered and sang "We Shall Overcome."[135] A quick flight to Chicago led to Mahalia Jackson's long-planned concert at McCormick Place, which began with a motorcade through the city featuring King, Jackson and Mayor Richard J. Daley. Performances and speeches by King, Jackson, Rev. Clay Evans, co-organizer Rev. C. L. Franklin, Eartha Kitt, Gregory (just released from a Chicago jail for protesting in front of Daley's house), Hibbler, Studs Terkel, and others ended at 2 a.m. with Aretha Franklin's performance of "Precious Lord" that, as one writer put it, "wrung them all inside out." The Chicago receipts totaled $45,000.[136]

Throughout the previous weeks, even during the less eventful periods of the movement, several unsung heroes continued their surreptitious work—Birmingham's DJs. Shelley "The Playboy" Stewart, whose commentaries on WEDR once prompted the Klan to cut the guide wires of the radio station, had fan clubs at many of the area high schools and juniors highs and used that notoriety to continue feeding movement information under the noses of teachers and principals. When not on the air, Stewart was often at his nearby record store, where he had a view of Kelly Ingram Park. The store was connected to the law offices of J. Richmond Pearson by a little-used hallway. Closely monitored by Connor and his henchmen, King and his associates would stroll into Stewart's record store and then disappear down the hallway for meetings with other movement officials in Pearson's offices. Stewart, White, or Faush received prearranged codes from movement leaders to play certain songs, ranging from the old protest spiritual "Wade in the Water" to the pop hit "Yakety-Yak," that signaled certain directions and instructions for listeners. Or a DJ would casually remark on the air, "Hey, you know I saw Reverend Gardner up on Sixteenth Street," which meant a specific event would be happening at Sixteenth Street Baptist Church.[137] The three DJs would also strategically broadcast "bogus" traffic reports, to inform listeners of streets that police had blocked downtown, thereby outmaneuvering Connor.[138] In April 1968, in a speech to radio announcers, King heralded the contributions of African-American radio announcers during the struggle, specifically mentioning White's work in Birmingham.[139]

Not nearly as well documented were the appearances by various gospel artists in support of the movement during the long struggle. Gospel historian Anthony Heilbut has cited in particular the support given by Jackson who, in addition to financially supporting the SCLC, was singing "We Shall Overcome" at her concerts, as well as the contributions by Julius "June" Cheeks and Birmingham native Dorothy Love Coates.[140] Singer James Alex Taylor of the Birmingham Sunlights recalls Sam McCrary of the Fairfield Four leading the singing at the movement meetings at New Pilgrim Baptist Church.[141] Another member of the Sunlights said he heard that both the Blind Boys of Alabama and the Golden Gate Quartet sang at different rallies as well.[142] Another early financial supporter of Shuttlesworth and the ACMHR was legendary gospel composer Thomas Dorsey ("Take My Hand, Precious Lord" and "Peace in the Valley"). Dorsey became active during the Montgomery bus boycott and wrote several politically pointed songs, including "Let Us Work Together, Let Us Sing Together." "Until everyone is free, no one is free," Dorsey once told *Ebony*.[143]

As May drew to a close, Birmingham was not the only place where civil rights–related activities took place, of course. Wallace announced plans to use some of the same state highway patrolmen who had wreaked havoc in Birmingham to bar the admission of twenty-year-old Vivian Malone from the University of Alabama in Tuscaloosa. Antisegregation protests took place in several North Carolina cities and police dogs were used on peaceful demonstrators in Greensboro. The quarterback of the North Carolina A&T football team, a student named Jesse Jackson, told reporters, "When a police dog bites us in Birmingham, people of color bleed all over America." As footage and photographs of Connor's dogs in Birmingham spread, American prestige plummeted abroad. In Cairo, an English-language newspaper published a series of photographs under the giant headline,

**FIGURE 8**

Under the watchful eye of a North Carolina state trooper, African-Americans sing protest songs and clap their hands on the lawn of the Executive Mansion in Raleigh, North Carolina, 1963. *News and Observer* Photograph Files, State Archives of North Carolina. Photo courtesy of the *Raleigh News and Observer* and State Archives of North Carolina.

**FIGURE 9**

A group of African-American and white
protesters marching down a sidewalk at night.
*News and Observer* Photograph Files, State
Archives of North Carolina. Photo courtesy
of the *Raleigh News and Observer* and State
Archives of North Carolina.

"SAVAGES!" ACMHR-SCLC leaders estimated that their expenses, mostly bond money and legal fees, in April and May totaled a staggering $300,000.[144]

In Danville, Virginia, Shuttlesworth and eighteen SNCC field secretaries (including Mary King, Ivanhoe Donaldson, and Bob Zellner) began arriving on June 8 to support civil rights activists who were facing a particularly intractable city government. Beginning with the first demonstration two days later, heavily armed police attacked protesters with a fury. During one particularly brutal night, hundreds of men, women, and children were hospitalized even as attacks on reporters kept most of the egregious events out of the eyes of the press. Hundreds were imprisoned at the Danville City Farm. That night, Cordell and Bernice Reagon, along with the SNCC Freedom Singers, arrived in town to sing at the mass meeting at the Bibleway Holiness Church, where they saw the effects of the carnage. After the meeting, fifty volunteers, mostly women, walked the two miles to the jail to conduct a prayer vigil at the jail and sing "Jesus Keep Me Near the Cross." Within seconds, firemen opened up high-pressure fire hoses on the women and police rushed in swinging their clubs. Of the fifty who marched on the night of June 10, forty-seven required medical treatment.[145] In the days that followed, the Danville mayor, an apparent admirer of Connor, declared, "We will hose down the demonstrators and fill every available stockade."[146] When federal marshals served Shuttlesworth with an injunction against further protests, the reverend declared they would continue to disturb the peace with "the joyful noise" of their singing. "If singing 'We Shall Overcome' is upsetting, let's upset the hell out of the community. It needs to be upset when it keeps people down."[147] While the events in Danville were little reported in the white media, the *(Baltimore) Afro-American* gave them front-page coverage, with photographs of the victims and a headline that screamed, "'Like a Slaughterhouse.'"[148]

As the tension-filled summer wore on and bail costs soared, the coffers of the SCLC, the ACMHR, and the SNCC again grew dangerously low. In response, a number of artists hosted and performed at another series of fund-raising concerts. A June 22 benefit, "A Salute to Southern Freedom" at Carnegie Hall, hosted by John Henry Faulk and featuring Jackson and the Freedom Singers, benefitted the SNCC. The subsequent review, by the *New York Times*' Robert Shelton, lauded both, calling Jackson "spectacular" and writing of the Freedom Singers, "Even if the quartet were not dealing in matters so urgent as the topic freedom songs of the integration movement, it would be outstanding for its singing."[149] Baseball legend Jackie Robinson, who had been to Birmingham several times, hosted a benefit for the SCLC in his Stamford, Connecticut, home the following day where forty-two musicians performed, including Dizzy Gillespie, Cannonball Adderley, and Dave Brubeck, and raised $15,000.[150] In July, a concert at the ILWU Auditorium in San Francisco featured the Vince Guaraldi Trio, the Carmen McRae Group, the Ahmad Jamal Trio, and others.[151]

On June 23, more than one hundred twenty-five thousand people (though organizers estimated the total was closer to two hundred fifty thousand) marched in a procession in downtown Detroit with King, with many more watching from the packed sidewalks. The marchers repeatedly broke into spirited versions of "We Shall Overcome" and "The Battle Hymn of the Republic." The parade ended at Cobo Hall where Rev. C. L. Franklin hosted a rally and fund-raiser. Speakers and performers included the Four Tops, Ramsey Lewis, Erma Franklin, and others. A mass choir sang freedom songs, including "We Shall Overcome," and closed with music dedicated to the memory of Medgar Evers. An offering was taken for scholarships for the late activist's children. The evening ended with a speech by King, which included many of the elements that would reappear as the "I Have a Dream" speech at the Washington Monument only a few weeks later.[152] At a September fund-raiser in Atlanta featuring Lena Horne, Motown Records rush released an LP of the speech titled *The Great March to Freedom*.[153]

The reverence that now accompanied every performance of "We Shall Overcome" in Birmingham, along with its ubiquitous nature, prompted the *New York Times* to a devote an article to the song on July 23, "Rights Song Has Own History of Integration." Written by Shelton, the article documented the song's sometimes convoluted history and the decision by Frank Hamilton, Guy Carawan, Pete Seeger, and the estate of Zilphia Horton to copyright and thus allocate any royalties accrued to the "freedom movement under the trusteeship of the writers." The article called "We Shall Overcome" the "Marseillaise" of the integration movement and included an eloquent testimony to the song's power from one of the architects of the Birmingham movement, Wyatt T. Walker:

> One cannot describe the vitality and emotion this hymn evokes across the southland. I have heard it sung in great mass meetings with a thousand voices singing as one. I've heard a half dozen sing it softly behind the bars of the Hinds County prison in Mississippi.
>
> I've heard old women singing it on the way to work in Albany, Georgia. I've heard the students singing it as they were being dragged away to jail. It generates power that is indescribable. It manifests a rich legacy of musical literature that serves to keep body and soul together for that better day which is not far off.[154]

One of the early agreements between the city of Birmingham and the movement was that integrated concerts be allowed in the City Auditorium. The SCLC, the NAACP, the Urban League, the SNCC, and other groups were set to cosponsor "American Guild of Actors and Entertainer's Salute to Freedom '63," featuring, among others, Jackson, Ray Charles, and Nat King Cole, on August 5. However, on July 15, the city announced that it would be painting the auditorium on that date and summarily cancelled the concert, the first to feature both white and African-American artists performing before an integrated audience in Birmingham. The concert, cohosted by radio station WNEW and now targeted to raise money for the upcoming March on Washington for Jobs and Freedom, was hastily moved to Miles College. Performers at Miles included Johnny Mathis, Nina Simone, Clyde McPhatter, the Shirelles, the Alabama Christian Movement Choir, and Charles; speakers included King, James Baldwin, Steve Allen, and boxer Joe Louis. During the closing set by Johnny Mathis, the stage collapsed, though no one was injured. Estimates of the crowd size on the football field ranged from seven thousand to thirteen thousand.[155] When the concert ended at 3 a.m., more than $10,000 had been raised, with more promised.[156]

The singing continued in the Birmingham mass meetings after the media spotlight had faded. Writer Margaret Long reported on one August night's rally, describing in great detail not just what was sung, but how. She noted that the singing was "Gospel, gay and honky-tonk at times" as the congregation sang "O Freedom":

> *O free*dom, *o free*dom, *o free*dom *over* me, and be*fore* I'll be a *slave,* I'll be *buried* in my *grave,* and go *home* to my *Lord* and be *free* . . . no segre*gation,* no segre*gation,* no segre*gation over* me . . . no more *weeping,* no more *weeping over* me . . . and no more shooting, burning churches, Jim Crow, Bull Connor, "I'll go *home* to my *Lord* and be *free!*"

Like few before her, Long recorded in rich, descriptive language that evening's performances of "All God's Chillun' Got Shoes" and other protest spirituals, capturing the fevered excitement of the music and its message: "The old jazz and gospel rhythms, the city sidewalk beat, and the ancestral black music, worked, vied, and raced faster and faster, with the piano plunking away, and the hands clapping like castanets in a tremendous assertion and a mounting suspense suggestive of Ravel's 'Bolero.'"[157]

## Aftermath

Change would ever be slow, grudging, and still occasionally violent in Birmingham. It would not accelerate until the passage and enforcement of the Civil Rights Act of 1964. In the wake of Birmingham, Kennedy once wryly noted, "The civil rights movement should thank God for Bull Connor. He's helped it as much as Abraham Lincoln."[158] Certainly the willingness to suffer and the sacrifices of the demonstrators, young and old, were essential, as was the movement's leadership. But in reflecting on Birmingham, King writes that "songs bind us together, give us courage together, help us march together."[159] Note that King writes those words in the present tense—the freedom songs, gospel songs, and protest spirituals songs that inspired, encouraged, sustained, and succored protesters then, he clearly believed, continue to serve those purposes . . . and more.

The participants, such as high school student Richard Simpson, told Charles Euchner that the success of the movement was directly tied to the singing: "How do you explain it? It was like a fire. It started out small. You start a fire, just fan it a little bit. Well, Birmingham was on fire. Once it got going it was no turning around. As that song sang, 'Ain't gonna let nobody turn me around.' All those things we sang about, we believed. If not, we would have just stopped, quit, and said, 'That's it.'"[160]

This park is the Jerusalem of the civil rights movement, the Mecca of the civil rights movement, the Iwo Jima of the civil rights movement. From now on, when we come here and hear the birds sing, they will be singing "freedom." When the water runs, it will run "freedom." When the wind blows, it will blow, "freedom." When footsteps touch the walk, they will say "freedom."

—REVEREND ABRAHAM WOODS AT KELLY INGRAM PARK, BIRMINGHAM, ALABAMA, SEPTEMBER 15, 1992[161]

# 5

## THE MARCH ON WASHINGTON FOR JOBS AND FREEDOM

*August 28, 1963*

*It was the beginning of something, and the ending of something.*
*It came 100 years and 240 days after the signing of the Emancipation Proclamation.*
*It came like a force of nature.*
*It came like a storm, like a flood, it overwhelmed and stunned by its massiveness and finality.*

—LERONE BENNETT

Gospel queen Mahalia Jackson of New Orleans was also there that day; she often sang on the most important occasions at which Dr. King spoke, the pair working in tandem, her voice a kind of hallelujah chorus, of a piece with his testimonies. The singing at the mass gatherings not only provided entertainment, it served as a way for audiences to participate in the event. Music's ability to reach the place in the heart that words alone simply cannot access made it essential to the spoken presentations and to keeping the human spirit awake. If the justice and morality at the basis of Dr. King's message couldn't reach its intended audience, perhaps some familiar words from a gospel song could get the job done.

—DENISE SULLIVAN

As A. Philip Randolph stood on the steps of the Lincoln Memorial on August 28, 1963, speaking to a crowd of a quarter of a million people, it was the culmination of more than twenty year's work for the grand old man of American labor. Randolph had first conceived of this magnificent spectacle in the early days of World War II. Just the suggestion of it had helped convince President Franklin D. Roosevelt to sign into law legislation that meant jobs for hundreds of thousands of African-Americans.[1] And it was on these steps that Marian Anderson had sung spirituals and patriotic anthems to a national radio audience, defying segregation in this most symbolic of all of Washington's monuments.[2] Anderson herself was seated near Randolph on this Wednesday and would, shortly, sing again. The March on Washington for Jobs and Freedom would signal a new phase in the American civil rights movement. But for Randolph and Anderson, it proved that—at least on this hot August day—the circle was, indeed, unbroken.[3]

The March on Washington is now best known for the thundering "I Have a Dream" speech by Dr. Martin Luther King, Jr. But before, during, and even after the day-long event itself, music was as essential and as vital to the goals of the organizers and participants as the speeches, sermons, and prayers. That this was so is due, certainly in part, to the organizing genius behind the March, the remarkable Bayard Rustin. Rustin, who sang with Josh White and Paul Robeson; who recorded an album of spirituals; who was a conscientious objector, a socialist, and a Quaker; and who was hounded by J. Edgar Hoover and denounced from floor of the Senate, was the man who would pull together one of the largest, and certainly the most famous, civil rights events of all time in a matter of months, with a handful of volunteers and virtually no budget. While Randolph was the spiritual head of the March, it was Rustin who worked the magic with the seemingly endless array of logistical issues and tough, on-the-spot decisions.[4]

Once word spread of the financial requirements of the upcoming March, numerous benefits were organized. Nat King Cole hosted and paid for a benefit on August 8 in Los Angeles that featured most of the movement leaders, including King. The benefit raised $4,000 and Cole added another $1,000.[5] The famed Apollo Theater featured another benefit on the evening of August 23[6] with an impressive lineup that included Thelonius Monk, Art Blakey, Billy Eckstine, and Quincy Jones. On August 25, at the famed Polo Grounds, a fund-raiser featuring Duke Ellington, Cole, Sammy Davis, Jr., Frank Sinatra, and dozens of other performers and speakers ran from noon until midnight.[7]

Meanwhile, during the frenzied preparations leading to the March, Rustin spent much time defending himself from the attacks of segregationists, including Senator Strom Thurmond. But the chain-smoking Rustin soldiered on. Just prior to the event, the *Afro-American* newspaper in Baltimore devoted most of the front page and two inside pages to advance coverage and featured a photograph of Rustin posed beside a map of Washington, DC, and centered under the headline, "200,000 Marchers D.C. Bound." Rustin was at the center of legal and political preparations; fund-raising, including money earmarked for "freedom trains" bringing workers from Jacksonville and New Orleans; logistics related to food, transportation, and sanitation; and coordinating among the many civil rights and religious entities represented. The newspaper featured long lists of premarch prayer vigils and rallies and the names of "celebrities" who had announced their intent to participate. Some, like Burt Lancaster, would be flying in from movie shoots abroad; others came from concert venues across the country.[8] *Ebony* magazine likewise devoted nearly an entire issue to the March, detailing the scale of the preparations, the political climate, and the various ways marchers arrived in Washington. In nearly every picture, the participants are singing. One train from Chicago featured a combo, including drummer, trumpeter, and stand-up bassist, leading the travelers in "old spirituals" and a particularly appropriate song long identified with Sister Rosetta Tharpe: "This train don't carry no liars. . . . This train is bound for glory."[9] The modes of transportation to the District of Columbia would include, by one estimate, thirty-seven special trains, eleven charter airplanes, 1,514 "blocks of buses" and an unknown number of personal automobiles, taxis, and bicycles.[10] The first wave of marchers arrived in Washington before dawn and their numbers grew steadily throughout the morning and early afternoon.

According to *Time* magazine, the morning of August 28 only became "lively" in Washington, DC, when one of the "Freedom Special" trains "roared in from Deep Dixie." The train, originating in Jacksonville, Florida, carried 785 marchers, including a host of young people who had spent time in southern jails. "They piled off the train singing the battle hymn of the Negro's 1963 revolution, 'We Shall Overcome.'"[11] Trains continued to arrive for hours at Washington's massive Union Station, each bearing singing passengers. Students from the Pittsburgh SNCC strolled through the concourse singing "We Shall Not Be Moved." They were met by a group of young NAACP members disembarking from a train from Chicago who sang "When the Saints Go Marching In." Each new arrival was greeted with applause and cheers from others in the vast concourse.[12] The United Auto Workers (UAW) chartered five airplanes for its participants. The planes were met by buses and the participants were given lunchboxes when they arrived in Washington, DC. A contingent of twenty-three young people, all recently released from jail and still in coveralls, came from Greenwood, Mississippi, the scene of some of the most violent responses to voter registration in the South.[13] The largest union representation was five thousand members of the Retail, Wholesale, and Department Store Union. The parent International Ladies' Garment Workers' Union (ILGWU) chartered both a sixteen-car train and an eight-bus convoy.[14] Rustin, who had arrived on the Mall before dawn, personally met a group of teenagers from Albany, Georgia, and a "busload" from Des Moines.[15] From the bloody and still-dangerous streets of Danville, a group of civil rights workers arrived singing "Ain't Gonna Let Nobody Turn Me 'Round."[16]

Rustin's music background played a pivotal role in two of his most crucial decisions. Working under the assumption that any crowd will soon grow restless if it cannot hear the speakers or singers, Rustin insisted on the best sound system available. The $20,000 for the sound system was donated by the UAW and the ILGWU and was installed and checked out repeatedly in the days before the March.[17] Rustin also used March funds to pay for an electric organ to be installed at the Lincoln Memorial. The organ proved to be so successful that the music company that provided the organ donated it to the government for future use at the memorial as a tribute to the March.[18] The night before the March, however, someone sabotaged the public address equipment. When the contractor said it would take days to repair, Rustin called Walter Fauntroy, who was in charge of the March's local operations. Fauntroy called Attorney General Robert Kennedy and Kennedy's representative at the Justice Department, Burke Marshall. Marshall then called the Army Signal Corps, which immediately sent a team of engineers. Working through the night, the Corps's specialists repaired the system by early the next morning.[19]

The best, most detailed planning in the world, of course, can never anticipate all eventualities, especially for something on the scale of the March on Washington for Jobs and Freedom. Many of the best-known Hollywood stars were late in arriving and were briefly stranded at National Airport. Burt Lancaster read a short statement (prepared by James Baldwin), flanked by Marlon Brando, Charlton Heston, Sidney Poiter, and Harry Belafonte, among others before a small crowd of newspaper reporters; they then slowly made their way toward the Mall, where they met with the press again.[20]

At 10 a.m., with tens of thousands of marchers still arriving at the Washington Monument, actor Ossie Davis served as the master of ceremonies. When several scheduled performers and speakers were late because of the crush of bodies, he asked Dorothy Dale of Birmingham to lead those assembled in "freedom songs."[21] In what became something of an informal jam session, Joan Baez, who would garner the most press coverage of the white folk performers, sang a solemn version of "Oh Freedom" and then sang "We Shall Overcome" with Bob Dylan singing in the later verses. Folk singer and "musical historian" Odetta, who had worked tirelessly for movement causes through the 1960s, performed a medley of protest spirituals under the title of "O Freedom."[22] The New York Times said that her "great, full-throated voice carried almost to Capitol Hill: 'If they ask you who you are, tell them you're a child of God.'"[23] Odetta was followed by Josh White, who invited Peter, Paul and Mary to perform Dylan's "Blowin' in the Wind," and they were soon joined by Dylan. "Blowin' in the Wind," already a hit on the record charts, is set to the tune of "No More Auction Block for Me," a protest spiritual recorded by both Odetta and Paul Robeson.[24] Dylan joined Baez to accompany movement veteran and singer Len Chandler for "Keep Your Eyes on the Plow—Hold On."[25]

Years later, Mary Travers called the performance the "softest spot" in her career. "If you could imagine . . . singing that song in front of a quarter of a million people, black and white, who believed they could make America more generous and compassionate in a nonviolent way, you begin to know how incredible that belief was. And still is."[26] During the March itself, Peter Yarrow said he was struck by the sheer power of the music: "I had the feeling, in those first marches that we were part of, that the songs were a different kind of rhetoric. There were a lot of people in America that were fence-sitters, that were just not about to think about the possibility of change and alteration, and were dead against it. When they heard the music, something human was touched and it was undeniable."[27]

Also walking up to the podium at the Washington Monument was singer/actress Lena Horne wearing, as she often did, her blue NAACP cap. Horne, who was not feeling well—though it may have been nerves from the size of the crowd and the gravity of the occasion—simply shouted/sang a single word, "Freee-*eeeee*-dommmmm!" and held it for "four or five seconds." Horne's "performance" was marked by attendees for years to come.[28]

In the final days before the March, Harry Belafonte had noticed that none of the local song leaders of Montgomery, Albany, Birmingham, and a hundred more movement battles in the South were represented. He hurriedly chartered a flight to bring the Freedom Singers from Los Angeles in time to perform at the Washington Monument. As the Freedom Singers watched, those same local song-leaders spontaneously filled the air "with the sounds of the jail-ins, sit-ins, and street marches of Southern campaigns," noted Bernice Johnson Reagon. The Freedom Singers sang "I Want My Freedom Now" in tribute to those often anonymous leaders.[29]

The crowd, which had been growing since dawn, continued to mill about at the Washington Monument waiting impatiently for the official parade to begin. At one break, someone urged the Mississippi delegation up to the podium to sing freedom songs. Among those who sang was a reluctant Anne Moody, only recently released from another stint in jail in Jackson.[30] Soon, the throng "extemporized its own diversion." Local high school bands played and after one performance, recently released demonstrators from Danville shouted "Move on!" The impromptu procession, led by the Kenilworth Knights, a Washington-area drum and bugle corps, "surged forward" on its own, leaving its still assembling "leaders" stranded long before the 11:30 a.m. scheduled start time.[31] What was supposed to be two lines down Constitution and Independence Avenues surged like a tidal wave across the entire width of the Mall toward the Lincoln Memorial.[32] Movement leaders hurriedly joined in the middle of the mass of people, though through artful staging for photographers it appeared they were in the front, leading the way. "We could not even see the front," John Lewis observed. "We came to the Lincoln Memorial, the leaders being pushed along by the people—as it should be."[33]

En route, reporters noted the number of times different groups spontaneously broke into "We Shall Overcome." One person who was particularly frustrated by the nearly impenetrable foot traffic was the organist at the Lincoln Memorial, whose copy of the sheet music for "We Shall Overcome" was delayed by the crowd of marchers. An "unidentified Negro minister" rushed to the organist's side and notated the melody line and soon the song resounded over Rustin's speakers as well.[34] The *National Guardian* called the demonstration the "gayest seen in Washington" and everywhere were groups, large and small, singing songs, "all of which, at one point or another, seemed to contain the word 'freedom.'"[35] It took from 11:30 a.m. to 2:30 p.m., according to one estimate, "for the quarter million people to walk four-fifths of a mile" from the Washington Monument to the Lincoln Memorial. Singing broke out constantly along the way. One cluster of people within the larger throng sang a variation of "Oh Freedom," mocking South Carolina's segregationist

Senator Sam Ervin ("No more Sam Ervin / No more Sam Ervin over me / And before I'll be a slave / I'll be buried in my grave / And go home to my Lord and be free"), while another nearby group sang "John Brown's Body." It was during this part of the March that writer Toby Stein, a nonsinger and childhood friend of James Baldwin, had an epiphany about the lyrics and music. "I listened, as I never had before when I heard them over the television, to the words of the songs," she said. "And they were so—simply—true. I couldn't very well *not* join in with my half-dead frog voice."[36]

The opening remarks at the Lincoln Memorial, as was appropriate, were delivered by Randolph. It would be his last major speech and it set the tone for the day: "Let the nation and the world know the meaning of our numbers. We are not a pressure group, we are not an organization or a group of organizations, we are not a mob. We are the advance guard of a massive moral revolution for jobs and freedom."[37] Marian Anderson, designated to sing "The Star-Spangled Banner" to open the Lincoln Memorial portion of the event, could not make her way through the wall of people heading to the Mall in time. In her place, Camilla Williams, the first black woman to sing with the New York City Opera, sang instead.[38] When Anderson, "in tears," arrived, she "sang a stunning version" of "He's Got the Whole World in His Hands."[39] There were those in the crowd who had been in attendance at the Easter 1939 concert when Anderson had sung the patriotic song "America" and a handful of spirituals and struck one of the early blows of the civil rights movement.[40] There was more music at the Lincoln Memorial, including music by the Eva Jessye Choir and repeat performances by Bob Dylan (who sang "Only a Pawn in Their Game," about the murder of Medgar Evers), Odetta, Peter, Paul and Mary, and Joan Baez. Speakers that day represented a number of social justice and religious organizations: Dr. Eugene Carson Blake, John Lewis, Rabbi Uri Miller, James Farmer, Whitney M. Young, Jr., Mathew Ahmann, Roy Wilkins, Rabbi Joachim Prinze, and Rustin.[41] But the two moments most marked by attendees then— and best remembered now—were the two spirituals sung by Mahalia Jackson and King's closing remarks, what would become known as the "I Have a Dream" speech.

Jackson and King had originally agreed that Jackson would sing "Take My Hand, Precious Lord," but her manager, Lou Mindling, had lobbied for something more upbeat. At some point, King had astutely judged the massive crowd's mood and whispered to Jackson and her accompanist, Mildred Falls, "Mahalia, sing 'I Been 'Buked.'" Jackson, resplendent in her new hat, moved to the podium and began to sing the old protest spiritual that had sustained and nurtured African-American hopes and dreams of freedom for more than a hundred years:

> "*I been 'buked and I been scorned, I been talked about, sure as you're born*—" Singing it into the maze of mikes, into America, out to the crowd, it was not hurt of the past but the now of the future that brought tears of joy to her voice so the vast, restless crowd became one listening body, rapt, intent. A plane roared low overhead. Mahalia raised her eyes . . .

*"I'm going to tell my Lord"*—"By God," murmured Studs [Terkel], "she's taking it on, the artist against the machine—and she's *done* it!" She sang it away—face brilliant, glowing, voice vibrant; not while she's telling *her* Lord!—and without a sound the crowd broke out white handkerchiefs, thousands of them waving in the air. With her last note, "More! More! More!" It could not be denied and she rocked them with *How I Got Over.* When she finished—dripping with sweat, panting—she got a standing ovation.[42]

For Lewis, who had earlier that afternoon delivered a controversial speech urging the administration to take stronger measures to protect African-Americans, it was "How I Got Over" that still resonates with him, decades later: "I can hear her now singing, just singing from the depths of her soul, 'How I Got Over.' There was a feeling, there was a feeling just being there in the presence of that sea of humanity that we had gotten over. There was something very moving about the music and the songs and the beat, the words, it gave you this sense we were on our way, on our way someplace."[43] On the steps in the "celebrity section," actor Sammy Davis, Jr., was "seemingly ready to shout" while Jackson sang.[44] Attorney Mortimer Zuckerman, inadvertently placed with the celebrities on the Lincoln Memorial platform, had a "magnificent view of the enormous crowd" and noted that the crowd was not "unified" at first and did not "coalesce" until Jackson sang. "She transformed the audience with the most extraordinary performance I have witnessed by any artist," he wrote years later. "Her voice, her presence and her gospel songs seized the crowd in a magnificent way."[45] Historian Lerone Bennett was equally moved. He called Jackson's performances one of the "keys" to the day's success. "There is a nerve that lies beneath the smoothest of exteriors, a nerve 400 years old and throbbing with hurt and indignation," he wrote in *Ebony.* "Mahalia Jackson penetrated the facades and exposed the nerve to public view." According to Bennett, the moment of recognition happened during "I Been 'Buked, I Been Scorned" and the lines, "I'm gonna tell my Lord / When I get home, / Just how long / You've been treating me wrong." It was then, he observed:

> A spasm ran through the crowd.
> The button-down men in front and the old women way back came to their feet, screaming and shouting. They had not known that this thing was in them and that they wanted it touched. From different places, in different ways, with different dreams, they had come and, now, hearing this sung, they were one.[46]

As for Rustin, who had been working feverishly for months in preparation for this day, film and news footage of the March show him "running around and talking" incessantly during the event itself. He only paused once during his labors—to hear Jackson sing.[47]

Randolph's two decade–long quest culminated with his heartfelt introduction of the day's final speaker, Dr. Martin Luther King, Jr. As King approached the microphones, the sounds of "The Battle Hymn of the Republic" resounded through the speakers.[48] More than fifty years later, the "I Have a Dream" speech, as it has come to be called, is perhaps as well known as Lincoln's "Gettysburg Address," and the images of King in full rhetorical glory preaching in front of the massive, brooding statue of Lincoln is indelibly burned into the nation's consciousness. In the "Gettysburg Address," Lincoln began "Four score and seven years ago . . ." and alluded to the Declaration of Independence. King alluded directly to both Lincoln's speech ("Five score years ago . . .") and the Declaration of Independence as well. He cited a host of biblical, philosophical, and theological allusions.[49] It was a monumental speech for a monumental occasion. But by now it was late in the afternoon and many had been standing in the sun for eight hours. Few on the steps of the Lincoln Memorial were as attuned to the moods of live audiences as Mahalia Jackson. She had carefully noted the "weight of history," the size of the crowd, and the presence of all three television networks on King as he worked through his prepared remarks. Instinctively, she "evoked a bit of holy boisterousness" and loudly encouraged her long-time friend to abandon the written speech. "Tell 'em about the dream, Martin!" Jackson shouted—her interjection "a sweet call and response," drawn from of their life immersions in the black church.[50]

When King abruptly departed from his prepared text and began the now iconic "I have a dream" passages, the weary crowd erupted: "It caught the cadence. It whooped and hollered as though Moses himself had come down from the Mount to tell them what life was going to be like. 'I have a dream'—the swell of noise from throats engulfed everything, and Dr. King had to stop."[51] As for Jackson herself, the African-American newspaper the *Michigan Chronicle* reported that she "chanted in the background, 'My Lord . . . My Lord . . . My Lord'" while King spoke.[52] Later, Jackson would describe the scene at the Lincoln Memorial as another Exodus: "It was like the vision of Moses that the children of Israel would march into Canaan." It is not insignificant, Bruce Feiler posits, that organizers had distributed song sheets for "Go Down, Moses" and several other spirituals to marchers. Nor was the symbolism lost on the millions of Americans watching televised coverage of the March that King concluded with the words from a spiritual that Zora Neale Hurston "put into the mouth of the Israelites as they set out for the Promised Land: 'Free at last! Free at last! Thank God Almighty, we are free at last!'"[53] With the words of the old protest spiritual—and it *had* to be a spiritual—the multitude erupted. "The Kingdom of God," Coretta King later recalled, "seemed to have come on earth."[54]

And then it was over. After final instructions from Rustin on how to maintain the momentum of the day and a closing prayer, the members of the SNCC who were there, the veterans of abuse and jail and the occasional victory in Georgia,

Alabama, and Mississippi—Bob Moses, Julian Bond, Dorie Ladner, Rachelle Horowitz, and the rest—formed a circle with Rustin's exhausted volunteers that "stretched to half the length of a football field." In the SNCC manner, they clasped hands and crossed one arm over the other, swayed, and sang "We Shall Overcome."[55] Jervis Anderson, one of Randolph's biographers, wrote that August 28, 1963, "expired upon the hauntingly beautiful strains of 'We Shall Overcome,' the black vesper hymn of that period. The song served as a benediction as the day officially ended, sung by hundreds of thousands of voices. It was one of the last times it would sound so sweetly or with its peculiar admixture of melancholy, yearning, and stubborn faith."[56]

As Jonathan Rieder has pointed out, King "nestled" the "I Have a Dream" speech between two spirituals. By asking Jackson to sing "I Been 'Buked, I Been Scorned," he "summoned the voice of the ancestors." And when he closed with "Free at last! Free at last!," he asked white marchers to sing with blacks so that they, too, "could experience both bondage and liberation." In this simple framing device, he suggests, the message of "I Shall Overcome" becomes the more inclusive "We Shall Overcome."[57]

## After the Speech

A quarter of a million people began the long process of wending their way back home. The music resounded down the Mall as the crowd left, leaving only the volunteers to clean the grounds. "Where 250,000 people had sat that day, there was nothing but the wind blowing the leftover programs and scattered them across the way, across the Reflection Pool," Ralph Abernathy recalled. "The wind was moving and blowing and blowing and keeping music. And we were so proud of the fact that no violence had taken place that day, and we were so pleased. This was the greatest day of my life."[58]

Kennedy had invited the leaders of several African-American organizations to a "stag" reception at the White House immediately after the conclusion of the March. It was a savvy bit of political gamesmanship. The leaders would have been ill advised to criticize the administration during their speeches even as they accepted its hospitality. The reception at the White House had all but made the once controversial March an "official" event, a "peaceful camp meeting in Washington to promote racial understanding."[59]

Nothing created by human hands is perfect, of course. Dick Gregory, already a veteran of numerous marches, jail time, and beatings, turned away and placed his hands over his ears during Dylan's performance. "I preferred to see Odetta up there," Gregory said. "She is a virtuoso musician, and she lived what we were there for. What was a white boy like Boy Dylan there for? Or—who else? Joan Baez? To support the cause? Wonderful—support the cause. March. Stand behind us—but not in front of us." Belafonte disagreed, saying that white performers sent a wider message of the inclusivity of the civil rights movement to those watching and listening that day.[60] The music played a minor role in the day's lone confrontation as well. Fifty members of the "nitwit" American Nazi Party, led by George Lincoln Rockwell, watched helplessly as the crowd swelled and police immediately cordoned them off of the Monument grounds. "I can't stand niggers," Rockwell raged, "I can't stand to hear 'We Shall Overcome.'" Rockwell finally led his "ridiculous" group away before the March even started.[61]

The fact that there were no women among the long list of speakers rankled and hurt some of the movement's strongest female supporters. That omission had been pointed out to Rustin, King, and others from the earliest planning stages and continued as a one-sided dialogue even during the day-long event.[62] "A Tribute to Negro Fighters for Freedom" was noted in the official program, with Movement heroes Daisy Bates (who spoke briefly), Diane Nash Bevel, Prince E. Lee (widow of murdered civil rights activist Herbert Lee), Rosa Parks, and Gloria Richardson sitting together. Myrlie Evers (wife of the murdered activist Medgar Evers) was also listed, but her flight was delayed.[63] Also in the "VIP section" was singer/actress and "celebrated expatriate," Josephine Baker, who returned to the United States after decades in France. Wearing the uniform of the Free French Army (she was a decorated veteran), Baker also spoke a few words.[64] But none of the major speeches were delivered by a woman.

Not all participants enjoyed peaceful return trips. Three busloads of marchers from Connecticut had their buses pelted with stones as they entered the Baltimore Harbor tunnel, though no one was injured.[65] Police also reported that four buses returning marchers to Philadelphia were attacked with rocks in the Rosedale area of Maryland. While there were no injuries, at least one window appeared to have been shattered by a bullet from a .22 caliber rifle.[66] African-American bus riders in eastern Maryland were denied service at a restaurant and several passengers on a bus returning to Mississippi were "roughed up" at a stop near Meridian—one even required medical care. Other riders were denied entrance to gas stations and restrooms in New York and elsewhere.[67]

And there was sadness on that day as well. Roy Wilkins, executive director of the NAACP, prefaced his remarks with the solemn announcement that Dr. W.E.B. Du Bois, author and one of the founders of the NAACP, had died at midnight on August 27 in Ghana, his adopted home. Wilkins asked for a time of silence and "a moment almost cinematic in its poignancy passed over the marchers."[68]

But by virtually all accounts, it was a day of kindness and generosity. Columnist Russell Baker marveled that "no one could remember an invading army quite as gentle" and the "extraordinary politeness that characterized the day was dramatized every time an elbow was crooked."[69] Birmingham gospel singer and activist N. B. Wooding said that a number of the "marching" Birmingham schoolchildren, including his daughters Patricia and Sandra Raye, were taken to the White House after the March, where Jackie Kennedy herself oversaw a meal for them. "Took care of them," he recalled. "She fixed lunch for them and everything."[70]

In the end, the question emerged as to whether the March on Washington for Jobs and Freedom—despite the size of the adoring and peaceful crowd and the glorious music and speeches—had accomplished everything Rustin and its supporters and organizers had hoped that it would. The *New York Times* interviewed several southern congressmen, none of whom believed the March would influence upcoming votes on Kennedy's proposed civil rights legislation.[71] But Clifford W. Depin, ILGWU district manager in Scranton, Pennsylvania, said that the day would have the "greatest effect" on the Marchers themselves: "We came here with about fifty members, and I'm not sure most of them were awakened to the real issues until we started to march and sing. That turned the trick."[72]

What was and is the ultimate impact of August 28, 1963? Ten years later, Rustin noted that just five months after the March on Washington, the Twenty-Third Amendment was ratified outlawing the poll tax. Five months after that, the 1964 Civil Rights Act was adopted. And within a year, the Voting Rights Act was signed.[73] Could any or all of these events be attributed in some way to a peaceful gathering of two hundred fifty thousand people on a day filled with extraordinary music and rhetoric? Like Depin, Lerone Bennett believed that the lone thing that could be known for certain was the impact of the March on Washington for Jobs and Freedom on the participants themselves, now and in some unknown future: "And they would remember. If the bridge held, and if it didn't rain, men and women would look back on this day and tell their children and grandchildren: "There was a March in the middle of the twentieth century, the biggest demonstration for civil rights in history—and I was there."[74]

Singing was the most powerful part of our mass meetings; we sang and sang and sang—freedom songs, church songs, church songs we made into freedom songs. Singing brought the people in and held us all together. It connected us to a Higher Power, and it lifted our spirits. Singing made us feel the need for freedom and inspired in us the belief that we could have it. Freedom songs provided the emotional link to the message. We'd preach freedom and then we'd sing freedom, and everybody got it. Without the compassion and honesty of freedom songs, I don't believe many people would have connected to the movement.

Singing for some people is an opportunity to express thoughts and feelings; black people sing mostly to satisfy a deep longing on the inside. Whether it's blues or gospel music or freedom songs, we sing to help us feel that things will get better. We sing for inspiration, as we've done for generations. Our love of music, I think, grew out of being used and oppressed. We had no material possessions. All we had that we could hang on to was music. The women in my family had always worked in the church, and they sang. *Black people never had anything but a song.* The songs of African Americans have given this country its truly American musical art. Our singing gave the civil rights movement its heart.

—UNITA BLACKWELL

## September 15, 1963: The Bombing in Birmingham

In the weeks that followed, the success of the March on Washington overshadowed all other events in the civil rights movement. But back in Birmingham, even the most microscopic advances by African-Americans, regardless of how tenuous, only served to further inflame the hate of a group of die-hard racists. That hatred exploded on Sunday morning at Sixteenth Street Baptist Church, the most visible symbol of the movement in the city.[1] Nineteen sticks of dynamite placed under a stairwell during Sunday school killed Denise McNair, 11, Carole Robertson, 14, Cynthia Wesley, 14, and Addie Mae Collins, 14, and injured more than two dozen other churchgoers. One of the most poignant moments of the entire horrific day came as rescuers worked desperately to remove debris from the wreckage. In the area where the nearly unrecognizable little girls were found, a church member found Sarah Collins, still alive but horribly burned and blinded. As she was loaded into the "colored" ambulance, Sarah sang, "Jesus Loves Me" and asked for her sister Addie. Angry, confused African-Americans gathered around the church almost immediately; a few threw some of the shattered bricks at the helmeted policemen. The police fired a volley over their heads. In response, many of those in the growing crowd defiantly sang the "We are not afraid" verses of "We Shall Overcome."[2]

Two more young African-Americans were killed in the hours of disorder and grief that followed. The church again became the symbol of protest and Governor George Wallace—whose vitriol and race hatred many blamed for the violence, including Martin Luther King and Roy Wilkins—sent the National Guard to keep the peace. This was the twenty-first bombing in Birmingham in eight years. Though no one had been killed in the earlier attacks, no one had been arrested, either. King and other civil rights leaders quickly returned to the city.[3]

Radio announcer Erskine Faush's scheduled on-air shift at station WENN, located just a block from the church, was not until later that day, but he rushed to the station once he heard the news. By the time he had arrived, police had already cordoned off the immediate area and stopped all traffic. They allowed him through and Faush went on the air and implored listeners to remain calm in the hours that followed.[4] Also across from the church in an unnamed hotel (presumably the Gaston Hotel) were the popular soul singers, Sam and Dave, recovering from a late show the night before. The duo was shaken but unharmed by the blast.[5] At a concert with the Harmonettes and Stanley Keeble in Chicago, Dorothy Love Coates heard the news and rushed to a telephone to call her mother, who lived in Birmingham. "Shall we come home?" she asked. Her mother responded, "No, Dorothy. You all go ahead on and sing. And those of us who are here, we're going to pray. And God is going to deliver us."[6]

In the tumultuous days that followed, each funeral reopened the wounds and the grief from the killings. Carole Robertson's family chose not to be a part of a proposed joint funeral service and instead held services Tuesday September 17 at St. John African Methodist Episcopal. More than eighteen hundred people attended, with many more listening outside. The Reverend C. E. Thomas, the church's pastor, prayed that "Carole's blood may become like that of Crispus Attucks," the first African-American to die in the American Revolution.[7] During his emotional remarks, the Reverend Fred Shuttlesworth said, "We are here because of an evil system which, while singing songs of Zion, and repeating philosophic phrases about love, justice and brotherhood, will allow innocent children to be blown into judgment rather than turn evil men out of office."[8]

**FIGURE 10**

Emergency personnel on the street in front of
Sixteenth Street Baptist Church following the
bombing on September 15, 1963 that killed four
young girls. *Alabama v. Chambliss* Trial Transcript, Collection 85, Archives Department,
Birmingham Public Library. Photo: Birmingham, Alabama, Public Library Archives.

On Wednesday, mourners filled Sixth Avenue Baptist Church hours before the service and police estimated that "thousands more" surrounded the church and lined the streets. The few white faces in the church included about fifty out-of-town pastors who sat near the back,[9] including the Reverend Joseph Ellwanger, a minister at St. Paul's Lutheran Church, who participated in the service.[10] The joint service began with the revival hymn, "Shall We Meet at the River" and included the singing of "Beautiful Garden of Prayer" and "He Leadeth Me."[11] King, who asked that those outside not sing during the memorial, said that the murders "may well serve as a redemptive force that brings light to this dark city."[12] However, the large crowd outside the church did begin to softly sing "We Shall Overcome" during the service. As the three small caskets were carried to the parking lot to waiting hearses, those outside the church began to sing more loudly with, as always, lyrics created for the moment: "Deep in my heart / I do believe / They won't die in vain / We shall overcome / Someday."[13] The *Birmingham Post-Herald* reporter noted that "a thousand voices strong, the song swelled up and downtown 5 p.m. traffic was routed away from the scene." As they walked toward the cemetery, the mourners added the verse, "They don't die in vain / They won't die in vain." The article noted that "about a thousand of the singers, overcome with emotion and stress, found relief in singing, 'Turn me 'round / Keep on a'walking / Keep on a'talking / Marching to Freedom Land'" as they marched.[14] SNCC members, in their trademark "bib overalls," followed behind the hearses. They led the growing crowd in an "up tempo and defiant" version of "Ain't Gonna Let Nobody Turn Me 'Round" as they walked to the gravesites, six miles away.[15] Virtually lost amid the national outpouring of grief and rage at the murder of the four girls, separate funerals were held Sunday, September 22 for the two African-American boys killed in the aftermath of the bombing, including thirteen-year-old Virgil Ware, shot in the back by two white Eagle Scouts, both 16, as he rode his bicycle in his neighborhood. Sixteen-year-old Johnnie Robinson had been shot by police for throwing rocks at cars.[16]

In the close-knit Birmingham African-American community, virtually everyone was touched by the loss. Carole Robertson was best friends with Eloise Ford Gaffney, one of the primary movers behind the Alabama Christian Movement Choir. Gaffney also took piano lessons with Cynthia Wesley. In her grief, which Gaffney said still surfaces more than fifty years after the bombing, she performed with the Movement Choir at the funerals.[17]

The morning of the bombing, Birmingham gospel singer Henry Burton was singing at a radio station when he received a telephone call saying that his father had suffered a stroke and told him to meet the family at Hillman Hospital. Burton found them in the segregated, black-only emergency room. As he stood by his father, who was lying on a stretcher on the emergency room floor waiting for a doctor, the hospital was shaken by a loud "boom." Five minutes later, the first ambulances arrived from Sixteenth Street Baptist. One woman shouted, "They done bombed Sixteenth Street Church!" The small African-American waiting room and ER quickly filled and the wounded were only transported upstairs to the white section of the hospital when a priest ordered the staff to do so. Burton saw the bodies of the young girls being wheeled in. Later that day, his father died as well.[18]

Two sacred songs in particular that emerged from that awful day came to resonate with and soothe the African-American community in the years to come. The first was by a Birmingham resident who both marched the city's bloody streets and sang gospel music across the country. Dorothy Love Coates is little known outside of gospel circles, though later in life she appeared in two national motion pictures, *The Long Walk Home* (1990) and *Beloved* (1998), in which she leads a group of former slaves in song.[19] No gospel artist was more outspoken to black audiences about segregation in her songs and sermon-songs: "Our Governor Wallace, child, he's so confused he cain't even see right, and as for Governor Maddox, church, he's *just pitiful.*" Dorothy and the Gospel Harmonettes vied with the Clara Ward Singers as the most popular female group on the gospel highway, despite—or, perhaps, because of—her fiery, fearless songs. Coates sang her compositions "He's Right on Time" ("He may not come when you want Him to / But He's right on time"), "That's Enough" ("They're trying to block and stop my progress / Most of the time"), "Lord, You've Been Good to Me" ("I know you brought me from a mighty long way") and others while marching, visiting churches to encourage voter registration, and occasionally spending long days and nights in jail.[20] But it was Coates's classic sermon-song "The Hymn" that most explicitly named the demons of the day:

> When the president was assassinated, the nation said, "Where is God?"

> When the little children lost their lives in the church bombing, the nation cried, "Where is God?"

> I've got the answer for you today: God is still on the throne.[21]

Gospel artist and television show host Bobby Jones vividly recalled the days following King's assassination in Nashville, where he saw Coates and the Harmonettes speak out about the events in Birmingham and sing "I'm Just Holding on and I Won't Let Go" as the "people in the audience were just going wild."[22] Gospel radio announcer Linwood Heath, who was broadcasting in Philadelphia at the time, also said that Coates was the one artist who "sticks out" in his memory from that era. With the Gospel Harmonettes, Coates's tours took her through Philadelphia, where she commanded respect both for her involvement in and outspoken support of the movement, including "The Hymn." According to Heath, "In the midst of her singing, in between songs, she would do . . . a little sermonette. It was just encouraging because she would always say that God still has everything in his hands; he's got it all in control. So she was very inspiring to us, up here in the North, because we knew she was in the midst of it all."[23]

The second gospel song most associated with the healing that eventually followed the terrible events of Sunday September 16, was the gospel hymn, "Peace Be Still," recorded by the Reverend James Cleveland with the Angelic Choir of the First Baptist Church of Nutley, New Jersey. Recorded live on Thursday at the nearby Trinity Temple Seventh Day Adventist Church in Newark, the album became one of Savoy Records' biggest sellers and, according to gospel historian Robert M. Marovich, "helped usher in the era of live gospel recordings."[24]

Topical songs, religious or secular, in part because many are recorded quickly in the heat of the moment, vary widely in quality. Some are little more than badly rhymed couplets recounting an event, while others dare to ponder deeper and ask otherwise unspoken questions. One of the most memorable songs to come from the bombing of Sixteenth Street Baptist Church was composed and sung by Richard Farina, once married to Mimi, Joan Baez's sister. In the days that followed the tragedy, Farina was moved to write "Birmingham Sunday": "On Birmingham Sunday, the blood ran like wine / And the choirs kept singing Freedom." Baez made it a staple of her concerts for several years.[25] Nina Simone wrote "Mississippi Goddam" in an hour following the news of the bombing. In her autobiography she says that the "entire direction" of her life "shifted" after the events of that day and that for the next seven years of her life she was "driven by civil rights and the hope of black revolution."[26] Jazz great John Coltrane was moved by the bombing to write an instrumental titled "Alabama," which he recorded November 18 for the *Birdland* album. One writer called it "his eulogy, a lament and an elegy, for the four murdered children in that Birmingham church."[27] Other movement activists found solace elsewhere. Anne Moody in Mississippi retreated to her room, questioned the existence of God, and repeatedly played Ray Charles's recording of "The Danger Zone": "Feeling sad all of the time / That's because I got a worried mind. / The world is in an uproar / The danger zone is everywhere."[28]

Despite the revulsion over the murders and the public display of grief, even in Birmingham, on September 25, two more bombs exploded in an African-American neighborhood in that city, the second timed fifteen minutes after the first and apparently designed to kill and maim as many first responders and neighbors as possible. The bombing came only a few hours before Kennedy's special representative was to meet with black and white leaders in an effort to defuse the still simmering tensions in Birmingham. Among the African-American representatives were to be businessman A. G. Gaston and attorney Arthur Shores, both of whose homes had been bombed previously.[29]

## November 22, 1963: A Death in Dallas

The spiral of violence did not end in Birmingham. On November 22, President John F. Kennedy was assassinated while driving through Dallas with his wife, Jacqueline Kennedy, and Texas governor John Connally. Few events in American history have caused a more profound shock and the subsequent despair was felt keenly in the African-American community where Kennedy was considered the first president since Lincoln to actively advocate and legislate for civil rights reform. An editorial on the front page of the *Afro-American* newspaper, based in Baltimore, echoed what others said, calling him a "martyr in the cause of human rights—civil, political and social equality of colored people." The writer likened the murder to those of Medgar Evers, George Lee, and Emmitt Till in Mississippi, saying there was "blood on the hands" of southern legislators and governors.[30] Another front-page story hailed the "many racial precedents" of the Kennedy administration.[31]

Few felt the loss as keenly as Mahalia Jackson, who had met, campaigned, and performed for the president on numerous occasions. In the midst of rehearsals for another appearance on the Danny Kaye television show in California, Jackson sobbed "inconsolably" at the news. A host of radio and television stations across the country asked her to go on the air and plead for calm. The following morning, she recorded "Deep River" with Kaye's orchestra, and it would be "years before Halie could sing 'Deep River' again." Two weeks later, she sang for the SCLC in Atlanta before the King and Abernathy families, who presented her with an award "recognizing her special place in the movement." Shortly thereafter, at the request of Columbia Records, she recorded "In the Summer of His Years" as tribute to the fallen president.[32]

According to Guido van Rijn's *Kennedy's Blues: African-American Blues and Gospel Songs on JFK,* so profound was the grief felt by African-Americans following Kennedy's assassination that Jackson's song was one of at least forty-seven songs about the president released in the days that followed. Many were quickly recorded and had only limited distribution. A sampling of the gospel songs released after November 23 includes "My Friend Kennedy" by Brother Sidney Harris and his Sunset Jubilees; "Take Courage" by Rosie Wallace and the Choir of the First Church of Love, Faith and Deliverance; "The Day the World Stood Still" and "Let Freedom Ring" by the Sensational Six of Birmingham; "Assassination" by the Dixie Nightingales; "Tribute to a Great President" by the Birds of Harmony; "Story of President Kennedy" by Brother Will Hairston; "J. F. Kennedy's Reservation" by Ronda Mitchell and Mrs. Lovell; "A Light That Shines" by Rosie Wallace; and "The Modern Joshua" by the Jewell Gospel Singers.[33]

But of all the gospel songs written and released to commemorate the too-short life of John F. Kennedy, none have endured and been as celebrated as the Dixie Hummingbirds' 45 rpm "Our Prayer for Peace," backed with "Come Ye Disconsolate" (Peacock 3013), released in early 1964. Written by James Walker, "Our Prayer for Peace" remained a staple of the Hummingbirds' concerts for more than fifty years, a dramatic, emotional gospel song with direct references to the assassination, a nation's grief, and a heartfelt call to repentance: "Let every man know, Father / Let them know that it is a sin / To hate his brother because / Of the color of his skin."[34]

Like the rest of the country, African-American artists quickly cancelled performances to honor the slain president. Band leader Count Basie, who had performed for Kennedy in the past, walked off the set of *Sex and the Single Girl* in tears when he heard of the assassination and cancelled a week's worth of dates. Nina Simone immediately cancelled her upcoming shows as well. Dick Gregory cancelled his remaining dates and flew to Washington, DC, for the funeral. Gospel artists Princess Stewart and Marian Williams and Stars of Faith each cancelled their upcoming performances. Langston Hughes requested that performances of his gospel show *Black Nativity* in New Haven be cancelled.[35] A "Stars for Freedom" show set for November 25 at the Santa Monica Civic Auditorium and featuring, among others, Frank Sinatra, Dean Martin, and Sammy Davis, Jr., was postponed and rescheduled for December 6. The rescheduled performance, now billed as a tribute to Kennedy, raised $69,000 for the SCLC, the NAACP, and CORE.[36] The State Department also cancelled the remainder of Duke Ellington's tour of the Middle East as part of a thirty-day national period of mourning.[37]

Yes, the heart of the world weighed heavy,
with the helplessness of tears,
For the man cut down in a Texas town,
in the summer of his years.

—"IN THE SUMMER OF HIS YEARS,"
MAHALIA JACKSON[38]

# 6

## MISSISSIPPI FREEDOM SUMMER

Night had a reputation in Mississippi. . . .
In Batesville, Chris Williams and others
were in the Miles backyard, arms linked,
singing Freedom Songs. "Get on Board,
Children" and "We'll Never Turn Back"
kept fear at bay, yet when the songs were
done, Robert Miles and "Junior" went
inside and came out with shotguns.

—BRUCE WATSON

"This Little Light of Mine"—It was sung in
churches, in freedom schools, on marches,
on picket lines, at jails and in Parchman
where hundreds of demonstrators were
jailed. The song became a force.

—L. C. DORSEY

Few theaters in the modern civil rights movement were as complex and wide-ranging as the long campaign in Mississippi. Like most stops on the "freedom trail," Mississippi's struggles began long before *Brown v. Board of Education.* The events in Mississippi often occurred simultaneously in the dozens of small actions taking place across the state, which meant that the vast majority of them are not as well known as the larger-than-life events in Birmingham or the March on Washington. Whether in Jackson or southwest Mississippi or the sometimes life-or-death voter registration struggles taking place in the state's small towns and villages, the heroic actions of local volunteers and their SNCC, SCLC, CORE, and NAACP counterparts provided an essential element in the struggle for civil rights. Early in the campaign, SNCC and CORE, the two most active groups in Mississippi, joined forces with the other civil rights organizations in the state under the umbrella heading the Council of Federated Organizations (COFO).[1] They would need all of the support they could muster. Movement veterans Guy and Candie Carawan termed Mississippi "the most difficult arena for the civil rights movement." That *any* progress was made in the state "where the most entrenched system of segregation and oppression was kept in place with the worst violence" makes the outcome all the more remarkable.[2]

Though the NAACP's Medgar Evers and others had worked heroically in Mississippi for years, most of the movement work in Mississippi began as a direct result of the tumultuous SNCC meeting at Highlander in 1961 when the factions supporting either voter registration or direct action nearly split the organization. A compromise brokered by Ella Baker led to the registration group beginning its efforts in Mississippi. As noted in the First Interlude, the SNCC, led by the charismatic Bob Moses, established a small, tenuous beachhead in McComb in the Ku Klux Klan–dominated southwest corner of Mississippi. Eventually, the murder of movement supporters and the extreme violence drove them out of the city.[3] Other groups worked quietly in the state during this period, including the biracial New World Singers, who held a freedom song workshop in Edwards. The group, which was the first to record Bob Dylan's "Blowin' in the Wind" and "Don't Think Twice, It's Alright," learned freedom songs while in Mississippi and returned to New York City, where the songs were shared with other musicians and published in the folk-oriented *Broadside* magazine.[4]

## Greenwood 1962

Regrouping after the difficult events in McComb and armed with a $5,000 Voter Education Project (VEP) grant from the Kennedy administration, SNCC sent Sam Block, just 23, to Greenwood in LeFlore County. Block arrived in October 1961 and quietly established his credentials among the African-American residents. In June 1962, he attended a voter registration workshop at Highlander's Knoxville campus, then returned to Greenwood, where he resumed canvassing and building a small core of supporters. The first meeting was held in mid-June at the Elks Hall. At the second meeting, a week later, Block began teaching the two dozen attendees freedom songs. Pressured by the white segregationist mayor, the Elks promptly ejected the group, though the organization claimed it was because "they didn't like all that singing." For a time, Block was often avoided in town, but he continued escorting blacks to the registration office at the LeFlore County Courthouse. After months of individual meetings and small church services, Hollis Watkins, Willie Peacock, and Block were eventually invited to a service at the First Christian Church, led by Rev. Aaron Johnson.[5] Fortified with Johnson's ringing endorsement, this became Greenwood's first mass meeting. "It was powerful," Peacock said. "We couldn't stop singing freedom songs. Those songs had a real message that night: Freedom doesn't come as a gift. It comes through knowledge and power—political power.

It comes from the vote."[6] In the following days, Block found himself approached by strangers on the streets wanting to know when there would be another meeting where they could "sing those songs."[7]

Block and Peacock quickly grasped the importance of music in reaching black Mississippi and soon were working to bring various singing groups to "movement-friendly" churches. Since both men were "fine singers," according to Andrew Young, they could enter a new church or a town "under the cover of a musical group" and sing and speak their way "through the black communities of the Delta, from Greenville to Greenwood."[8] "After our first meetings, I realized how much those songs I had learned, those freedom songs, could help pull us together," Block said. "It was an organizational glue. I asked people to think about a song they might want to sing that night and then change that song. Think about freedom, interject your own feelings, your own words. . . . Out of that came freedom songs we'd be singing all across Mississippi."[9]

By August 16, meetings were in full swing, registrations were being attempted and police harassment was a daily occurrence. That evening, Block was joined by Luvaughn Brown and Lawrence Guyot, two more SNCC workers, when a mob armed with guns and chains surrounded their modest offices. When the three men heard the stamp of feet and shouts coming up their stairwell, they made one of the movement's most legendary escapes, climbing out a window, onto the roof, and down a television antenna. When a frantic Moses and Peacock arrived early the following morning, the offices were trashed, but their friends had escaped. The office was broken into repeatedly in the days that followed and their landlord was threatened by police. Block was urged to leave town.[10]

It was during this period that Block, Moses, and other SNCC members met Fannie Lou Hamer of nearby Ruleville. Hamer, another early supporter of the movement, had earlier joined seventeen other African-Americans on an old school bus chartered by the SNCC to take them to Indianola to register. As was the usually case, the registrar rejected all of the applicants. On the return trip, a Mississippi Highway Patrol officer flagged down the bus. Hamer instinctively began leading the riders in "Have a Little Talk with Jesus" as the patrolmen approached. Both Moses and the driver were arrested—the driver's "crime" was for "driving a bus with too much yellow in it."[11] Hamer continued singing, leading the passengers in "This Little Light of Mine," "Freedom's Coming and It Won't Be Long" and "Down by the Riverside." "That's Fannie Lou!" someone shouted "with delight," "She know how to sing."[12]

Hamer's efforts toward registering African-American voters eventually forced Fannie Lou and her husband, Pap, out of Ruleville. Hamer continued her work in several small Mississippi towns, each time being forced out by official harassment.[13] In the process, she developed a reputation among SNCC members for her fearless and effective work for the movement. When the home that sheltered her and two SNCC volunteers was fired on by nightriders, Hamer and the two young women sang, *"Oh freedom / Oh freedom / Ohhhhh, freedom over me / And before I'll be a*

**FIGURE 11**

The great warrior/song-leader of the Mississippi Freedom Summer, Fannie Lou Hamer, photographed in 1964. Mississippi Freedom Democratic Party Records, 1962–1971, Wisconsin Historical Society, WHi-97978. Photo: Wisconsin Historical Society.

*slave / I'll be buried in my grave.*" "This *empowers* you," Mississippi volunteer Dorie Ladner said of Hamer's singing. "Without music, you don't have anything. We were used to singing and getting everyone to join in. You can talk for only so long, but you need to sing or march to get people involved. If we were getting ready to go out for a protest march, we're going to start a song before we leave that door." SNCC members and volunteers regrouped after the various attacks and resumed their voting registration efforts in Greenwood, bolstered at night by the regular mass meetings.[14]

Of Hamer, who survived desperate poverty as a child and who would in the years to come endure numerous beatings and incarceration as a civil rights activist in Mississippi, Bernice Johnson Reagon once wrote, "Her work as an organizer was grounded in her own testimony. She called and urged others to join in battling racism, poverty, and injustice. A natural and fearless community leader, master orator, and song leader, she used her stories and songs to nurture the air we breathed as fighters."[15] Andrew Young called her "our most effective recruiter of Mississippi participants" and wrote that there was "something special" about her speaking and singing gifts. "And she could really sing—she knew all the old church songs of the Mississippi Delta; music was really her entrée into the movement." Hamer's outreach to new churches consisted of beginning with gospel songs, then moving to the newer freedom songs, asking the congregation to join in the singing. Only after the singing was completed would she talk about voter registration and ask for volunteers.[16]

Eventually, the Kennedy administration deemed that the number of voters being registered was insufficient and, without specifically naming the violence and intimidation as the primary cause, the VEP withdrew its funding. Once again, a group of entertainers led by Harry Belafonte stepped in to raise the "minimal financing" necessary to continue the registration work in the state.[17] Organized labor, including the United Auto Workers, the AFL-CIO, the Packinghouse Workers, and other unions donated generously to both CORE and SNCC in Mississippi as well.[18]

In October, officials in LeFlore County unilaterally halted distribution of surplus commodities to the desperately poor, mostly African-American recipients who depended on those supplies. More than twenty-seven thousand people were affected and the move was widely regarded as retaliation for the continued mass meetings and voter registration efforts in Greenwood. The move prompted a national response, with the SNCC, churches, and other organizations denouncing the action, then working to replace the essential commodities. Among those involved was popular comedian Dick Gregory, who spoke in Jackson in November and immediately donated money and organized fund-raising activities.[19] SNCC's impressive response to the crisis, both in the physical distribution of the commodities and in their unceasing fund-raising efforts, stemmed the worst of the food insecurity issues for LeFlore County's poorest residents. It also paid off in improved respect for SNCC in the community as residents noted that the organization provided "direct aid, not just 'agitation'" and spurred renewed voter registration efforts. By February 1963, hundreds of African-Americans were attempting to register at the Greenwood courthouse. The police responded with intimidation and arrests, including the arrest of Block for "making statements calculated to incite the breach of peace." But Block's arrest had the opposite effect—hundreds of black residents attended the trial and attendance at the mass meetings swelled. On February 28, Moses, SNCC worker Jimmy Travis, and Randolph Blackwell of VEP left the Greenwood office, only to be assaulted by white men in a car. Multiple shots were fired and Travis was hit in the neck and head, but survived.[20]

## Greenwood 1963

Though much of the nation's attention was on Birmingham in April and May 1963, the violence against African-Americans in Mississippi continued, prompting black congressmen Representative Robert C. Nix and Representative Charles C. Diggs to travel to the state on a fact-finding tour. The congressmen charged Congress to respond to what they claimed were "64 acts of murder, shootings, beatings, riots, burning and intimidations" in the state since 1961. Diggs and Nix noted in particular the attempted lynching of nine-year-old Gloria Laverne Floyd and the separate "brutal" beatings of two other African-American young people in Mississippi. On national television, Gregory and singer Al Hibbler reported on the violence against blacks in Greenwood. Demanding equal time, the mayor of Greenwood denied their allegations on NBC-TV's *The Today Show* the following day and argued that Greenwood City Hall employed a "nigger janitor" and a "janitress" and that both had "been voting for years."[21] While national coverage of the violence against blacks for attempting to register in Greenwood was spotty, the African-American press, including the *Afro-American* in Baltimore, dispatched several reporters and photographers to Mississippi. The newspaper devoted front-page coverage to Greenwood throughout April and in the April 13 issue allotted an entire page to photographs of the participants. In one photo, a line of people, including several ministers, their arms crossed and their hands clasping those on either side, are shown singing "We Shall Overcome." The caption cites the "fervor of songs of freedom" and reports that the songs "inspire movement leaders as well as followers."[22] In the same issue, the *Afro-American* reported on the continued violence and said that "outsiders," whose knowledge of what was happening in Greenwood and LeFlore County was limited by what they read, would be "wise to follow the lead of a song sung at the mass meetings to impress upon the people" the importance of continuing the voter registration fight: "Ain't no harm to keeping your mind staying on freedom / Walking and talking with my mind staying on freedom / Going to register with my mind staying on freedom / Hallelujah, hallelujah."[23]

Among those serving time in Greenwood's jail during this period were Moses, Guyot, Peacock, and SNCC field secretary James Forman, who kept a diary detailing his incarceration with eight other people in a cell in March and April. The SNCC prisoners organized classes and book discussions, and of course, they sang. Each evening at lights out, the cellmates sang "We'll never turn back / We have served our time in jail / With no money to go our bail." On April 3, following a visit by Justice Department representative John Doar, the group sang throughout the day, "You Better Leave Segregation Alone," "Freedom Is Coming" and "I will let Chief Larry know, before I go / I'll have my civil rights / Which side are you on, boy? Which side are you on?" That evening, federal marshals transferred the SNCC members to the Washington County Jail in preparation for testifying at their injunction hearing the following morning. One song that night recorded the event: "Well, I stayed in jail and thought I'd change / Here comes the Marshals and put me in chains." On the morning of April 4, Forman writes that Moses led the singing and that other prisoners requested freedom songs. The group was released later that day, following what Forman described as an agreement between the Justice Department and Greenwood officials.[24]

Elsewhere, Young, Dorothy Cotton, Diane Nash Bevel, Hamer, and others traveled through the South, conducting citizenship classes in small towns. Young taught the group the freedom songs he had learned while working for the movement in other cities, including "Follow the Drinking Gourd," and Hamer led the singing at the stops and frequently led the discussions. "This was a folk workshop," Cotton recalled, "so even if we were talking about the Constitution, we started our sessions singing and [Hamer] was a powerhouse." In May, Hamer received additional leadership and voter registration training in Charleston, South Carolina. The two-week program was led by Bernice Johnson Reagon, scholar Vincent Harding, and Guy and Candie Carawan, who taught those in attendance still more freedom songs. While returning to Greenwood following the Charleston programs on June 9, the bus carrying a small party of riders, including Hamer and Annell Ponder of the SCLC, stopped in Winona, Mississippi. When some of the riders tried to eat at the station café, they were arrested, taken to the Montgomery County Jail, and over a period of several days, each was savagely beaten, sometimes by the police, sometimes by trustees. Hamer was humiliated and beaten relentlessly with blackjacks. It was a beating of such intensity and fury that the aftereffects would pain her for the rest of her life. Unable to sleep in her cell following the assaults, Hamer still managed to lead the singing (including "When Paul and Silas Were Bound in Jail") and join a hunger strike. Young posted bail and the activists were finally released on June 12.[25]

Throughout the year, the Freedom House in Greenwood continued to be the command center for COFO activities. Endesha Ida Mae Holland, an early supporter, remembered the spontaneous singing that often erupted in the crowded, chaotic offices. At one mass meeting, she recalled hearing Block speak, seeing a donation taken for the "freedom works and for the church's building fund," and joining numerous civil rights songs led by the SNCC workers, including "Keep Your Eyes on the Prize, Hold On," "This Little Light of Mine" and "Wade in the

Water." "Meetings like these encouraged people to join the movement and stay in it," Holland wrote in her memoir. "It was hard to turn back once you had heard such soul-wrenching speeches and joined in such fervent singing." Other activities, including the protests on behalf of jailed civil rights workers and voting registration abuses, were preceded by lengthy instructional meetings, where participants were told how to dress, how to respond to abuse, and how to incorporate the principles of nonviolent protest. Holland writes that after a series of bombings of African-American businesses, she went on her first protest march. "We'd been singing freedom songs since we started marching, and by now we'd managed to get the fear out of our voices," she added. "'Ain't scared of your jail / 'Cause I want my freedom."[26]

In the state capital of Jackson, demonstrations, marches, and sit-ins were building, fueled by support from students from Tougaloo College and area high schools. Among those arrested in early June was Tougaloo student Anne Moody, whose autobiography about growing up in Mississippi is rife with invaluable details and observations. Moody was part of a large group that included ministers and civil rights activists who were thrown into the now infamous Jackson jail. Female inmates soon discovered that the showers did not have curtains, so they improvised with chewing gum and tissue paper. More than four hundred high school students were among those arrested and taken to the nearby fairgrounds, where they were kept in an open-air compound. The female students in the jail itself sang freedom songs for hours. After first threatening them, the jailer showed them the stark solitary confinement chambers. "If you don't stop that damn singing, I'm gonna throw all of you in here together," he told the students. The following day, students at nearby Lanier High School began singing freedom songs during their lunch break. When they would not quit, school officials called the police, who loosed their dogs on the school grounds. Parents from adjoining houses joined the students in "fighting off" the dogs, using bricks, rocks, and bottles. Again, dozens were arrested.[27]

On the evening of June 11, 1963, President Kennedy, perhaps prompted by the violence in Birmingham and throughout Mississippi, and by Governor George Wallace's "defeat" in failing to prevent the enrollment of two black students at the University of Alabama in Tuscaloosa, gave his staff just a few hours to prepare a speech he wanted to deliver that night on national television. "We are confronted primarily with a moral issue," he said. "It is as old as the scriptures and is as clear as the American Constitution."[28] Some writers believe the president's most direct call for civil rights–related legislation was also in response to the sudden popularity in the media of King's "Letter from Birmingham Jail," even though such a bold stand could possibly have cemented Kennedy's defeat at the polls during the next election.[29] Regardless, and at long last, the administration publicly unveiled comprehensive civil rights legislation that would prohibit discrimination in public restaurants, theaters, and hotels. Rights activists in Jackson, Mississippi, Albany, Georgia, and Cambridge, Maryland, responded with active resistance to segregation, which was met with more violence and arrests. In Jackson, more than six hundred students were hauled off in garbage trucks following peaceful sit-ins and demonstrations.[30]

But even as Kennedy spoke, an assassin planned to murder civil rights activist Medgar Evers. Evers, with the support of the NAACP, had earlier begun a Birmingham-styled action in Jackson, including sit-ins, which had spurred a series of small concessions by local authorities. On May 28, his home was fire bombed, spawning protests the following day and a spate of violence against the demonstrators, with hundreds beaten and arrested. On the evening of June 12, Evers was gunned down from behind as he returned from another rally and meeting.[31]

In response, civil rights groups in Jackson called for a march on Saturday June 14, though the NAACP advised against it. King and other SCLC officials arrived that morning and received a police escort to the Masonic Temple for a memorial service, where an estimated four thousand people crammed into the building or stood outside. Once the service was over, the great mass of people began walking toward the Collins Funeral Home, where the body would be returned. Police armed with "carbines, automatic rifles, shotguns and dogs" met hundreds of mourners near the end of the march. A group of women stood in front of the funeral home where Evers's body lay, singing "We Shall Overcome" and "Before I'd be a slave / I'd be buried in my grave / And go home to my Lord and be free." Evers's memorial service at Pearl Street AME was attended by hundreds more, including representatives from the major civil rights organizations and international media.[32] Among those present was Lena Horne, who had been with Evers at a voter registration rally the night before his assassination and had presented the NAACP with a sizable donation at the rally. Horne sang "This Little Light of Mine."[33] Reporters at the service, moved by Myrlie Evers's impassioned plea that her husband's assassination not be in vain, raised more than $650 among themselves for the Evers family.[34] The service ended with an emotional version of the spiritual, "This May Be the Last Time."[35] And while city officials had granted permission for a ceremonial march along the funeral route, it was with the stipulation that there would be no singing. Still, bystanders along the route and members of the procession spontaneously broke into a dirge-like "Oh, Freedom" and an up-tempo "This Little Light of Mine" and surged onto the street in the 103-degree heat. Police responded harshly to the impromptu demonstration, prompting Kennedy's representative, John Doar of the Justice Department, to frantically intervene. Dozens were injured and jailed.[36] Present at the demonstration was SNCC volunteer Dorie Ladner, who was one of those singing "This Little Light of Mine" on North Capitol Street. "It was defiant," she said. "The music soothed the beast."[37]

Evers, a decorated veteran of World War II, was buried with full military honors at Arlington Memorial Cemetery on June 19. The Evers family was invited to the White House and a number of members of Congress were in attendance at the gravesite ceremony, which ended with the singing of "We Shall Overcome" by the crowd of more than a thousand mourners.[38] That same day, Kennedy sent to

Congress a comprehensive civil rights bill that would take almost exactly one year to pass, though Kennedy would not live to see the day.[39]

Among the many musical tributes paid to Evers in the days that followed, two reverberated beyond Jackson. Bob Dylan's "Only a Pawn in Their Game" describes both the murder and the murderer ("But he can't be blamed / He's only a pawn in their game").[40] Also written in the aftermath of the Evers assassination was "Ballad of Medgar Evers," composed by Matthew Jones. Based loosely on the old folk song "Jesse James," the SNCC Freedom Singers sang "Ballad of Medgar Evers" on subsequent tours. The song was later released on Smithsonian LP R023.[41]

During the statewide protests that followed Evers's death, more than two hundred people were arrested while kneeling to pray in Greenwood, including Holland. Most were taken without a trial directly to a LeFlore County work farm. Segregated once again by race and sex, Holland found herself in overcrowded cells with civil rights activists from the North and white college students, as well as "streetwalkers and thieves from Gritney, Baptist Town, Gee Pee" and the county. After the group was warned by the jail's chief officer about Holland's activism ("You others better git her to tell y'all that I'm not gonna have no sanging or no back talk!"), Holland organized cleaning parties and educational opportunities for her cellmates. Upon the protesters' release, SNCC organizers held a mass meeting to celebrate. "We sang up a storm," Holland writes, "freedom songs mixed with church hymns."[42]

In July, Pete Seeger, as he had done in several other cities where the struggle for civil rights was playing out, visited Greenwood. He sang at a small Baptist church, at the NAACP meeting in Jackson, and again in an open-field "song fest," along with Bob Dylan, Theodore Bikel, Jackie Washington (who would later change his name to J. Washington Landron), Josh White, the Freedom Singers, and a small crowd of COFO staffers, volunteers, and curious onlookers before television cameras and a *Life* magazine photographer. During his days in Mississippi, Seeger wrote to *Broadside* magazine that the "most popular song by all odds was 'This Little Light of Mine, I'm Going to Let It Shine,'" which he said he heard "dozens of times a day and, once it was started, it would go on for ten and 15 and 20 minutes with people singing new words and repeating old ones." Seeger cited Bertha Gober's "slow and deeply moving" "We'll Never Turn Back," which was "sung by thousands at the funeral of Medgar Evers." In addition to "We Shall Overcome," Seeger also noted the popularity of the rewritten protest spirituals and freedom songs, "Everybody Wants Freedom," "Keep Your Eyes on the Prize, Hold On," "I'm Goin' to Walk the Streets of Jackson One of These Days," "Oh, Freedom," "We Shall Not Be Moved" and others. "In each case," he added, "they keep putting new words into the old songs, including a lot of names of friends or foes in the integration battle. To hear them singing these songs with hands clapping and bodies swaying and faces lighted up with a fierce joy of the Freedom struggle was an experience I'll never forget."[43]

The night before the July 6 Delta Folk Music Festival, several of the singers and many of the volunteers joined the regular mass meeting at a Greenwood church. Among the songs sung that evening was a "lined hymn," "Amazing Grace." Lined hymns are an ancient tradition in both black and white churches, where a song leader sings or speaks a line and the congregation sings it back. In the midst of the singing, the local sheriff and his deputies burst into the church, hoping to intimidate those assembled. Instead, the congregation "responded by giving more fervor to the songs and prayers and testimonies, determined not to give in to fear." While lined hymns had been sung at sites throughout the various civil rights actions, nowhere were they more a part of the mass meetings than in Greenwood. The lined hymn sung most often at movement events was "A Charge to Keep I Have." In Greenwood, the "common meter hymn 'Must Jesus Bear the Cross Alone,' was also sung regularly and the singing was often led by Hamer when she was in town."[44]

The festival itself was sponsored by the SNCC as the city's first integrated public gathering, in part to raise the spirits of Greenwood's African-American population following the Evers assassination. Police harassment—"no parking" signs were placed on each side of the roads leading to the festival site—kept the gathering small. And while few of the poor blacks may have heard of the headliners, Moses (who had once served as tutor of R & B star Frankie Lymon) and the SNCC staffers clearly enjoyed their performances.[45]

Robert Shelton returned again to the "the racial crisis in the South" to write about the protest music for the *New York Times,* noting that folk singers from the North have become involved and that the "new songs" are not only "weapons in the civil-rights arsenal" but have also developed into "valuable commodities in the music industry." "Northern singers," he suggests, now include the "spontaneous hits" of the movement in their concerts, television appearances, and recordings: "We Shall Overcome," "Oh, Freedom," "Woke Up This Morning with My Mind Set on Freedom," and "This Little Light of Mine." But the songs penned by Dylan and others had become, in Shelton's opinion, equally compelling. Peter, Paul & Mary's version of Dylan's "Blowin' in the Wind," released on June 18, was "the fastest-selling single in the history of Warner Brothers Records," with three hundred twenty thousand copies sold in eight business days and "with sales in the South surprisingly heavy." Also cited was the trio's "If I Had a Hammer," "another anti-discrimination plea," written by Seeger and Lee Hays. Shelton pointed to the success of the Chad Mitchell Trio's "Alma Mater (Ole Miss)" and Tom Paxton's "The Dogs of Alabama" as further evidence of the power of the new music. African-American artist Len Chandler "galvanized a throng of 11,000 at a street hootenanny in Cambridge, Massachusetts" with a series of songs dedicated to Evers. Shelton called the "new anti-segregation lyricists . . . the direct descendants of the Hutchinson Family," who introduced abolitionist and other protest songs to the North in the years before the Civil War.[46] The *New York Times'* actual coverage of the event the following day noted that "one of the more popular songs" was Dylan's "Only a Pawn in Their Game," his tribute to Evers.[47]

As the summer wore on, horror stories about the conditions in the Greenwood jail began to emerge. In early August, fifty-eight protesters from both the country prison farm and the Mississippi State Penitentiary, better known as the dreaded Parchman Farm, were finally released following their arrests in June for a "breach of peace" when they had tried to register to vote. Most were students and all were in varying degrees of physical distress, including several with medical emergencies and severe dietary deficiencies. Others had spent weeks in the dreaded "hot box," a small, virtually airless metal container, or hanging by the hands and arms from their cell's bars for the crime of singing freedom songs.[48]

As was the case in other early movement actions, only a few recordings were made of the mass meetings in Mississippi in 1963.[49] One, taped sometime in the fall of 1963 at an unnamed Greenwood Baptist church, begins with Peacock introducing the evening's main speaker, Hamer, and requesting that she lead the congregation in what had already become her "theme" song, "This Little Light of Mine." Hamer's "powerful contralto" voice "filled the room" and within two phrases, the entire congregation joined: "Everywhere I go / Shine, shine, shine / All in the jail house / This little light of mine." According to Reagon, the protest spiritual "swelled as it continued, and one could sense the energy level of the congregation being stirred." Hamer and her singing would, for many, become the dominant voice and image for the Mississippi movement. Peacock then introduced Freedom Singer Matthew Jones, who sang a version of "Keep Your Eyes on the Prize, Hold On" that he had composed for Greenwood:

> *Greenwood people bowed in jail*
> *Got no money to go their bail.*
> *Keep your eyes on the prize,*
> *Hold on, hold on, hold on.*
> *Keep your eyes on the prize, hold on.*

The congregational response was so great that Peacock requested another song from Jones, the long-popular labor song, "We Shall Not Be Moved." Once again, those present quickly joined in the singing:

> *Governor Johnson, we shall not be moved*
> *Governor Johnson, we shall not be moved.*
> *Governor Johnson, he shall be removed.*
> *Just like a pail of garbage in the alley,*
> *He shall be removed!*

At the conclusion, Reagon records that Hamer broke into "Go Tell It on the Mountain," once again with lyrics spontaneously composed to address the situation in Greenwood in particular and Mississippi in general. Other speakers and songs followed through the evening, including movement staples "Wade in the Water" and "Come by Yah." Reagon's memories of Hamer's sermon are as vivid as those of her singing and she writes that it was interspersed with spontaneous renditions of

"Certainly, Lord," "I Woke Up This Morning with My Mind Stayed on Freedom" and others. The role of congregational singing in the movement, Reagon says, was "crucial." On this fall evening in 1963, more than sixty percent of the evening was given to singing. The mass meeting closed, as most such meetings from that era closed, with the singing of "We Shall Overcome."

*The Story of Greenwood, Mississippi*, recorded by Guy Carawan for the SNCC in 1963, is an excellent record of the mass meetings from the COFO operations in Mississippi that year. In addition to the music of the mass meetings and sections of various sermons and speeches (including Gregory), the disk does have some freedom songs featuring Hamer. Unfortunately, because of the original length restrictions of vinyl LPs, most of the segments are truncated. *The Story of Greenwood* does give a taste of the diversity of musical styles within the broad category of "freedom songs" and the passion in the performances and sermons.[50]

A few other examples of the singing that helped inspire Greenwood in 1962 and 1963 have been recorded. According to the notes accompanying the Smithsonian/Folkways compilation *Voices of the Civil Rights Movement: Black American Freedom Songs, 1960–1966,* the wide range of black sacred music expression was utilized in Greenwood, from arranged spirituals to quasi-calypso to classic black gospel to the more familiar, ever-evolving freedom songs. In addition to several protest spirituals led by Hamer, the two-disk set features sermons, quartets, and mass meeting congregational singing. Peacock serves as song-leader on "Get on Board, Children," "Come By Yah," and "Calypso Freedom" (a remake of Belafonte's "Banana Boat Song") from "fall/winter 1963." Block leads an unnamed congregation on "Freedom Train" from what appears to be the same session.[51]

The year 1963 was also one of the peak years of the folk music revival across the United States, including the "Hoot Tour" of mostly Southern venues by an aggregation of musicians that included the Journeymen (with John Phillips), Glenn Yarbrough of the Limeliters, the Geezinslaw Brothers, and others. When Phillips (later of the Mamas and Papas) announced to the crowd at the University of Alabama that they were going to perform a song by Josh White, audience members chanting "Nig-Ger, Nig-Ger" drowned him out. In another city, their bus was met by a group of baseball bat–wielding white students shouting, "Nigger lovers go home." One of the last tour dates in November was in Jackson, where the group received a telegram from the SNCC affiliate in Memphis saying that a Jackson city ordinance banned African-Americans from the civic auditorium. The tour members voted to boycott and were promptly met by roving groups that smashed their hotel's windows while chanting "Nigger lover." Phillips recalls that the artists proposed to their booking agent that they instead perform a free concert in the campus church at nearby Tougaloo College, where a cross burning just outside the college's grounds greeted them upon arrival. The performance itself, however, was "profoundly moving." Phillips writes that black students requested freedom songs and, at the conclusion, the entire cast joined hands and sang "We Shall Overcome" on the church podium. "There were tears in most of our eyes as well,"

Phillips notes. "It felt as if our harmonies could carry a hundred miles into the night, soaring together with an emotional power that nearly ripped the church roof off."[52] According to Scott McKenzie, another member of the Journeymen, the artists discovered years later that the morale at Tougaloo had been "very low" and the artists' decision to honor the boycott and instead perform at the college had been a significant event for the embattled students and activists.[53] Other artists, including popular jazz trumpeter Al Hirt, cancelled their concerts when the Jackson auditorium's policies were publicized. When the stars of the hit television series *Bonanza* cancelled an appearance in Jackson for the same reason, Jackson's mayor urged citizens to boycott the show.[54]

Throughout the remainder of the year, COFO continued its dangerous routine in Greenwood and LeFlore counties, working within the African-American community, building trust, and taking more residents to register to vote, only to be rebuffed, often violently, time and time again by Greenwood and Mississippi authorities. Through it all, Peacock, Watkins, and Block continued to attend mass meetings and sing. "When you sing," Peacock told Seeger, "you can reach deep into yourself and communicate some of what you've got to other people, and you get them to reach inside of themselves. You release your soul force, and they release theirs, until you can all feel like you are part of one great soul. Sometimes when Hollis and I were leading a song, we could feel it. We were together with the people, and they would not let us go, you knew you could not cut the singing short until it reached a conclusion. The singing could go on for hours." Not even their frequent stays in jail stopped the singing or organizing, Peacock said. Both activities continued in the cells. Mass meetings in Greenwood always ended with "We Shall Overcome." "It is a song [that] says whatever we have been through and whatever we have to go through and whatever conflicts we've had in the heat of the day," Peacock said, "now we are refocusing and rededicating ourselves to our main object." For Watkins, the song assumed a powerful spiritual dimension during those long months in Mississippi; it was "the end result of all of the hard fighting." "We are going to overcome, no matter what, no matter how; no matter how hard or how difficult or how long, we *shall* overcome," Watkins added. "We sang it with our arms crossed with the right over the left, to show that the right will finally be victorious, and by holding each other's hand, the common bond pulled together all of the people."[55]

In October, three black students from Tougaloo College quietly entered several white churches in Jackson. All were promptly arrested by a zealous policeman, even though pastors of the churches had no policy against integrated services. After spending four days in jail, the three were bonded out by civil rights attorney William M. Kunstler, who fought a running legal battle with a number of prosegregation judges. At a mass meeting on the Tougaloo campus to celebrate the students' release, one of the jailed students, Joyce Ladner (sister of Dorie), sang an emotional version of "We'll Never Turn Back" and was soon joined by those in attendance. When Joyce began the final verse, Kunstler writes, "I suddenly realized that my eyes were wet. I was completely carried away, and I sensed that I was experiencing one of those rare occasions in a man's life when he yields completely to the inspiration of a moment." The meeting was, he adds, "one of the most moving I have ever attended."[56]

Ultimately, out of money, exhausted, and facing increasing violence while still showing only a handful of successful attempts at voter registration, COFO members, led by the SNCC, agreed with Moses's suggestion to recruit a thousand college students to work on voter registration in Mississippi in the summer of 1964. Despite the emotional malaise and depression in the days following the Kennedy assassination, more than three hundred workers attended an SNCC leadership conference on Thanksgiving weekend in Washington, DC, and heard firsthand the problems and dangers they would face them in Mississippi. Toward the end of the conference, Hamer was called to speak. Still limping from her injuries, she struggled to the podium. Hamer told her story, including the recent beating, and concluded with "This Little Light of Mine." Among those present was Eleanor Holmes Norton, who had heard virtually all of the major civil rights activists speak. Norton said she believed only King was Hamer's equal as an orator. "She also, let us not forget," Norton said, "would break out into song at the end of her things, and I'm telling you, you've never heard a room flying [like one] that Fannie Lou Hamer set afire."[57]

Another important meeting took place over three days in Greenville in November 1963 where the SNCC's Mississippi staff, along with representatives from CORE and the SCLC, met to decide an issue that had been vexing the organization in the past year—the role of whites in the movement. The conversation was heated at times, with Moses, Hamer, Guyot, and others arguing for the continued inclusion of white staff members and volunteers. The meeting concluded at midnight on the final night of the retreat. Among the participants was Howard Zinn, a white, who recorded the events. Those present were exhausted, but they rose, stood in a circle, locked hands and sang multiple stanzas of "We Shall Overcome." "I had heard the song sung many times at various meeting with deep passion, but never quite like this," Zinn writes. "I felt that people were gripping each other's hands tighter than usual. When they came to the stanzas 'We shall brothers be' and 'Black and white together,' the voices somehow grew louder, more intense. People looked at one another. A few broke hands and applauded. The song came to an end, and the people at the meeting, talking in low voices, moved out together into the darkness."[58]

Within a few years, the climate would change to such a degree that even the singing of "We Shall Overcome" would not be enough for SNCC to include white volunteers in its ranks. The song itself came under attack from some African-Americans as well, including Malcolm X, who believed that it would only be effective when sung while holding a gun. In the month following the Greenville meeting, COFO and SNCC representatives, including Hamer, toured cities in the North hoping to raise both financial and political support. On December 20, they were joined by the Freedom Singers at Williams Institutional CME Church in Harlem. After the Freedom Singers had performed and Hamer had delivered her powerful testimony, Malcolm X spoke and referred to Hamer's horrific beating in Mississippi: "We don't deserve to be recognized and respected as men as long as our women can be brutalized in the manner that this woman described," he told the small audience, "and nothing being done about it, but we sit around singing 'We shall overcome.'"[59]

In the midst of the unrelenting violence in Mississippi, the first "Sing for Freedom and Workshop," under the auspices of the SNCC, the SCLC, and the Highlander Folk School, convened at Gammon Theological Seminary in Atlanta, May 7–10, 1964. Directors Guy and Candie Carawan credited a visit by the Freedom Singers to a Johns Island Festival in December for inspiring the workshop.[60] The goal, according to Guy, was to continue to "expose the leading singers from the different areas of the South" to the freedom songs emerging from each movement center. Among those who sang, lectured, and shared songs old and new were the Albany Singers, Len Chandler, Charles Sherrod, Bessie Jones and the Sea Island Singers, Phil Ochs, Theo Bikel, Tom Paxton, Andrew Young, Bernice Johnson Reagon, Dock Reese, Carleton Reese, and Cleopatra Kennedy and the Birmingham Gospel Choir. During one of the sessions, Young told participants, "We all know you can't trust a Negro on a negotiating committee who doesn't like his people's music. We found that out in Birmingham . . . CORE tried to organize Plaquemine, Louisiana, but they did not do too well. Their people were mostly from the North, and really did not know how to sing. When we came into Plaquemine we had hundreds in the streets in a few days. That's because we learned how to sing in the old church way." A songbook compiled during the workshops was prepared to send to towns and cities in the midst of various movement actions. "The singing of freedom songs has ceased to be solely a means for strength and unity in the face of brutality and harassment," wrote Josh Dunson in *Broadside* magazine. "It is slowly becoming a wedge with which the treasure chest of Afro-American culture is being opened."[61]

Based in part on the work done in Hattiesburg since 1962 by SNCC workers Curtis Hayes and Hollis Watkins and CORE's Dave Dennis, COFO leaders chose this southern Mississippi town for the launch of the Mississippi Registration Project (often called Freedom Summer). While the bulk of volunteers would not arrive until after training sessions in June, the SNCC celebrated the beginning of the project on Wednesday January 22, 1964, with activities that centered on the organization's Freedom House in an African-American neighborhood. In addition to voter registration efforts, plans called for SNCC staffers and volunteers to be joined by representatives from CORE, SCLC, and the National Council of Churches. As staff members and volunteers began arriving at the Freedom House on Tuesday, they passed a gauntlet of children singing, "We will go-o-o to jail / Don't need no bail / No, no, no, no / We won't come out / Until our people v-o-o-o-te!" At the mass meeting that night, the church was filled beyond capacity, with the overflow standing outside the windows and doors. At one point, the lights failed and, in the darkness, a single voice intoned, "We shall not, shall not be moved." Within seconds, the entire congregation was singing. A flashlight provided the light at the pulpit until the lights returned later that evening. Speakers included Ella Baker, Lawrence Guyot, Aaron Henry, John Lewis, two rabbis, dozens of ministers from across the United States, and others. At the meeting's conclusion at midnight, the congregants joined hands and sang "We Shall Overcome" before walking into the darkness.[62]

## Freedom Summer and the MFDP

Following a nationwide call for help, COFO's two one-week orientation sessions for Mississippi volunteers were originally scheduled for mid-June at Berea College in Kentucky, but Berea alumni pressure forced the group to instead scramble for a backup site. COFO settled on Western College for Women (now a part of Miami University) in Oxford, Ohio, June 13 to 27. The sessions were financed by the National Council of Churches. A host of movement veterans, including Bob Moses, Julian Bond, Mary King, James Forman, Hollis Watkins, and Hamer welcomed the hundreds of eager, idealistic students (called "the volunteers") who arrived in Oxford for the June orientations. In addition to training in nonviolence response and the intricacies of the Mississippi political and legal systems, attendees heard freedom songs and inspirational messages, often from Hamer. Hamer greeted new volunteers, singing, "If you miss me from the back of the bus / You can't find me nowhere / Come on up to the front of the bus / I'll be riding up there." Moses, already a legend among civil rights workers for his courage and tactical genius, spoke at length at the first session, and his words carried a soft-spoken power: "When Mrs. Hamer sang, 'If you miss me from the freedom fight, you can't find me nowhere; Come on over to the graveyard, I'll be buried there . . . ,' that's true," he said.[63]

The first wave, two hundred fifty mostly white college-age students, arrived at a place where much of the leadership was provided by equally young African-Americans, most of whom had survived vicious campaigns in Albany, Birmingham, Mississippi, and elsewhere. One student, Lew, wrote home that the volunteers and staff were initially "unfriendly and unextending" until after dinner: "tremendous enthusiasm was generated when we all began singing." The group sang for two hours and all previous "cliques" and distance began to disappear. Another student wrote home about the "brutal" role-playing, but loved the singing: "What 'We Shall Overcome' is to the national movement, 'We'll Never Turn Back' is to the Mississippi workers. It is a slow song, measured out in grief and determination." The student, Jim, noted that the final verse mentioned Herbert Lee, the black voter registration worker who was murdered in Liberty, Mississippi, in 1961:

*We have hung our head and cried,*
*Cried for those like Lee*
*Who died*
*Died for you and died for me,*
*Died for the cause of equality,*
*But we will never turn back*
*Until we've all been free*
*And we have equality, and we have equality.*[64]

Another volunteer was Ron Ridenour, then a student at UCLA. Ridenour and a friend fulfilled the requirements for nonviolence training and drove his 1953 Chevy to Oxford, where they found that 80 percent of the staff were black and 80 percent of the volunteers were white, along with dozens, perhaps hundreds of lawyers and clergy. Of the first week-long session, which began June 13, Ridenour writes movingly of the training and experiences at the intensive preparatory workshop, as well another equally important component, the music: "After the orientation meeting, people broke into song. In the following days, meetings and workshops were often interrupted by song: gay and sad songs, songs of folk in struggle sung off-key by some and exquisitely by many, but always sung with vigor. Some would break off singing and recount a story that signifies the song, while others would hum and clap in the background, and everyone would join in on the chorus. One word—Freedom—stirred and captivated everyone there. The old 'negro spirituals,' with roots from the time slaves found solace in them, gave new meaning to demonstrators struggling for freedom today, braving billy clubs and jails."[65]

Among the hundreds of volunteers in Oxford were three young men, two white civil rights workers, Andrew Goodman and Mickey Schwerner, and James Chaney, a black Mississippian. On the evening of Friday June 19, staff and students gathered in Oxford for a final group sing before the first "graduates" left for Mississippi early the following morning. The music, led by Matthew Jones of SNCC's Freedom Singers, included "We'll Never Turn Back."[66] According to Len Holt, the singing continued right up until the early morning departure. "Old verses were remembered," he writes, "new verses were created. They sang of triumphs, of defeats, of fallen martyrs and rising heroes. They sang of jails, of picket lines. While groups with arms across each other's shoulders in the wide circle tried to remember a song that hadn't already been sung, there were just hums and moans like those found in little country churches. But the dawn, which they tried to stop with the anguish of their hearts transposed into the wails of their vocal cords, came anyway."[67]

At 3 a.m. on Saturday morning, eight volunteers, including Goodman, Schwerner, and Chaney, left for Meridian, arrived at 5:30 p.m., and checked into their living quarters.[68] On a lonely road near Philadelphia, Mississippi, the three were arrested, then disappeared on Sunday, June 21, while investigating the burning of an African-American church. Goodman and Schwerner, who had spent time working in the movement, had expressed concerns about their safety that morning. By Thursday, the FBI was quoted as saying, "We're now looking for bodies."[69]

Back in Oxford, the tenor of the second wave of orientation sessions, already somber, turned grim. Historian Vincent Harding's sessions were straightforward. "There has been no word of the three people in Neshoba," he told Sally Belfrage and the other volunteers. "The staff met all night," he said. "When we sing, 'We are not afraid,' we mean we are afraid. We sing 'Ain't gonna let my fear turn me 'round,' because many of you might want to turn around now."[70]

At the end of the week, a badly shaken Moses spoke movingly to the last group of volunteers preparing to board buses southward. He talked of his anguish for creating the situation that led to the apparent murders of the three men, of his fear that others may die; then left the auditorium in total silence. Wrote one volunteer, "Finally, from far in the back, a single girl's voice started to sing, 'They say that freedom is a constant sorrow.'" Other voices joined and those in the room embraced and sang the song to each other. "The group sang in one voice," the writer noted, "each individual singing not for himself but for the group. As I sang and I felt the love of the group, I realized that I loved all equally and that the difference was that I knew some better than others. And I knew better than ever why I was going to Mississippi and what I am fighting for."[71] Another song arose almost immediately afterward. Jean Smith and Judy Richardson stood and walked slowly toward the front, with Smith singing:

> *I don't know why*
> *I have to cry sometimes.*
> *I don't know why*
> *I have to cry sometimes.*
> *It would be a perfect day,*
> *But there's trouble all in my way.*
> *I don't know why*
> *But I'll know by and by.*

Smith says that by the time she reached the front of the room, those assembled had learned the song and were singing with her. And, by then, "the frightened atmosphere had changed into one of resolve and we were together again."[72] Stuart Rawlings's emotions careened widely as well. His journal diary on June 25–26 shows him calculating his fears in percentages—two hundred COFO volunteers in Mississippi in the first week, with three of them already missing and presumed dead. But as a group of volunteers watched a segment of the *CBS Evening News with Walter Cronkite* where their work was featured, they spontaneously joined hands and sang "We Shall Overcome" until one African-American asked them to hum. "You know what we're all doing," the man said, "we're moving the world. We're all here to bring all the peoples of Mississippi, all the peoples of this country, all the peoples of the world . . . together . . . we're bringing a new revolution of love, so let's sing out together once again now, everybody hand in hand." Rawlings says that he walked into the night with the strains of "We Shall Overcome" still continuing behind him and thought, "These people were me, and I was them. Absolutely nothing came between us, as our hearts felt the call to work toward a better world . . . I felt that I could and would devote my life to this kind of revolution. Alleluia."[73]

In addition to the physical demands on the COFO volunteers by the end of the grueling two-week training sessions and the emotional cost from the disappearance of the three volunteers, the sponsoring organizations were, yet again, facing a huge financial drain on their resources. In desperation, Jim Forman, the de facto leader of the SNCC, called his most reliable resource, Harry Belafonte, pleading for at least $50,000 in the next three days. Belafonte donated most of the money, tapped a few of his friends, then organized a quick fund-raiser, and raised the money. Afraid to use the white supremacist–controlled banks and knowing the obvious dangers of wiring that much money to an individual, Belafonte decided to hand deliver it, along with his long-time friend, actor Sidney Poitier. Arriving at night, and met by a few SNCC members, the caravan departed for Greenwood. They were soon tailed by segregationists, whose trucks continually battered the SNCC vehicles. Following the harrowing chase, the two stars walked into the Elks Hall in Greenwood where exhausted volunteers cheered their every move. "The crowd took up a freedom song, and then another," Belafonte writes in his autobiography, "the spirituals that had given these brave volunteers comfort and encouragement day after day." Belafonte delivered the satchel with the money to wild cheers. However, outside, a number of vehicles filled with Klan members sat idling in the street. The two stars spent an uneasy night sharing a single bed, then returned to New York the following day after visiting Greenwood's SNCC headquarters.[74]

COFO dispersed the Oxford volunteers across the state, with many assigned to Hattiesburg, Greenwood, and even smaller towns. Belfrage's assignment was as the Freedom School librarian in Greenwood. On her first evening, she attended a mass meeting, which opened with freedom songs, continued with a fiery sermon urging those present to register to vote, and resumed with old hymns, with the pastor lining out the words. "There was very little resemblance between the sounds of the freedom songs and the hymns," Belfrage noted. "The voices changed in quality from determination to resigned, from fresh and young to generations old, from exuberant with hope to fatalistic with suffering." Then Block, already scarred and weary from his work in Mississippi, stood up and led more freedom songs. Though the congregation was more "oriented toward hymns," Block "wanted them to sing the songs of freedom as fully and naturally as they sang of Jesus." Block interspersed his message amid the songs. "The moral came through the music and the people gave themselves the message of the meeting," Belfrage writes. The evening closed with a message from Stokely Carmichael, more freedom songs, and "We Shall Overcome," which ended "every meeting of more than a half a dozen" participants. "We sang out all fatigue and fear, each connected by this bond of hands to each other, communicating an infinite love and sadness."[75]

Many of the volunteers were assigned to Ruleville, where Rebecca and Joe McDonald, Mary Tucker, Ruby Davis, and Hamer were based, working fearlessly for voter registration and operating both the library and the Freedom School. Among those posted there was Tracy Sugarman, a talented artist and a military veteran. When he arrived, the talk in both the white and black communities was of the three missing volunteers. At the first mass meeting, Charles McLaurin, one of the SNCC's first black field secretaries, led in the singing of "Go Tell It on the Mountain" and spoke passionately on the importance of voter registration. "A kind of inevitable logic worked through the text and the singing, and the 'mass meeting' became a created whole," Sugarman writes. "A unity of purpose and a sharing of aspiration grew almost visibly in the humid hothouse of Williams Chapel." Other songs were sung, including "Ain't Gonna Let Nobody Turn Me 'Round," and ending with the entire congregation surging to the altar, holding hands and singing "We Shall Overcome."[76]

In addition to its other activities, COFO sponsored and supported Hamer's Ruleville-based campaign for a seat in the House of Representatives against a segregationist congressman who had been in office since 1941. The threats and official harassment immediately intensified. Ruleville's mayor interrupted a service at Hamer's church, Williams Chapel, accompanied by fifteen policemen, two reporters, and a police dog, to threaten Hamer in public. Her campaign, which was continuously subject to official intimidation and violence against her tiny staff and supporters, was one of six organized by local activists and conducted on a shoestring budget. Hamer campaigned widely to a population that was largely unable to vote. Not surprisingly, all six lost to their segregationist opponents by wide margins. The experience assisted in the formation of the Mississippi Freedom Democratic Party (MFDP), created first as an organizing tool, then as a direct challenge to the all-white, prosegregation slate of Mississippi Democratic delegates to the party's national convention later that summer.[77]

Hamer was selected as the vice-chair of the MFDP delegation and the biracial group met repeatedly throughout the summer to create and publicize its platform. Meanwhile, at their state convention, the "regular" Mississippi Democrats reaffirmed their party's commitment to segregation, stating that the "separation of the races is necessary for the peace and tranquility" in the state. The state Democrats rebuffed every effort by the MFDP (often called the "Freedom Democrats") to work together and even the *Delta Democrat-Times* in Greenville noted the extremism of the regular party delegates, calling them "a combination of John Birch-Citizens Council professional types."[78] At the MFDP's state meeting in Jackson, movement veteran Ella Baker delivered a "stirring" keynote address, urging listeners to prepare for the struggle ahead. After her speech, "there was a march of all the delegates around the convention hall—singing Freedom Songs, waving American flags, banners and county signs," one participant wrote in a letter home: "This was probably the most soul-felt march ever to occur in a political convention, I felt, as we marched with a mixture of sadness and joy—of humility and pride—of fear and courage, singing 'Go Tell It on the Mountain,' 'Ain't Gonna Let Nobody Turn Me 'Round' and 'This Little Light of Mine.'"[79]

The star of the national Democratic convention in Atlantic City, the incumbent Lyndon B. Johnson, was aware of what was happening in Mississippi and worked tirelessly to retain enough southern votes to hold off a challenge from the presumptive Republican nominee, Barry Goldwater. Johnson's strong support of civil rights legislation—and Republican front-runner Goldwater's opposition to it—would make many of the traditionally Democratic southern states support the Republican ticket for the first time since Reconstruction. After epic battles in the House and Senate, Johnson signed Kennedy's Civil Rights Act of 1964 into law on July 2.[80] The signing took place on national television and Johnson warned that the nation was now experiencing "a time of testing" and signed the bill with seventy-two different pens, one of which he gave to Martin Luther King, who was standing behind him. Those watching the television at Vicksburg's Freedom House erupted into cheers. They sang "We Shall Overcome" and then, "just for fun" they sang "We *Have* Overcome," though events in Mississippi would soon prove that there was much still to overcome.[81]

In the days that followed the passage of the Act, four members of Congress, including Don Edwards, whose son was a volunteer in Ruleville, arrived in Ruleville and Greenwood to celebrate the passage of the Civil Rights Act on the Fourth of July. More than a hundred people heard the congressmen and John Lewis speak in the charred remains of Williams Chapel, which had been fire-bombed a week earlier. An enthusiastic crowd sang freedom songs, including "Ain't Gonna Let Nobody Turn Me 'Round," "Certainly, Lord," and "Come and Go with Me," and Charles McLaurin, from nearby Drew, quoted Hamer, whose small house was across the road from Williams Chapel: "These people will be a light to Drew just as a few people were the light in Ruleville a couple of years ago. The reason so many are coming to Ruleville to see what is happening is that that little light did not go out."[82]

The Mississippi Freedom Democratic Party, which included both black and white representatives, left for Atlantic City in mid-August. Among the representatives was folk singer Len Chander, who recorded that the delegation sang much of the way to New Jersey, including the freedom songs "Roll, Freedom, Roll," "This Little Light of Mine," "Ain't Gonna Let Nobody Turn Me 'Round," "Freedom Is a Constant Struggle," and "This May Be the Last Time."[83] The Freedom Democrats' challenge to the right of the segregated Mississippi delegation to be seated provided most of the drama at a convention where Johnson's ascendency was assured. For his part, Johnson wanted to avoid the embarrassment of a general walkout of white southern delegates should the MFDP be seated. Johnson also hoped to prevent a heated, behind-the-scenes battle before the credentials committee, where the MFDP might receive the support of the delegates from other states.[84] Like the rest of the MFDP, once Hamer arrived in Atlantic City, she worked the other delegates, spreading the word of conditions in Mississippi, trying to garner support for their cause. In one emotional sequence, television cameras caught Hamer singing "Go Tell It on the Mountain (To Let My People Go)" on the Boardwalk and "showed a woman calling forth some inner vision of a political system that might—must—let her people go." Also shown singing and holding a sign with Hamer were Anne Devine, Victoria Gray, and Bernice Johnson Reagon. The emotional footage was widely replayed throughout the summer.[85] The Boardwalk near the convention center remained the impromptu nerve center for the Mississippi delegation, where delegates, friends, and supporters sang freedom songs virtually nonstop. Other convention delegates had to pass by the spot to enter the center. Later, a man from her hometown of Mayersville and a member of the "regular" Mississippi delegation, told MFDP delegate Unita Blackwell that he, his wife, and children were so "entranced" by the music that they turned down a chance to hear the Beatles, who were also in Atlantic City that week, to hear the group sing.[86]

Before national television cameras, the 110-member credentials committee heard eight-minute speeches of support for the Freedom Democrats from the SCLC's King, CORE's Farmer, and others, most notably Hamer. Hamer told the committee of her struggles in the registration battles, of the shots fired into her home and the homes where she had sought refuge. In graphic terms, she told of her horrific beatings by the police, Highway Patrol, and their trustees. With tears in her eyes, she said, "All of this on account we want to register, to become first-class citizens, and if the Freedom Democratic Party is not seated now, I question America, is this America, the land of the free and the home of the brave where we have to sleep with our telephones off the hook because our lives be threatened daily because we want to live as decent human beings, in America?" Hamer's televised presentation was suddenly cut short—Johnson called an "impromptu news conference" that preempted the hearing. However, the networks replayed her testimony on the nightly news. MFDP members rejected a compromise that would put two of their delegates on the convention floor and the committee reluctantly voted to seat the "official" state delegates. Eventually, the Freedom Democrats were given delegate tickets as nonvoting "honored guests" and some were given credentials by sympathetic delegates, including North Dakota and Michigan, allowing them on the floor. The MFDP members, including Hamer and Moses, stood silently on the convention floor in protest.[87] At a press conference following the close of activities, the MFDP delegates and Hamer sang "Go tell it on the mountain . . . let my people go" before answering questions. According to Blackwell, Hamer said, "We will not take the compromise. We didn't come all this way for no two seats. All of us is tired."[88]

On the final night before their return to Mississippi, Belfrage joined Hamer and a number of the MDFP delegates in their usual spot on the Boardwalk singing "We Shall Overcome," "remembering all the impossible times, unlike any others, we had sung it before," Belfrage recalls. "The only song that has no clapping because the hands are holding all the other hands. A suspension from color, hate, recrimination, guilt, suffering—a kind of lesson in miniature of what it's all about. The song begins slowly and somehow without anticipation of these things: just a song, the last one, before we separate. You see the others, and the instant when it comes to each one to think what the words mean, when each nearly breaks, wondering: shall we overcome? The hands hold each other tighter. Mrs. Hamer is smiling, flinging out the words, and crying at once. 'Black and white together,' she leads the next verse, and a sort of joy begins to grow in every face; 'We are not afraid'—and for just that second no one is afraid, because they are free."[89]

Johnson swept the election handily, winning all but the five states of the Deep South (including Mississippi) and Goldwater's home state of Arizona. The president invited a number of African-American artists to perform at his inaugural balls and in the White House, including gospel stars Clara Ward and the Ward Singers and jazz singer Sarah Vaughan. At one point, Vaughan sang for the president and the prime minister of Japan. After the concert, one of the First Lady's aides found Vaughan crying in her dressing room. When the aide asked if there was something wrong, Vaughan replied, "Nothing is the matter. It's just that twenty years ago when I came to Washington, I couldn't even get a hotel room, and tonight I sang for the President of the United States in the White House—and then he asked me to dance with him. It is more than I can stand."[90]

Throughout the hot summer, volunteers worked feverishly across Mississippi, staying with mostly poor African-Americans, enduring the near daily tormenting by police and white citizens—and learning the power of song firsthand. One volunteer wrote of a visit to a "real whoop and holler church" in Holly Spring on July 6: "The sermon began as a talk and ended as a song. The preacher jumped up and down and had tears running down his face. He finally was overcome by the sheer power of his word[s] and started to sing 'This Little Light of Mine' in the middle of a sentence. We joined him, and people came up to grab his hands. I was one of them. This was the only House of God I had ever run into in my life. Amen! It was real, powerful, and glorious." From Canton, "Jo" writes on July 10 that she stayed with two elderly sisters who lived under the threat of bombing and harassing phone calls. "I overhead one of them on the telephone," Jo writes, "'My guhls probly think I'm out of mah head; I been singin' all morning, every song I knows—I just has to.'"[91]

The violence and hate meant that the volunteers and staff members were forced to live tightly controlled, ever-vigilant lives, constantly aware of their surroundings and the very real possibility of murder in every shadow, around every corner. In that setting, one volunteer wrote, music replaced much of what they had known and loved before Mississippi: "The music . . . would have to take the place for them, all summer, of swimming, solitude, sex, movies, walking, drinking, driving or any of the releases they had ever grown to need; and would somehow have to come to mean enough to drive off fear."[92]

African-American folk singer Chandler's weeks in Tupelo taught him still another facet of life in Mississippi. That summer, Chandler sang constantly at mass meetings, outside on a flatbed truck, and at every small voter registration meeting in the area. Shortly after July 4, he found himself at an afternoon mass meeting in an un-air-conditioned church, with the temperature in excess of one hundred degrees. "I had never experienced singing like the singing of Mississippi," he wrote. "Those people could kill you." The singing, accompanied by "children, teenagers, old people in their sixties and seventies," continued through the afternoon, with people "playing tambourines and swaying and shouting on one song for thirty minutes." Chandler, singing, playing his guitar, and sweating profusely, focused on a short black woman in a "stringy-brim, straw hat and a flowered cotton dress" who continued to sing more and more forcefully. "I swore that I was not going to let some little old lady wear me out. The whole church was rocking, verse after verse. We made up verses then started at the beginning again. Somewhere I turned a consciousness curve and was transported. I became a transcendental surfer riding the crest of a never-ending musical wave. I had joined them in the zone." It was only after the meeting that Chandler was introduced to the indomitable singer, Fannie Lou Hamer.[93]

Despite the terrorism and constant abuse, or perhaps because of it, the nightly mass meetings in black churches across the state drew hundreds of African-Americans "singing, shouting, chanting 'Freedom Now.'" The SNCC moved its headquarters from Atlanta to Greenwood in time for what organizers called Freedom Day on July 16. In Greenwood, Mississippi's new anti-picketing law was tested by dozens of people. Their efforts were met by billy clubs, electric cattle prods, and mass arrests. In the police vehicles and buses, those arrested clapped and swayed and sang "Oh, freedom / Oh, freedom, over me." As the day wore on and more arrests were made, volunteers, COFO members, and black citizens alike sang "Ain't gonna let Chief Lary turn me around / Keep on a-walkin', keep on a-talkin' / Marchin' on to freedom land" as they were pushed around and threatened in the police station. Belfrage was among those arrested and, as was typically the case, the new prisoners were segregated by race and sex. The African-American women sang "Ain't scared o' your jails because I want my freedom" and the white prisoners joined them until the jailer threatened them with tear gas and shut the windows. As the arrests continued, the black prisoners were transported to the county jail, but more arrived at the city jail for several days and Belfrage writes that the singing continued until their release nearly a week later, despite increasingly deteriorating conditions that left most of those released ill or infirm.[94]

On the evening of Freedom Day, the remaining volunteers at the Freedom House watched Republican presidential candidate Barry Goldwater speak at his party's convention in the Cow Palace in San Francisco. Goldwater loudly opposed the Civil Rights Act of 1964 and the Cow Palace shook with applause with his signature line, "extremism in the defense of liberty is no vice." The convention closed with the playing of "The Battle Hymn of the Republic."[95]

While most of those arrested spent their time in the city and county jails of Mississippi, an unfortunate few ended up in the Mississippi State Penitentiary—Parchman Farm—the most brutal of old plantation-styled southern penitentiaries and no stranger to Freedom Riders and civil rights workers over the previous few years. Among those who spent time in Parchman was Endesa Ida Mae Holland, whose thirteen arrests included time for "disturbing the peace," "inciting a riot" and "unlawful assembly." Within Parchman's bare concrete cells and in the back-breaking outdoor labor, a medieval code of punishment and intimidation ruled. Nearly as violent as their jailers were the black "trustees" who meted out much of the daily abuse. Holland's particular tormenter told her upon arrival, "Ain't gonna have no sangin', no prayin', no talkin' 'mongst yo'selves." In addition to the bad food (when it was not being withheld), female inmates were issued six squares of toilet paper once a week. As in other prisons, the covert singing of freedom songs and hymns were the lone release. After a particularly cruel period follow-ing a visit by Governor Ross Barnett, the sick and abused inmates were close to despair when a single voice intoned, "Nobody knows / The trouble I seen / Nobody knows / My sorrow." "Before long," Holland writes, "our whole cell block was sing-ing softly—sorrowfully—into the burning night." Holland and her friends were kept for thirty-three days in Parchman, and were only released due to the efforts of John Doar of the Justice Department. On the bus ride home, they stopped in Ruleville, where they met Hamer. Hamer sang "This Little Light of Mine," hugged and kissed "every last stinking one of us" and whispered into Holland's ear, "You got the light of freedom."[96]

There seemed to be no end to the violence in Mississippi. The tortured remains of Schwerner, Chaney, and Goodman were finally found August 3 in an earthen dam near the town of Philadelphia, and only then because of a tip. By one esti-mate, during Mississippi Freedom Summer, six civil rights workers were murdered, eighty people were beaten, thirty-five were shot at (with at least three receiving bul-let wounds), thirty-five churches were burned, thirty homes and other structures were bombed (seventeen in McComb alone, where the violence raged unabated for another year), and thousands were arrested. The Justice Department and FBI were notably absent through much of the state, prompting a particularly ironic sign to be posted in the Jackson Freedom House: "There's a town in Mississippi called Liberty. There's a department in Washington called Justice."[97]

Chaney, who had suffered an "inhumane beating" before being shot three times, was buried in a private ceremony following a second autopsy.[98] A memo-rial march in Meridian on Friday August 7 drew hundreds of mourners who sang "We Shall Overcome" inside the packed church. In a state that had seen the mur-ders of Emmett Till, Medgar Evers, Herbert Lee, and an unknown number of African-Americans in recent years, the singing was interspersed with the wracking sobs of those weeping over yet another loss and the shouts of those who were angry at the injustice of it all.[99] The funerals for Schwerner and Goodman took place in their hometown of New York City on Sunday August 9. At Goodman's service, Rabbi Arthur J. Lelyveld of Cleveland, who had himself gone to Mississippi as a representative of the National Council of Churches and had been beaten with a lead pipe in July, delivered the main eulogy. At the end of the service, the three mothers, Chaney, Schwerner, and Goodman, rose, linked arms, and walked out of the auditorium together as the mourners outside softly sang "We Shall Overcome." Schwerner's funeral service was held that evening at the Community Church and speakers included James Farmer, John Lewis, William Kunstler, and Dave Dennis. "Evil societies always try to kill their consciences," Farmer told the grieving families. At the conclusion of the service, the mourners and those outside again sang "We Shall Overcome."[100]

While performing in Meridian on the day following the discovery of three bodies, Pete Seeger was told that each had been positively identified. He made the solemn announcement to his listeners, most of whom had not yet heard the news. "We must sing 'We Shall Overcome' now," he said. "The three boys would not have wanted us to weep now, but to sing and understand this song."[101] And in Moss Point, once considered a "good area" for volunteers because of a relative lack of violence, Lawrence Guyot spoke at a mass meeting, saying, "What will it take to make you people move? A rape? A shooting? A murder?" As the congregation of more than three hundred stood at the end of the service and sang "We Shall Overcome," a car drove by the church, firing through the open door. A young African-American girl was hit in the side, but survived. A police patrol and sheriff's deputy sitting outside the building had disappeared shortly before the shooting.[102]

Through it all, folk artists in particular continued to perform in Mississippi, despite the danger. In addition to Seeger, the Mississippi Caravan of Music criss-crossed the state throughout the Freedom Summer. Among those who participated at different times were Chandler, Judy Collins, Carolyn Hester, Peter LaFarge, Phil Ochs, Cordell Reagon, Barbara Dane, Joe Harrison, Jackie Washington, and others. An article by Bob Cohen on the Caravan, the cultural arm for the Mississippi Freedom Project, reported that singers also became involved in Freedom Schools at each stop, as well as holding workshops for local musicians and singers. "It seemed to me that the farther out in the country and the more ramshackle the wooden church," Cohen writes, "the greater was the singing. I'm thinking particularly of a mass rally in Ruleville, hometown of Mrs. Fanny Lou Hamer . . . where the singing nearly blew off the roof." Cohen, who with Wendy Heyel coordinated the Caravan from their office in Jackson, added that, "when Mrs. Hamer finishes singing a few freedom songs, one is aware that he has truly heard a fine political speech, stripped of the usual rhetoric and filled with the anger and determination of the civil rights movement. And, on the other hand, in her speeches is the constant thunder and drive of music." Surprisingly, the Caravan of Music participants faced little of the direct harassment experienced by most white volunteers during the Mississippi summer.[103]

Collins, Dane, and Hamer were among the few who made it to both Ruleville and Drew the first week of August. On a bus to Drew to sing at a voter registration meeting, Collins later recalled being consumed "by total fear and the understanding that what we were doing was dangerous. I knew that I would probably be shot at or killed or beaten." The riders sang "Ain't Gonna Let Nobody Turn Me

'Round" and Collins wrote that "it is something to know that there is nobody that can turn you around except yourself and the singing, the music is what makes a lot of this conviction possible." Even as their small gathering of seventy-five people was constantly surrounded by cars full of Klansmen circling the meeting, Hamer spoke and sang "This Little Light of Mine." The music and words in the face of fear left Collins "purged and united."[104] Sugarman, who was also there, marveled at the courage of those who had chosen to participate the first night in Drew, and wrote of the singing with remarkable insight into the evolution of the protest spiritual: "They built their shrine with their religious faith, summoning their courage by singing the spirituals which had been reshaped to the great design of the 'Movement.' River Jordan is segregation—and they're gonna cross, gonna cross. Heaven is freedom, and hell is Mr. Charlie and the police dogs. 'Ain't gonna let nobody turn me round. . . .' Saul and David marched with Emmett Till and Medgar Evers and all those who have been ''buked and scorned.' All had to be willing to pay with pain for a ticket on the 'Freedom Train.'"[105]

On her final night before returning to New York after their short stay in Mississippi, Collins writes she joined Dane and sang Malvina Reynold's popular movement song, "It Isn't Nice" to a man in a pickup truck who threatened to kill the workers. They then left for a mass meeting that lasted late into the evening. "We all went home with no voices left at all," Collins writes, "we had sung until there was nothing left. It was the best way in the world to lose your voice. It means so much, the music." Dane's most vivid memories from those dangerous days and nights with the Caravan are also of Hamer "weaving together song and talk and song again; making the spirits of her weary, sweaty neighbors visibly rise as their hearts connected." To Dane, Hamer embodied the concept of a "singer" as "not just one who sings, not only a great voice, but a shaman, preacher, teacher, healer, taking responsibility for community and continuity, making sure that life itself will go on with any sense of the reasons for it. As she reminded them again of the rightness of their struggle and led them into the cadences of call and response so old and yet so new, you could almost touch the ties that bound them ever closer into a community with the strength to resist and triumph."[106]

The constant unrest in Mississippi made life difficult for most African-Americans, especially those who had to travel. Chicago's Pilgrim Jubilees often played Clarksdale at the behest of legendary black radio announcer Early Wright. Police would follow the group's car each time they arrived and escort them back out of town after the concert. The group suffered the same issues that other African-Americans experienced in the state—substandard, segregated facilities (when facilities for blacks were available at all), lack of access to restaurants and hotels, and constant harassment by local police and the Mississippi Highway Patrol. "Any little thing," Cleave Graham of the Jubilees said, could expose the group to "potentially life-threatening harassment and degradation."[107] After a disagreement at a restaurant in Greenwood, the Salem Travelers, another Chicago-based group, found themselves fleeing the town, pursued by a host of angry and presumably armed citizens.[108]

Ultimately, it is Hamer who remains the person most associated with the free-dom struggle in Mississippi. Reagon said that Hamer was known to the SNCC long before she arrived in Mississippi and that Hamer was one of the "special people" who "changed the way I looked at myself and the world I lived in." When Hamer died in 1977, Reagon wrote a song in her honor, accompanied by the following statement: "Every once in a now and then somebody moves in such a way that makes us jerk up and take note. Fannie Lou Hamer made some decisions during the early part of the sixties that made us stand up and follow, feeling a little stron-ger and going a little farther because of the price she paid for the stances she took. Mississippi will never be the same; I will never be the same. Black song was wedded with struggle in her hands."[109] Sugarman made more than a hundred drawings during the Mississippi Summer, but only two capture a "fleeting image" of Hamer since, he wrote, an artist "needs at least a few moments of repose to make a portrait sketch, and repose was as foreign to Mrs. Hamer as luxury." Instead, Sugarman's memories of her are "filled with frenetic movement and gigantic energy."[110]

## Music

While the work of the volunteers during the Freedom Summer led to relatively few African-Americans actually being registered to vote, numerous commentators noted the sense of empowerment the events of the summer bestowed on many blacks in Mississippi. Certainly, the heroism, sacrifice, and patience of the COFO, the volunteers, and the courage of local people who dared to defy Mississippi's entrenched segregationist power system played a major role in bringing about change, as did the enactment of the Civil Rights Act of 1964. But the one constant among all participants was the music. In an article in the August 31 edition of *Newsweek* titled "Without These Songs . . ." the uncredited writer cites the work of the Mississippi Caravan of Music and tells of the impact of musicians Seeger, Chandler, Collins, Dane, and others. At a meeting in Greenwood, Cordell Reagon "admonished" listeners at a mass meeting: "Without these songs, you know we wouldn't be anywhere. We'd still be down on Mister Charley's plantation, chop-ping cotton for 30 cents a day." Facing a hostile reception among whites in Drew, Collins admitted that she was afraid until she and members of the Eastgate Singers began to sing "Ain't gonna let nobody turn me 'round . . . marching up to Freedom Land." "It was then that I found out just a little of what freedom music can really mean," Collins said. "The music was the only way to settle the terror—to direct it." Elsewhere, other musicians told of discovering new singers, songwriters as young as eleven and twelve, and newly encouraged blacks bravely registering to vote for the first time.[111] As was usually the case, many of the singers and speakers in Drew were arrested and then released a few days later, only to be arrested again.[112]

Charles M. Payne's towering history of Mississippi, *I've Got the Light of Free-dom,* identifies the power of the music at the mass meetings as being one of the

**FIGURE 12**

Freedom Singers Chuck Neblett (left) and Matthew Jones listen to the music and teaching in a Hattiesburg church during the Freedom Summer, July 1964. Photo: Herbert Randall Freedom Summer Photographs, McCain Library and Archives, The University of Southern Mississippi.

**FIGURE 13**

Free Southern Theater guitarist Roger Johnson
crosses his arms and joins hands with legendary folk singer and activist Pete Seeger to sing
"We Shall Overcome" at Mount Zion Baptist
Church, August 4, 1964, during the Freedom
Summer in Hattiesburg, Mississippi. Photo:
Herbert Randall Freedom Summer Photographs, McCain Library and Archives, The University of Southern Mississippi.

primary catalysts for change. "It would be hard to overestimate the significance of the music of the movement," he writes. "The changing fortunes of the movement and the morale of its participants could have been gauged by the intensity of the singing at the meetings." The music in the mass meetings came to mean different things to different people. Volunteer Arance Brooks cited the physical benefits of great singing at the packed meetings. "I loved it. I just felt so much better when everybody would go . . . I slept better. The singing and everything, I just loved it." Payne writes that he believes that the music "operated as a kind of litany against fear." Freedom songs fearlessly sung in the meetings "offered a context in which the mystique of fear could be chipped away."[113]

Because of the length of the struggle, a number of different protest spirituals and freedom songs have come to be associated with Mississippi. For the Smithsonian Folkways compilation *Sing for Freedom: The Story of the Civil Rights Movement Through Its Songs,* compilers Guy and Candie Carawan chose a reworked version of the old labor song, "Which Side Are You On," with verses adapted for Mississippi, and sung by the Freedom Singers. Also included on the CD is Hollis Watkins singing "I'm Gonna Sit at the Welcome Table" and a passage from a Mississippi mass meeting in 1964 that features preaching, prayer, and the congregation singing "Guide My Feet," which the Carawans say was "associated with Mississippi" because "the race was so long and dangerous."[114] Also strongly identified with Mississippi is Greenwood hero Block's adaptation of an old spiritual, "Freedom Is a Constant Dying": "They say freedom is a constant dying / O Lord, we died so long / We must be free / We must be free." Historian C. Eric Lincoln calls the song a good example of one of the "militant protest songs veiled in lamentation."[115] Reagon, then an SNCC field secretary and member of the Freedom Singers, said that Bertha Gober's arrangement of "We've Been 'Buked and We've Been Scorned," written in tribute to the slain Mississippi organizer Reverend Herbert Lee, "was sung sometimes more than 'We Shall Overcome' because it expressed the constant threat surrounding those involved in the struggle for freedom" in the state.[116] Nina Simone's fiery "Mississippi Goddam" became "the anthem" of the Freedom Summer for the volunteers. "Everybody in the Movement just sort of took that as a tribute to the Mississippi Summer Project," one participant recalled.[117]

The Freedom Singers recorded only two complete albums in their various incarnations, both on Mercury Records and both out of print and difficult to find. The original five members met in October 1963 at a Chicago studio for a whirlwind recording session. Released in time to be reviewed in the "Special Merit Picks" for the December 14, 1963 issue of *Billboard* magazine, *We Shall Overcome* featured the best-known songs of the freedom movement. On the cover, singing in front of a wooden fence, Rutha Harris, Bernice Johnson Reagon, Cordell Reagon, Charles Neblett, and Bertha Gober stand in the classic "We Shall Overcome" stance, with arms linked and crossed.[118] A second album, *The Freedom Singers Sing of Freedom Now!* was recorded in the spring of 1964 at the SNCC's Fourth Annual Conference at Gammon Theological Seminary in Atlanta, with liner notes written by

Studs Terkel during the difficult time when the fates of Schwerner, Chaney, and Goodman was still uncertain. The tone of the writing and the choice of the songs is darker, less upbeat than the earlier release. Songs include "They Laid Medgar Evers in His Grave" ("In Jackson, Mississippi, in 1963 / There lived a man who was brave / He fought for freedom all of his life / But they laid Medgar Evers in his grave"), "Soon—I Will Be Done" ("Soon I will be done with the troubles of the world / Goin' to freedom land") and "We'll Never Turn Back" (the "theme song" of the Mississippi Summer Project, according to Terkel's liner notes). "To hear these voices," he writes, "is to suffer a terribly moving experience."[119]

As with many of the sites in the freedom struggle, Mississippi was not changed in a year or even ten years. Federal laws were disobeyed, lengthy lawsuits followed, violence continued, and the freedoms found elsewhere only gradually spread through the state. The sheer length of the struggle and the ferocity of the opposition wore down many of the volunteers and workers, embittered some, frustrated most. In the end, the ambiguous nature of what constituted "success" in Mississippi touched all of those involved. In the violence of Ruleville that summer, a volunteer named Heather wrote to her brother of the terror and threat of violence that shadowed her every move. Even as her parents begged her to come home, she somehow found the strength to pen these words to him:

> "We are not afraid. Oh Lord, deep in my heart, I do believe, We shall overcome someday" and then I think I began to truly understand what the words meant. Anyone who comes down here and is not afraid I think must be crazy as well as dangerous to this project where security is quite important. But the type of fear that they mean when they, when we, sing, "we are not afraid" is the type that immobilizes. . . . The songs help to dissipate the fear. Some of the words in the songs do not hold real meaning on their own, others become rather monotonous—but when they are sung in unison, or sung silently to oneself, they take on new meaning beyond words or rhythm. . . . There is almost a religious quality about some of these songs, having little to do with the usual concept of god. It has to do with the miracle that youth has organized to fight hatred and ignorance. It has to do with the holiness of the dignity of man. The god that makes such miracles is the god I do believe in when we sing "God is on our side." I know I am on that god's side. And I do hope he is on ours.[120]

# 7

## SELMA, ALABAMA

We were singing. Somehow, I can't explain it, through the singing and the sense of our solidarity we made a kind of psychological barrier between us and the mob. Somehow we made such a wall of strength that they couldn't physically push through it to hit us with their sticks. It wasn't visual, but you could almost see our singing and our unity pushing them back. You could see it most clearly when we passed this wedge they made. You could see those Klan leaders trying to push into us. They got within a few feet of us, but they couldn't get closer. By our singing, we actually pressed them back from us, pressed them away from us. Eventually, the only way they could get through was to bombard us with rocks. When we started to retreat, and we stopped singing, it was like they had broken our bubble. They moved in on the back of the march and started to beat us up.

—BRUCE HARTFORD

### Selma 1963

As with other sites in the southern freedom struggle, various forces had been working in Selma, the seat of Dallas County, long before it received national attention.[1] Father Maurice F. Ouellet, a Catholic priest, had been the voice for African-Americans since 1961, conducting a lonely campaign that primarily generated indifference and the occasional rebuke from the rest of the city's clergy. Despite threats and ostracism within the white community, Ouellet attended civil rights rallies, spoke from the pulpits of black churches, and sang their hymns and protest songs. Working independently of Ouellet was Dr. John L. Newton of the

First Presbyterian Church, who waged a much quieter campaign.[2] All of this took place in a county with a population that was 57 percent African-American, but with 1 percent eligible to vote. In neighboring Wilcox County, blacks composed 78 percent of the population and none were eligible to vote.[3]

The SNCC first chose Selma for its next round of movement activities in 1963 because organized opposition to voter registration was clearly deep-rooted and local law enforcement frequently resorted to violence to suppress civil rights for African-Americans. Immediately after the Supreme Court's *Brown v. Board of Education* ruling in 1954, whites in Dallas County had formed one of Alabama's largest Citizen's Councils, with more than three thousand members committed to opposing equal housing and other rights for blacks. Even though the Kennedy administration had filed its first voter registration suit against Dallas County in April 1961 and a district judge had subsequently ruled the presence of "gross discrimination" against African-Americans, virtually no blacks were yet registered in the county. Selma was also home to Sheriff James G. Clark's volunteer "sheriff's posse," a deputized all-white paramilitary that numbered more than a hundred armed men and that had already made violent appearances in Birmingham. Even Eugene "Bull" Connor, the scourge of blacks in Birmingham, was originally from Selma.[4]

Leading the early days of SNCC's Selma operation were Reverend Bernard and Colia Liddell Lafayette. He was a veteran of both the Nashville sit-ins and Freedom Rides; she had been active in Mississippi. With support from Frank Holloway and Worth Long, the Lafayettes began their work in the fall of 1963 with a Voter Education Project grant, citing the "fear-stricken" African-American population. Within days of their first voter education class, the violence began.[5] Thirty-two schoolteachers tried to register and all were promptly fired by the city. Blacks were arrested for picketing, riding in an automobile, or simply being seen downtown. Long was badly beaten by a sheriff's deputy in the county jail. A young black girl was knocked off a stool at a store and struck repeatedly with an electric prod as she lay unconscious. When the SNCC's Jim Forman came to Selma for the first mass meeting in May, Clark's posse ominously surrounded the church. Given Clark's reputation for violence, most of the three hundred people in Tabernacle Baptist Church remained inside the building late into the evening until it appeared that the posse had finally left the area. When John Lewis and seven other SNCC staffers and supporters were subsequently jailed, the organization called for a "large scale offensive" believing, as they had discovered in other movement actions, "fear decreased with numbers."[6] Large-scale demonstrations resumed on September 24, 1963, when officers armed with clubs and guns arrested one hundred fifty-six marchers singing "Nobody's Gonna Turn Us 'Round" in two antisegregation demonstrations. Another one hundred fifty marchers were arrested the following day. As Forman told reporters, "This is going to get tough."[7]

Undeterred, representatives from both the SNCC and the SCLC selected October 7 as "Freedom Day" in Selma. A new Freedom Choir led the music at the mass meetings, singing what by now had become "standard" freedom songs. One of the featured soloists was Bettie Mae Fikes, a sixteen-year-old Selma native who had hopped aboard a Freedom Riders bus at age fifteen. A "powerful contralto," Fikes was best known for her rendition of "This Little Light of Mine," performed "in a distinctly Selma style." On the appointed day, more than three hundred African-Americans protested and waited in line to register. Speakers included Dick Gregory and James Baldwin, but despite the presence of Justice Department representatives, virtually no blacks were able to register.[8]

*Movement Soul: Sounds of the Freedom Movement in the South, 1963–1964* features a number of short excerpts from speakers and singers in Selma 1963, including an evening mass meeting in October with more than three hundred people. The music is led by Sikes and "This Little Light of Mine" contains verses identifying the protagonists in the freedom struggle in that city: "Tell Governor Wallace," "Tell Jim Clark," "Tell Judge Moon," and "Tell Mayor Hinz." During the recording, Clark and his posse stood outside the church.[9] A week earlier, as the congregation had left the service, "the posse, swinging their clubs, chased people off the streets and into their houses." Howard Zinn, who was in attendance, called the music of Selma "the most beautiful singing I had heard since the mass meetings in Albany." Clark's men also heard Gregory speak for two hours to the packed church. Gregory called southern police officials "peons, the idiots who do all the dirty work, the dogs that do all the biting." It was, Zinn said, "a lesson in economics and sociology, streaked with humor."[10]

For "Freedom Day," SNCC officials made a concerted push to attract as many African-Americans as possible to apply to register. By mid-morning, more than three hundred and fifty applicants formed an orderly line at the courthouse. They were faced by dozens of sheriff's deputies and armed irregulars, as well as Clark himself, resplendent with an eagle on his green helmet, "a big gold star on his shirt, the Confederate flag stamped on his helmet, an open collar, epaulets on his shoulders . . . [and] gun at his hip," according to Zinn. Forman and Lewis were joined by James Baldwin and his brother David, and two lawyers from the U.S. Department of Justice. At mid-afternoon, the Clark posse had attacked a group of reporters and photographers. By 4:30 p.m., after a full day of standing in line, not a single applicant had been registered, nor had the Justice Department representatives done anything, save for attempt to bail one of the SNCC staffers out of jail. At the mass meeting that evening, Zinn writes that mood was curiously buoyant, perhaps because that many blacks had dared assemble in Clark's Selma. Those SNCC members and reporters who had not been arrested sat in the packed pews and heard a children's chorus sing "This Little Light of Mine" and the Selma Freedom Chorus sing, "If you miss me, can't find me nowhere / Just come on over to the county jail, I'll be sittin' over there" and "Kumbaya": "Selma needs you, Lord, kumbaya! / Selma needs you, Lord, kumbaya! / Selma needs you, Lord, kumbaya! / Oh Lord, kumbaya!" Zinn, clearly moved by the service, noted that the meeting closed with

"We Shall Overcome."[11] Eventually, spread too thin in Birmingham and elsewhere, movement activists decided to postpone a full-scale action in Selma until 1965.

## 1964

Following the Mississippi Summer, John Lewis writes in William R. Beardslee's *The Way Out Must Lead In* that the SNCC "started turning inward as an organization." The rising conflict over the place of whites in the movement, the constant financial strain, and the emotional and physical scars of Mississippi all had taken a toll. "When there was a low period without a target," he writes, "sometimes frustration set in and people turned inward on themselves." The SNCC had survived and flourished by fostering a sense of unity around a common target, such as Bull Connor in Birmingham or the restaurants in Nashville. With a formidable opponent, "people could direct all of their energies and all of their attention toward it." Despite the events in Mississippi and long simmering struggles elsewhere, a number of SNCC staffers continued to feel the call of Selma. Lewis writes that when a "crisis" would strike—"a crisis affecting a particular individual, or a particular city, or movement of people"—the response within the organization was to sing. The decision to enter Selma was one such crisis and "We Shall Overcome," "Freedom Is a Constant Struggle," "I Ain't Gonna Let Nobody Turn Me 'Round" and "Before I'll Be a Slave, I'll Be Buried in My Grave" were all sung repeatedly. Then, he writes, the members would reach some kind of consensus. "Songs tended to give people a sense of togetherness, a sense of unity and 'sustaination.' Music had a way of quieting some of the feelings, disrobing people of some of their fears."[12]

In early December 1964, Dr. Martin Luther King, Jr., received the Nobel Peace Prize in Oslo, Norway. King accepted it on behalf of the civil rights movement and "all men who love peace and brotherhood." He donated the prize money associated with the award—about $54,000—to the movement and told an audience that included King Olav V of Norway that he was only a "trustee" for the movement's "humble children."[13] The King party sang often while in Norway and Sweden, sometimes for their hosts and sometimes just for the sheer joy of being together. Coretta King tells of a quintet with her husband, Andrew Young, Ralph Abernathy, Wyatt T. Walker, and Bernard Lee singing freedom songs "in beautiful harmony." It was, she said, "something they often did to break up the seriousness of staff conferences and retreats." The entire entourage then sang a series of freedom songs, spirituals, and hymns, including "Oh, Freedom," "Ain't Gonna Let Nobody Me 'Round," "Were You There When They Crucified My Lord," and "Balm in Gilead," which Coretta said Martin often quoted when he "needed a lift." The party left for Stockholm and the Kings went to a small Baptist seminary, where Martin preached and closed with the singing of "We Shall Overcome."[14] Response to the award ranged from the recording of the Duke Ellington–penned song "King Fit the Battle of Alabam'" to a statement from Bull Connor in Birmingham that the

Nobel Peace Prize committee "must be scraping the bottom of the barrel" with King's selection.[15]

## Selma, January 1965

On his return to the United States from Europe, one of King's first stops on Monday January 18 was Selma. He told a "clapping and singing" crowd of eight hundred that a "massive test" of the 1964 Civil Rights Act would begin in the city in the days ahead and that the registration drive would be "Selma's opportunity to repent" from its dismal record on human rights.[16] Among those "clapping and singing" was Sheyann Webb, then just in the third grade. Webb was introduced to Hosea Williams, who had heard her sing several freedom songs, all of which she already knew by heart: "Ain't Gonna Let Nobody Turn Me 'Round," "This Little Light of Mine," "O Freedom" and others. Webb was soon invited to be one of the featured singers at the mass meetings. When she sang "Ain't Gonna Let Nobody Turn Me 'Round" that night, she was joined by her friend Rachel West. Years later, West recalled those heady days: "The singing at those meetings had a purpose; it wasn't just for entertainment. Those songs carried a message. They were different from Negro spirituals, which—as beautiful as they are—told of some distant hope while carrying the burdens of this life. Freedom songs cried out for justice right now, not later." Soon, Webb and West were improvising with the older singers, "Ain't gonna let George Wallace turn me 'round / I'll keep a-walkin', I'll keep a-talkin' / Marchin' up to freedom land.'"[17] Whenever King spoke at Brown Chapel African Methodist Episcopal Church in Selma, he asked for Webb. "Every time he came around, I used to sit on his lap in the pulpit and lead a favorite tune of his, 'Ain't Gonna Let Nobody Turn Me 'Round,'" she recalled. "And every time he'd come and get ready to leave, he'd say, 'Sheyann, what do you want?' And I'd say, 'Freedom.'"[18]

Within a week of the first mass meeting, two hundred twenty-nine people had been arrested, mostly by Clark and his men. On January 22, more than a hundred African-American teachers lined the steps and sidewalks of the Dallas County Courthouse, only to be physically repulsed by officers who shoved, jabbed, and struck demonstrators. After a second attempt to line up was forcefully rebuffed, demonstrators marched to Brown Chapel, where they were met by hundreds of cheering students and supporters waiting for a mass meeting and all singing "Ain't Gonna Let Nobody Turn Me 'Round." The following day they were also met by what, on the surface, appeared to be their first good news. A federal judge angrily ordered Clark to stop interfering with black applicants in the registration process, warning that "violence on either side will not be tolerated." However, District Judge Daniel T. Thomas's order allowed Clark the leeway to prevent protesters from interfering with "the normal flow of business." So, not surprisingly, by January 26, thirty-four more protesters were arrested for refusing to leave the line for registration offices. Among those arrested was Lewis. It was, according to the

**FIGURE 14**

Legendary singer and activist Fannie Lou
Hamer and others singing while walking in
support of the Mississippi "March Against
Fear," begun by James Meredith in June 1966.
Jim Peppler, *Southern Courier* Photograph
Collection, Alabama Department of Archives
and History. Photo: Alabama Department of
Archives and History, Montgomery, Alabama.

*New York Times,* his thirty-seventh arrest as part of the movement. The following day, another twenty-four were arrested, bringing the total over the previous ten days to two hundred eighty. The protests and arrests continued with no movement toward voter registration, despite a second order from Thomas, amending the original injunction, clarifying the number of people who could line up to register to vote at any one time, and prohibiting Clark's men from obstructing other peaceful protests. The judge's orders appeared to have had little impact on Clark's actions.[19] During one of these protests at the courthouse, West stood with a small group of protesters. When Clark ordered them to disperse, West recalled, "There wasn't a sound for a few seconds, just the wind blowing. Then, from down at the far end, somebody started singing and it caught on all along the ranks." The group sang "We Shall Not Be Moved" as Clark raged, "Shut up! Stop that now! You niggers cut that out!" When the singing continued, Clark shouted for a while longer, then held up a hand. "If you don't stop, if you don't stop right now, I'm going to arrest every one of you." After a pause, West's group moved on.[20]

The mass meetings continued, even as the weather worsened and there were precious few signs of progress. In her account of the last days of January, West writes, "White folks probably never understood how important songs were to us, how they played such a role in binding us, bringing out what courage we had when things looked bleak. That night, after singing that song through several times, I was ready to march again, no matter how cold it was outside, no matter how cutting the wind might be. There was truly a deeper meaning to the songs we would sing, a religious one. That 'little light' in each of us, I believe, was that spiritual strength and determination we instilled in ourselves that the Lord Almighty was walking with us, that we were never alone, that we were right." West also wrote fondly of her favorite of the white volunteers, a young seminary student from New Hampshire, Jonathan Daniels.[21]

LaFayette, who had been working in Selma for more than two years, also wrote movingly on the importance of music during those dark times. He calls music "the language of the soul," and essential in "developing a sense of togetherness at the mass meetings." Participants "transformed their songs of meditation to songs of justice." "Songs have a way of soothing frustrations, pain, and suffering, but they also can illustrate the power of resistances and determination." At the Selma mass meetings, LaFayette notes, the music and singing were "designed to promote involvement rather than to provide a concert or to entertain. Music was measured not by the quality of the voices but rather by the power of the spirit."[22]

## February

On Monday, February 1, King and more than seven hundred seventy protesters were arrested, including more than five hundred students who left their schools to protest Dallas County's voter registration suppression at the courthouse. An earlier, smaller group of fifteen had begun at Brown Chapel and reached the courthouse. Clark appeared in time to read them an order from Circuit Judge James A. Hare saying that court was in session and if they did not immediately disperse, they would be held in contempt. When the protesters responded with "Ain't Gonna Let Nobody Turn Me 'Round," Clark and his deputies led them to Hare's second-floor courtroom, still singing. Hare promptly held them in contempt and had them arrested. Subsequent waves of protesters descended on the courthouse throughout the day. The following day, another thousand, mostly students, were arrested, both in Selma and in nearby Marion at the Perry County Courthouse. A high school student, Charles Mauldin, led the Selma students in their march as they sang, "Ain't gonna let Jim Clark turn me 'round" and, during another song, sang the line "I love Jim Clark in my heart." At which point the notoriously dour Clark, according to the *New York Times,* smiled. Many of those arrested were promptly hauled to a work camp sixty miles away and held under $100 bond. More than three hundred of the students were arrested for truancy for "serenading" Clark and his "special posse" for thirty minutes outside the Selma courthouse. They followed Clark's officers, still singing freedom songs, into the local armory. In Marion, students assembled in front of the jail and were singing freedom songs when an Alabama state trooper approached. "Sing one more song and you are under arrest," he said. The SCLC's James Orange turned to the students and responded, "Sing another song." Orange and the students were arrested, placed in school buses, and driven away.[23]

On Thursday, February 4, a federal judge issued an order that suspended the use of the nearly impossible "literacy test" designed to stymie African-American voters and instructed the Dallas County board of registrars to process at least one hundred applications each day the board was in session. The following day, the SCLC placed a large advertisement in the *New York Times* and other newspapers, "A Letter from Martin Luther King from a Selma, Alabama Jail." In the letter, King noted that his incarceration followed just a few weeks after receiving the Nobel Peace Prize and that there were more African-Americans in jail with him than there were on the city's voting rolls. The letter concluded with a plea for funds to support the SCLC's work in the South. Back in Selma, King was finally released on Friday. Movement leaders called for a cessation of demonstrations over the weekend, but vowed to renew them on Monday if the county did not comply with the court's orders. More than three thousand three hundred protesters, mostly black, had so far been arrested during the campaign, though all but twenty had been released from jails and work camps in Dallas County. Throughout the week, the overcrowded cells had rung "with the inmates' noisy music." The remaining twenty were still being held in contempt of court charges for demonstrating while court was in session. Over the weekend, a group of fifteen congressmen visited Selma to investigate conditions.[24]

Demonstrations resumed on Monday and the Reverend James Bevel of the SCLC was arrested for demonstrating outside the courthouse and ordered to spend five days in jail. Later in the week, he became ill and was taken to an

African-American hospital, where he was chained to a bed and accompanied by an around-the-clock guard. On Wednesday, February 10, a group of one hundred sixty-five demonstrators, children and teenagers, stood in a silent vigil outside the courthouse, a few holding signs urging Dallas County to ease voter registration restrictions on African-Americans. Suddenly, at mid-afternoon, Clark and about twenty members of his posse emerged from the courthouse and motioned for the young people to follow him. The forced march progressed from a rapid walk to a full run as Clark led the protesters more than two miles into Dallas County. Most of the police rode in cars, spelling those who assaulted the students with cattle prods and nightsticks along the way. At last, the exhausted young people fled into a private yard by the road and refused to go any farther. Reporters had been kept from Selma by a blockade at the Edmund Pettus Bridge. When later asked about the bizarre incident, Clark said that he had been taking them to another facility in the county when "they escaped." Reporters found many of the students still in the yard, singing freedom songs. That evening, two mass meetings were held in response to Clark's actions, and civil rights organizers cancelled a planned march in Birmingham to converge on Selma instead. Demonstrations resumed on Thursday, but no arrests were made. Clark himself was hospitalized on Friday for "exhaustion." More than two hundred African-Americans, including many of the young people from Wednesday's forced "march," held a prayer vigil for Clark outside the courthouse. One demonstrator told reporter John Herbers, "It just wasn't the same without Jim Clark fussing and fuming. We honestly miss him." The following day, King was also ordered to bed in Atlanta for what his doctor called "exhaustion."[25]

Like Greenwood and a dozen other towns in Mississippi before it, the violence in Selma was part of a never-ending cycle, like a song on repeat on a record player. The Reverend Samuel Welles writes of numerous instances of abuse and recalls that he lived in a constant state of fear. On one occasion in February, a group decided to sing and pray at the Dallas County Courthouse. Five blocks from the courthouse, heavily armed police lined a barricade. A policeman walked up and struck Welles in the eye with his fist, knocking him down. Welles staggered to his feet, just as the police began beating members of his small group. Welles told his people to return to the church. "Then the police really started whipping us," Welles said. "The police started beating women with big sticks. That's the first time in my life I've seen a man hit a woman with all his might." As they fled back to the church, the police followed. Welles was struck again and again. That night, those who were able marched again. "We started out singing 'Nearer My God to Thee.' That's the song the people were singing when the *Titanic* sunk. The same policeman caught me the second time in the dark and hit me on the other side of my face. He stomped and kicked me so hard that I had pain in my side for years after that."[26]

And so the unequal engagement continued. King's urbane aide, the Reverend C. T. Vivian, was smashed in the mouth by Clark himself for calling the sheriff a "brute" and comparing him to Hitler for refusing to allow more voters to register. Vivian was then arrested on the scene for "criminal provocation" and contempt of court. King, now out of bed, that evening delivered the "strongest" speech of the campaign, enjoining demonstrators to engage in "broader forms of civil disobedience," and local leaders urged blacks to boycott downtown stores. In Marion on the evening of February 18, three generations of an African-American family were beaten in one night for their efforts and one, Jimmie Lee Jackson, was critically wounded during the aftermath of a demonstration. Jackson had joined his family and four hundred others at a mass meeting at Zion's Chapel Methodist Church. After the services, the group marched the one block to the Marion City Jail. Alabama state troopers brutally halted the march and during the subsequent chaos, Jackson was beaten and shot in the stomach. Among those present in the furor was Clark. When asked why he was in Marion, Clark responded, "Things got a little too quiet for me over in Selma tonight. It made me nervous."[27] Alabama by now had turned into a two-front engagement, with activities in both Selma and Marion. While Selma drew much of the national media, violence against blacks and newspaper reporters escalated on an uninterrupted basis in Marion. Arrayed against the demonstrators were police, state troopers, Klansmen, and Clark's auxiliary paramilitary group—"anybody, really, who felt like beating folks up," recalled one marcher.[28] With these forces roaming the streets of both cities looking for trouble, Captain Wilson Baker, Selma's Commissioner of Public Safety—and widely considered the lone moderate among the city's law enforcement officials— convinced Hosea Williams and other black officials to remain on the predominately African-American side of Selma after the shooting. "Jimmie Lee Jackson is near death tonight after a night march," Baker pleaded with congregants outside Brown Chapel. "You say you are nonviolent people, so go back into the church."[29]

After the events in Marion, Alabama governor George Wallace banned nighttime demonstrations in the state. But when a group of young people attempted to march on the Selma courthouse just before dark on Tuesday February 23, Baker again convinced them to return to Brown Chapel instead, displaying an "attitude of firmness and diplomacy" instead of violence or arrest. Baker was continually at odds with "Col." Al Lingo, Director of the Alabama Highway Patrol, and his irregulars, now back in Selma after fomenting much of the violence in Marion the previous week. The students, numbering more than one hundred, reluctantly returned to the church, singing, apparently without a hint of irony, "Ain't Gonna Let Nobody Turn Me 'Round." Also that week, the *New York Times* reported that, for the first time, white moderates in Selma had begun meetings to search for ways to end the violence. Perhaps spurred by the behind-the-scenes work of Federal District Judge Daniel H. Thomas, who had longtime ties in the city, and the presence of additional registrars, two hundred and sixty-six African-Americans registered to vote on Monday, March 1. This was accomplished despite a driving rain and Clark's refusal to allow most of the applicants to wait inside the courthouse during the downpour.[30]

When Jackson died of his wounds on February 26, a host of SCLC officials, including King and Bevel, attended the two funerals (Brown Chapel in Selma and Zion Methodist in Marion), where he was called a "martyr" and given a "hero's burial." At the second service, Bevel proposed for the first time a march from Selma to Montgomery, beginning on Sunday, to dramatize the difficulties in voter registration and honor Jackson's death. The service opened with "In the Sweet By and By" and closed with the overflow congregation standing, holding hands, and singing "We Shall Overcome" as Jackson's parents and grandparents listened.[31] Jackson was buried on March 3 in Marion and thousands viewed the body. The funeral procession passed the café where he had been shot.[32]

King and Abernathy, along with many of the SCLC leaders, generally stayed at the home of Sullivan and Jean Jackson while in Selma. On the particularly difficult days, when King would find himself "in a distressed state and in need of picking up," he would often call Mahalia Jackson. According to Jean, Mahalia would "counsel, console and sing to him," especially his "favorite" song, "Amazing Grace."[33]

Behind the scenes, Wallace met with Lingo to discuss the level of appropriate force that could be used should the Selma protesters attempt another march. Lingo then met with Clark. When Baker got wind of the meeting, he told Selma Mayor Joseph Smitherman that Lingo and Clark were intent on turning Sunday's march into a "blood-letting" and he "wanted no part of it." Wallace then issued a statement prohibiting Sunday's march on U.S. 80 in the interests of "public safety." At a press conference, Wallace said that he had authorized state troopers to use "whatever measures are necessary to prevent" the march.[34]

On the morning of Saturday March 6, Selma residents awoke to see something perhaps never before experienced in the Deep South—seventy-two white Alabamians demonstrating for equality for African-Americans. The group, which called itself the Concerned White Citizens of Alabama (CWCA), was led by the Reverend Joseph Ellwanger of St. Paul's Lutheran Church in Birmingham, a longtime civil rights activist. Appalled by Jackson's death, Ellwanger organized the group, primarily composed of ministers and university professors. The small band, which included Ellwanger's pregnant wife Joyce, formed a line around the courthouse, where they found themselves between an estimated five hundred black protesters and more than a hundred jeering, threatening whites armed with baseball bats and lengths of pipe. Ellwanger read a statement calling for the registration of blacks throughout the state and the group sang "America the Beautiful." In an effort to drown out the CWCA, whites broke into a ragged chorus of "Dixie." The CWCA and several hundred African-Americans across the street from the courthouse responded with "We Shall Overcome." Before the song was completed, however, segregationists began shoving the protesters and attacking reporters and cameramen. Only a quick appearance by Baker and his men prevented further violence. The CWCA returned to the Reformed Presbyterian Church, where SNCC members and others met them to "rousing applause." And when the Ellwangers returned to St. Paul's in Birmingham, the congregation had a party and sang "When the Saints Go Marching In" as the couple entered.[35]

King's return to Selma prompted a series of meetings with his advisers and supporters. Both SNCC and SCLC staffs could feel the "disillusionment and impatience . . . surging through the black community" following Jackson's funeral. Over SNCC objections, the SCLC leadership agreed to Sunday as the date for the march from Selma to Montgomery to present Wallace with voter registration petitions and, more importantly, to keep the pressure on both Alabama and the federal government. King left for Washington to meet with the president and later said that the two had conferred on a voting rights bill that Johnson indicated would be presented to Congress shortly. After the meeting, King flew to Atlanta, leaving Hosea Williams in charge of preparations, not wanting to embarrass the president by leading the march or becoming an issue in the administration's efforts to marshal congressional support for the bill.[36]

### Sunday, March 7

On the morning of what came to be called Bloody Sunday, more than two thousand people squeezed into Brown Chapel AME in the eerily quiet city. For once, the phalanxes of police and armed irregulars were nowhere in sight. The mood was somber following the terror and confusion of the previous days and Williams warned those present not to fight back. During a period of silent prayer, a single voice, a "thin soprano," cut through the quiet, "God will take care of you / Be not dismayed whate'er betide / God will take care of you." The rest of the congregation joined the soloist: "Beneath His wings of love abide / God will take care of you." More than five hundred of those present rose and left the church, still singing softly, and walked down Sylvan Avenue holding their tiny American flags.[37] At the front of the long line, which included both children and the elderly, was Williams. He was accompanied by the SNCC's John Lewis, who was marching not as an SNCC staffer but as an individual in this SCLC-sponsored march. Sensing a problem as they neared the Alabama River, Williams whispered to Lewis, "John, can you swim?" Lewis replied, "No." "I can't, either," Williams said, "and I'm sure we're gonna end up in that river."[38] Some marchers carried "an assortment of packs, bedrolls and lunch sacks"; all were bundled up against the chill. As they approached the Edmund Pettus Bridge, named for Selma's Civil War hero, they passed dozens of Clark's heavily armed posse members standing on the side streets and in alleys. Still marching two-by-two, the protesters were met at the bridge by what Lewis called "a sea of troopers." Major John Cloud approached Williams and Lewis and told them, "This is unlawful assembly. Your march is not conducive to the public safety. You are ordered to disperse and go back to your church or to your homes." Williams asked, "May we have a word with the major?" Cloud responded, "There is no word to be had." After a few moments, Cloud said, "You have two minutes to turn around and go back to your church." The entire column, only a few of whom had heard the exchange, stood quietly in response. In less than two minutes, the major shouted, "Troopers, advance." Donning their gas masks, the officers charged forward, flailing away with their billy clubs and bullwhips. "This time I felt it was really, really the end," Lewis recalled. Lewis was smashed in the head by a billy club and fell. "The troopers rushed forward," reported Roy Reed, "their blue uniforms and white helmets blurring into a flying wedge as they moved. The wedge moved with such force that it seemed almost to pass over the waiting column instead of through it. The first 10 or 20 Negroes were swept to the ground screaming, arms and legs flying, and packs and bags went skittering across the grassy divider strip and on the pavement on both sides." Clouds of tear gas billowed over the scene. The whites watching the melee "whooped and cheered." Clark's voice could be heard screaming, "Get those god-damned niggers! And get those god-damned white niggers!"[39]

At the initial charge, those farther back in the column turned to run, only to be met by still more of Clark's and Lingo's irregulars, who attacked them on Selma's streets, sidewalks, and front yards with bullwhips and nightsticks. Several women lay by the side of the bridge, including Amelia Boynton, one of the leaders of the Selma Movement. When the women did not respond to the trooper's initial demands to get up, they were hit with more tear gas canisters. Choked by the gas, the line of protesters crumbled. Four ambulances had accompanied the marchers, but the vehicles were blocked by troopers two blocks from the bridge. Eventually, one ambulance was allowed to cross and it weaved through the road, avoiding the hats, overnight bags, and umbrellas dropped by panicked marchers, as it headed for the bridge. The rampage continued for several hours, the entire scene enveloped by a thick fog of choking tear gas, with Clark and Lingo's posses now beating those who had escaped the initial surge of troopers. Reporters from various newspapers recorded numerous incidents of wanton violence and cruelty, including the use of bullwhips on fleeing women. When Clark's men tried to physically force the dazed and battered protesters back into Brown Chapel, bystanders responded with rocks and bricks. Only the intervention of Baker, whose men physically restrained Lingo's and Clark's forces from entering the church, saved further violence. At the church, Lewis, bleeding profusely from a head wound, recalled, "I made a little speech in the church. I made a statement to the effect that 'the United States Government can send troops to Vietnam but cannot protect the poor people of Alabama.'" The initial estimates placed the number hospitalized at seventeen, with at least another forty requiring medical attention, many on the floor of Brown Chapel. At the mass meeting that evening at Brown Chapel, those who braved the roving patrols of Clark's men and posse were angry. Williams, who was one of the few who was not injured, told the crowd of more than seven hundred, "I fought in World War II and I was captured by the German army, and I want to tell you that the Germans never were as inhuman as the state troopers of Alabama."[40]

That same evening, as many Americans were watching the movie *Judgment at Nuremberg*, ABC News interrupted the broadcast with a report detailing the assault, clearly showing the attack on the quiet column by troopers, "the flailing clubs, the stampeding horses, the jeering crowd, the fleeing blacks." President Johnson met with his advisers, including the Justice Department, crafting a response.[41] Late that night at Brown Chapel, the injured and angry sat in the pews and on the floors, still receiving treatment in the makeshift hospital. Some of the children continued to cry from the emotion and effects of the tear gas. Young Sheyann Webb was there, holding her friend Rachel, listening to the sounds of Lingo's men patrolling the streets:

> All of a sudden, somebody there started humming. I think they were moaning and it just went into the humming of a freedom song. It was real low, but some of us children began humming along, slow and soft. At first I didn't even know what it was, what song, I mean. It was like a funeral sound, a dirge. Then I recognized it—"Ain't Gonna Let Nobody Turn Me 'Round." I'd never heard it or hummed it that way before. But it just started to catch on, and the people began to pick it up. It started to swell, the humming. Then we began singing the words. We sang, "Ain't gonna let George Wallace turn me 'round." And, "Ain't gonna let Jim Clark turn me 'round." "Ain't gonna let no state trooper turn me 'round." Ain't gonna let no horses . . . ain't gonna let no tear gas—ain't gonna let nobody turn me 'round. *Nobody!*

Webb said the sound of the singing drew people from the nearby apartments to the church because, she said, they knew "something was happening": "We was singing and telling the world that we hadn't been whipped, that we had won. *Just all of a sudden something happened that night and we knew in that church that—Lord Almighty—we had really won, after all. We had won!* I think we all realized it at the same time, that we had won something that day, because people were standing up and singing like I'd never heard them before."[42]

Throughout the night, "possemen" continued to roam through Selma's poorer neighborhoods, "clubbing" blacks and shouting, "Get out of town!" at African-Americans. "We want all niggers off the streets!" As the news of the events in Selma spread, both the national and international reactions reflected the anger and horror many felt. From Atlanta, King called the events "a reign of terror" and said that troopers "brutalized" African-Americans on a "peaceful, orderly march." King also announced plans for another march, only this time with the full protection of the federal government. Selma city officials had earlier asked Federal District Judge Frank M. Johnson, Jr., to sign an order prohibiting further marches. However, King's announcement that there would be more marches despite the order and the horrific scenes from the night news had galvanized the movement's supporters and hundreds streamed into the city. The SCLC and other organizations appealed and asked for an immediate ruling on the order. The following day, Lingo, the state director of public safety, admitted that his troops were present as well and that their use of force, and the force used by Clark's officers and irregulars, had been cleared in advance by Wallace. Across the country, thousands joined in protest marches against the police action in Selma. In Detroit, Governor George W. Romney and Mayor Jerome P. Cavanagh led an estimated ten thousand people through downtown.[43]

Mahalia Jackson dictated a long telegram to Johnson, imploring the president ("God has given you the power to free us and all people.") to provide protection for the marchers.[44] From Copenhagen, jazz legend Louis Armstrong told reporters that he had become "physically ill" watching the mounted police beating the helpless marchers. "They would beat Jesus if he was black and marched," Armstrong said. Armstrong, who financially supported movement causes, was at the peak of his popularity with the release of his version of "Hello Dolly." He asked, "Tell me, how is it possible that human beings treat each other in this way today? Hitler is dead a long time—or is he?"[45]

And, like thousands of others, when reporter and novelist George B. Leonard saw the graphic footage, he was both horrified and enraged. "A shrill cry of terror, unlike any sound that had passed through a TV set," he wrote of the grainy images on his television, "rose up as the troopers lumbered forward, stumbling sometimes on fallen bodies." Leonard immediately booked a flight from San Francisco and later wrote vividly of the hours he spent speaking with other like-minded pilgrims in airports, on airplanes, and in shared rental cars—all heading for Selma. To protect the arriving supporters, movement officials in Selma devised an intricate plan to smuggle as many demonstrators as possible into the city without drawing the attention of law enforcement. Finally at Brown Chapel, Leonard writes that he thought of the song "John Brown's Body," even as he met and later walked with Charles Evers, James Farmer, James Forman, and Ralph Abernathy. "Perhaps the worst sin in life," King told Leonard and those assembled at the church that night, "is to know right and not to do it."[46]

Judge Johnson, an independent-minded federal jurist who was hated by Wallace and whose home was guarded each night by a federal marshal, ordered several days of hearings on the injunction, beginning Thursday March 11. He also ordered the announced Tuesday march—and all other marches, protests, and demonstrations—cancelled until a ruling was issued. Opinion within the SCLC was sharply divided on whether to abide by the judge's order. Some, like Forman, argued that the long delay would allow "the campaign's spirit to fade." After twelve hours of discussion with his advisers and movement-related lawyers, King and the advisers moved to Monday evening's mass meeting, where he announced that the Tuesday morning march would take place after all. What followed was one of the more controversial incidents of the Selma movement. All morning on Tuesday, the SNCC "freedom chorus" stood on the steps of Brown Chapel singing "Ain't gonna let nobody turn me 'round / I'm gonna keep on walkin', keep on talkin' / Marching up to freedom land." Those in the gathering crowd expected to march. As one minister said, "We didn't come from all over the country just to stand around Selma." Among those arriving in town that morning was Mario Savio, who would later gain fame for his work in the "free speech movement," as part of a contingent from the University of California, Berkeley, along with the wives of several congressmen and cabinet officials. The Reverend Fred Shuttlesworth arrived from Birmingham in time to march. King finally entered Brown Chapel at 1 p.m., passing through a "freedom chorus" of supporters still singing ""Marching up to freedom land." He told the still growing crowd, "I have no alternative today." The decision had been made to march. At 2 p.m., King led an estimated two thousand people, including newly arrived white protesters, all singing "We Shall Overcome," to the now infamous bridge. Once there, the entire group sang again. "If you have never heard 2,000 Negroes and whites sing 'We Shall Overcome,' hands joined and swaying in eight-abreast rows on U.S. 80 just east of the Alabama River, there is little that can be said to convey the experience," one participant wrote. Waiting at the bridge was a contingent of law enforcement officials. King stopped the procession. Several prayers were offered, then King solemnly and surprisingly turned around and led the mile-long procession *back* to Brown Chapel Methodist AME, singing, as Charles E. Fager has noted, a rendition of "Ain't Gonna Let Nobody Turn Me 'Round" that sounded more than "a little ironical." Both King and Wallace had been in separate negotiations that morning with the White House and both had apparently agreed to the abbreviated march. However, SNCC staffers and others, many still in pain from the Sunday assaults, had not been informed of the agreement and forcefully expressed their displeasure at the apparent "retreat." Still, even as some marchers wept in disappointment, King told the mass meeting that evening at Brown Chapel that marchers had won a "great triumph" and the day's abortive march was "the greatest demonstration for freedom, the greatest confrontation so far in the South."[47]

After the mass meeting, twenty clergymen, of the hundreds of religious leaders who were still continuing to converge on Selma, convened for supper at Walker's Café, a "soul food" restaurant on the unofficial "safe" side of town, where they ate and talked with movement volunteers, reporters from African-American publications, and local residents while Sam Cooke's "A Change Is Gonna Come" played on the jukebox. After the meal, four of the clergymen inadvertently strayed into white-held territory and were attacked by a group of whites.[48] One man, the Reverend James J. Reeb, a Unitarian minister from Boston, suffered a particularly savage blow to the head with a club or lead pipe. All four clergymen were hospitalized, but Reeb soon sank into a coma and, only after long delays, was taken by ambulance to Birmingham. Reeb had been among those moved by footage of the attack on the Pettus Bridge and decided to come to support the movement in Selma.[49]

The Selma campaign then entered a strange and deadly impasse, a *Sitzkrieg* where both sides uneasily awaited Judge Johnson's decision. Throughout Wednesday, March 10, different groups attempted smaller marches in the city. One crowd of three hundred, led by Abernathy, was stopped repeatedly in its efforts to march on the Dallas County Courthouse. That evening, following the mass meeting at Brown Chapel, the congregants surged into the streets singing "We Love Everybody." A reporter noted that one of the troopers "snapped his fingers in rhythm to the song." In Montgomery, more than five hundred SNCC members and supporters protested outside the state capitol building.[50] Back in Selma, one group of demonstrators was stymied on their march to the courthouse at the corner of Selma Avenue by Smitherman, Baker, and seventeen "nervous-looking" city policemen, on the edge of the housing project that flanked Brown Chapel. Movement leaders urged their followers not to leave their district and Baker strung rope across the intersection, blocking their way to the courthouse. The roped-off area quickly became the focal point for demonstrations. Even the rope itself was dubbed "the Berlin Wall" and waves of protesters over the next few days and nights used the protest spiritual "Joshua Fit the Battle of Jericho" as the basis for a new freedom song: "We've got a rope that's a Berlin Wall, Berlin Wall, Berlin Wall / We've got a rope that's a Berlin Wall, in Selma, Alabama / We're gonna stand here till it falls, till it falls, till it falls. . . . Hate is the thing that built that wall, built that wall, built that wall. . . . Love is the thing that'll make it fall, make it fall, make it fall." The singing and praying continued through the night, despite a cold rain.[51]

On the evening of Thursday March 11, Baker himself told those holding vigil at the Berlin Wall that Reeb had died in a Birmingham hospital. Baker arrested Reeb's four assailants, but they soon bonded out on an obscure Alabama law. One of those arrested, Elmer L. Cook, had seventeen previous arrests for assault and battery on his record. Brown Chapel quickly filled for an impromptu memorial service. At the Berlin Wall, protesters continued singing throughout the evening. When the rains resumed, they produced plastic sheeting to shield themselves until Baker ordered the sheets removed. The protesters complied, then joined in singing "We Shall Not Be Moved."[52]

The standoff in the streets continued until the third day, Friday March 12, when the Berlin Wall finally came down, cut by Baker in the midst of yet another chorus of the freedom song by the same name. Baker complained that he was "just tired of them singing about it all the time and making such a symbol of the damn thing" and implored the protesters not to violate the judge's order to march. The demonstrators, who numbered about two hundred, cut the rope into souvenirs and quickly improvised new words for "Joshua Fit the Battle of Jericho": "The invisible wall, the invisible wall, the invisible wall / The invisible wall is a Berlin wall / In Selma, Alabama / The trooper's cars, the trooper's cars, the trooper's cars / The trooper's cars are a Berlin wall / In Selma, Alabama." Later in the afternoon, Smitherman and the city council voted not to allow a memorial march honoring Reeb. In Washington, DC, hundreds of protesters marched along Pennsylvania Avenue singing "We Shall Overcome" and chanting "Freedom" as President Johnson told reporters he had placed seven hundred federal troops on alert, should Selma erupt in violence again.[53]

The informal perimeter, which actually extended for two city blocks around Brown Chapel, was manned by state troopers and city policemen and augmented by Alabama Alcoholic Beverage Control Board agents and conservation officers. Through the long days and nights, the officers standing uncomfortably or dozing in their cars were serenaded with "I Love Everybody in My Heart" as demonstrators clapped their hands and stomped their feet in "that steady, inexorable rhythm" and repeatedly shouted, "I love all the troopers," "I love all the posse," and even "I love Jim Clark in my *heart*," "with both the melody and the philosophy combining to draw out the last word for emphasis, and sounding about as genuine as anyone could under the circumstances," writes Fager. "You can't make me doubt them," went the next verse, "Cuz I know too much about them / No, you can't make me doubt them in my heart." The demonstrators, at different times featuring top religious leaders from various denominations and faiths, stood just feet away and prayed constantly for troopers and assorted other officers. By the end of the week, the officers and agents manning the makeshift lines were imploring the governor to replace them with the National Guard.[54] For the eager young activists stationed at the barricade, the long hours were spent in singing and "contriving" ideas and schemes to further the movement's aims: "Let's sing all night." "Let's don't eat tomorrow." "Let's see if we can get somewhere without getting arrested." "Let's write a song."[55]

On Sunday March 14, massive protests raged across the country and demonstrators called on the President and Congress to protect marchers in Selma. One of the largest gatherings—more than twenty-five thousand people—met at the historic abolitionist Arlington Street Church in Boston, with most standing in silence outside on the grass of the Boston Common, to attend a memorial service for James Reeb. Back in Selma, shoving and pushing between the opposing forces continued long into the night, with supporters of the movement continuing to stream into town. When a group of demonstrators moved toward the courthouse, the former president of Notre Dame, the Reverend John J. Cavanaugh, and Baker went nose to nose in a direct confrontation. Among those arriving was a group of nuns from St. Louis. Novelist Gay Talese writes that one of Selma's most "unforgettable" moments came when the nuns "learned, or . . . tried to learn" spirituals and freedom songs. He marveled at the sight of "tiny, red-faced nuns standing arm in arm with tall Negro boys, swaying from side to side, clapping hands, kicking feet slightly and singing out, 'If you want FREE-dom, stomp your feet.' (Thump, thump, thump); If you want FREE-dom, you got to shout. ('Yeah, yeah, yeah.')" Talese and other writers also noted the constant sounds of freedom songs throughout the city. Also on Sunday, Selma officials said they would again enforce the city's ban on marches and demonstrations, making mass arrests rather than dispersing crowds. As a result, Baker reinstituted the police blockade on Sylvan Street, near Brown Chapel, where singing and praying protesters had kept an around-the-clock vigil for days. Baker erected a "flimsy wooden barrier" where the rope dubbed "the Berlin wall" had once been strung. "I wanted to give them something to sing about," Baker said. The Selma memorial service for Reeb was held on Monday afternoon. During the service, Abernathy received word that Judge Thomas had ordered the city to permit a memorial procession in Reeb's honor to the courthouse, effectively immediately. Those in attendance, which included Walter Reuther of the United

Auto Workers and Archbishop Iakovos of the Greek Orthodox Church, walked solemnly to the courthouse. As prescribed by the judge, a prayer was said, King offered a short homily, and a single, heartfelt chorus of "We Shall Overcome" was sung before the marchers returned to Brown Chapel.[56]

Monday March 15 marked a significant date in the movement. After months of wrangling with Congress, and spurred by the international revulsion at the violence against peaceful protesters on the Pettus Bridge, President Johnson now believed he had a voting rights bill that would pass. Throughout the day, legislators spoke in favor of or against the proposed legislation. At 9 p.m., working from an original draft by Richard N. Goodwin until an hour before a national broadcast before all three television networks, Johnson gave one of the most powerful speeches of his presidency. Inserting stories from his life in rural Texas, denouncing the violence against protesters in Selma, applauding the heroism of African-Americans in that city, and calling for quick passage of the legislation, Johnson's forty-five minute speech before the joint session of Congress was interrupted forty times by applause, twice with standing ovations. But one phrase in particular resounded most strongly among rapt black listeners throughout the country: "But even if we pass this bill, the battle will not be over. What happened in Selma is part of a far larger movement which reaches into every section and state of America. It is the effort of American Negroes to secure for themselves the full blessings of American life. Their cause must be our cause, too. Because it's not just Negroes, but really it's all of us, who must overcome the crippling legacy of bigotry and injustice. And we shall overcome." Outside of the Deep South, the response to the speech was overwhelmingly positive, even laudatory. Lewis remembered that "tears actually came to Dr. King's eyes when President Johnson said, 'We shall overcome.' It was a great speech, probably one of the finest statements in support of voter rights for all people." One of King's aides later told Goodwin that "no speech by a white man had ever moved him, but now he felt the Negro cause was actually going to succeed." Rachel West and her family and friends took a break from their demonstrations at the Berlin Wall to watch the speech. When Johnson said, "And we shall overcome," she recalled that "all the people in the room, my sisters, my parents, the ministers, all cried out and applauded." The president's daughter, Lynda Bird Johnson, said, "It was just like that hymn, 'Once to every man and nation comes a moment to decide.'"[57]

In Montgomery, where the bulk of SNCC supporters had moved after the split over the original march, daily demonstrations and protests were invariably followed by beatings and arrests. The SNCC's Forman denounced the proposed voting rights bill and claimed that Johnson's use of the words "We shall overcome" robbed the song of its "integrity" and reduced it to a "tinkling empty symbol." Even as the country was applauding the president's speech, mounted sheriff's deputies rode into one hundred fifty demonstrators in Montgomery's African-American neighborhoods. On Tuesday, mounted state and county police, some "flailing with nightsticks and ropes," waded into another six hundred protesters on a residential street heading for the courthouse, aided by a number of "possemen" on foot. The *New York Times* and other news outlets featured prominent pictures of the action on their front pages, with black and white demonstrators bleeding, fleeing, and calling for help. Almost immediately, Montgomery officials apologized for the melee, calling it a "mix up." Just a few blocks away, Judge Johnson continued to hear testimony concerning the proposed Selma to Montgomery march. Alabama state troopers testified that the marchers would "pose a traffic hazard." Lingo and other state authorities declared that they had used only "the bare minimum necessary force" during the March 7 attack on the Pettus Bridge and had actually prevented a "massacre" by protecting the protesters from a "waiting white mob." Still bandaged and bruised, Lewis testified to the contrary. To augment Lewis's statement, SCLC lawyers showed clips from the brutal assault taken by the CBS News team, including those of Lewis. Lewis watched Johnson's face during the showing, and later said he saw the judge's reactions change from "disgust" to "rage" before ordering a recess. On Tuesday, over the objection of Alabama state officials, attorneys for the proposed march presented Johnson with a detailed, five-day plan for the march. Johnson said he would reveal his decision the following day.[58]

On Wednesday, March 17, Judge Frank Johnson did just that. In addition to allowing the Selma to Montgomery march to take place, Johnson prohibited state officials from interfering. He noted that the federal government had expressed a willingness to respond to a request for additional protection for the marchers. Johnson also attacked the behavior of Clark and his posse throughout the events in Selma. In Montgomery, more than sixteen hundred people marched on the Montgomery County Courthouse, where King, Lewis, and others met with Montgomery Sheriff Mac Sim Butler for seven hours. When they emerged, Butler apologized for the department's actions the previous day and said that the city's volunteer sheriff's posse would no longer be employed to "handle" demonstrations. For their part, demonstrators agreed to apply for "official" parade permits for all future marches in Montgomery. And at that evening's mass meeting in Selma, Hosea Williams announced that the march would begin on Sunday, March 21.[59]

A frenzied period of preparation for the mammoth march ensued. Since Judge Johnson had ordered that only three hundred marchers would be allowed to traverse a particularly narrow, two-lane section of U.S. Highway 80, those three hundred had to be chosen by movement leaders—a difficult and delicate task given the already bruised egos among the main participants. Sites for camping had to be secured, also a troubling task where African-Americans still faced reprisals. Food, bedding, transportation, water stations, electric generators, portable toilets, and medical facilities had to be purchased or donated and arranged for a marching army that continued to grow daily with new arrivals in Selma. As they waited for Sunday, the new demonstrators slept on the floor and pews of Brown Chapel, in the homes of African-Americans, or even in their automobiles. In the Brown Chapel basement, piled high with supplies, groups sat around singing freedom songs to pass the time. At Friday night's mass meeting, Reverend John B. Morris's tape recorder captured a spiritual rendition of "Amen," complete with the joyful clapping, along with encouraging words from King and Bevel. Nor was George Wallace idle, filing appeals, convening emergency sessions of the Alabama legislature, and demanding that Washington pay for the state's expenses, but none of his tactics ultimately succeeded.[60]

### Sunday, March 21

Sunday dawned cold in Selma, with a temperature in the 40s, as thousands of people surged toward Brown Chapel African Methodist Episcopal Church. King was slated to conduct an 8 a.m. interdenominational service, followed by a 9:30 a.m. sermon, with the fifty-one mile march scheduled—though not expected—to begin at 10 a.m. The church quickly filled and hundreds gathered in the streets singing, "I want to go and march today, march today / I want to go and march today, in Selma, Alabama / We stand here with black and white, black and white, black and white / We stand here with black and white, in Selma, Alabama / In your heart, you know we're right, know we're right, know we're right / In your heart you know it's right, in Selma, Alabama / Step aside and let us by, let us by, let us by / Step aside and let us by, in Selma, Alabama." During the sermon, which actually began at 11, King recited lines of an old protest spiritual, "Walk together children / Walk together and don't you get weary / And it will lead us to the promised land." In their respective places along the route were two military police battalions, one hundred FBI agents, nearly one hundred federal marshals, and hundreds of soldiers from the newly federalized Alabama National Guard, even as two Army helicopters flew "low, flat arcs" over the chapel. The procession, estimated at thirty-two thousand people, slowly unwound from downtown and reached Edmund Pettus Bridge at 1:15 p.m. At the front of the line was a small mob of reporters and photographers, followed by King, Dick Gregory, Ralph Bunche, Lewis, actor Pernell Roberts, Rabbi Abraham Heschel, and other religious, political, labor, and movement leaders. The group sang the entire way, the sound of "We Shall Overcome" overwhelming the small knots of jeering whites who held signs that read "Nigger King Go Home," "Too Bad, Reeb" and "Meridian, Miss. Hates Niggers." Among those marching was actor Gary Merrill. "Why did I come?" he told a reporter. "Because I was too young for Lexington and Concord." Sunday's march lasted only seven miles; the massive column was so long that five different freedom songs could be sung simultaneously along the line with no confusion. That evening, transportation volunteers returned all but three hundred marchers back to Selma. Supper each night was coordinated by D. Elwyn Allan Smith, a Presbyterian professor at Pittsburgh Theological Seminary, and his cohort of pastors and seminarians. The singing of freedom songs and protest spirituals had continued throughout the day. It was, writes William G. Roy, inevitable: "There is probably no better context for making music than a long march. Mass meetings are mainly for speeches and dialogue; freedom rides have groups of people thrown together for long periods of empty time, but also allow individual activities like reading. Marching not only gathers large groups for long periods but invites the entraining coordination of chants and songs. Thus the Selma march displayed to a nation the movement at its most musical." For some, like Andrew Young, there were other considerations. Young continually raced up and down the length of the nearly mile-long procession. "If the people toward the back were lagging," Young writes, "or hadn't caught the song started in the front, I would walk and sing with them, 'Ain't gonna let nobody turn me 'round / I'm gonna keep on a-talking, keep on a-walking, marching up to freedom land.'"[61]

### Monday, March 22

Monday morning, as campers stirred, their shoes and boots crunched a light frost. Highway 80 narrowed to two lanes. As the marchers moved slowly into much-feared Lowndes County, the column broke into "We are not afraid" even as spotter planes buzzed overhead and jeeps and soldiers continued to flank the parade. Still, "the singing kept up" and desperately poor African-Americans emerged from their shacks, often dressed in rags, to cheer the marchers. The three hundred marchers, mostly African-Americans who had been jailed or beaten during Selma's registration battles, were scheduled to sleep on the property of seventy-eight-year-old Rosie Steele, who said she no longer feared white retaliation: "I almost feel like I might live long enough to vote myself." No African-American had registered to vote in Lowndes County until the previous week, though the county was 80 percent black. In New York, the *Times* published a large advertisement promoting "Broadway Answers Selma!," a benefit for Reeb's family, SNCC, and other civil rights–related organizations and programs. The concert, set for April 4, was scheduled to feature more than fifty singers and actors, including Carol Burnett, Art Carney, Maurice Chevalier, Sammy Davis, Sir John Gielgud, Walter Matthau, Robert Preston, and Barbra Streisand. NBC News began assembling a microwave tower in tiny Lowndesboro, midway between Selma and Montgomery, and a representative said that the network would begin broadcasting live footage of what was now called the Alabama Freedom March within forty-eight hours. Near the end of the day's march, demonstrators passed a group of whites, including a woman dressed as a stereotypical African-American cook. The small group laughed and pointed at the marchers until those closest began to sing, "Ain't Gonna Let Nobody Turn Me 'Round," and improvised one line as "Ain't gonna let Aunt Jemima turn me 'round."[62]

### Tuesday, March 23

A light drizzle turned to a driving rain by mid-morning as the three hundred marchers, including a limping King, suffering from blisters on his left foot, passed the halfway mark to Montgomery. Their destination was a farm owned by black Birmingham millionaire A. G. Gaston. Despite the deluge, the rain "merely challenged" the marchers, wrote Roy Reed, one of three *New York Times* reporters covering the event. "Their freedom songs rang out louder than ever." The marchers passed numerous hecklers along the way. When the jeering became abusive, the demonstrators responded with rousing verses of "We Shall Overcome." The presence of the MPs and troopers kept most angry whites at a safe distance, although at one point a white man ran along the road shaking his fist and screaming "Niggers, niggers, niggers, niggers, niggers!" at the marchers. The column simply sang louder. The procession passed a "dilapidated one-room" school for African-Americans. The thirty-four students filed outside and sang "We Shall Overcome" back to the column as it trooped by. Lewis, who was still recovering from the effects of the concussion he had received on the Pettus Bridge, marched doggedly through the rain. Later, he recalled one of the marchers' favorite songs from Tuesday: "I've been in the storm / I've been in the storm so long / I've been in the storm too long / Yeah, give me one more day / Give me one more day / Give me one more day to pray." The improvising continued throughout the march, Lewis said. "People would just start another line; people were very, very creative." One of those lines, he said, was "Oooh, Wallace, you never can kill us all / Segregation is about to fall." By Tuesday evening, a host of entertainers had been confirmed for the Wednesday evening concert on the outskirts of Montgomery, including Mahalia Jackson, Leonard Bernstein, Pete Seeger, Harry Belafonte, Odetta, Len Chandler, Dick Gregory, Joan Baez, Tony Bennett, and Sammy Davis, Jr., among others. Many of the actors and singers indicated that they would also join the procession for its entry into the city and sing outside the capitol building.[63]

One of Lewis's treasured memories of the march was singing a marching song by Chandler, written to "beat back" the rain: "Pick 'em up, lay 'em down, all the way from Selma town." The Reverend Henry Silva, who had once served as a bodyguard for King and was present at most civil rights–related activities, remembered the singing the most vividly of all of the activities along the route. "You knew you were in a dangerous situation," he later recalled, "but the adrenaline charge you get from listening to great preachers and great singing took away the fear. It made you part of something bigger." At King's personal invitation, Pete Seeger also marched the entire way. "It was Pete Seeger's thing come true," said a fellow marcher. "He went nuts trying to take down all the songs." Seeger recalled hearing "three of four freedom songs drifting up from different places along the line" and scurried to listen. "They were creating one great song after another—before our very eyes!" he wrote. "Imagine: they were changing 'You Can't Make Me Doubt Him' into 'I Love Everybody.'" That evening, in the sodden camp, Seeger drifted among the campfires, "jotting down lyrics like an anthropologist." The threat of attack by segregationists forced marchers to wear armbands and all were given strict instructions to remain at the campsite. "But they carried on," one organizer wrote. "People sang like they might never get another chance." Few of the three hundred were able to sleep in the ankle-deep mud at the campsite, and the marchers who returned to Selma or were driven on to Montgomery to spend the night had to find what accommodations they could. Gladys McFadden and the Loving Sisters, one of gospel's top groups, were among those who were taken to a hotel in Selma. The situation back in the city, she said, was tense, with crowds still roaming the streets, sometimes clashing with police. Locked in her hotel room, McFadden wrote "Crying Days Will Be Over After While" to commemorate the day. Mavis Staples has said that her father wrote "Marching up Freedom's Highway" for the march from Selma. "It felt like we were supposed to be there," she has said, "like we were supposed to be singing these songs." According to gospel singer Reverend Jeff Brown, other gospel artists marched at different times, including his group, the Sunset Travelers. Brown said he remembered singing "Take My Hand, Precious Lord" for King during the journey.[64]

**Wednesday, March 24**

Wednesday dawned warmer and brighter as thousands rejoined the march where U.S. 80 widened to four lanes once again. The final campsite, on the edge of Montgomery, was at the City of St. Jude, a complex of buildings including a school, church, and medical center operated by the Catholic Church. Just as marchers reached the city limits, another deluge of rain swamped them, but "the marchers pushed down the street joyfully, singing 'We Shall Overcome' at the top of their lungs." One of the most famous photographs of the Selma movement was taken on Wednesday and hundreds of Associated Press newspapers featured the shot of two men carrying American flags flanking the one-legged James Letherer of Saginaw, Michigan, who walked on crutches the entire fifty-one miles, and folk singer Chandler playing "Yankee Doodle" on a fife or small flute ("Wallace said we couldn't march / We knew he was a phony / Now we're marching all the way / To make him eat baloney"). At the "vanguard" of the massive march were the three hundred chosen to march the entire route and who sang freedom songs most of the way. "In the long perspective of this flat land," wrote one reporter, "it looked as if the line of flag-waving, singing, hand-clapping people went on forever." Some, as they reached the church grounds, began singing for the first time, "We *Have* Overcome." By late afternoon, St. Jude's large playing field was packed with an estimated ten thousand marchers and supporters and the understaffed, overworked volunteers were unable to get the food to the growing throng, once again standing in deep mud. An impressive array of famous cinema and stage personalities and musicians greeted the crowd, told an inspirational story or a joke, sang a song or two, and introduced the next star in line. A buoyant Harry Belafonte even sang "Kingston Town." In a now predictable bit of churlishness, Governor Wallace declared Thursday to be a holiday for all female state employees in Montgomery.[65]

The concert Wednesday evening, on a flimsy stage composed of donated coffins, unfolded before an estimated ten thousand movement supporters standing in a sea of mud, surrounded by an uneasy alliance between Alabama National Guardsmen and federal troops and observers.[66] Belafonte purchased the entire evening's house of Sammy Davis, Jr.'s, *Golden Boy* on Broadway so Davis could perform and continue the march the following morning.[67] Tony Bennett, also at Belafonte's invitation, performed Jule Styne's "Just in Time," shared a "bedraggled" hotel room with African-American jazz singer Billy Eckstine on the route, and marched with the others into Montgomery. Bennett and Eckstine found themselves walking next to Frank Sinatra's bodyguard Jilly Rizzo, who said Sinatra had sent him to join the march. Rizzo produced a pair of brass knuckles, in case, he said, someone did something "funny."[68] Dick Gregory, who had expressed his unhappiness at white artists performing at the March on Washington, later said that Peter, Paul & Mary's performance was one of the highlights of the concert in Montgomery. "Most of these black folks had never heard of Peter, Paul & Mary. But I knew when they got up on that stage, the songs they did were so close to the black spirituals . . . that's why they were always a big hit. Their music had the rhythm that we had in the Baptist church. They were one of the few folk groups that black folks could understand." Peter Yarrow particularly recalled the trio gathering around a single microphone and performing an uncommonly slow version of their hit "Blowin' in the Wind." "We sang it slowly," he said, "in the rhythm of that weariness, of that long march. And I remember feeling that our lives made sense."[69] Nina Simone cancelled a Village Gate show, hired a private plane, and arrived with her band just before their scheduled slot. Lit by an Air Force searchlight, Simone could see "gangs of armed white racists" prowling just beyond the perimeter. When her guitarist pulled up the stage apron looking for a plug for his amplifier, he saw, for the first time, the coffins and gasped, "Oh, my God." The drummer smirked and said, "Welcome to Montgomery." When Simone sang the line "Selma's got me so upset" from "Mississippi Goddam," the crowd roared.[70] One of the observers that day, Alan Levine, was concerned with the Alabama troops he saw. Each "guardsman's trigger finger," he noted, "tightened on the trigger of his rifle" when Simone sang "Mississippi Goddam." Nearly fifty years later, Levine said no performance he has ever seen since has rivaled Simone's "passionate denunciation of segregation" that night for "bravery and eloquence."[71]

**Thursday, March 25**

On the triumphal entry into Montgomery the next morning, many of those present—and the march had swelled to twenty-five thousand—knew they were experiencing a historic moment. Coretta Scott King reflected on how, ten years earlier, the Montgomery bus boycott had begun in Montgomery and how the occasion "had a very special meaning" for her.[72] "To me, there was never a march like this one before and hasn't been once since," John Lewis said. "It was a sense of community moving there. And as you walked, you saw people coming, waving, bringing you food or bringing you something to drink. You saw the power of the most powerful country on the face of the Earth."[73] Seeger marched into the former capital of the Confederacy with African-American folk singers Len Chandler and Jimmy Collier. At one point, Seeger, his notebook poised, asked a woman who had been singing if she could tell him the words to "Oh, Wallace." "The words?" she said. "Why, there are no words!" Nonplussed, Seeger asked her, "Well, do you know any of the verses?" She said, "Why sure. You just make 'em up. Here's a few." As Seeger wrote furiously, she paused. "Don't you know you can't write down freedom songs?" Seeger continued to try, eventually capturing at least some of the lyrics. If a song was only sung for a few minutes, he noted, it meant that "the spiritual isn't moving the singers." If a freely improvised freedom song is "going well," it might last ten minutes or longer. Anyone along the march was free to start a song and the song would continue "as long as anyone within earshot wanted to keep it going." Seeger and his wife Toshi found themselves just ahead of a group of teenage girls who sang constantly throughout the day. While the teenagers would occasionally sing a song they had learned in school, such as "America the Beautiful" or "Theme from *Exodus*," more often they sang freedom songs: "Ain't Gonna Let Segregation Turn Me 'Round," "Hold On," "Which Side Are You On?," "Woke Up This Morning," or "We Shall Overcome."[74] Collier, who walked with Seeger much of the way, said that despite the presence of the troops, the marchers had been scared the entire journey from Selma. "You know what happens when people are really scareder than shit?" he asked writer David King Dunaway. "They sing like they're not going to ever be able to sing again. And they eat, and it was that kind of atmosphere. People were really scared but they felt that they had to carry on. So the music was very important to making people feel good. Many of the songs were old Union songs, you know, right out of the thirties and so on, just different words."[75]

The Alabama Freedom March from Selma to Montgomery culminated at noon on the steps of the capitol building. King was flanked by most of the best-known movement leaders in the United States, including Rosa Parks, A. Philip Randolph, and Bayard Rustin, along with dozens of popular musicians and actors. Troops surrounded the sea of people, standing guard atop buildings and patrolling the side streets, but relatively little trouble was reported. Marchers were instructed to leave Montgomery as soon as possible after the rally, which lasted three and a half hours, though it would be Saturday before some of the demonstrators were able to secure transportation out of the city. Wallace had originally agreed to receive a petition calling for the state to end segregation, but instead sent an aide to accept it.[76]

The speech King gave on the steps remains one of his most enduring and provided a fitting bookend for a campaign that began in a small Alabama town whose message eventually reached Washington, DC, where it provided an important impetus for Congress to pass the Voting Rights Act. The speech, really more of a sermon, is a masterpiece of oratory, and Ralph Abernathy, who had been with King since the bus boycott on these same streets years earlier, was by his side. As was often the case, the sermon included references to the music of the movement:

"They told us we wouldn't get here, and there were those who said we would get here only over their dead bodies, but all the world today knows that we are here and that we are standing before the forces of power in the State of Alabama saying, 'We ain't goin' to let nobody turn us around.'" According to Abernathy, following a massive roar by the crowd, a venetian blind in Wallace's office parted slightly. The speech ended with what Abernathy called one of King's "finest climaxes."[77] "I know you are asking today, 'How long will [justice] take?' King asked the crowd. 'I come to say, it will not be long. How long? Not long because you still reap what you sow. How long? Not long 'cause mine eyes have seen the glory of the coming of the Lord, trampling out the vintage where the grapes of wrath are stored, Our God is marching on.'" The lyrics from "The Battle Hymn of the Republic," based on "John Brown's Body," delivered on the steps of the capitol of the Confederacy, completes the song's evolution from "patriotic standard" to hymn to freedom song, and the allusions were not lost on the African-Americans in the vast audience in Montgomery or watching on television.[78] Andrew Young recalled that the closing words, the entire throng "roared in unison" when King concluded with "the blood-and history-soaked refrain."[79]

Writer Margaret Long, whose insightful articles for *The Progressive* had chronicled the movement for several years, proclaimed that the concert on the steps of the "Cradle of the Confederacy" was "the most rousing and beautiful singing of the Movement in the South" featuring "select young talent from our singing insurrections and some of the nation's great folk singers and Negro artists." She believed the presence of so many "stern-faced Alabama boys obliged as Federalized National Guardsmen to protect the march," as well as "the hundreds of capitol employees standing spellbound for hours on the steps" was so cathartic that it "seemed to inspire everyone to sing with the verve and power of the professionals." She particularly noted the protest spiritual, "You Gotta Move When the Spirit Say Move," a "rollicking, confident combination of old words and new threats": "You got to *work* when the spirit say *work,*" "*preach* when the spirit say *preach.*"[80]

However, the celebration of the day was again muted by sadness as word spread of yet another murder. Viola Gregg Liuzzo, wife of a union official from Detroit and a longtime activist, was shot to death Thursday evening after delivering another group of demonstrators back to Selma. With Liuzzo had been Leroy Moten, an African-American teenager, who saw a group of men in another automobile pull up beside Liuzzo's 1963 sedan and open fire with a high-powered rifle. Liuzzo, a member of the SCLC, was part of the march's transportation committee. The following evening, her body was transported by Teamsters president Jimmy Hoffa's plane back to Detroit. As the body was loaded, a solemn group of civil rights workers stood on the tarmac and sang "We Shall Overcome." President Johnson called her husband, Anthony, to express his condolences. That night, Johnson took the airwaves again to "declare war" on the Ku Klux Klan and announce the arrest of four Klan suspects in the murder investigation. Moton, who had accompanied Liuzzo in transporting demonstrators for most of the final days of the march, said they had been harassed by whites throughout the day. Moton was later forced to leave Montgomery after he began receiving death threats as well. Memorial services for Liuzzo were held in Selma at Brown Chapel and at Trickem Baptist Church in Lowndes County, just a few miles from the site of the attack. The mass meeting that followed was the first of its kind in the county. At her Detroit funeral on March 31, King, Roy Wilkins of the NAACP, James Farmer of CORE, and Lewis of the SNCC, along with Hoffa and Walter P. Reuther of the United Auto Workers were all in attendance. The service ended with the singing of "We Shall Overcome." Among those Liuzzo had driven on Thursday was Tony Bennett, who said she had dropped him off at the airport just prior to her murder. When Len Chandler passed the spot of Liuzzo's murder on the lonely road on his way out of Montgomery, he began writing a song that was completed by the time he reached Atlanta: "It was Jackson on the roads of Alabama / It was Reeb on the roads of Alabama / William Moore is dead and gone / And this killing still goes on / Now Liuzzo's on the road of Alabama."[81]

### Selma Aftermath

Under the direction of Mayor Smitherman and the still imposing presence of Clark, Selma fought and gave ground only grudgingly in its civil rights battle through the hot summer of 1965. Most of the volunteers eventually left and local activists were exhausted, battered, or both. Smitherman and the city council repeatedly rebuffed any call for substantive change in the city's segregation laws, even as federal registrars arrived to insure that blacks could register to vote.[82]

When the Voting Rights Act of 1965 finally cleared through Congress by comfortable margins, Lewis was among those summoned to the White House on August 6 to observe the signing in the President's Room, where Lincoln had signed the bill freeing the slaves pressed into service by the Confederacy one hundred four years earlier. Bearing scars that would remain with him the rest of his life, he received a pen, as did King, Rosa Parks, Vivian Malone, and others. The law suspended literacy tests in twenty-six states, including the Deep South, appointed federal examiners to replace local officials as voter registrars, and authorized the attorney general to take action against local or state authorities that required a poll tax. Lewis called the passage of the Voting Rights Act the "culmination, a climax of a very long road, a road that had led from Montgomery through the South, only to end in Montgomery once again." Johnson and Attorney General Nicholas Katzenbach promised immediate enforcement. Paradoxically, Lewis said he believed that the Selma to Montgomery march and the murder of Viola Gregg Liuzzo marked the end of the belief in nonviolence as the operating principle of most SNCC members. The SNCC's integrated leadership model also crumbled, with virtually all of the white volunteers and staffers being asked to leave shortly thereafter. "It had been Selma that held us together as long as we did," Lewis writes. "After that, we just came apart."[83]

**FIGURE 15**

Johnson's office is the site of a meeting on the day the Voting Rights Act was signed, August 6, 1965. With the president are John Lewis, James Farmer, and two unidentified men. Photo courtesy of the Lyndon Baines Johnson Presidential Library (Yoichi Okamoto).

Following a special called session of the Mississippi legislature to respond (that is, to find "loopholes," according to one observer) to the president's Voting Rights bill, weary SNCC and Mississippi Freedom Democratic Party members had first taken to the streets in Jackson in July to protest. More than eight hundred were arrested, many were beaten, and most were kept in the summer heat for "processing." One SNCC worker was in the "chow line" when he was suddenly knocked to the floor and beaten by an officer who snarled, "Next time, move faster." Another was taken from a holding area and beaten repeatedly outside because he "refused" to stop singing. Others told tales of pregnant women beaten until they miscarried, grotesquely overcrowded conditions, and systematic abuse.[84] Nor was the SCLC having a much better time of it. Bruce Hartford's work in Grenada was actively opposed by the KKK and the White Citizen's Council. Once, while returning to Grenada, Mississippi, via Highway 80 in Lowndes County, he saw a truck filled with angry-looking men sporting rifles and Confederate flags. The truck pulled up dangerously close to their rear bumper just as a thunderstorm struck, its high winds lashing the VFW microbus Hartford was driving. "So we sang," he said. "We sang, 'Wade in the Water.' And we rocked that car for forty-five miles. Singing was my release."[85]

In California, race-related riots erupted in the Watts area of Los Angeles on August 11. Before they would end a week later, thirty-four people had been killed, more than a thousand were injured, and damage was in the millions of dollars as the National Guard was called in to help restore order. The shocking scenes on television news were in stark contrast to the images of the peaceful singing protests in Alabama.[86]

But the Selma initiative had one more surprise. On August 14, twenty-nine protesters, including Stokely Carmichael and Ruby Sales from the SNCC, and the Reverend Jonathan Daniels, a young seminarian who had arrived in Selma in May, were arrested in Fort Deposit, protesting ongoing registration abuses in the small town where the Voting Rights Act had not yet been implemented. They were taken and jailed in nearby Hayneville, where Carmichael and Daniels were cellmates. The group was finally released on August 20, though no one from the SNCC had contacted them about making bail. While waiting for transportation, Daniels, Sales, Joyce Bailey, and Father Richard F. Morrisroe, a Roman Catholic priest, attempted to buy cold drinks in J. D. Varner's Cash Store. In the store was Tom L. Coleman, a member of one of the many volunteer law enforcement groups in the county. When Coleman drew his revolver on Sales, an African-American, Daniels shoved her to the floor and was hit instead. Morrisroe and Bailey fled, only to have Coleman continue firing. Morrisroe was hit repeatedly in the back. Daniels died on the scene; Morrisroe survived after eleven hours of surgery. The story received national attention and an angered President Johnson ordered the Justice Department to investigate. The SNCC immediately assigned ten of its most experienced field secretaries to Lowndes County to accelerate the voter registration activities. A series of memorials for Daniels followed in the days ahead, culminating with a funeral in his hometown of Keene, New Hampshire, on August 25, where hundreds attended the service.[87] A message of condolence from Johnson was read and a portion of a paper Daniels had written about his experiences in Selma was shared with the congregation, including a passage in which Daniels wrote that his decision to go to Selma was a part of trying to "tell a story, to sing 'a song of myself.'" At the graveside, a tearful Stokely Carmichael joined hands as those present sang "We Shall Overcome."[88]

In the year that followed, more than nine thousand African-Americans registered to vote in Selma and, when election day arrived, the new voters helped vote Sheriff Jim Clark out of office and Wilson Baker in.[89]

## The Recorded Legacy of Selma

By 1965, the importance of freedom songs was such that a systematic effort was being made to record the music of the Selma campaign. Two extraordinary recordings of the events were issued shortly after the Alabama Freedom March's triumphant conclusion in Montgomery. The first, *Freedom Songs: Selma, Alabama*, was recorded and produced by Carl Benkert, who served as the night watchman for the march and made audio recordings of the events. Benkert's documentary recording is significant because of his careful documentation in the liner notes indicating where and when each song, sermon, or chant takes place. The accompanying booklet includes both Benkert's transcriptions of the songs and introductions, and candid photographs of the participants by Toshi Seeger. As with previous live recordings from the movement, the aural quality is often poor, as the small recording devices were inadequate to capture the music and singing with the degree of clarity of a professional recording. Also as before, most of the songs are truncated to allow as many as possible to fit within the time constraints of the standard vinyl LP.

From Monday, March 15, *Freedom Songs* features demonstrators maintaining their vigil a block from Brown Chapel AME, led by Hosea Williams, singing "God Will Take Care of You" and the old spirituals "Steal Away" and "Nobody Knows the Trouble I've Seen." At the rope called the "Berlin Wall," protesters sing "Come by Here," "Berlin Wall," and an up-tempo version of "We Shall Not Be Moved." From inside Brown Chapel, at a memorial service for Reverend Reeb, mourners sing "Oh, Freedom," "If You Miss Me from the Back of the Bus," and "Woke Up This Morning with My Mind Stayed on Freedom."

Recordings from Tuesday March 16 begin with the James Orange leading a small group outside of Brown Chapel in a dark and slightly menacing "Which Side Are You On, Boy?" and "Keep Your Eye on the Prize," which features two young female soloists, presumably Sheyann Webb and Rachel West. The following recordings were made on the steps of Brown Chapel after yet another march attempt was foiled by Sheriff Clark: "Everybody Wants Freedom," "Go Tell It on the Mountain"

**FIGURE 16**

Dr. Martin Luther King, Jr., and Andrew Young
compare notes while a choir sings during a
church meeting in Greenville, Alabama in
December 1965. Jim Peppler, *Southern Courier*
Photograph Collection, Alabama Department
of Archives and History. Photo: Alabama
Department of Archives and History, Montgomery, Alabama.

**FIGURE 17**

Activist Edward Rudolph
and others standing and
singing on the porch
of the Autauga County
Improvement Associa-
tion office in Prattville,
Alabama, on the day
of a civil rights march,
June 29, 1967. Jim Pep-
pler, *Southern Courier*
Photograph Collection,
Alabama Department
of Archives and History.
Photo: Alabama Depart-
ment of Archives and
History, Montgomery,
Alabama.

("I would not be a posse man / I'll tell you the reason why? / I'm afraid my Lord might call for me / And I couldn't get ready to die"), the "Freedom Now" chant, and "Which Side Are You On, Boy." The Wednesday March 17 recordings are of "Oh Wallace," "Get on Board," and "Ain't Gonna Let Nobody Turn Me 'Round."

The proceedings of the final day of Benkert's recordings, Thursday, March 17, were made at Zion Methodist Church in Marion. An evening mass meeting "was filled to overflowing" by residents and supporters, many of whom had been working in the counties north of Selma. Songs included on the LP are "This Little Light of Mine" and another version of "Which Side Are You On, Boy," with the haunting line, "My daddy was a freedom fighter / And I'm his freedom son / I'll stick to this freedom fight / Until every battle's won." The service ends with "We Shall Overcome." However, Orange and a group of young people remained at the church and Benkert captured them singing "Ain't Gonna Let Nobody Turn Me 'Round," "Oh, Wallace," and a final version of "Which Side Are You On, Boy" that emphasizes its labor origins—"Don't 'Tom' to Mr. Charlie / Don't listen to his lies / Us black folks, we haven't got a chance / Unless we organize."[90]

The second release, *WNEW's Story of Selma*, with Len Chandler, Pete Seeger, and the Freedom Voices, is the first civil rights movement recording to discuss the creation of the freedom songs. With its jacket adorned by the now iconic picture of Chandler playing the fife, Letherer (who is interviewed) on his crutches and flanked by two men waving American flags, *WNEW's Story of Selma* is based on New York radio station WNEW's coverage of the events in Alabama. Reporter Mike Stein invited Chandler, Seeger, and the Freedom Voices (four unnamed SNCC field workers) to New York to tape a news special on April 18. The interviews and the songs, still fresh in the minds of the participants, are augmented by field recordings from the march. The LP (later released on CD by Smithsonian Folkways) is by far the most polished, both in sound and presentation, of the various civil rights releases. Chandler and Seeger have an easy, accessible charm as they describe how freedom songs were created and sung. The informative booklet, also with photographs by Toshi Seeger, transcribes both the interviews and the various freedom songs, including "Hold On," "We've Got a Rope That's a Berlin Wall," "I Love Everybody," "If You Want to Get Your Freedom," "Oh, Wallace," "Ain't Gonna Let Nobody Turn Me 'Round," "Do What the Spirit Say Do," and "Murder on the Roads of Alabama."[91]

## INTERLUDE

*St. Augustine, Florida; The Meredith March; Popular Music*

During the human-rights struggle in the 1960s, the freedom songs uplifted us, bound us together, exalted us, and pointed the way, and, in a real sense, freed us from the shackles of psychological bondage. They captured and kept alive the yearnings, dreams and fervency of a people under stress. Indeed, the civil rights movement was fueled by the singing of black people. Traditional spirituals and gospel hymns were used exactly as they had come down through the years, or were adapted or completely rewritten. Freedom songs were also composed anew. A strong black tradition of composing in performance and in the midst of need led to new words being added or a line being changed to address a specific issue. Song leading became an organizing tool, helping to mobilize the dedicated or to motivate the reticent. Never has there been a social or political struggle as rich in protest songs as the southern civil rights movement, because of the magnificence of black congregational singing, nourished as it was by a legacy of struggle, resistance, endurance and faith. It was a movement that could be said to have had its own culture. Freedom songs both gave and reflected back the political fire and spiritual longings of countless individuals in untold mass meetings, addressing real frustrations whether of making a personal commitment or of fear and dread.

—MARY KING

No more long prayers, no more Freedom songs, no more dreams—let's go for power.

—STOKELY CARMICHAEL, 1966

The civil rights movement and the music of the movement continued to change and evolve, as movements and music are wont to do. Some important arenas were little marked at the time, their impact only understood by later scholars. Other events were simply overshadowed by bigger stories in the movement, such the Mississippi Freedom Summer or the violence in Selma, leaving even major newspapers and television networks hard pressed to assign enough reporters to cover them all. Still other movement actions—equally important, equally bloody—occurred on days when national or international news events dominated the front pages and nightly news broadcasts and were thus relegated to the back pages. And finally, there were the shifts in attitude, culture, and perception that take place slowly, occurring concurrently with the more visceral action in the streets and barricades and churches across America. One such shift was taking place among the embattled foot soldiers of the SNCC and even among some members of the SCLC leadership.

### St. Augustine, Florida, 1964–65

Overshadowed by the events in Birmingham, rural Mississippi, and Selma, St. Augustine's bloody campaign lasted through the spring and summer of 1964, though the violence and the oppression of African-Americans in that city continued for several years more. Pat Watters called it "the South's last great demonstration campaign" and active protests had begun as early as 1961, despite particularly violent reprisals by the Ku Klux Klan.[1] Longtime activist Dorothy Cotton called it "the roughest city we've had—forty-five straight nights of beatings and intimidation. In church every night we'd see people sitting there with bandages on." The nighttime protest participants were invariably attacked by much larger crowds of whites armed with chains, bats, and broken bottles. "After we were attacked," she notes, "we'd come back to the church and somehow always we'd come back bleeding and singing, 'I love everybody.' It was hard."[2]

Even as the Civil Rights Act of 1965 worked its way through Congress, activists had for several years attempted to challenge the overt racism and segregation in the city. The SCLC's Andrew Young was among those sent to assess the turbulent situation in St. Augustine, already notable for the number of the injuries and arrests sustained by African-American marchers. On his first night in town, he was asked to lead a small demonstration of thirty teenagers and mostly older women to the Old Slave Market. As had happened in the past, they were met by Sheriff L. O. Davis, who told them he was unable to offer Young's group any protection from a waiting crowd of "four or five hundred" angry whites. Initially reluctant to participate on his first night in town, Young offered a prayer at the mass meeting, supported by the group's singing of "God Will Take Care of You." "We sang out an affirmation of faith that was about to be tested," Young writes in his autobiography. "I finally realized that there was no turning back for any logical or pragmatic reason. We marched, still singing softly, "God will take care of you." And I thought to myself, *It's one thing to sing this in church where it's easy to believe it, but the song says through every day, and this is nighttime in St. Augustine.*" As these events usually ended in St. Augustine, many of those in Young's small band were badly beaten that night.[3]

One of the most troubling images of St. Augustine was a nighttime march through the city's African-American neighborhoods by two parades of whites, surrounded by a protective phalanx of hundreds of Florida state troopers. The procession, which included many of those responsible for the nightly attacks on nonviolent demonstrators over the past year, featured violent segregationist Halstead "Hoss" Manucy. Marchers held signs that read "Kill the Civil Rights Bill," "Put George Wallace on the Supreme Court," and "Don't Tread on Me." At the second all-white parade the following night along the same route, blacks lined the streets, held signs as well ("I Am an American" and "Equality for All in '64"), and sang "I love everybody / I love everybody / I love everybody / I love everybody in my heart / You can't make me doubt him / You can't make me doubt Him / You can't make me doubt Him in my heart." At the end of long procession, those watching along the streets sang "We Shall Overcome" to the marchers.[4]

In one of the more intriguing events of the St. Augustine campaign, eighty-eight protesters were arrested on April 1, 1964, including the Reverend William Sloane Coffin, a chaplain at Yale University, and seventy-three-year-old Mary Peabody, wife of Episcopal Bishop Malcolm Peabody and mother of Endicott Peabody, the governor of Massachusetts. Peabody posted bond after spending two nights in jail, but most of the nearly three hundred demonstrators who had been protesting segregation and discriminatory practices in the city remained behind bars. Martin Luther King, Jr.'s, presence at mass meetings that spring reinvigorated the battered movement. In May, King spoke to a mass meeting and alluded to the violence in St. Augustine and the increasingly specific death threats he continued to receive. "Well, if physical death is the price that I must pay to free my white brother and all of my brothers from a permanent death of the spirit," he said, "then nothing can be more redemptive." His sermon, Watters reports, was halted briefly by "overwhelming" applause from the congregants. "We have long since learned to sing anew with our foreparents of old that, 'Before I'll be a slave / I'll be buried in my grave / And go home to my Father / And be saved.'" King and seventeen others were jailed trying to receive service in the Monson Motor Lodge Restaurant. During his short stay behind bars, King wrote "A Letter from the St. Augustine Jail," inviting his friend Rabbi Israel Dresner, a former Freedom Rider, and others to join him in protesting the conditions in the city. A number of rabbis joined the protests and on June 18, sixteen were arrested, along with twenty-five other people, outside of the Motor Lodge. When an integrated group of demonstrators entered the Lodge's pool, a policeman jumped in to haul them out. Some of the protesters were beaten and struck with cattle prods during the demonstration and the picture of the diving deputy made the front page of the *New York Times*.[5]

Once again protesters filled the city and county jails to overflowing, and Sheriff Davis kept them, including the elderly and the injured, in an open pen with a single outdoor toilet, unshaded against the Florida summer sun. When a reporter asked him about the "inhumane" treatment of the demonstrators, Davis replied, "If we keep 'em inside the jail all day like we did on Monday, they sing and cheer until two o'clock in the morning. But when they're out taking exercise all day, they're ready to sleep at night."

St. Augustine's troubles would have doubtless continued indefinitely if not for the courageous actions of Federal District Judge Bryan Simpson. Sickened by the flagrant disregard of the rule of law and brutality against African-Americans, Simpson eventually enjoined the banning of the nighttime marches, ended the practice of charging exorbitant fines and lengthy jail sentences against protesters, and worked to eliminate the most egregious violence against blacks. Simpson firmly "demanded that the city and state provide protection" of the constitutional right to demonstrate—a rarity in the South during the movement—though the violence continued for some time.[6]

Several songs entered the civil rights movement canon through St. Augustine. While the protest spiritual "I Love Everybody" had been widely used in earlier movement actions, protesters relied heavily on it in the face of unchecked brutality in the city, somehow finding the grace to sing "The Klan can't make me doubt Him" each night. "It was hard to sing 'I love Hoss Manucy' when he'd just beat us up, to say a little bit about what love really was," recalled Cotton. "He's still a person with some degree of dignity in the sight of God, and we don't have to like him, but we have to love him. He's been damaged, too. So we sing it, and the more we sing it, the more we grow in ability to love people who mistreat us so bad." The other song that became identified with St. Augustine was the old protest spiritual "Wade in the Water," which soon accompanied attempts by African-Americans to integrate the city's public beaches. Despite a large police presence, blacks who dared "trespass" on white beaches were openly attacked by white mobs. After one particularly savage attack, Cotton writes that her small group left for a time, then returned the following day still singing, "Wade in the Water."[7]

### Newport Folk Music Festivals

On the surface, the alliance between the (mostly white) folk musicians and the (mostly black) men and women who sang protest spirituals and freedom songs on the front lines in the civil rights battles would seem an unlikely one. But the roots of the two art forms are indisputably intertwined. Pete Seeger, for example, spent his life chronicling, performing, and promoting the authentic musical expression of all people in their daily lives. Founded in 1959 in Newport, Rhode Island, as a three-day festival, Newport attracted forty-seven thousand listeners for the concerts of July 26–28, 1963. Performers that weekend included the Freedom Singers, Bob Dylan, Joan Baez, Jackie Washington, Theodore Bikel, Pete Seeger, Bessie Jones and the Sea Island Singers, Phil Ochs, Dave Van Ronk, Peter Yarrow, and labor singer Jim Garland, all of whom had been active at different times in the civil rights movement. Just days ahead of the March on Washington, the *Washington Post* spotlighted Dylan's protest songs "With God on Our Side" and "Masters of

**FIGURE 18**

The Freedom Singers (from left): Rutha Mae
Harris, Bernice Johnson (partially hidden),
Cordell Reagon, and Charles Neblett are joined
by Pete Seeger (far right) in performance at the
1963 Newport Folk Festival. Photo: Daniel A.
Gómez-Ibáñez © 1963.

War." Vanguard Records released a six-record set of the performances, including the Freedom Singers' "Woke Up This Morning with My Mind Stayed on Freedom" and their rendition of "We Shall Overcome," which included many of the best-known artists at Newport that week: Dylan, Peter, Paul & Mary, Bikel, and Seeger.[8]

By 1964, the Folk Festival outdrew its parent, the Newport Jazz Festival, and was playing an important role in introducing African-American artists to a white audience. More than seventy thousand attendees heard the Moving Star Harp Singers, the Swan Silvertones, Johnny Cash, Judy Collins, and Peter, Paul & Mary, among the more than two hundred performers. Odetta closed the final concert, leading the audience and most of the folk stars from previous shows in two freedom songs, "a symbolic finale merging music and social meaning."[9]

The 1965 concerts are best known as the festival where Bob Dylan performed several songs with a full rock band and the subsequent controversy over whether the audience was booing Dylan, the length of his set, or the overloaded sound system. With the presence of more than one hundred fifty artists, including the Chambers Brothers, Baez, Seeger, and Odetta, and more than seventy-six thousand paid admissions, the year marked the apex of the folk movement as sales soon thereafter began to decline in the face of the rising popularity of rock and roll. Attendance the following year dipped markedly. Three gospel groups, the Dixie Hummingbirds, Claude Jeter and the Swan Silvertones, and Dorothy Love Coates and the Gospel Harmonettes, all performed. But the closing ceremonies were marred by an incident at midday on the festival grounds at the SNCC booth. Uniformed policemen from the neighboring town of Pawtucket "forcibly ejected about a dozen members of the civil rights group from the park." Members of the Newport police broke up the scuffle. The small event is worth noting because of the presence of Stokely Carmichael, not John Lewis, as the new national chairman of the SNCC. Carmichael worked with Newport police to identify the outside policemen involved.[10]

Bernice Johnson Reagon has said that her performances with the Freedom Singers at Newport were important experiences both in her life and in the life of Bob Dylan: "We were young then. It was very hard for us to understand the meaning of Newport in terms of music and culture. It was a forum for music of the people. We were doing songs that never made the hit parade, but are still around today. We were perceived as warriors. People perceived us as performers who were, with their words and voices, challenging a system that needed to be changed."[11]

### James Meredith and the March Against Fear, June 1966

In May 1966, James H. Meredith, the tough-minded Army vet who was the first African-American to attend the University of Mississippi, declared his intention to walk from Memphis to Jackson, Mississippi. Walking through small towns and rural communities, Meredith's twin goals were to draw attention to the slow rate of African-American voter registration and to encourage registration at every stop. Meredith's proposed march was not sponsored by any civil rights–related organization and it was his intention to keep the procession small. "We shall arrive," he said as he left Memphis on June 4, traveling down U.S. Highway 51. Meredith's nearly solitary march would have gone unmarked and little noticed had he completed his journey. But on the second day of his trek, just two miles south of Hernando and twenty miles into his march, Meredith was ambushed by a white man, Aubrey J. Norvell. Norvell appeared out of the woods and fired on Meredith three times with a shotgun, peppering Meredith with "60 to 70" pellets. A front-page photograph of Meredith crawling off the highway and screaming in pain would later earn photographer Jack R. Thornell a Pulitzer Prize for News Photography.[12] Immediately after the shooting, the Congress of Racial Equality, the Southern Christian Leadership Conference, and other civil rights organizations announced that they would be joining Meredith when he resumed his march. However, when King, Dick Gregory, Fannie Lou Hamer, Carmichael, and a number of other well-known activists tried to resume the march on June 7, they were roughly treated by officers of the Mississippi Highway Patrol.[13]

During the course of the march, the group passed the section of the highway where Meredith had been shot. Instead of the standard freedom songs, King, who had been forced to leave SCLC's work in Chicago to come to Mississippi, writes that marchers began arguing the merits of violence as opposed to nonviolence. At one point, the long column paused and the strains of "We Shall Overcome" drifted the entire length of the march. "The voices rang out with all the traditional fervor," King writes of the moment, "the glad thunder and gentle strength that had always characterized the singing of this noble song. But when we came to the stanza which speaks of 'black and white together,' the voices of a few of the marchers were muted. I asked them later why they refused to sing that verse." As King recalled the conversation, the response then came back: "This is a new day, we don't sing those words anymore. In fact, the whole song should be discarded. Not 'We Shall Overcome,' but 'We Shall Overrun.'"[14]

The marchers were welcomed into Grenada on June 14 by African-Americans lining the streets, swaying and singing, including "Walk for your children, brother / Make them free." More than six hundred African-Americans were registered, doubling the total registrations in the entire county. At a mass meeting that evening at New Hope Missionary Baptist Church, one unnamed civil rights worker shouted to the congregation, "We're supposed to be singing about freedom! You never had this town before. Now you've taken it over in a day. That's freedom. So sing about it!"[15]

As the procession approached Philadelphia, one of the march's several detours off of Highway 51, the leaders requested the protection of federal troops for a pilgrimage to honor the three civil rights workers who had been murdered near there the previous summer. There were numerous reports of African-Americans responding with violence to attacks by whites, and King was assaulted by a mob when he approached the Neshoba County Courthouse on June 21. Police watched

**FIGURE 19**

Fannie Lou Hamer singing to a group of people
in Mississippi during the James Meredith–
inspired "March Against Fear," June 1966.
Jim Peppler *Southern Courier* Photograph
Collection, Alabama Department of Archives
and History. Photo: Alabama Department of
Archives and History, Montgomery, Alabama.

**FIGURE 20**

Ralph Abernathy, Coretta Scott King, Martin
Luther King, Jr., Floyd McKissick, and others
participate in the "March Against Fear" in
Mississippi, June 1966. Jim Peppler *Southern
Courier* Photograph Collection, Alabama
Department of Archives and History. Photo:
Alabama Department of Archives and History,
Montgomery, Alabama.

passively and made no move to intervene. On June 24, as the two thousand marchers tried to pitch their tents for the evening on the grounds of an African-American elementary school singing "We Shall Overcome," they were attacked by club- and rifle-wielding highway patrolmen who repeatedly sprayed them with teargas.[16]

Also joining the march was veteran civil rights reporter Paul Good, who said that the "Two, four, six, eight / We wanna integrate" chant had been replaced by "Ho-ho, whatta you know / White folks gotta go." As the column trooped into Grenada, the freedom song "I love everybody / I love everybody / I love everybody in my heart" was replaced by "I love everybody / I love everybody / I love everybody in my heart / I just told a lie / I just told a lie / I just told a lie, in my heart." Another group of Meredith marchers sang, "Jingle bells, shotgun shells / Freedom all the way / Oh what fun it is to blast a trooper man away." For Good, the "most disturbing, even frightening" chant of the march was the repeated cries of "Black Power!" from members of the SNCC. The march did have some positive outcomes, Good reported, as extra federal registrars helped more than thirteen hundred African-Americans register to vote in Grenada during the course of the march. When the march reached nearby Greenwood, the site of so much violence during the Mississippi Freedom Summer, Carmichael, Hosea Williams, and King joined in a sometimes tense discussion over the more militant tone taken by Carmichael and Williams.[17] During a fiery speech by Carmichael, the SNCC's Willie Ricks jumped up on the platform. Ricks cried out to the large crowd, "What do we want?" The response, instead of the movement's long-cherished "Freedom now!" was the roar "Black Power!" In his book *Where Do We Go from Here?*, King identified Greenwood as the "arena for the birth of the Black Power slogan," and the unraveling of the agreement among the various civil rights organizations intensified.[18] After Greenwood, the singing in tents pitched near the highway briefly resumed, including "Oh, Freedom," "Ain't Gonna Let Nobody Turn Me 'Round" and "If You Miss Me from the Back of the Bus" though not for the duration, as in previous marches. "Unlike the Montgomery March," Good added, "there were few guitars and little singing at night around the campfire; when you are living a folk epic you don't have to sing about one."[19]

Meredith resumed marching, now with a much larger procession, on June 25. That evening, a crowd of "eight to ten thousand" joined marchers for a rally at Tougaloo College. Among those present were actors Marlon Brando, Sammy Davis, Jr., and Burt Lancaster, some of whom arrived in Frank Sinatra's private airplane. Also present were Belafonte, Gregory, and singer James Brown. On a stage so crowded "one could hardly tell the performers from the audience," the crowd parted "like Moses" for Brown. Already known as the "hardest working man in show business," Brown was a longtime supporter of the movement through his friend, SNCC program director Cleveland Sellers. In addition to financial contributions to the movement, Brown had previously met King privately on several occasions. Taking the microphone, Brown complimented Meredith on his courage and performed a brief set with his group that included "I Got You (I Feel Good)" and "Try Me." He also made a $1,000 contribution to defray some of the costs of the march.[20]

When Meredith lead a column of "singing Negro men" into Jackson on June 26, the tenor of the march—and perhaps the civil rights movement—had changed markedly. An estimated twelve to fifteen thousand marchers, many in their "Sunday best," walked into town accompanied by a small brass band performing "When the Saints Go Marching In" and hundreds of members of the Mississippi National Guard, the highway patrol, and other law enforcement officers. Both King and Meredith spoke, but members of the SNCC and the SCLC periodically tried to shout each other down with dueling cries of "Black Power!" and "Freedom, freedom!" At different times, Meredith shoved two of King's aides, Andrew Young and Robert Green, both of whom had joined the march "to smooth over differences" within the various groups represented.[21]

Through the course of the march, more than four thousand African-Americans had registered to vote, though more than three hundred thousand remained to be registered. Behind the scenes, representatives of the SNCC, the SCLC, the Mississippi Freedom Democratic Party, the NAACP, and CORE had held intense, angry negotiations on the speakers for the day's event. The hard feelings would continue in the difficult years ahead.[22]

"Now it is over," writes Julius Lester. "The days of singing freedom songs and the days of combating bullets and billy clubs with love. 'We Shall Overcome' (and we have overcome our blindness) sounds old, outdated and can enter the pantheon of greats along with the IWW songs and union songs. As one SNCC veteran put it after the Mississippi March, 'Man, the people are too busy getting ready to fight to bother with singing anymore.' They used to sing 'I Love Everybody' as they ducked bricks and bottles. Now they sing: 'Too much love / Too much love / Nothing kills a nigger like / Too much love.'"[23]

## Popular and Gospel Music

Pop star Sam Cooke was one of many artists who made the transition from gospel to pop or R & B music in the early 1960s, joining the ranks of Aretha Franklin, Wilson Pickett, and others. While not at the forefront of the civil rights movement, as early as 1961 Cooke had, with Clyde McPhatter, refused to perform at a segregated concert in Memphis. Written in response to the events in Birmingham and the March on Washington, Cooke first performed "A Change Is Gonna Come" on *The Tonight Show with Johnny Carson* in early 1964. By the Mississippi Freedom Summer, it had become an anthem of the movement. The song was selected for inclusion on the LP *The Stars Salute Dr. Martin Luther King,* along with contributions from Frank Sinatra, Belafonte, Ray Charles, and others, as a fund-raiser for the SCLC.[24] Of "A Change Is Gonna Come," music historian Dave Marsh has said that the song "ranks with Martin Luther King's best speeches as a verbal encapsulation of the changes black perspective underwent in the Sixties."[25]

The Staple Singers were the best-known gospel-soul group consistently releasing civil rights–related material. In addition to "Freedom Highway," the group recorded and released "I've Been Scorned" (1961), "This Little Light of Mine" (1964), "What You Gonna Do" (1965), and "Why Am I Treated So Bad?" (1965). The group performed with King on several occasions in rallies or church settings. King was said to be particularly partial to "Why Am I Treated So Bad," invariably asking Roebuck "Pops" Staples, "You gonna play my song tonight?" However, gospel historian Anthony Heilbut claims that no gospel group was more "intimately" involved with King and the movement than Gladys McFadden and the Loving Sisters. By the mid-'60s, the Staple Singers were booked months in advance, often playing two hundred or more concerts a year, making them unavailable for most rallies and benefits. Conversely, the Loving Sisters regularly made themselves available to the movement. "There were all these reviews making it seem as if [the Staples] were working with Dr. King, and it's not fair to the Loving Sisters who did the lifting," Heilbut adds. The Loving Sisters toured with King throughout 1965 and later recorded a tribute album for him.[26]

But few popular songs became as identified with the movement as those of Curtis Mayfield. With his group the Impressions, Mayfield released the album *Keep on Pushing* in 1964 and the title track, along with the group's rendition of "Amen," was a favorite among movement activists. Called a "milestone" in Mayfield's lyrics, "Keep on Pushing" "provided spiritual support to King and the civil rights movement" to the wider popular audience.[27] In 1965, the Impressions released *People Get Ready*. Mayfield said that the gospel-influenced title track was written in response to the March on Washington and the deadly church bombing in Birmingham. Music critic Stanley Crouch attributes the song's impact on activists to Mayfield's message. "'There's a train a-coming, get ready,'" Crouch writes. "So, regardless of what happens, get yourself together for this because you are going to get a chance. Your chance is coming." "The train that is coming in the song speaks to a chance for redemption," adds Juan Williams, "the long-sought chance to rise above racism, to stand apart from despair and any desire for retaliation—an end to the cycle of pain."[28] Civil rights activist Gordon Sellers called the song "warrior music" and said that "it was music you listened to while you were preparing to go into battle. [Mayfield] was writing at a time we were struggling. But he knew we were struggling for the right things." According to SNCC veteran Stanley Wise, "Curtis always seemed to be right on time. You could see his records on every movement turntable."[29] *Rolling Stone* magazine placed the song at Number 24 in its list of "The 500 Greatest Songs of All Time." In the summer of 1966, some Chicago churches and recreation centers featured a rewritten version of "People Get Ready" with lines like "there's no hiding place when the movement comes" and reviled "Toms or any sorry Negroes, comin' to me saying they won't go." Singer, composer, and activist Jimmy Collier says that the Impressions were known as "movement fellows" and that phrases such as "people get ready" and "keep on pushing" had specific meanings to activists that were not readily understood by white teenagers or DJs. Mayfield gave activists permission to use this song and a number of his compositions as "metaphors for the civil rights struggles."[30]

**FIGURE 21**

Mavis Staples and the Staple Singers were favorites among civil rights activists. Forty years later, Mavis was still singing freedom songs. Picture taken at the Aladdin Theater in Portland in October 2004. Photo courtesy of Bob Gersztyn.

Musical tastes within the movement itself were changing. During the summer of 1965, at the Southern Community Organization and Political Education (SCOPE) training sessions for the mostly northern volunteers in Atlanta, Margaret Long observed that the interracial singing "seemed predominantly and wildly rock and roll, pounding with thunderbolts of hand-clapping." Even the volume, according to Long, was changing. The four hundred mostly Northern volunteers heard music "amplified by a skull-splitting sound system which drowned the words, blurred the melody and blared away the earthly gaiety of rock and roll, but apparently increased the excitement of the meetings." Also present was the SCLC's Andrew Young, who said, "If I had to say whether Billy Graham or Elvis Presley has done more for integration, in some ways I'd have to pick Elvis," and added that rock music had done more than any other form of African-American musical expression "to span the culture gulf between young blacks and whites."[31]

# 8

## CHICAGO, ILLINOIS

You can cage the singer, but not the song. . . . All of the songs were inspirational. All of the songs had one purpose. It was to reach deep into our moments of the greatest anguish and to say we've had worse moments than this. We can endure.

—HARRY BELAFONTE

*You conspire to keep us silent in the field*
*    and in the slum*
*You promise us the vote and sing us*
*    "We Shall Overcome"*
*But John Brown knew what freedom was*
*    and died to win us some*
*That's why we keep marching on*

*Move on over or we'll move on over you*
*Move on over or we'll move on over you*
*Move on over or we'll move on over you*
*And the movement's moving on*

—LEN CHANDLER'S PARODY
OF "JOHN BROWN'S BODY" /
"GLORY, HALLELUJAH"

Chicago was big, difficult, complex, and unlike anything Martin Luther King, Jr., and the SCLC had ever experienced before.[1] A series of complex considerations, decisions, and pressures, along with a liberal dose of intuition, led King and the SCLC to Chicago: the presence and ongoing work of civil rights activist Albert A. Raby and the Coordinating Council of Community Organizations (CCCO), the American Friends Service Committee (AFSC), the Chicago chapter of CORE, the Woodlawn Organization, and the long-standing intransigence of Chicago School Superintendent Benjamin C. Willis, which had led to some early successes mobilizing protesters against the city's policy of segregated schools.[2]

There were other reasons to choose Chicago. During King's five-city "People to People" tour, which began in Chicago and included Cleveland, New York, Philadelphia, and Washington, DC, in July and August 1965, the reception had varied widely. In Chicago, a series of speaking engagements culminated with an enthusiastic crowd of more than a thousand at Friendship Baptist Church on Chicago's West Side on July 24. The following day, thousands more heard him on the South Side and that evening more than ten thousand people were in attendance in an outdoor venue in the mostly white Chicago suburb of Winnetka. The Chicago leg of King's journey ended on July 26 with tens of thousands, though estimates vary, marching with King to Chicago City Hall, the largest civil rights rally in the city's history. During the rally, King referenced an old blues song, "We sang 'Going to Chicago' until there were as many of our people in Chicago as Mississippi. Now we see the results. Chicago did not turn out to be a new Jerusalem. . . . One hundred years after the Civil War we're still protesting social, economic and educational injustices." Chicago's civil rights activists and the African-American population, for the most part, warmly embraced King throughout his whirlwind tour of the city. Other stops, especially New York and Philadelphia, were not so welcoming. Harlem's Representative Adam Clayton Powell bluntly told King he was not welcome in New York.[3]

There were personal reasons to choose Chicago as well. James Bevel, the SCLC's "eccentric" genius, worked with the well-regarded West Side Christian Parish, an inner-city outreach ministry. Bevel's wife, Diane Nash Bevel, one of the heroes of the movement, was originally from Chicago. Bevel's team included singer and songwriter Jimmy Collier, who had proven so effective in Selma. Also in Chicago was another movement veteran, Bernard LaFayette. And, as Ralph and others have noted, nearly a million African-Americans, mostly from the Deep South via the various Great Migrations, lived in Chicago—more blacks than in the entire state of Mississippi.[4]

Mary Lou Finley, an SCLC staffer who joined with the Chicago Freedom Movement, said Collier was responsible for bringing southern-style freedom songs to one of the first meetings of the organization at Pleasant Valley Farm outside the city in September 1965. "People Get Ready" was sung repeatedly, with lyrics tailored to Chicago concerns. Finley called Collier "the moving spirit" for the music of the movement. As with other meetings, the Pleasant Valley sessions ended with the arms-linked singing of "We Shall Overcome." It was, Finley said, "very powerful in creating a sense of group cohesion and group commitment and that in spite of our differences, we were all together." The southern activists, Finley said, had "come out of extremely difficult situations and faced into those with an enormous amount of courage. I think the courage was one of the things that struck me so intensely. And then, in the way in which the courage is in the music, the affirmations of courage that come through the songs I think really helped people to hold onto that courage."[5]

Then there were the practical concerns. Chicago was the home of gospel music with a host of outstanding, passionate mass choirs and supportive gospel artists. One of the cities originally under consideration as the SCLC's next campaign, Rochester, despite its more "manageable size and Kodak funding," was ultimately bypassed because, according to Andrew Young, it did not have the "good movement choir" needed to "make an impression."[6]

One final consideration weighed in Chicago's favor: the presence of Mahalia Jackson. "This was the house that Martin said was his haven," one of Jackson's friends said, "his favorite place in all the world to relax." Of King's relationship with Jackson, a mutual friend noted, "Martin got *many* things from her—the freedom to laugh, good food, wit, and a sense of privacy. Just headed toward Mahalia's house, he would start laughing gleefully; just anticipating the moment when he's going to be arriving. It's difficult for many people to comprehend this need for carefree, relaxed *pleasure.* She was unaffected, she would say what she had to say—most times, it was funny; she was such a humorous person—and yet she was deep and serious when she was serious. Another thing he appreciated is that when Martin asked Mahalia for an opinion, Mahalia would give him the truth—the truth being her honest opinion." Jackson encouraged King to come to Chicago. She often cooked elaborate New Orleans-style meals for King and his entourage and their evenings included gospel sing-alongs. "Talk about soul food," Jackson said in her biography, *"this* is soul food."[7]

In the end, Chicago was chosen, despite the strenuous objections of one of King's closest advisors, Bayard Rustin. For all of King's rhetoric about the movement's ability to "inspire" and "mobilize" African-Americans in the city, Rustin responded, "You don't know what you are talking about. You don't know what Chicago is like. . . . You're going to be wiped out."[8]

The various groups, including King, the SCLC, the CCCO, and other civil rights leaders met near Chicago on October 6 to plan and coordinate their ambitious plan to address, in particular, the city's segregated, dangerously inadequate housing situation where vast neighborhoods remained mired in deep poverty. At the meeting, Collier taught the Chicago activists the most powerful movement songs. King said that he believed that Chicago Mayor Richard Daley was too shrewd to allow himself to be used as "symbol," such as Jim Clark or George Wallace, to unite African-Americans and generate the necessary financial support to maintain an operation of this scale.[9] "In the North we will not be aided as much by the brutality of our opponents," he told the more than one hundred fifty people in attendance, "but Chicago still has an Egypt, although the pharaohs are more sophisticated and subtle." Few in the audience missed the reference to Daley, sometimes called an "American pharaoh." "There are giants in the land, but we can possess the land of freedom," King added. "Let us be dissatisfied with things as they are. Then, in some bright future, we will say with a cosmic past tense, 'Deep in my heart, I *did* believe, we *would* overcome.'"[10]

Various pressing duties, as well as a long overdue European trip with Coretta, kept King from Chicago until early 1966. Despite the vigorous efforts of local activists in what came to be known as the Chicago Freedom Movement and the work of Bevel and other SCLC staffers, the movement stalled during King's absence. James Orange worked with the city's powerful gangs, hoping to convert them to the "gospel" of nonviolence. Orange was beaten three times by gang members "to test" his "sincerity about nonviolence." When Orange did not retaliate, his commitment to nonviolence "broke the ice" with the gang members. At one meeting, members of the Blackstone Rangers derided Orange's request that they sing freedom songs. "You think you're too bad to sing?" Orange shouted back. "Well, I'm badder than all of you, so we're going to sing." The physically intimidating Orange then walked into the middle of the gang members. "It looked as though he might really *be* badder than all of them," one reporter wrote of the incident.[11]

When King returned to Chicago, it was to rent a "slum apartment" for his family on the West Side in an attempt to dramatize the Freedom Movement's "anti-slum drive." Neighbors, especially children, continually flowed into the apartment, some just to gawk at the man locals called the "Pied Piper of Hamlin Avenue." On at least one occasion, the children sang "moving spirituals" with Martin and Coretta.[12] Collier, Billy Hollins, and other SCLC staffers began going door-to-door in the apartment's North Lawndale neighborhood in an effort to organize residents. The actual headquarters for the group would be across town on the South Side. In February, the movement took control of a particularly decrepit West Side "slum building" without the owner's permission, calling it a "trusteeship" and began using rents to fix problems in the building. The controversial action drew attacks and threats of lawsuits from a variety of groups within Chicago, including judges and real estate officials.[13]

Elsewhere, without the support of many of Chicago's largest, most powerful African-American churches, whose pastors feared to jeopardize their mutually beneficial relationship with the Daley machine, organizers found it difficult to rally support. One of the few pastors to actively engage with the Chicago Freedom Movement, the Reverend Clay Evans, pastor of Fellowship Missionary Baptist Church and president of the Baptist Ministers Conference of Chicago and Vicinity, brought along a young veteran of the Greensboro, North Carolina, campaigns, seminary student Jesse Jackson. Evans soon paid a price for his support. The necessary city licenses and certifications for Evans's in-progress sanctuary soon stopped or were denied, leaving his congregation without a home for seven years as the steel skeleton rusted on the site. Some pastors discreetly supported the institution of the SCLC's Operation Breadbasket, which had been successful in Atlanta and Philadelphia in instituting boycotts and actions designed to generate better jobs for blacks. Most major labor organizations in the city were also disinclined to challenge Daley, save for the United Packinghouse Workers and a few others. The District 1 branch of the UPWA actually joined the CCCO.[14]

Efforts in Chicago's massive neighborhoods quickly depleted SCLC and CCCO coffers. A Freedom Festival, hosted by Harry Belafonte and Jackson, drew twelve thousand people to the International Amphitheater on Saturday March 12. The

festival raised more than $100,000, thanks to gifts from Evans's Fellowship Church and James Wright of the United Auto Workers, Teamsters Local 743.[15] Jackson also sponsored a gala at the city-controlled McCormick Place on May 27. At Jackson's urging, Daley himself made an appearance, while King was joined by Fred Shuttlesworth and Ralph Abernathy. Jackson, "clucking like a mother hen," assembled and oversaw the entertainment by Sidney Poitier, Eartha Kitt, the Chad Mitchell Trio, Dick Gregory, Aretha Franklin, and Al Hibbler.[16]

As spring arrived in Chicago, King was distracted from his work by both James Meredith's nearly fatal march in Mississippi and the May 21 election of Stokely Carmichael as head of the SNCC over incumbent John Lewis. While Carmichael did not advocate violence, he was elected with a platform that opposed the SNCC's use of nonviolent demonstrations as change agents. "To ask Negroes to get in the Democratic Party," he said, "is like asking Jews to join the Nazi party." Raby and ten busloads of activists left Chicago for the triumphant entry of Meredith into Jackson on Sunday June 26, the culmination of Meredith's unpredictable quest that had begun three weeks earlier. King was also dealing with a public "breach" with CORE's Floyd B. McKissick over the use of Carmichael's term "black power."[17]

Most discouraging, however, was the sheer size and scale of Chicago and the ambitious, disparate aims of the Chicago Freedom Movement. At a mass rally on July 10, King dramatized the group's demands for a "just and open city" that included immediate action on ending real estate "red-lining" (which kept African-Americans in narrowly prescribed areas), increasing employment opportunities for blacks, creating a citizen review board to review police actions, and the resignation of Willis, along with various other civil rights and justice–related actions. The crowd, an estimated forty-five thousand (though some sources suggest the attendance was closer to sixty-five thousand), was supportive of speeches by King, McKissick, and Meredith, and performances by Jackson (singing under a black umbrella to protect her from the brutal heat), Peter, Paul & Mary, Stevie Wonder, B. B. King, ten singing nuns from Mundelein College, DJ Pervis "The Blues Man" Spann, Nancy Wilson, Johnny Nash, and others. "Mahalia Jackson sang that day as if the heavens were coming down on Soldier Field," an awe-struck organizer said. "You can't explain that feeling, but you knew then that things are going to change; it must change. You felt that God was with us." The crowd also included a two-hundred member contingent of Blackstone Rangers with placards and bedsheets that read "Black Power," "We Shall Overcome," and "Freedom Now" but were illustrated with drawings of machine guns on them. Overall, the event was festive and up-tempo, with some audience members dancing on the sidelines during the music. West Side resident Milton Ray attended the concert and said that the rally marked a "turning point" for the movement in Chicago. At the conclusion, thousands trooped downtown in the 98-degree heat singing "Ain't gonna let nobody turn me 'round" to attach the meeting's demands to the doors of City Hall. Handouts had also been distributed to marchers with new lyrics to Curtis Mayfield's "Meeting over Yonder." Finley remembered "We Shall Not Be Moved" and "Which Side Are You On" being sung during the march. Like previous rallies, the event was sponsored in part by the UAW, the Packinghouse Workers, meat cutters, and other unions, whose members also made up a significant portion of the crowd. The symbolic posting of the demands at City Hall signaled the long awaited "action phase" of the Chicago Freedom Movement. Meetings began with Daley's representatives, who promised much, at least publicly, while residents on the South and West Sides continued to see few results.[18]

The scorching summer ground on, fraying tempers throughout town. Disagreements over the use of fire hydrants by children and youth in a near West Side neighborhood drew thirty police cruisers and quickly resulted in sporadic violence, with the arrest of six "battered" teenagers. King, whose family was having dinner with Mahalia Jackson at the time, raced with Jackson to the closest police station, where they negotiated the teens' release. That evening, at Shiloh Baptist Church, King was heckled during his sermon and, amid the noise of "urban chaos" outside the church walls, hundreds of angry people walked out during his speech. The violence and rioting, now on both the West and South Sides, continued for days. King, Jackson, Coretta King, Charles Billups, Orange, and other SCLC staffers continued to walk the streets, talking to rioters. Despite riots in other cities because of the heat wave, Daley blamed King's staff for the unrest and asked for the assistance of the Illinois National Guard.[19]

Daley continued to claim that the city was doing something about the slums and the poor quality of education in African-American schools, but progress, if any, was masked by endless committee meetings, stonewalling bureaucrats, official denials, and the occasional outright hostility. In the final days of June, the CCCO organized a series of nonviolent sit-ins and protests targeting real estate offices that the AFSC had identified as supporting segregated housing. A major march on the morning of Saturday July 30 left from New Friendship Baptist Church, heading for Marquette Park. More than four hundred fifty people, including Mahalia, joined the march, many encouraged by Jackson's exhortations on radio station WBEE to African-American women: "Clean your kitchen, clean your house, and then go march for something better!" But at Sixty-Seventh Street, they were met by hundreds of screaming brick-, rock-, and bottle-throwing whites who countered the marcher's freedom songs with, "I'd love to be an Alabama trooper / And that is what I'd truly like to be / Because if I were an Alabama trooper / I could shoot niggers, one, two, three." While police separated the groups and arrested seven whites, there were several injuries. What frightened Jackson the most, however, was the sight of American citizens holding signs with swastikas. When CCCO officials begged her not to march again, she wrote a letter to Daley, with whom she had had a long relationship: "We need you here when we get back. In the name of the Lord let them march, but give them protection. We don't have a toothpick to fight with." Daley politely responded, thanking her for her comments and enquiring as to her health.[20]

A second march on Sunday fared even worse. An estimated five hundred fifty black and white activists, including nineteen priests, left their automobiles at

Marquette Park, then marched through the all-white Gage Park en route to Halvorsen Realtors. They were met by thousands of angry whites who again assaulted the marchers with racist signs and chants, bricks, bottles, rocks, and firecrackers. More than fifty people, including two policemen, were injured; fourteen whites were arrested. Gang members flanked the marchers and claimed to have prevented more injuries by batting down the thrown debris. Police repeatedly tried to disperse the whites, who chased the marchers brandishing a noose, burning a cross in the street, and screaming "KKK." "It's worse than Mississippi or Selma," one marcher said. "Down there, white people had guts enough to wade in and physically assault you. Up here, they hide behind buildings and hurl rocks, bottles, cherry bombs." When the battered marchers returned to Marquette Park, they found dozens of their cars vandalized, overturned, or destroyed, with two—including one rented by Andrew Young, who saw its headlights shining through the murk—pushed into the park's lagoon. Marchers said that police had promised that a detail would remain to protect the automobiles. Finally returning to the relative safety of the "black side" of town, Wentworth Avenue, battered demonstrators were met by a crowd of African-Americans, including numerous children, singing "We Shall Overcome." Many of the exhausted marchers began to sing as well.[21]

On the evening of Thursday, August 4, King returned to Chicago from church and SCLC responsibilities elsewhere. The previous days had been marked by mostly peaceful open-housing protests, though the venom from white onlookers was unsettling even to veteran marchers. At New Friendship Baptist Church, "the air was electric with the spirit and conviction of the Movement" and two thousand supporters roared through speeches by Raby and Bevel as Jackson sang and led the congregation in song. King responded with one of his most "inspiring" speeches, telling listeners that they too deserved good homes and schools. Energized, Friday's march began with more than six hundred demonstrators led by King, Raby, and Jackson and included many rabbis and priests. The procession was protected by nearly a thousand police officers. As they approached Marquette Park, they were attacked by an even larger crowd of angry whites throwing a fusillade of dangerous objects, including firecrackers and knives. King was hit in the head with a fist-sized rock almost immediately, but gamely continued as the battle raged on Chicago's Southwest side. Some whites chanted, "Two, four, six, eight, we don't want to integrate" and wore Nazi symbols and helmets. Others screamed, "Burn them like Jews!" The police were assaulted and one small group was nearly overwhelmed by furious whites until reinforcements arrived to rescue them. Dozens of marchers were injured and police made nearly forty arrests as violence against blacks continued long into the evening. A bandaged King told a reporter, "I've never seen anything like it in my life. I think the people from Mississippi ought to come to Chicago to learn to hate."[22]

David Wallace, a seminary student who was active with Operation Breadbasket, remembered one mass meeting during this period held at union leader Addie Wyatt's Vernon Park Church of God in Christ. Previous marches had not gone well and many of the demonstrators were bruised and discouraged, but Wyatt had participated in the southern campaigns and was not cowed by Daley's "machine." Ben Branch, a saxophone player with a long list of R & B, blues, and gospel recording sessions, had founded the Operation Breadbasket band. As Branch's band performed, Mahalia Jackson appeared to encourage the marchers and joined with Branch's group, singing "Joshua Fit the Battle of Jericho." "Boy, I mean, she sang," Wallace recalled. "She was really into it and just lift that place up. It had a balcony . . . all of the way up to the pulpit. It was packed, main floor, balcony . . . you talk about binding people together. People were strengthened to go out and know that they were likely to come under such fire as we'd been in before. Her singing and Dr. King's preaching just kind of brought all that together and people were fortified to go forth."[23]

The sheer scale of activities in Chicago continually taxed the resources of the CCCO and the SCLC, with monthly expenses exceeding $10,000.[24] Throughout 1966, Coretta King performed freedom songs and spirituals at a series of "Freedom Concerts," primarily in the Northeast. The fund-raisers netted the SCLC $20,000.[25] Bevel was also forced to call Harry Belafonte on several occasions, begging for another concert or fund-raiser to raise another $25,000 to sustain the movement "through the next project, through the next round." "I don't think people knew how much he contributed," Finley, then Bevel's aide, said of Belafonte. "He was always there to bail things out when they were going badly. And that's even more important: somebody you can call when you really need help."[26]

Exhausted, both sides slowly staggered to the negotiating tables over the next few weeks, even as smaller marches continued. Police fired their weapons in the air and fought thousands of whites attacking a much smaller group of marchers in the all-white Belmont-Cragin neighborhoods, a predominantly Eastern European enclave in Chicago's Northwest Side. Plans for marches in the Bogan and Cicero areas finally drove Daley to call for negotiations. Cook County Sheriff Richard B. Ogilvie vowed to prevent any march in Cicero and claimed that he had information that residents there would "make Gage Park look like a tea party." The first meeting was arranged by the Chicago Conference on Religion and Race with the Commission on Human Relations, the Chicago Real Estate Board, the city's mortgage bankers, and religious leaders, along with representatives from Daley's office and the Chicago Freedom Movement. Proposals and counterproposals were exchanged in the lengthy meeting on Wednesday August 17. As detailed in David R. Garrow's meticulous account of the events in *Bearing the Cross: Martin Luther King, Jr. and the Southern Leadership Conference,* the testy negotiations nearly broke down on several occasions, only to be saved more than once by King's eloquence. The greatest test to the negotiations came when a judge, at Daley's request, ordered an injunction on further marches on August 20, allowing only a single demonstration each day, to be composed of no more than five hundred people, and held only between the morning and evening rush hours. Police were also to be given notice twenty-four hours in advance. Activists denounced the injunction as "unconstitutional" and filed motions to have it overturned. Subsequent protests abided by the judge's order but the CCCO resumed calls for a march in Cicero, which had a history of racially motivated violence. At the prospect of a march in the all-white suburban city, Illinois Governor Otto G. Kerner mobilized units of the state National Guard. With Cicero hanging over their heads, negotiators met again on August 25 and, eventually, agreed to a ten-point plan to end discrimination in residential housing sales. The Real Estate Board agreed to end its stated opposition to open housing. The so-called Summit Agreement, however, required that Chicago activists accept "on good faith" alone that subsequent meetings would occur and, if occurring, would lead to substantive change in Chicago's vast slums. For their part, many activists believed that there had been yet another "sell out" of the African-American community to the city administration. A bruised and weary King could only characterize the pact as "the first step in a thousand mile journey."[27]

After the announcement, the CCCO held a "Victory Rally" in a West Side church, just two blocks from a section of Roosevelt Road where rioting had gutted most of the storefronts. Paul Good, who had covered the movement in the South, writes that King and various other activists spoke and the congregation sang "This Little Light of Mine," but the mass meeting lacked the sense of relief and joy of mass meetings in Birmingham or Selma. "The atmosphere was heavy with those simpler days when the thrust of spirit had seemed enough and the complexities thrown up by unyielding white power had not betrayed black trust and divided the movement," Good writes. "But now it was a different and complex day, and most Negroes were interested in reaping an overdue harvest."[28]

Three months after both parties had signed, a city councilman was able to tell his colleagues in a public meeting, "There is no Summit Agreement." It was simply "a goal to be reached," nothing more.[29] Ultimately, the goal of transforming Chicago may have been too ambitious, especially when all but a handful of African-American pastors allied themselves with Daley. The vicious attacks on the CCCO and King by the powerful Baptist leader Rev. J. H. Jackson meant that, unlike most previous movement battlegrounds, the CCCO never worked with the full support of the black church.[30]

Despite the general perception that the Chicago Freedom Movement was a failure, there were successes in Chicago, though they were not as flashy as in Birmingham or Selma. Jimmy Collier said that the SCLC's goal, from the beginning, was to reach "the largest audience possible" for the message of open housing. As one of the last great civil rights protests, Chicago certainly captured the attention of the nation's media. And, as James R. Ralph has noted, just as Selma had presaged the Voting Rights Bill of 1965, the Chicago open-housing pact, however tenuous, was a "prophetic" connection to the congressional debate over the inclusion of a fair-housing section in the Civil Rights Bill of 1966.[31]

There was also the matter of Operation Breadbasket, which had found a prominent home in Chicago. Adrian Dove called it a "combination religious service,

**FIGURE 23**

From the office of the Reverend Clay Evans,
a photograph of the signing of an agreement
between Operation Breadbasket and the A&P
grocery store chain to employ more African-
American workers. King (third from left) and
Jesse Jackson, who spearheaded Operation
Breadbasket (second from right), were party
to the signing, along with representatives from
A&P. Photograph courtesy of the Reverend
Clay Evans.

concert and civil rights meeting." Clay Evans's protégé, Jesse Jackson, had led Operation Breadbasket as it signed historic accords with dairy firms, soft-drink bottlers, big supermarket chains, including A&P, and other major Chicago employers to hire more African-Americans.

Breadbasket's original home was the McGifford House dining hall at Chicago Theological Seminary, but space requirements soon forced a move to the basement of Evans's Fellowship Missionary Baptist Church. The regular Saturday morning food pantry and informal concert were soon attracting top artists in every genre. Mavis Staples says that King himself asked them to perform in the early days of the project. "People in Chicago don't know Jesse Jackson," he told Pops Staples, "but if they know you and the family will be there to sing, the people will come out. Pops, if you do this for me, I'll owe you one." According to Mavis, Pops replied, "Doctor, you don't ever owe me nothing." King also persuaded powerful Chicago radio station WVON to broadcast from Operation Breadbasket each week. The Salem Travelers with Robert Dixon were among the gospel groups who performed on Saturday mornings. Some groups continued to perform when Operation Breadbasket split with the SCLC and became Operation PUSH in 1971. Eventually, Saturday mornings drew crowds of four thousand or more with regular and extensive media coverage. The event became a mandatory stop for musicians, politicians, and other celebrities, including Cannonball Adderley (who recorded his *Country Preacher* album at Operation Breadbasket), Quincy Jones, Ramsey Lewis, Aretha Franklin, Rance Allen, Jerry Butler, Nelson Rockefeller, the Staple Singers, Curtis Mayfield, and Isaac Hayes. "It got to the point where anybody who wanted to do anything in Chicago felt like they needed to come by Operation Breadbasket and touch base," Wallace said.[32]

As the spiritual home of gospel music, one of the bonuses of the Chicago Freedom Movement was the active involvement and support of gospel musicians. In addition to Mahalia Jackson, Evelyn Gay and the Gay Sisters organized several fund-raising programs during 1966 and beyond. The Reverend Maceo Woods and members of his congregation also participated in the rallies, mass meetings, and fund-raising events, as did the Roberta Martin Singers, Albertina Walker, Inez Andrews and the Caravans, the Reverend Stanley Keeble, Willie Taplin Barrow, and the Strings of Harmony. The Chicago-based Reuben Burton and the Victory Travelers were also active and recorded several civil rights–related songs during this period, including "I Signed a Contract with Jesus," "I Know I've Been Changed," "What Are You Going to Do When Jesus Comes," "I Have a Newborn Soul" and "I Need Jesus." Burton recalled that the Travelers performed at several benefits for the movement at Evans's Fellowship Missionary Baptist Church. Burton and the Travelers also marched in some of the protest marches, including a bloody trek on Independence Avenue. In addition to benefits and rallies, Inez Andrews said that the Caravans participated in planting gardens and food distribution for Operation Breadbasket.[33]

Ben Branch, a top session musician and bandleader, had been one of the earliest supporters of the movement, attending when there were only twenty or thirty people. "It just so happened I was the only musician there in the meeting," Branch said, "and I spoke to him [Jackson] about helping with these musicians. He said, 'Well, maybe we should try to organize it and get a group of them together.'" Branch brought his current group, Ben Branch and the Down Homers, to the next meeting and those musicians became the foundation of the Operation Breadbasket Orchestra. The group eventually expanded to include more than seventy-five members and could split into two separate bands. From the Saturday morning concerts at Fellowship, the orchestra traveled wherever the movement needed music and support before it eventually settled in the much larger venues in Chicago to accommodate the crowds. Branch said he had first met King during one of the fund-raising rallies that included Belafonte, Aretha Franklin, and Marlon Brando. At one of the Operation Breadbasket morning sessions, Branch and the orchestra played an arrangement of "Take My Hand, Precious Lord" for King. The first time King heard it, he told Branch to play the chorus several more times. From that moment, it became the song that King always requested when he saw Branch. "When I was a kid, I always wanted to sing this song in my church," Branch recalled. "This was really the height of my ambition, to do this in church, to sing this song. Just to show you how if you have faith and believe in God how sometimes things can really come about that you're just not aware of. Now this has been a part of my life all of my life with this one song; and all of a sudden that dream just came into my life."[34]

The Operation Breadbasket Orchestra's other signature numbers included "Motherless Child," "If I Can Help Somebody," and "We Shall Overcome." Regular musicians included Donny Hathaway, Gene Barge, Wayne Bennett, Richard Thomas, and his son Eric. Eventually, the Saturday morning events were moved to the Parkway Ballroom because of the size of the crowd. Movement regulars on Saturday mornings included James and Charles Bevel, who sang freedom songs. "In Breadbasket, the music was there," recalled Hermene Hartman. "The music was what attracted me. You came back for the music. The music was a capturing point. The music provided a theme. The words of the songs were paired with activity and events and situations of happenings of the day. Expressing a mood, expressing a tone, expressing a rationale, if you will, of what we were doing and why."[35] Under the direction of gospel great Albertina Walker, the Operation Breadbasket Choir, later the Operation PUSH Choir after the organization's split with the SCLC, also flourished.[36]

According to Gay, the songs sung in Chicago mass meetings often differed from those he had heard sung in the southern freedom movement. During the "offerings" at the movement, the jubilee song "He's Got the Whole World in His Hands," with the lyric "Come on with your money / Don't be afraid to give / God's got the whole world in his hands" was usually sung. Other Chicago mass meeting songs included "I Can Hear Jesus Calling Me," Eugene Smith's "I Know the Lord Will Make a Way, Oh Yes He Will," and the old spiritual "You Gotta Move." "We're Gonna Have a Good Time," with the lines, "When the war is over / We're gonna shout, trouble's over / We're gonna have a time," was sung at rallies to inspire marchers. Evelyn Gay's song "God Is on Our Side" featured the Chicago-specific lines "God told Pharaoh to let my people go / Pharaoh disobeyed and God let him know / That he was King Almighty and the Lord God is his name / If you will only trust him / He'll send the latter rain." Gay said that "God Is on Our Side" was sung for King on numerous occasions. "The music had to sell the people," Gay said. "Us being a musical people, we had to hear the music. Sometimes the words and verbiage got a little tiring. But if you listen to that song—you can go farther with a song because that song will stay with you longer than those words." Gay also recalled Mahalia Jackson singing W. Herbert Brewster's "How I Got Over" at the Chicago rallies and mass meetings.[37] At other times, Chicago marchers adapted familiar freedom songs. After the Gage-Marquette Park rallies, demonstrators sang, "Ain't going to let no King Richard turn me 'round."[38] "This Little Light of Mine" became "I Don't Want to Be Lost in the Slums" in Chicago: "The reason I sing this song, I don't wanna be lost / The reason I sing this song, I don't wanna be lost / The reason I sing this song, I don't wanna be lost / I don't wanna be lost in the slums."[39]

Jimmy Collier became the Chicago Freedom Movement's most readily identified song-leader and composer. "The Chicago movement found its voice in the songs of Collier," writes Tammy Kernodle. "As vividly as songwriters like Matthew Jones had been in documenting the sights, sounds, and experiences of the southern movement, Collier did the same in expressing what black life was like in the slums of Chicago."[40] Collier had joined King early in the Chicago Freedom Movement, still sporting the same battered guitar he had used in Selma. King and Ralph Abernathy felt sorry him, Collier recalls, and pooled their money to buy him a new guitar. "Chicago was a tough nut. And the North, in general, proved to be difficult organizing. The music never changed, except that there was probably a little more rhythm and blues. But it was still the spirituals [that] were the core of what was being sung on the picket lines and whatnot." Collier sang wherever the CCCO operated: community centers, settlement houses, school auditoriums and classrooms, street rallies, picket lines, and churches.[41] In addition to leading the singing of freedom songs, Collier was an accomplished composer and his "Burn, Baby, Burn," about the Watts riots, was already in the movement's repertoire. Collier said the frustrations felt in Watts were also felt by the African-Americans living in Chicago. "And with this song," he writes, "part-way through, after they've sung the song and got out some of their hate and some of their vengeance, we try to put in our own pitch about using nonviolence to change things. We say you've got to learn, baby, learn, and what you really want to do is build something rather than tear down."[42] Two of Collier's songs most identified with Chicago are "Lead Poison on the Wall" ("The landlord does nothing to stop it all / That death on the walls") and "Rent Strike Blues" ("Everybody black and white / 'titled to a decent place to stay").[43]

# 9

## MEMPHIS, TENNESSEE

*O graveyard, O graveyard,*
*I'm walkin troo de graveyard;*
*Lay dis body down.*

*I know moonlight, I know starlight,*
*I'm walking troo the starlight;*
*Lay dis body down.*

*I go to the judgment in de evenin' of de day,*
*Lay dis body down.*

*And my soul an' your soul will meet in de day,*
*When we lay dis body down.*

—OLD SPIRITUAL

The year that followed the Chicago Freedom Movement was as tumultuous for Dr. Martin Luther King, Jr., and the SCLC as it was for the rest of the nation.[1] The situation in Chicago was never fully resolved, necessitating several return visits; violence flared again in Grenada, Mississippi, where African-Americans were still being denied the vote; Johnson's latest civil rights bill was again scuttled when Republicans in the Senate declined to support the open-housing title; and in Georgia, avowed segregationist and restaurateur Lester Maddox was elected governor.[2] For the movement at large, the most significant event of 1967 may have been King's decision to publicly oppose the escalating war in Vietnam. In March, he joined five thousand antiwar marchers in a demonstration in Chicago, calling the war "a blasphemy against all that America stands for" and saying that the cost of Vietnam hindered both the civil rights movement and antipoverty programs. During a sermon at New York's historic Riverside Church on April 4, King called for a boycott of the war in Vietnam. In his most public denunciation of the war, King noted that African-Americans were "dying in disproportionate numbers" in the conflict. The almost overwhelmingly negative response to his declaration left King "badly shaken, even stunned, by the ferocity of the pro-war attack." Many of King's long-time supporters, Bayard Rustin, Whitney M. Young, Jr., and even baseball great Jackie Robinson, either refused to comment on his statement or disassociated themselves from it. The directors of the NAACP voted unanimously to reject the suggestion that the movement "merge the civil rights and peace movements." An editorial in the *New York Times,* whose extensive coverage of the movement had been essential, decried the "fusing" of the antiwar and civil rights movements and claimed that King's words "could very well be disastrous for both causes."[3]

Further complicating matters, the "long hot summer," what James H. Cone has called a "black insurrection," struck most major U.S. cities, leaving dozens dead, thousands injured, and neighborhoods gutted and burned from the rioting. Especially hard hit were Detroit and Newark. It was the worst summer of President Lyndon B. Johnson's political life as well. One biographer said that the Newark riots "threw Johnson into a mood of near despair." Antiwar demonstrations grew in size and violence, even as military commanders requested and received authorization to increase American forces in Vietnam to five hundred twenty-five thousand by mid-1968.[4]

King and the SCLC convened in Atlanta on August 18, facing serious challenges from the growing "black power" movement and the ever-present fundraising difficulties, which had been heightened by the organization's public stance against the war. At an opening night gala marking the group's tenth anniversary, the featured singer was Aretha Franklin. Though not as outspoken as Mahalia Jackson or the Staple Singers, Franklin had supported the movement financially, especially the SNCC. Franklin's hits "Respect," "I Never Loved a Man (the Way I Love You)," and "Chain of Fools" had made her the number one female artist in the country and epitomized the positive aspects of the "black power" movement. The SCLC was eager to make that association. Amid the grim financial and operational news, Sidney Poitier spoke and said of King, "The courage of this man has made a better man of me." It was King's policy statement, however, that drew the headlines: The SCLC would embark on a new campaign to "dislocate" American cities employing "mass civil disobedience." Throughout the days in Atlanta, the organization discussed how best to move in 1968.[5]

The SCLC eventually settled on the Poor People's Campaign, an initiative designed to address the changing landscape of American race relations and the rise of the black power movement, while still keeping a focus on nonviolent actions. On December 4, the proposal was announced. The Poor People's Campaign would involve relocating several thousand poor people from different states to a "highly visible shantytown" in Washington, DC, during May and June 1968. The SCLC and campaign leadership proposed a series of nonviolent demonstrations that would lead to mass arrests and encourage similar such actions across the country. Again, the public and media response to the initiative was mixed at best. A *New York Times* editorial directly opposed the idea, especially the threat of "massive dislocation" of the capital, stating, "This is one more case in which the means are not justified by the ends."[6]

New Year's Eve found King in Chicago with Mahalia Jackson. Along with Bernard Lee, Chauncey Eskridge, and Russell Goode, they attended a small party at the home of one of Jackson's friends. "Martin was in a mood to sing," Jackson's biographer Laurraine Goreau writes. "He sang for Mahalia some of the gospel songs he liked best. Then Mahalia sang his favorite, 'Take My Hand, Precious Lord,' the song that was like a prayer to her. Then they sang together." At five minutes to midnight, Jackson left the room to pray until midnight, as was her custom. When she returned, King said, "This is going to be a *terrible* year," then began another song. "Mahalia came to join him, and they sang together."[7] The early months of 1968 were consumed with the planning for the Poor People's Campaign, despite Rustin's continued arguments against the plan, saying that any action designed to "disrupt transportation" and block government buildings would lead to "further backlash and repression," in addition to hindering critical fund-raising efforts.[8]

In the midst of the turmoil and preparations for the Poor People's Campaign, few noticed—and fewer media outlets reported—an incident on January 31 in Memphis.[9] Twenty-two black sanitation workers were sent home when it began raining, though white workers remained on the job. An hour later, the rain stopped. The white workers received a full day's pay, while the African-American workers received nothing. Even at $1.70 an hour, this was a financial blow as nearly half of all sanitation workers qualified for welfare. On February 1, two sanitation workers, both black, were "ground up like garbage" by a malfunctioning city garbage truck. Their families were offered an additional month's salary and funeral expenses, but nothing more. The two incidents, the latest in a long line, precipitated a request to the city council and Memphis's imperious mayor, Henry Loeb, for improvements in their dangerous, dirty working conditions. The mayor flatly refused. On February 12, thirteen hundred African-American sanitation workers walked off the job, demanding a pay raise, merit (instead of race-related) promotions, and recognition of their union, the American Federation of State, County and Municipal Employees (AFSCME). Again, city officials refused to see them and hired nonunion workers to collect the garbage.[10] The workers' demonstrations became associated with a series of long-standing grievances in the black community and their marches soon had the notice of civil rights leaders. Rallies at the United Rubber Worker's Hall continued daily and black churches hosted mass meetings several times a week for the next two months. A march by a thousand sanitation workers on February 24 was met by nightstick-swinging policemen, tear gas, and mace. The city responded by obtaining an injunction prohibiting union leaders from joining in the protests. The attacks on strikers grew in frequency and intensity until February 26, when more than a hundred African-American ministers called on blacks to boycott downtown businesses, businesses owned by the city councilmen, and the two daily newspapers, both of which resolutely backed the white establishment.[11]

As for King, he continued to cross the country, often accompanied by Gladys McFadden and the Loving Sisters, raising support for the Poor People's Campaign. "We were in every state with him," McFadden recalls, "and Klansmen were trying to run us off the road."[12] On February 28, King spoke to the Minister's Leadership Training Conference in Miami. He was doubtless aware of the constant criticism and how, to some, his nonviolent crusade was appearing increasingly irrelevant in a day when "black power" dominated the media discourse. King, however, never lost hope in the movement or its music, and forcefully said so:

> I am not going to stop singing "We shall overcome," because I know that "truth crushed to the earth shall rise again." I am not going to stop sing-ing "We shall overcome," because I know the Bible is right, "you shall reap what you sow." I am not going to stop singing, "We shall overcome," because I know that one day the God of the universe will say to those who don't listen to him, "I'm not a playboy. Don't play with me. For I will rise up and break the backbone of your power." I'm not going to stop singing, "We shall overcome," because "mine eyes have seen the glory of the com-ing of the Lord. He's trampling out our vintage where the grapes of wrath are stored. Glory hallelujah, his truth is marching on."[13]

It was during the first week of the strike that Bill Lucy, the highest-ranking African-American in the national AFSCME organization, proclaimed what would become the defining image and cry of the strike, "I Am a Man." Steve Estes attributes the power of the slogan, bolstered by photographs of hundreds of white placards held by strikers, can be attributed, in part, to a "theme of the Delta blues that had pumped out of Beale Street clubs and juke joints since before World War II," and epitomized by the Muddy Waters' song, "Mannish Boy."[14] Memphis was also home to the influential civil rights pioneer W. Herbert Brewster of East Trigg Baptist Church, whose songs, sermons, and gospel pageants had been promoting racial equality since the 1940s.[15] These elements, coupled with continued police violence against strikers, prompted the formation of the Community on the Move for Equality (COME) by more than one hundred fifty ministers under the direction of longtime SCLC ally James Lawson, the pastor of Centenary Methodist Church. College and high school students soon began participating in the demonstrations as well. The strike, which the sanitation workers had begun, evolved into a full-scale movement that addressed a long list of grievances in Memphis. On March 14, a number of activists came to Memphis to address the nightly mass meetings, including the SCLC's Rustin and Roy Wilkins, executive director of the NAACP. Wilkins told the strikers, "Don't foul your nest. Don't go out and tear up the town. Just don't give an inch in your demands." Rustin, "bathed in sweat and arms high above head," led in the singing of "This Little Light of Mine." The nine thousand people in the Mason Temple rocked with "wild cheers," and the meeting continued with "hymns, freedom songs and Black Power signs." At the conclusion, Rustin, "a grand singer," led those assembled in singing more freedom songs, including "Ain't Gonna Let Nobody Turn Me 'Round." In mid-March, as the economic boycott began to affect downtown businesses, attacks on the churches hosting the meetings began to rise as well, along with "isolated but ominous incidents of fire bombings, bottle throwing and trash fires" in African-American neighborhoods. At Lawson's invitation, King came to Memphis to speak to fifteen thousand people at the Mason Temple. The crowd received his remarks enthusiastically, even as King admitted his own struggles over the previous year: "Sometimes I feel discouraged having to live under the threat of death every day. Sometimes I feel discouraged, having to take so much abuse and criticism, sometimes from my own people." However, the response at the "lively rally" was so compelling that Lawson, COME members, and some of his own aides on the podium urged King to return to the city to lead a mass march on March 22. After the disappointments of the past two years, local church leaders implored him to come and support their efforts. The unions were equally supportive. And, as David L. Lewis notes, "'We Shall Overcome' was still sung in Memphis and there was no coalition of CORE and SNCC to shout down those gentle lyrics." Despite his overcommitted schedule, and buoyed by what he had seen and heard, King agreed to return. Back at the Lorraine Motel that evening, where African-American musicians and politicians had stayed while in Memphis since the 1950s, King was met by two old friends, Ben Hooks and Samuel "Billy" Kyles, both Memphis ministers. "I've never seen a community as together as Memphis," he told them. At midnight, a girls' choir from Texas, dressed in "pajamas and bathrobes," serenaded King outside his room with songs with a "Hallelujah" motif. The next morning, King began another whirlwind tour of the South to promote the Poor People's Campaign.[16]

The sanitation workers, their ranks swelled by white union members and students from area colleges and high schools, determinedly continued their picket lines, marches, and protests, usually singing freedom songs and adaptations of labor songs. Occasionally, a puckish sense of humor found its way into the lyrics, as witnessed by this adaptation of the old protest spiritual/union song "We Shall Not Be Moved": "Pork chops, pork chops, greasy, greasy / We can beat Loeb, easy, easy / Loeb shall, he shall, he shall be removed / Just like a can of garbage in the alley / Loeb shall be removed."[17]

A freakish sixteen-inch snowfall in Memphis and across the South postponed the much-publicized March 22 demonstration. King continued his barnstorming tour promoting the Poor People's Campaign, from Mississippi to Harlem, where he admitted to reporters that he was "overly tired" from the travel and was sleeping only two hours per night. He still returned to Memphis to keep his commitment to march on March 28.[18]

**FIGURE 24**

In Memphis, Dr. Martin Luther King, Jr., walks
with marchers in early April 1968. Photo courtesy of Preservation and Special Collections,
University Libraries, University of Memphis.

In the ten days since King's last visit, negotiations with the city had gone nowhere, with even small agreements scuttled by Loeb. On Thursday morning, more than six thousand demonstrators (though movement estimates were much higher) departed from Clayborn Temple African Methodist Episcopal Church shortly after 11 a.m., led by King and heading for City Hall. "King's face exhibited his exhaustion and discomfort," writes David J. Garrow. Singing "We Shall Overcome" and holding placards, the march appeared at first like hundreds of previous civil rights demonstrations across the South. Also present, but not a part of the march, were hundreds of teenagers from different Memphis high schools. School officials estimated that twenty-two thousand students played hooky or left school early. Some of the placards along the march route were vulgar or confrontational, in stark contrast to the union's ever-present "I Am a Man" signs. As the long procession approached Beale Street, windows along the route were suddenly shattered and a small group of individuals began looting the stores. Parade marshals rushed back to stop the vandalism. Elsewhere, police clashed with high school students who were intent on joining the march. As police worked to halt the looters, more violence erupted. Soon, clouds of tear gas dispersed the crowd, as police indiscriminately attacked suspected looters and peaceful marchers alike. More than sixty-four people were injured and two hundred eighty-two were arrested. One young man was shot and killed by police, who claimed he attacked them with a knife. In the hours that followed, police units continued to use tear gas, roughly herding the marchers back toward Clayborn Temple, which enraged still more demonstrators and onlookers. Almost immediately, suspicion was raised about the identity of those who had disrupted the march, leading some to speculate that they had been in the employ of rogue elements in the city, local antisegregation groups or the "short fuses of fatigued forces on the fringe of the black freedom movement." The foremost Memphis gang, the Intruders, denied instigating or participating in the looting. King and the leaders of the demonstration escaped harm, but King was said to be "discouraged" by the violence. Acting on a law that had only been approved that day, Loeb declared a 7 p.m. curfew and Tennessee Governor Buford Ellington called up four thousand National Guard troops and a number of highway patrolmen at Loeb's request. That night, King became "despondent" about the day's events. "I had never seen him so depressed," Ralph Abernathy later said.[19]

In the following days, King vowed to return to Memphis to mount a "massive" civil rights march to demonstrate, again, that such protests could be conducted in a nonviolent manner. Subsequent demonstrations by the striking sanitation workers, most carrying the "I Am a Man" placards, took place without incident under the watchful eye of National Guardsmen. The *New York Times* used the incident to again editorialize against the proposed Poor People's Campaign. The turmoil in Memphis was nearly forgotten on the evening of March 31 when Lyndon Johnson, after debating the merits of such a monumental decision for months, announced that he would not seek a second full term as president. The increasing opposition to the War in Vietnam and health concerns had eventually led him to the decision.

During a sermon the next morning at the National Cathedral, King pledged to the cancel the Poor People's Campaign, if Congress or the now lame-duck President made specific proposals and a "positive commitment that they would do something this summer" to assist in antipoverty efforts.[20]

On Sunday March 31, most of King's staff returned to Memphis and the Lorraine Motel. James Orange, the SCLC member who had worked so successfully with gangs in Chicago, and other SCLC staff members met with the leadership of the Invaders at the Lorraine Motel. The Invaders and Lawson had had an acrimonious relationship and Orange worked to insure the group's support and cooperation for the proposed second march, now set for Monday April 8. The Invaders, in return, wanted financial support for their own organizing efforts and an official voice in COME. They could not, however, guarantee a peaceful march.[21] On Monday, hundreds of African-Americans viewed the body of Larry Payne, sixteen, the only casualty of the previous Thursday's disturbance. While tensions in Memphis had eased, National Guard troops bracketed Clayborn Temple African Methodist Episcopal Church, where many of Thursday's protesters had fled following the abortive march.[22]

On April 3, a federal judge issued a restraining order against "out-of-state residents," including King, Abernathy, Hosea Williams, Bevel, Orange, and Bernard Lee, along with their "servants, agents, employees and those in concert with them from organizing in or engaging in a massive parade or march in the city of Memphis."[23] King responded "angrily," and suggested that the SCLC may defy the order, as it had in Birmingham in 1963. King urged labor to support the planned demonstration, saying that the situation was such that civil rights organizations were now forced to expand the Memphis action beyond just the striking sanitation workers—and urged all parties to "go all out" in placing economic pressure on the city. Back at the Lorraine Motel that afternoon, King, still fatigued, met with SCLC associates and representatives from the Invaders, and eventually asked Abernathy to represent him and speak at a rally at the Mason Temple. The stormy weather kept the crowd small, perhaps two thousand, though Beifuss suggests it was closer to three thousand, including many Public Works employees. When Abernathy saw the television cameras and reporters, he sensed that the audience was disappointed at not hearing King himself. He called King, who wearily drove to the Mason Temple, as Abernathy improvised a laudatory thirty-minute introduction. Amid the rolling storm's thunderclaps, King arrived about 9 p.m.[24]

King's impromptu remarks that evening have come to be known as the "Mountain Top" speech by some, the "Jericho Road" speech by others, studied by scholars and religious leaders alike, parsed and dissected for what some believe was a premonition of the events that followed. King told the enthusiastic crowd that, given the choice to live at any time in history, he would want to be living now. He cited the use of "Ain't Gonna Let Nobody Turn Me 'Round" and "Over My Head, I See Freedom in the Air" when standing before the dogs and water cannons in Birmingham. He told of singing "We Shall Overcome" in Birmingham's paddy wagons and how those jailed were "moved by our words and songs. There was a power there which Bull Connor couldn't adjust to." And, in speaking of the injunction not to march again in Memphis, he said, "We aren't going to let any injunction turn us around."[25] Near the end, King said, "Well, I don't know what will happen now. We've got some difficult days ahead. But it really doesn't matter with me now. Because I've been to the mountain top." Moments later, referring to the same Moses he has been compared to since Montgomery, King continued: "I just want to do God's will. And he's allowed me to go up to the mountain. And I've looked over. And I've seen the Promised Land. I may not get there with you. But I want you to know tonight, that we as a people will get to the Promised Land." To his audience, this was a clear reference to Deuteronomy 34:1–8, where, after the long exodus from Egypt, God allows Moses to see the Promised Land from atop Mount Nebo (also called Mount Pisgah), but tells him that the old warrior will never "cross over there." And finally, his voice rising in a booming preacher's cadence, King shouted, "So I'm happy tonight. I'm not worried about anything. I'm not fearing any man. Mine eyes have seen the glory of the coming of the Lord!" For the closing of his final public speech, King invoked "The Battle Hymn of the Republic," and, as Beifuss reports, "The sound of the crowd comes up, engulfs, surrounds, pushes, catches, threatens, all turning on him, lifting him up." Some of the assembled ministers and union leaders on the stage broke down in tears. Uncharacteristically, King remained in the drafty Mason Temple after his sermon and shook hands and talked with those in attendance that night.[26] The Reverend Harold Middlebrook, who observed that King had looked "harrowed and tired and worn and rushed" when he entered Mason Temple, said that King's eyes were full of tears as he finished his speech. The Reverend James Jordan said that while he had seen other preachers in tears after emotional sermons, he had never seen King cry: "This time it just seemed like he was just saying, 'Goodbye, I hate to leave.'"[27]

### Thursday, April 4

Thursday, April 4, 1968, Dr. Martin Luther King, Jr., slept late into the morning. Meetings continued in Memphis, including the second gathering of black and white clergy who had hoped to present a statement to the mayor urging him to consider a resolution to the sanitation strike. The movement's attorneys appeared before Judge Bailey Brown and the city's attorneys in an effort to have the injunction for the proposed march reversed. By 4 p.m., the judge announced that he would give his written opinion on Friday morning, but that he was inclined to allow the march to proceed, as long as certain conditions were met. The sanitation workers strike continued, now in its fifty-third day, and Mayor Loeb continued to rebuff all attempts to negotiate. At the Lorraine Motel, it was business as usual in Room 306. King met with staffers and a handful of militants, and shared a catfish lunch with Abernathy. Union representatives arrived from an afternoon meeting. The Reverend Billy Kyles arrived and discussed the dinner he would host that evening at his home. Andrew

Young and attorney Chauncey Eskridge reported on the court hearing, which had gone well. King remained in his room, dressing for the evening.[28]

During the day, Ben Branch had arrived from Chicago. King specifically requested the Operation Breadbasket band for the Memphis engagement. Branch, Dave McCullough, Wayne Bennett, Al Fook, and Gene Barge had originally left on Wednesday, but the inclement weather had delayed their arrival in Memphis until Thursday April 4. The group was denied permission to rehearse at the Firestone Union Hall, so they drove to the Lorraine, where they rehearsed in the restaurant. While they rehearsed, a number of the ministers staying at the hotel drifted by, each wanting to sing. "The ones I can remember are the ones that were trying to sing and trying to tell you how to play," Branch recalled. "And they were trying to tell us, 'Look, man, you're down South; you guys up in Chicago, you can't play like that down here.'" Kyles remembered the impromptu group singing several old gospel favorites, including "Yield Not to Temptation," "I'm So Glad Trouble Don't Last Always" and the spiritual, "I've Been 'Buked and I've Been Scorned." Among those present was the Reverend Jesse Jackson, who told Branch to ignore the other preachers: "Don't say anything to them. Just wait till tonight. They'll see. They'll see." Before moving to Chicago, Branch had fronted one of the most successful bands in Memphis and was well known in the city. After the rehearsal, Branch was among those who had been invited to join King and the other ministers and SCLC leadership for the early "soul food" supper before the evening's mass meeting. Just before 6 p.m., King and Kyles stood outside King's room on the second floor and saw Branch walk toward his car. From the courtyard, Jackson said, "Dr. King, here's old Ben Branch." King responded, "Yeah, that's my man, that's my man." King then looked directly at Branch and said, "Man, look, tonight, I want you play that 'Precious Lord' tonight like you never played it before.'" Branch said, "Dr. King, I do that all of the time." King nodded and said, "No, but tonight, especially for me, I want you to play it pretty tonight." King paused, said something to Jackson, then looked at Branch again. "Man, I tell you, *tonight* I want that song. I mean, I want you to play it *pretty* tonight, play it pretty." Branch, by now somewhat nonplussed, emphatically responded, "I'm gonna do that." King nodded and said, "Don't forget. I mean, I want 'Precious Lord.' Play it tonight."[29]

King turned toward his room just as the assassin's bullet struck him in the face. Among his last words had been to request Thomas Dorsey's elegiac heart-cry, written in the hours following the death of his wife and newborn baby.

The days following King's murder were as agonizingly endless as his passing was short. He was pronounced dead in the operating room within an hour. He died in the same emergency room where James Meredith, the first African-American to enroll in the University of Mississippi, was taken following the ambush on his quixotic March Against Fear. The FBI, which had spent years hounding and demonizing King at J. Edgar Hoover's orders, ordered a worldwide manhunt for the gunman, who left behind a great deal of evidence, including the discarded murder weapon, a 30.06-caliber rifle. Loeb ordered that curfew be reinstated and the National Guard was called out again, but rioting began almost immediately in Memphis as the word spread. Soon "disorders" were being reported in a host of American cities. Coretta King tried to fly to Memphis when she received the news, but was stranded at the Atlanta airport by storms. Atlanta Mayor Ivan Allen drove her home, where she received grieving friends and watched the extensive television coverage of the events unfolding in Memphis and elsewhere. A visibly disturbed Lyndon Johnson took to the airwaves to "deplore" King's "brutal slaying" and urged listeners to "reject the blind violence that has struck Dr. King, who lived by nonviolence."[30]

Once King had been pronounced dead, those closest to King, including Young, Abernathy, Kyles, Hosea Williams, Jim Bevel, and Lawson, left the hospital and eventually "converged" on the Lorraine around 1 a.m. where they decided to support Abernathy as King's successor of the SCLC. Lawson recalled that Abernathy suggested they spend time praying and singing together, including "We Shall Overcome." "We did a fellowship circle before we ended," Lawson said.[31] The men then tried to reach their friends in the media to ask that King's commitment to nonviolence be stressed in the developing coverage. "The dreamer has been killed," Young said, "but not the dream."[32]

In Detroit, Rosa Parks heard the news while listening to the radio. As the city erupted in violence, she held her mother and cried. They sat in her living room and played Sam Cooke's "A Change Is Gonna Come" over and over. Parks credited Cooke's song with "saving her sanity": "His smooth voice was like medicine to the soul," she said. "It was as if Dr. King was speaking directly to me." Parks flew to Memphis the same day and worked tirelessly with the dispirited sanitation workers. Belafonte later offered her a ride on his private plane for the funeral services in Atlanta.[33] In Nashville, the Staple Singers were about to leave for a concert when they heard the news. After the show, the group had planned to drive to Memphis to join King and the sanitation workers. In the hotel room, Pops Staples tried to embrace his children. "We were out of control," Mavis recalled. "We couldn't talk to each other for the longest time about it without crying." The group cancelled the concert, then drove nonstop back to their homes in Chicago.[34] In New York, Robert Dixon and the Salem Travelers and the Reverend James Cleveland were performing at the Apollo when the announcement was made. The famed venue shut down immediately. The Travelers and Cleveland were forced to remain at the Cecil Hotel for ten days as riots and unrest in New York and their hometown of Chicago brought the cities to a near standstill.[35]

The rioting spread across the country, a seemingly irresistible force. Senator Robert Kennedy arranged for a plane to fly Coretta King to Memphis from their Atlanta home. She met her husband's closest advisors at the R. S. Lewis Funeral Home as a steady stream of people poured in to view the body. A lengthy procession of automobiles escorted King's body to the airport, flanked by Memphis police and National Guardsmen. Attorney General Ramsey Clark met the group at the airport, but no representative from the City of Memphis was present. On the tarmac, about one hundred fifty people held a brief, emotional service, most unable to contain their tears. They sang a ragged version of "We Shall Overcome" over the roar of the jets, but some of the mourners "collapsed" as they tried to sing the refrain, "Yes, we will not fight / Yes, we will not fight / God is on our side / Today."[36]

Back in Atlanta, friends and loved ones filled the King household. Senator Kennedy installed three additional telephone lines to handle the hundreds, perhaps thousands of well-wishers calling Coretta. Harry Belafonte flew down immediately. "I just want to be there at your side and do any little menial thing to serve you in any way I can," she recalled him saying. "I want to share this sorrow with you, and I want you to know you can call on me for anything you need." Television stars Bill Cosby and Robert Culp from the hit television series *I Spy* arrived and spent the day playing with the King's children. Those who arrived at the modest house to pay their respects ranged from Robert, Ethel, and Jacqueline Kennedy to Richard Nixon. Still others, including Wyatt T. Walker and SCLC staff members, arrived to begin the Herculean task of organizing the myriad funeral arrangements.[37]

The murder "galvanized" national support for AFSCME and labor earmarked hundreds of thousands of dollars for the exhausted sanitation strikers. A number of public figures blamed King's assassination and subsequent riots in part on Loeb's refusal to recognize the union and its grievances. Illinois Governor Otto Kerner blamed the riots on white politicians who would not "take the first step" to resolve the issue. On Friday, Johnson instructed the Undersecretary of Labor James Reynolds to fly to Memphis to settle the issue. As Reynolds left Washington, DC, smoke billowed over the capital where ten people had died and a thousand buildings had burned in the worst devastation since the British invasion of 1814. The rioting and destruction continued elsewhere; Chicago was particularly hard hit. A year after the event, longtime movement activist Floyd McKissick was still angry and unapologetic over the demonstrations and riots. "Dr. King's death brought more bitterness than perhaps any single event in recent Black history," he writes. "If Martin Luther King, apostle of peace, could be slaughtered, then not one Black Man in America is safe." But not even the combined weight of Johnson's office and the Labor Department could make Loeb budge. He had been elected on the promise of refusing to recognize the union. Besides, he added, the city had spent all of its money on a new City Hall.[38]

Friends and admirers of the slain civil rights leader honored his legacy in a variety of creative ways. Senator Kennedy, speaking that evening in Indianapolis, delivered a six-minute, off-the-cuff tribute that remains a model of insight and clarity and, in the minds of many, helped that city avoid the destructive riots that were sweeping across the country. Kennedy, who had lost a brother to an assassin's bullet, spoke movingly of the pain he felt and the pain those in the audience were feeling when he shared the awful news.[39] In Boston, soul singer James Brown and public television station WGBH teamed together for a concert on April 5 that was taped and shown repeatedly. A visibly shaken Brown, who had performed for the March Against Fear at Tougaloo College in Mississippi and had known King, took the stage that evening and said, "We got to pay our respects to the late, great, incomparable—somebody we love very much, and I have all the admiration in the world for—I got a chance to know him personally—the late, great Martin Luther King." As with Kennedy's words, the combination of the concert and repeat showings is credited as a factor in Boston's relatively measured response to the murder.[40] In Atlanta, Robert Woodruff, the soft drink "tycoon" who was the anonymous benefactor of many of the city's nonprofit and civic ventures, called Mayor Allen. "Whatever you need will be taken care of," he said, referring to the costs of the funeral. When King's body is returned to Atlanta, he cautioned Allen, the city "is going to be the center of the universe."[41] Gospel singer and composer Gladys McFadden of the Loving Sisters knew there would be expenses in the days ahead as well. She contacted her neighbors, friends, church and family members in Arkansas with the announcement that she was going to the funeral "and if anybody wanted to contribute to the needs of the children, to donate, and they did." McFadden then drove to Atlanta, took the money to the King home and gave it to Coretta in person.[42]

### Friday, April 5

President Johnson declared Sunday a national day of mourning and met with African-American leaders in an attempt to defuse the rioting that had spread to most major American cities. National Guard troops were sent to Chicago and Detroit, while regular Army troops were called to Washington, DC. Johnson was among an estimated four thousand people, including most members of the Cabinet, the Supreme Court, and the leadership of virtually every African-American organization who attended a memorial service for King at the National Cathedral. As the cathedral filled for the noon service, the organist played "We Shall Overcome," "slowly, as a dirge." Citing King's request to play "Take My Hand, Precious Lord" just before his death, the gospel song was played and sung to an emotional response. Other memorial services were held throughout the capital and the heavy bells of the churches and cathedrals resounded throughout the day. After the service, Johnson called for a joint session of Congress to address the urgency he felt to pass the remaining "long-stalled items on his domestic agenda," including a "landmark civil rights bill." "No words of ours and no words of mine can fill the void of the eloquent voice that has been stilled," Johnson told reporters. "But this I do believe deeply: the dream of Martin Luther King, Jr., has not died with him."[43]

### Saturday, April 6

Now in a silk-lined coffin with a glass top to allow viewing, King's body was transported from Hanley Funeral Home to Spelman College in Atlanta. At the chapel, Coretta King, Belafonte and his wife Julie, and a few others were the first of what would be many thousands to view his remains. At Belafonte's urging, Coretta released her first public statement at a press conference at Ebenezer Baptist Church, urging the SCLC to continue its work under Abernathy, and saying how her faith had sustained her. "The day that Negro people and others in bondage are truly free," she added, "on the day want is abolished, on the day wars are no more, on that day I know my husband will rest in a long-deserved peace." Later that day, when Belafonte suggested that she join the march in Memphis, still scheduled for Monday, she "immediately" agreed. For the first time, the pastors of many of Atlanta's "old-guard" white churches, "segregated by custom if not law" called Mayor Allen at home to tell him that they would open their sanctuaries and buildings to the tens of thousands of mourners expected to arrive in the city in the days that followed. Shortly thereafter, Emory University, Georgia Tech, and Columbia Seminary also announced plans to open their dorms, dining halls, and gymnasium for the out-of-town visitors. Also in Atlanta, the SCLC leadership struggled with what seemed to be an insurmountable set of problems, including how to "assist in the logistics of what amounted to a state funeral," but without state funding, and then pick up the pieces after King's assassination and continue his dream.[44]

### Sunday, April 7

Memorial services for King were held across the United States on Palm Sunday. In New York, more than ten thousand people came to the band shell in Central Park to hear Mayor Lindsay deliver the eulogy and together sing "We Shall Overcome." Twenty-five thousand people, nearly half of them white, gathered in Newark's Central Ward as part of a "Walk for Understanding." In Atlanta's Ebenezer Baptist Church, the Reverend Martin Luther King, Sr.'s, opening prayer bemoaned the "strange, bewildering times in which we live." King's brother, A. D.'s, sermon included a line from one of Martin's favorite hymns. "America is a sick nation today," he said. "But we can find a balm in Gilead to heal the sin-sick soul." A reporter for the *New York* Times said that "the most emotional" moment in the service came when a soloist sang "Take My Hand, Precious Lord." From the front pew, seated beside Alberta Williams King, Martin's mother, Mahalia Jackson stood and sang the gospel song "Until Then," with the moving line "This troubled world is not my home." Biographer Laurraine Goreau's description of the moment is particularly poignant: "Mahalia stood and, alone, sang her sermon—a song out of the gospel whose spirit of love had been Martin's and was her true religion; the heart might break—the faith in man that God created could not. Evil was loose, but God was on the side of angels." In lieu of a benediction, trumpeter Dizzy Gillespie played an instrumental version of "Nobody Knows the Trouble I've Seen." That evening, in Memphis, COME members, city and police officials, union representatives, and the Civil Rights Commission worked long into the night on the logistics of Monday's march, now overseen by Bayard Rustin, whose experience with the March on Washington was invaluable. Outside, the violence in Memphis had finally quelled, leaving behind three deaths, dozens of injuries, two hundred seventy-five stores damaged and looted, and extensive fire damage, primarily on the black side of town.[45]

### Monday, April 8

The Memphis Memorial March of April 8 began gathering at 9 a.m. at Clayborn Temple under grey skies for the solemn procession to City Hall, where workers had spent the night erecting a large platform. Five thousand National Guardsmen lined the streets. The heart of the civil rights movement was there, along with a host of religious leaders, political figures, union representatives and members, actors and musicians. When the vast column began moving at 11 a.m., the bulk of the marchers were African-Americans, men and women, including the sanitation workers, holding their now iconic "I Am a Man!" signs and others that read, "Honor King: End Racism." Police estimated the number of people in the procession at nineteen thousand, but news organizations said the figure was between thirty-five and forty thousand. Rustin's estimate was that there were forty-two thousand mourners in the march, which stretched for nine blocks, eight people abreast. The most significant no-show was Mayor Loeb. "There were dense crowds of people along the route who did not cheer or wave," Coretta King wrote, "but stood silent in Martin's memory." Kyle led in the singing of another one of King's favorite songs, "O Lord, Hold My Hand" ("Guide my feet while I run this race"). Belafonte introduced Coretta King at City Hall. "How many men must die before we can really have a free and true and peaceful society?" she asked the giant crowd, her voice finally breaking with emotion. "How long will it take?" Rustin led the throng in choruses of "Amen." The event took three hours, with a number of speakers, including UAW president Walter Reuther, who held a $50,000 check for the union as the crowd roared. Abernathy "took their sadness and worked with it," Beifuss writes. "We are bound for the promised land and we aren't going to let nobody, whether it be Mayor Loeb, whether it be the Governor or the police force, whether it be Lyndon Johnson or the Congress of the United States, we aren't going to let nobody turn us around!" he shouted. That evening, King's body was removed from the Sisters Chapel at Spelman College in Atlanta for the memorial march the following day. Long lines had viewed the bier since Saturday. No official estimate was made of the number of people who had viewed the body.[46]

### Tuesday, April 9

Ultimately, what the King family, the SCLC, and the City of Atlanta had decided upon was for a private service at Ebenezer Baptist Church, then a three-and-a-half-mile walk through downtown Atlanta to Morehouse College, King's alma mater. Atlanta officials expected about fifty thousand people to take part in the long march and that the relatively open space of the school's Quadrangle would provide enough room for them all, but the chief of police predicted nearly three times that many would participate. Early Tuesday morning, Jackie Kennedy visited the King home, and the two widows shared a long embrace. Along the route of the procession, hundreds of police and National Guardsmen took their places. Georgia Governor Lester Maddox assigned one hundred sixty additional National Guardsmen to surround the capitol building. Later, he was said to have ordered troopers that if marchers had tried to approach the building to "shoot them down and stack them up." Many of the movement's longtime "celebrity" supporters were already in Atlanta, including Belafonte, Sidney Poitier, Stevie Wonder, Joan Baez, Marlon Brando, Nina Simone, Sammy Davis, Jr., and others. Eastern Airlines reported that thirty-three chartered jets were scheduled to land that day; the Greyhound Bus Company reported more than one hundred buses had been chartered. New York Governor Nelson Rockefeller alone chartered fourteen limousines and a fifty-seat bus. Auburn Avenue facing Ebenezer was crowded with ten thousand people long before the scheduled 10:30 a.m. service and marshals and friends worked from extensive lists provided by the King family to admit only a thousand into a church designed to hold seven hundred fifty. Among those outside was Sheyann Webb, the "littlest freedom fighter" from Birmingham. Abernathy officiated and the one hundred sixty-voice choir and congregation sang some of King's favorite hymns, "When I Survey the Wondrous Cross," "In Christ There Is No East Nor West," "Softly and Tenderly," and "Where He Leads Me, I Will Follow." Soloists sang the gospel songs "I Trust God" and "If I Can Help Somebody." In lieu of a sermon, a tape of King's February 4, 1968 sermon in Ebenezer was played, where King had mentioned how he would like to be remembered. Titled "Drum Major Instinct," the sermon was followed by another one of King's favorite songs, "Balm in Gilead."[47]

King's coffin, on a rough Georgia farm wagon pulled by two mules, then led the crowd, now estimated at a quarter of a million (Andrew Young called it "frighteningly enormous"), down the quiet streets of downtown Atlanta. The *New York Times* estimated that about ten percent of those present were white. Thousands of volunteer marshals shepherded the massive throng through the streets, while Atlanta police discretely directed traffic several blocks away. The major television networks broadcast live coverage of the slow processional march, capturing the frequent strains of "We Shall Overcome" throughout the day. The city reported no incidences of trouble or violence, despite Maddox's warnings. As the marchers passed the capitol building, the *Atlanta Journal*'s Paul Hemphill "imagined" Maddox, "scared to death, peering out at us through the Venetian blinds" as the mourners broke into "Swing Low, Sweet Chariot." Among those marching was SCLC staffer "Big" Lester Hankerson, who joined in the singing of "When Dr. King Goes Marching In" and other freedom songs during the long procession. "They were the kind of songs that helped build courage in front of rows of helmeted

**FIGURE 25**

Longtime financial supporter and King family
friend Harry Belafonte walks with other
mourners during the funeral procession for
Martin Luther King, Jr., in Atlanta, April 9,
1968. Jim Peppler *Southern Courier* Photograph
Collection, Alabama Department of Archives
and History. Photo: Alabama Department of
Archives and History, Montgomery, Alabama.

**FIGURE 26**

Stokely Carmichael, his wife, singer Miriam
Makeba, and activist Cleveland Sellers (dark
glasses) walk down Atlanta's Auburn Avenue
with mourners during the funeral procession
for Martin Luther King, Jr., April 9, 1968.
Jim Peppler *Southern Courier* Photograph
Collection, Alabama Department of Archives
and History. Photo: Alabama Department of
Archives and History, Montgomery, Alabama.

policemen" a reporter noted, "and they were the kind of people who had followed Dr. King." Aretha Franklin led the marchers in "We Shall Overcome." Dizzy Gillespie "belted out" the freedom song "Oh, Freedom!" as he marched. For Hunter Pitts "Jack" O'Dell, who wrote extensively about the movement and was a participant in numerous civil rights actions, the most powerful image of the procession was the multitude "half humming, half singing" the spiritual "This May Be the Last Time," as they followed by the wagon: "It may be the last time / May be the last time, children / It may be the last time / May be the last time, I don't know." At different times marchers also sang "This Little Light of Mine" and "Keep Your Eyes on the Prize." While not all of the well-known supporters made the march, marshals and marchers helped blind singer Ray Charles navigate the crush of people. Singer Eartha Kitt soon took off her heels and walked in stocking feet. The 80-degree heat sent many to the six first-aid stations strategically placed along the route. A broken water main provided some relief. Civil rights attorney Gordon Baxter walked behind the mules the entire way. "We walked real slow," he said, "and we sang the song to the cadence of it. And it was as beautiful as anything that you've ever heard out of the furl-the-banner legacy of the dying Confederacy, as beautiful as anything you've heard from Lee's march or any other of the grand music played a little too slow. And this song just rose up out of their voices as they came up out of the valley and on to the hillside of Atlanta: 'We Shall Overcome.'" "This was," Coretta King writes, "his last great march."[48]

When the massive crowd finally reached Morehouse, Abernathy made the decision to abbreviate the long-planned program. Mahalia Jackson, physically ailing and clearly emotionally distraught standing so close to the open casket, sang "Take My Hand, Precious Lord" to "massive applause." "She sang out her sorrow," writes Goreau, "sang a plea for forgiveness of mankind, sang for the soul she knew was sitting at Jesus' side. Save me a place, Martin. Save me a place." "I think she sang more beautifully than I had ever heard her sing before," wrote Coretta King in her autobiography.[49]

Television coverage remained constant throughout the long day, allowing, as one reporter noted, "the day of grief that saw Atlanta's cup of emotion overflowing" to be shared by a national audience. "The final sight of tens of thousands at the campus joining hands for the singing of 'We Shall Overcome' was a humbling spectacle of human unity." Some reporters "instinctively had joined in the singing." The television audience for the day was estimated at one hundred twenty million, half of the total U.S. population. At the end of the service, the chairman of the Memphis city council, Downing Pryor, slipped away from the crowd and began the long walk to find his car. He had asked and received permission to park it on the front yard of an African-American family's home. After finding his automobile, he asked the family if he could sit on their porch and rest for a moment. They were watching the end of the service on television and invited Pryor to join them. When the cameras showed the singing of the Morehouse alma mater, the family stood and Pryor stood with them. "Then they got into holding hands and singing 'We Shall Overcome,'" he later told Beifuss. "And there was one verse in it about black and white blending together . . . and when it was over, I said that I really felt like I had added to it. I was a stranger, but they said, 'No, we think it's nice that you were here. Where are you from?' Then I just said Tennessee. 'Where in Tennessee?' I said, 'I am from Memphis.'" Pryor's host, a minister, said, "Well, I am surprised that you would come today." But, Pryor then added, "He made me feel very comfortable and very good."[50]

Only a small group of family and close friends accompanied the casket to South View Cemetery, an African-American cemetery built by former slaves in 1886. Stenciled into the marble—the actual engraving would come later—was a line from yet another spiritual, "FREE AT LAST! FREE AT LAST! THANK GOD ALMIGHTY, I'M FREE AT LAST!" (The crypt would later be moved to a permanent home between the King Center for Nonviolent Social Change and Ebenezer Baptist Church on Auburn Avenue in Atlanta.) On Wednesday, after many hours of final arguments, the Civil Rights Law of 1968, later called the Open Housing Act, narrowly passed the House of Representatives. It had passed the Senate some weeks earlier. Johnson signed it into law the same day. On April 16, after a sixty-five-day work stoppage, the union and the City of Memphis finally announced a settlement. Pressured by corporations inside and outside Memphis, the federal government, national unions, and public opinion after King's murder, the city council—without Loeb—approved the settlement. The AFSCME voted to accept the deal, which was full of compromises that favored the city but achieved one of its most hard-fought goals, the inclusion of the line "The City shall make promotions on the basis of seniority and competency." As Michael K. Honey notes, "White supremacy thus fell, in twelve simple words."[51]

One of the success stories of racial reconciliation had been Stax Records in Memphis, where black and white artists created music that was loved and embraced by blacks and whites alike. Color had never been an issue in the humble little studio on East McLemore Avenue among musicians, on the tours, or among the songwriters. King's death changed that. "Suddenly," writes white songwriter Dan Penn, "our music—when I say our music, I mean black and white people cutting it, writing it and putting it down together, was gone. Until that moment . . . As far as I knew, that was the most fun being had on earth. . . . Suddenly, after Dr. King's death, it was over."[52]

Eileen Southern, one of the great historians of African-American music, said that King's assassination had left black Americans "numb" when they "began to realize that nonviolence was powerless against the entrenched racism in the United States." With that realization, she writes, there was an end to the singing. "Only for one day was there singing again—on April 9, 1968, the day of the funeral of the martyred Martin Luther King. The crowds marched through the streets of Atlanta, Georgia, behind the mule-drawn caisson, blacks and whites holding hands and singing, 'We Shall Overcome.' It was almost as if they thought King's death would set things right."[53]

**FIGURE 27**

Ralph Abernathy leads the funeral service
for Martin Luther King, Jr., at South View
Cemetery. Also participating are Benjamin
Mays (left) and Fred Shuttlesworth, April 9,
1968. Jim Peppler *Southern Courier* Photograph
Collection, Alabama Department of Archives
and History. Photo: Alabama Department of
Archives and History, Montgomery, Alabama.

# EPILOGUE

The plans for King's beloved Poor People's Campaign, never particularly well defined even before his death, were insufficient to deal with the harsh reality of the actual event when it finally came to be.[1] In one of his last interviews, King told the sixty-eighth convention of the Rabbinical Assembly that the initial goal had been to bring three thousand poor people to Washington, DC. That was later amended to bring the entire community of Marks, Mississippi, to the capital. "They don't have anything anyway," he told one questioner. "They don't have anything to lose." The pop-up village on the Mall in Washington, DC, would have a Freedom School and be supported, as King envisioned it, by a small army of people handling food, education, and sanitation, and lobbying for a bill of rights for the poor. The event would culminate with another massive march on Washington on June 15. Even as the campaign was "deluged" with volunteers, friction between Abernathy and other members of the SCLC resulted in an "embarrassing racial polarization." The massive tent city was erected on the Mall in Washington, DC, and dubbed Resurrection City U.S.A., and Coretta King led the first protest March on Mother's Day, May 12. At the official opening, Abernathy had defiantly declared the inhabitants would "plague the Pharaohs of this nation. . . . We'll stay here until 'We Shall Overcome' becomes 'We Have Overcome.'" However, as Action Director Hosea Williams often repeated, "We are a movement, not an organization" and organizational woes plagued the venture for its entire two-month existence.

Volunteers tried to rekindle the spirit of previous civil rights actions and provided multiple opportunities for singing freedom songs, even as Resurrection

**FIGURE 28**

Participants from Nashville board buses on
May 8, 1969, to join the Poor People's Cam-
paign in Washington, DC. Photo: *Nashville
Banner* Archives, Nashville Public Library
Digital Collection.

City's own radical politics perplexed and staggered organizers. Nonstop rain soon turned the grounds into mud. Fights broke out among the factions, there were arrests and assaults, and the open nature of the complex meant that the poorly guarded tents were often robbed or destroyed. Uncollected garbage and sewage became embedded in the mud, outsiders infiltrated the camp, and some young people were sent home for "harassing visitors and whites" on the grounds.[2]

There were some successes during Resurrection City's short life, despite the well-documented efforts by the FBI and Park Police "to discredit this campaign and to create a state of fear and panic among the general public." There were several instances of successful lobbying campaigns related to the event, and the challenges of poverty received unprecedented public awareness.[3]

In the end, the cold and drafty mosquito-ridden tent city, which lacked both adequate sanitation and showers, "depended on music to keep up its spirits." Nightly concerts in the large cultural arts tent, called the "Many Races Soul Center," were usually led by the Revered Frederick Douglass Kirkpatrick and movement veteran Jimmy Collier. Collier served as the camp's cultural director. Kirkpatrick had been a member of the Deacons of Defense in Southwest Louisiana before joining the SCLC and led one of the contingents to Resurrection City and, like Collier, was a gifted songwriter. Kirkpatrick wrote, among other songs, "Cities Are Burning": "Everybody's got a right to live / And before this campaign fail / We'll go down to jail." Frequent visitors to the Soul Center tent included movement stalwarts Bernice Johnson Reagon, Mike Seeger, and Pete and Toshi Seeger, who had their own tent in the Appalachian section of the camp. Reagon "soon had Tent City singing and shouting, rocking and clapping to the beat of old spirituals, the original freedom songs whose lyrics she referred to not as 'negro dialect' but as 'Afro-American language.'" The Seegers wandered from campfire to campfire, singing and encouraging residents, recalled Collier. Throughout the duration of Resurrection City, Fitzpatrick and Collier also performed at a number of Washington and New York–area churches with what Collier called their "little Poor People's Campaign act," promoting the event. Also involved was music historian Alan Lomax. Lomax "sketched out a cultural program" modeled on the Henry Wallace presidential campaign. He urged local groups to send their "best singers and musicians" to Washington. Lomax also oversaw the printing and wide distribution of some of the most important freedom songs, including "We Shall Not Be Moved," "We Shall Overcome," and "I Ain't Gonna Let Nobody Turn Me 'Round" to residents and visitors. In the initial planning stages, Sunday revival meetings and singing games for children were organized and the entire campaign would be documented on film and recordings. The Newport Foundation donated money to bring artists like the Carawans, Dock Reese, Fanny Lou Hamer, the Sea Island Singers, and "a dozen singing preachers." Also invited was Muddy Waters and his band, who drove overnight to reach Resurrection City. Lomax found them next to the stage, still in their car and fast asleep, the following morning. But chaos in Resurrection City meant that few of the ambitious plans came to fruition.[4]

A number of well-known gospel and mainstream artists performed for free at various Resurrection City functions, including Gladys McFadden and the Loving Sisters, who had accompanied King on his initial visit to Marks, Mississippi.[5] The Mighty Clouds of Joy performed a benefit concert for the participants at Constitution Hall, dressed in overalls instead of their usual matching colorful suits or tuxedoes.[6]

In the midst of the turmoil on the Mall in Washington, DC, an assassin's bullets struck down Senator Robert F. Kennedy in California on June 5 while on the campaign trail for the Democratic Party's nomination for President. Kennedy, who had been one of the Poor People's Campaign's most prominent supporters, died the following day. The family decided to use trains to convey Kennedy's casket to the burial site at Arlington National Cemetery. The funeral procession, which drew massive, somber crowds the entire route, made a final stop at Resurrection City. "At the foot of the Lincoln Memorial, there was a group of schoolchildren (with) middy blouses and skirts," recalled Resurrection City resident Marian Logan. "They were singing 'Battle Hymn of the Republic.' And I looked and I saw the hearse coming along right in front of the foot of the Lincoln Memorial. People from Resurrection City started singing 'Battle.' As they marched over the bridge into Arlington, it was one of the most dramatic, profoundly moving moments I've ever known in my life." King's assassin, James Earl Ray, was finally captured at a London airport by officers of Scotland Yard on June 8 after evading arrest for more than two months. The announcement of his arrest was made on the same day as Robert Kennedy's funeral. "Bobby Kennedy's assassination just brought everything to a halt," observed Andrew Young.[7]

The Poor People's Campaign's last gasp was a rally on June 18 at the Lincoln Memorial. The residents of Resurrection City, now in its fifth week, formed "the lonely vanguard" at the front of the marchers to the monument. Coretta King addressed the crowd, estimated at fifty thousand, saying that this was "the last opportunity to save the nation and the world from destruction." Pete Seeger and Mahalia Jackson both sang at what was billed "The Solidarity Day" march. Abernathy's fiery sixty-five minute speech included a threat to defy the government's original permit—set to expire on Sunday June 23.[8]

The following day, more than five hundred demonstrators impulsively staged a sit-in at the doors the Department of Agriculture at 5 p.m., blocking the exits. Eighty-seven protesters were arrested and police threw tear gas before SCLC members arrived to "cool tempers" and end the apparently "spontaneous" demonstration. The demonstration caught the FBI, which had infiltrated the camp and instituted extensive surveillance throughout Resurrection City's short history, by surprise. After repeated confrontations between "militant youths" and DC police, Abernathy pledged on Sunday to "purge" the settlement of "those people who are not committed to nonviolence." When the permit issued by the Department of the Interior expired on Sunday, Abernathy and about five hundred followers vowed to remain in the makeshift plywood city. When police began the process of tearing down

Resurrection City at 10 a.m. Monday, Washington's midtown area flared into looting and violence. Nine hundred District National Guardsmen joined more than a thousand policemen in quelling the rioting. Resurrection City's residents—those that remained—were not implicated in the unrest. Abernathy and his five hundred supporters, in a last act of civil disobedience, were arrested without incident as they stood singing freedom songs, including "Oh Johnson, You Never Can Jail Us All," "Ain't Gonna Let Nobody Turn Me 'Round," and "This May Be the Last Time." The campaigners were taken peacefully to the jail in buses, where they continued to sing, walking past heavily armed riot police. The eleven-wagon mule-pulled caravan from Mark, one of the centerpieces of the Poor People's Campaign's original vision when it left Mississippi on May 13, arrived on the Mall on Wednesday. Abernathy received a twenty-day jail term after entering a plea of no contest for the charge of unlawful assembly.[9]

When we colonize the moon there will be little green people joining their antennae together and they'll be singing (or chirping) something. And it will be "We Shall Overcome."

—JULIAN BOND

I n the months since I began writing the final chapters of this book, High John the Conqueror has taken the freedom songs and protest spirituals to Hong Kong for the Umbrella Revolution, as well as to the churches in Ferguson, Missouri, to the protests on Staten Island, and elsewhere. In the years since I began writing these two volumes, I have come to believe in the transcendent, transformative power of this music.

Those who sang it in the alleys of Beirut and at the barricades in Birmingham believed in the power of these songs to change the hearts and minds of those who opposed them. Sometimes that change happened. Sometimes it was slow in coming. Sometimes the change is imperceptible. There are people in the countries of the Arab Spring who may despair of real change ever coming to their homelands. When Bishop Desmond Tutu was elected president of the All Africa Churches organization in Togo in August 1987, "the whole place erupted and we sang that song," Tutu recalled. When South Korean students demonstrated in the streets of

Seoul that fall, they too sang "We Shall Overcome."[1] And around the world, people continue to sing, "In my heart, we shall overcome *someday*."[2]

One of the great chroniclers of the civil rights movement, Taylor Branch, spoke at Baylor University in 2007 and I had the great good fortune to spend time with him. He told the packed hall of how the shipyard workers in Gdansk, Poland, took the nonviolence lessons of the movement and helped end the Cold War. He told how "We Shall Overcome" was sung on the Berlin Wall and in Tiananmen Square. And he said, "What I want to argue is that this movement set into motion miracles that are unappreciated to this day in scope and content, and that we do not appreciate them at our peril." Miracles. *Miracles?* His Pulitzer Prize–winning trilogy *The King Years* is about people and movements and laws and protests and, occasionally, song. But it never mentions miracles.[3]

"Miracles" is a difficult word for academics and scholars. We are more comfortable with the empirical, the quantitative—facts and figures. It is much easier to measure the effectiveness of a civil movement by tallying the number of voters registered or comparing the number of civil rights–related laws passed after a certain date than it is to deal with a sea change within a human heart. Surveys can ascertain what people *say* they believe about a topic, but it is much more difficult to know what they truly believe. And when the word "miracle" is bandied about, the researcher's task becomes more difficult still.

In volume 1, I discuss the emergence of a movement to change America. It primarily consisted of African-Americans unjustly denied the true benefits of democracy. This multifaceted, sometimes feuding, sometimes unfocused movement sprang from the black church, was aided by the labor unions, and was assisted only occasionally and often grudgingly by a few members of the judiciary and the legislative branches. This movement challenged a deep-rooted racism fostered by a system that would use any means, including murder, to destroy it.

To transform the United States, the twentieth-century civil rights movement used the courts, public opinion, demonstrations, protests, sit-ins . . . and song. Its weapons were the courage of the participants, their unwavering religious faith, their staunch belief in nonviolent tactics . . . and song. This movement was sustained by faith and hope expressed in prayer, in sermons, and in song.

It is in examining those essential elements, with a focus on the music, that the *miracle* of the movement can be found. In their influential essay, "Movements and Cultural Change," Ron Eyerman and Andrew Jamison address this very issue: "Not only are songs significant and largely untapped resources for the academic observer; they are also channels of communication for activists—within movements, but also between different movements, and, indeed, between movement generations. Music enters into what we have called the collective memory, and songs can conjure up long-lost movements from extinction as well as reawakening forgotten structures of feeling." The nameless composers of the protest spirituals are long gone. Those who composed and sang the freedom songs on the streets of Albany are in their seventies and eighties. And yet, those same songs reemerged naturally in Ferguson during the protests and in the church services and marches that followed the death of Michael Brown. Those same songs reappeared a world away and in an entirely different faith tradition in Egypt during the Arab Spring. "Tradition," Eyerman and Jamison posit, "the past in the present, is vital to our understanding and interpretation of who we are and what we are meant to do." Those songs may lie dormant in the larger culture, but remain ever at the ready in the "residues and margins of society," where they retain their power to transform. "Such structures of feeling can be embodied and preserved in and through music, which is partly why music is such a powerful force in social movements and in social life generally. Music in a sense *is* a structure of feeling."[4] The Reverend Donald Solomon, A. G. Gaston's longtime associate in Birmingham, said it this way: "Singing goes with us, wherever, whatever we're doing. That's what we do. That's our thing, gospel singing. So it would naturally flow into the movement. And it did."[5]

As noted in the previous chapters, the organizational and sustaining impetus of the movement was rooted in the black church, a church founded in the rejection of the peculiar form of religion presented by the slaveholders, and later sanctified in activism. "Freedom songs, like the spirituals, captured the liberative aspect of God," writes Jon Michael Spencer. "They constituted a revolutionary liturgy of song, which ushered religion out of the churches of the black Protestant mainstream and onto the streets of human supremacy." Had this "liberative aspect" remained *inside* the churches, it never could have engaged and confronted the pervasive cultural racism in the United States. "Musically, the freedom songs were the paradigm of militancy; blacks were not just singing about freedom but were systematically seeking it."[6] C. Eric Lincoln and Lawrence H. Mamiya declare that the "lyric religion" of the freedom songs was a "principal stimulus in the sustained efforts of the civil rights movement." At the same time, they add that the freedom songs, based on the protest spirituals, "were the first openly . . . militant music to come out of the Black Church." The singing had to be supported with active, churchgoing black Americans.[7]

Civil rights activists, both those from the African-American church and those who professed no particular faith, integrated religion into the movement. As shown, the black church was the primary organizing entity in this community. It also provided financial support, volunteers, and a safe haven in an otherwise dangerous world. This "raw material," as Kerran L. Sanger calls it, came about, in part, because those activists purposefully "chose to present a view of the world in which religion and God played an important role." When freedom songs and protest spirituals were sung at mass meetings and on marches, "the religious or godly was manifested through the acts of women and men." This was made possible in the 1950s and '60s because people of faith believed—as the slave-poets did before them—that "God was on the side of civil rights."[8] The Reverend Clay Evans, King's staunch supporter in Chicago and a masterful singer and composer himself, cites the biblical examples of Moses and David as songwriters when he talks about the importance of music to the church: "Music was one of the main things that brought us over. Singing and praising God are important. Music does something for people. In the movement, music kept them inspired. It gave them hope. Music gave them physical, mental and moral strength." As for the freedom songs and protest spirituals, they matter, he says, because the music matters. "Look at those songs," he adds. "They have meaning. Music had meaning then and today, both secular and sacred music. I can't explain it, the depths of it, but it has great meaning. Music says to me what I've been saying to myself."[9] One of King's greatest strategists, Wyatt T. Walker, declares that the "entire nonviolent movement was religious in tone" and that the music was essential in the effort to "reflect and reinforce the religious base on which it stood."[10] In another article, this one written in 1963 during the height of the movement itself, Walker adds that the "religious orientation" of the movement "intensifies" the effect produced."[11] One of the last verses in the practical little New Testament book of James was often cited by black pastors in the movement, particularly in the elegant language of the King James Version: "The effectual fervent prayer of a righteous man availeth much."[12] Music scholars Dave Marsh and Daniel Wolff were not the first to observe that it is "no coincidence that the golden age of gospel corresponds to the golden age of the Civil Rights Movement." For Africans to travel from slavery to sharecropping to Jim Crow laws and restrictions, their religious faith had to sustain them—*something* had to—and it needed to both "promise salvation in the next life" and "offer the possibility of hope in this one, too. That's why the Civil Rights Movement had to center itself on black churches. That's why it could."[13]

The influential hymnal *Songs of Zion,* published in 1981 as a supplement to *The Methodist Hymnal,* offers a unique glimpse inside the African-American church. It contains the well-loved Protestant hymns of Watts, Wesley, and Crosby, classic gospel songs, spirituals, and contemporary gospel songs, as well as praise and worship choruses. The introduction, written by J. Jefferson Cleveland and William B. McClain, pays tribute to the prominent place music has played in the lives of African-Americans since their arrival centuries ago: "Singing is as close to worship as breathing is to life. These songs of the soul and of the soil have helped to bring a people through the torture chambers of the last three centuries. They reflect the truth of an old African dictum: 'The Spirit will not descend without music.'"[14]

If the movement and the music and the black church are inseparable, why did it take until the Montgomery Bus Boycott in 1955 for the modern civil rights movement to gain momentum? As illustrated in volume 1, a number of forces were at work leading up to the boycott: various lawsuits, the groundbreaking *Brown v. Board of Education* ruling, the infusion of union support and labor songs, and the hundreds of movement actions arising across the country by small local organizations dedicated to justice. Doubtless there was singing at these lesser-known protests as well. What was different in the 1950s was a concept that was introduced in Montgomery—the addition of the nonviolence doctrine, as identified by Gandhi and as articulated by the young "face" of the boycott in that city, Martin Luther King, Jr. For the black church to maintain the moral high ground in this struggle, it had to uphold a particularly profound and demanding expression of Christianity, one rooted in Jesus's abhorrence of violence. Joseph Lowery writes that he believes that it is the New Testament teachings of Jesus of Nazareth that "gave non-violence respectability in this country and credibility" from a theological standpoint.[15]

There is strong historic precedence for the teaching of nonviolence. The spirituals, as we have seen, are remarkably free of anger, accusations, or finger-pointing. Composer John Wesley Work wrote this paragraph in *Folk Song of the American Negro,* published in 1915, and notes that this had always been a defining trait of African-American music: "Another characteristic of the Negro song is, as has been stated before, that it has no expression of hatred or revenge. If these songs taught no other truths save this, they would be invaluable. That a race which had suffered and toiled as the Negro had, could find no expression for bitterness and hatred, yes, could positively love, is strong evidence that it possesses a clear comprehension of the great force in life, and that it must have had experience in the fundamentals of Christianity." He concludes with a quote from Alfred Lord Tennyson's *Sea Dreams:* "One shriek of hate would jar all the hymns of heaven."[16] In the hands of the civil rights movement, nonviolence became a sacred tool. At each major movement action, organizers demanded that supporters renounce violence and solemnly agree not to respond to force with force. In Birmingham, at the rehearsals for the sit-ins, during the training before the Mississippi Summer at Western College for Women in Oxford, Ohio, in Selma and in Memphis, movement veterans rejected volunteers who could not pledge to adhere to the principles of nonviolence. Merge that immersion in the tenets of nonviolence with the traditional power of the black church and the church's reliance—some might say dependence—on sacred song, and it becomes a potent weapon in the spiritual arsenal of the civil rights movement. "The spirituality was the root of the civil rights movement," said gospel singer James Alex Taylor. "I think the spirituality helped effect change by being the force that kept everyone disciplined."[17] Taylor uses the word "disciplined" here in the sense that those who were being abused in Birmingham, as he was, were able to respond nonviolently.

Also a factor in the success of the freedom songs and protest spirituals in accomplishing the goals of the civil rights movement, however "success" is identified and defined, is the historic continuity of this music, what Eyerman and Jamison call the "collective memory." The protest spirituals provide an instantly available repertoire for oppressed people, regardless of religion, race, gender, or nationality. Birmingham gospel singer Henry Burton recalled growing up in rural Hale County, Alabama, watching and listening to his grandparents picking cotton. As they picked, they hummed and "moaned" spirituals and gospel songs. "I didn't understand it, but it stayed with me," Burton said. "Why were they doing this? I didn't know until later on that this was the way that they talked to the Lord, with those songs and those moans. This was like in slave [times]. My determination was that all black people, wherever they were . . . this was the way that they made contact with God. By moaning and groaning and singing."[18] Gospel singer Candi

Staton, who would go on to a successful career in popular music, said that the music of the civil rights movement was the African-American "crying out to God for help." "We were so hungry for freedom. We were so hungry we were crying out for God, who was our father, 'Please, just give us crumbs from the master's table. Just open some doors for us. Help us get through. Help us to be accepted.' That's all we wanted was our bread, our freedom."[19]

This music is a "river of song," as T. V. Reed calls it, flowing from the pre–Civil War era through every civil rights movement–related engagement and beyond, enabling listeners and historians to begin to understand the "forces at play at various times, what ideas were central and how they evolved, as well as to capture some sense of what the movement felt like to those who enacted it."[20] That is not to say that this is a linear progression. The "river of song" twists and turns and nearly loops on itself like the Mississippi. By the time of Memphis and Resurrection City, the freedom songs, while not lost, were certainly less prominent. But they remained available, just below the surface.

When Birmingham composer and musician Eloise Gaffney also used a water analogy while speaking of the music of the movement during our interview, my wife, Mary, asked her to explain further. Gaffney called the freedom songs an "ever-flowing stream." "You know," she told us, "it rolls away but then it constantly comes back. So it's like a wave that continues. Even though it happened way back then, the music is still just as fresh as the morning dew. It's still fresh. That water is still fresh and it refreshes every day."[21] The same songs that the Pilgrim Travelers sang to support the Montgomery bus boycott[22] were sung by the New York delegation's supporters of candidate Eugene J. McCarthy inside the International Amphitheatre at the 1968 Democratic National Convention in Chicago.[23] In both cases, the songs were sung because the singers believed that singing them mattered.

Still another difference that separated the 1950s and '60s-era civil rights movement from previous efforts to achieve racial equality was the introduction, for the first time, of the labor movement—and the labor movement's songs—into the equation. As discussed in Chapter 3 of volume 1, once African-American workers were finally admitted to the unions, a remarkable transference took place between labor songs and protest spirituals. Musician and activist Alex Dobkin, who joined the civil rights struggle from the labor movement, had a "diehard, lifelong aversion" to organized religion, but soon recognized the value of the black church and its music while on the Mississippi Folk Music Caravan in 1965. "Church music was absent from my childhood," she writes, "and I have never felt entirely comfortable singing it. However the union songs, adapted by civil rights workers, had traditionally served as 'spirituals' to me growing up in my community. As I joined in with the familiar chorus of 'Which Side Are You On?' I felt more strongly entitled, more deeply connected."[24] Whether it is the public singing of "Solidarity Forever" or "The Internationale" on the first of May or the singing of "We Shall Overcome" at a demonstration in South Carolina, the goals are the same. Both "serve to reunite and to remind participants of their place in the 'movement' and also to locate them within a long-standing tradition of struggle and protest." When the two movements (always with the understanding that there were some unions that discriminated against African-Americans for years after the civil rights movement) united, it created another powerful impetus toward full citizenship rights for all Americans.[25]

What specifically did the singing of freedom songs accomplish? Singer and activist Julius Lester said that "freedom songs should comfort the disturbed and disturb the comfortable." Similarly, Peggy Seeger said that "Folk music . . . is not a comfortable music. That's why it frequently sounds funny in the mouths of comfortable people."[26] Within those general definitions, there are a numerous kinds of freedom songs, each with certain distinctions. The majority are based on spirituals, while others are based on old hymns, gospel songs, pop, rhythm and blues songs, and folk songs. "Which Side Are You On?" and "We Shall Not Be Moved," for instance, have their roots in the labor movement. As discussed in volume 1, "John Brown's Body" and "The Battle Hymn of the Republic" were both grafted into the movement from other sources still. Virtually all were accompanied by vigorous, sometimes polyrhythmic clapping. Two notable exceptions were the elegiac "We Will Never Turn Back" and the closing hymn of the movement, "We Shall Overcome" which, by tradition, was sung standing with arms crossed and linked. Even the words slipped easily among and within the various freedom songs; in a live performance, a rhymed couplet associated with "This Little Light of Mine" could appear in "On My Way to Freedom Land."

Of those freedom songs based on spirituals, there is an additional layer of history, emotion, and resonance. Sanger has written convincingly of the rhetorical power of the spirituals and that "singing spirituals provided slaves with one way to reclaim rhetorical power in their lives, communicating among themselves an affirming and positive self-definition." The singing of all spirituals, whether they contained the "double-voiced" or hidden messages or not, was an act of resistance. While the words to the spirituals did not apparently openly defy or challenge the planters or their overseers, singing them enabled slaves "to appear to work within the system while effectively resisting it." Freedom songs, of course, *could* openly challenge the authorities, for example, "Ain't Gonna Let Nobody Turn Me 'Round." That said, there is an unbroken connection between the original spirituals and the freedom songs based directly on those spirituals. Sanger suggests that slaves sang the spirituals strategically, purposefully choosing to "reveal themselves to each other," to establish their worth as human beings, to safely communicate among themselves, to create a sense of community, to foster and nurture creativity, and to serve as a religious outlet, especially as the spirituals helped "identify slaves with the key figures in Christianity." As discussed in volume 1, this belief that they were chosen by a God who sympathized with their plight was a powerful, sustaining tool during the horrific centuries of American slavery. The final strategic use of the spirituals noted in Sanger's essay was to convince the singers that they themselves were "capable of enacting change in their own lives"—that God would and could work through them to bring freedom.[27]

Sanger's overview of the primary purposes of the spirituals parallels the ways the freedom songs were used during the civil rights movement. Each time a freedom song was sung, it was sung with the understanding—or at least the fervent belief—that one or more of the purposes listed above would take place. Gaffney, a friend of the young girls who were killed in Birmingham, as well as a musician and composer and staple of that city's legendary mass choir, said the *need* to sing freedom songs was driven by the belief that the very act of singing, with God's help, was itself effecting change: "I think that is a part of the black heritage: sing with feeling and anointing. That is what carried us because when you think back on the dangers that we faced, you have to just have the power from God to keep you there. And we sang those songs and we sang those songs and we meant what we said. We knew that God was going to lead us to a better place. 'Precious Lord, take my hand, lead me on'—we have to know that and feel that in our hearts that those words really *were*. We have to bring those words to life."[28] Vincent Harding writes, "So the singing itself was powerful, was community."[29]

But as I hope these two volumes have shown, the differences between spirituals and freedom songs are paper thin. The intent—*freedom*—has always been the same. Within the black community there has always been tacit understanding that songs, sacred or profane, could have more than one meaning. A story is told of the great gospel singer Bessie Griffin, who was raised by her grandmother in the African-American Baptist church in New Orleans in the 1930s and '40s. When she misbehaved, Bessie was disciplined as any child would be disciplined. However, instead of "sassing" her grandmother or rebelling, Bessie would sing "I Been 'Buked and I Been Scorned," "I Wish I Had Died When I Was Born," or "Sometimes I Feel Like a Motherless Child." Her grandmother would listen and say, "I know what you doing." For, as writer J. E. Johnson notes, "message-loaded work songs" were part of her grandmother's DNA as well.[30]

As Mary and I interviewed participants about the music of the movement fifty years after those heady, dangerous days in Birmingham, Chicago, and elsewhere, I was particularly interested in determining the why and how of the freedom songs. How and why were they used? How and why did these particular songs contribute to the success of the movement? And as I read the hundreds of contemporary accounts of the civil rights actions across the United States in the 1950s and '60s, I looked for answers to those same questions. A brilliant scholar like David Garrow has researched nearly every facet of the movement, but he devotes virtually no space to the role of the music in the struggle, even though the vast majority of interviewees from the Montgomery bus boycott through Memphis repeatedly cited the music as a palpable agent of change. Their responses differed only in assessing the degree to which the music mattered. Singer, songwriter, and activist Jimmy Collier initially said that black sacred music comprised 60 percent of the effective work of the civil rights movement; then, after a pause, decided on a figure of 50 percent. "And I say that because you can't take away the ability of the Dr. Kings and the Julian Bonds and [John] Lewises and those people that could speak and move people and explain things and get people motivated to do things," Collier told me. "But the music carried the rest. It was the . . . river that carried all kinds of people and pulled them together in going the same direction. And it did it quickly, it did it efficiently, it did it without as much argument and friction."[31]

Collier was the only interviewee to attempt a percentage when assessing the impact of the freedom songs to the movement, but all were adamant about the importance. And each interviewee emphasized a slightly different aspect of the music. Chicago gospel singer and pastor Reuben Burton cited the music's power to "lift people": "That's what carried them. They had a song to sing, and a prayer in their hearts to go with. That's what carried them. That's all they had to go on, to keep them uplifted. As Jesse [Jackson] always says, 'Keep hope alive. Keep the joy. Sing a song. Pray a prayer.' And those types of songs would fit right in with what was going on. And that's what kept it going."[32] Cleopatra Kennedy, one of the featured soloists for the Alabama Christian Movement for Human Rights Choir, said much the same thing, citing the "spiritual side of the music" and its ability to keep participants "up." "Any time you're singing a song, and you can feel that, it's doing something great for you," she said. "You enjoy that feeling. It makes you feel good inside and every time you sing it, you're looking for that same good feeling . . . because it's a part of you. The more you do it, the more it will become a part of your life. And that keeps you going."[33] Another legendary Birmingham gospel quartet member, John Lawrence, also stressed the music's ability to "lift burdens off of people when the preachers can't get through to them. Singing lifts your burdens . . . especially when they're marching and they're going through . . . deep trouble. And you can start singing [and] that'll help comfort their minds. It takes some of that fear out of them."[34]

Still another gospel artist from Birmingham, Roscoe Robinson, who participated in many of that city's movement events, identified the ability of "We Shall Overcome" to "uplift" the demonstrators and worshippers in difficult times as one of the signature ways the music was essential to the movement. "It was something that made me feel within that it was a future date of something that was coming that was going to be great for me and actually great for my people," he told us. "Every time I hear it, I'll sing it—sometimes right now, in the house, by myself." I asked Robinson if he believed that the words of "We Shall Overcome" were true. "Sure I believe it," he said. "I believe it because I believe in God."[35] Shreveport gospel singer Eddie Jackson called "We Shall Overcome" "the beat of the drum." "It brought people together on one accord of what this was all about."[36]

Chicago musician and minister Maceo Woods said that the music of the movement was a "unifying experience," that it could "overshadow" any disagreement. "I would venture to say that music has a magnetic force," he added. "This music draws . . . as opposed to repelling. And even people who maybe felt themselves a little beyond it or above it . . . found themselves because they were in the same situation. And I think it brought a lot of them to the Holy Ghost."[37] Dick Simpson, who led protests at the University of Texas in Austin, also cited how singing the protest spirituals built "morale camaraderie" among participants. "It built the sense of unanimity and purpose—and 'group-ness.'"[38] Vincent Harding hailed the use of the singing of freedom songs in the "creation of community across age groups" in the movement.[39] In the words of the great activist, scholar, and musician Bernice Johnson Reagon, singing and community, in the context of freedom songs in the movement, are simply one and the same: "The song is not a product. The song exists as a way to get to the singing. And the singing is not a product. The singing exists to form the community. And there isn't anything higher than that that I've ever experienced."[40]

In Birmingham, gospel singer Barry Leon Taylor identified the ability of the protest spirituals to tamp down the anger against those who reviled and oppressed him as one of most important aspects of freedom songs. "I think the United States owes its salvation to all types of gospel music," he said. "Gospel music was a saving grace for the United States."[41] "The songs that we sang had more influence than anything else in enabling us to endure what the white people put on us," one participant told William R. Beardslee. "Without the songs, we might have gone berserk."[42] Ann Lee, whose extended family members included both friends and distant relatives of Mahalia Jackson, is even more adamant. "Music *was* the civil rights," she said. "Civil rights was the music, and that's just the way it was. And this is out in public, but behind closed doors, too. It gave them strength. It gave them courage." Her family, she said, believed that the act of singing actually gave movement participants supernatural protection from harm. "The power of the Holy Spirit was a shield while you were singing, and . . . it would protect while you were marching, or while you were in a dangerous situation. People need that. They believed that the song and the praise alone will sustain you, period. Because it was the power of the Holy Spirit through praising and singing."[43]

Through more than one hundred and twenty interviews, certain themes emerged from the question of the how and why of the freedom songs and protest spirituals: their ability to motivate, to explain, to "uplift" and lift the burdens, to comfort and calm, to provide hope, to provide protection, and to create unity. "The music was for your soul," Hermene Hartman said. "To calm it, to justify it, to ignite. To excite it."[44] Rosephayne Powell, a scholar of the spirituals, declared a certain inevitability in the emergence of the freedom songs, beginning with the Montgomery bus boycott. "I believe because that was a time that God wanted to move," she said. "The same way in slavery: When He got ready to move us, a song was always there. When it was time to revolt, there were songs that were being sung."[45] French scholar and economist Jacques Attali posits the same thing, but from an entirely different perspective: "Music is prophecy. Its styles and economic organization are ahead of the rest of society because it explores, much faster than material reality can, the entire range of possibilities in a given code."[46] The music, this *particular* music—freedom songs and protest spirituals—was already there, waiting for the time it was needed when the civil rights movement began to emerge.

None of this lessens the impact or importance of the NAACP's painstaking work in the judicial process, the legislators who risked the wrath of angry or indifferent constituents to pass progressive laws, the nearly anonymous local groups that toiled for years to pave the way for the movement, the charismatic leadership of the civil rights organizations, the reporters for the local and national newspapers, television and radio stations who bravely and accurately reported the news, or the religious leaders who supported the cause despite pressure from above and below. What this celebration of the place of the protest spirituals and freedom songs does, instead, is celebrate the power of the people in the nonviolent protest marches, at the barricades, in the prisons, and at the mass meetings. They were, at last, irresistible and unmovable, like the tide. They were sustained by their courage, the knowledge that they were embarked on a holy calling, and the glorious songs they sang. I love this moving declaration of the power of that singing. It comes from an interview with movement hero Prathia Hall, who would later become one of America's great, prophetic preachers:

> Music was a lifeline, a source, a well from which we could draw, a source of courage and strength in the face of eminent danger. With these forces of death with their guns loaded and sometimes drawn, surrounding you and taking down your name or license plate number, to be able then to sing and the relationship between the songs of the movement and the songs of the church is of one fabric, that's a continuous thread. What the Freedom Singers and the various movement projects did was simply add to the words, develop the subtle variations in the melodies . . . almost a living expression of what we're living right now. In the movement rallies there would be some slight variation from the old prayer meetings that . . . has a different phrasing of the melody, those pregnant pauses, those are underlying, underscoring. It's almost like you're gulping for breath in the face of fear.[47]

Note the common thread among many of these interviews. Hall spoke of "a well from which we could draw." Reed wrote of a "river of song." Collier described the music as a "river that carried all kinds of people and pulled them together." Reagon wrote of the centuries-long freedom struggle of African-Americans as a story that continues "bathing their courage and determination in songs that ring truest when used for major and radical change."[48] In his definitive book on the spirituals, Lovell cited all of the spirituals that celebrated the transformative, redemptive power of water such as "Wade in the Water," "Down by the Riverside," "Roll, Jordan, Roll," and many more besides, but he noted that while "Deep River" is "one of the most beautiful of spirituals," it is also "one of the most deadly to the institution of slavery": "Deep river / My home is over Jordan / Deep river, Lord / I want to cross over into campground." Slaveholders and overseers must have been particularly "obtuse" to miss the real meaning of this spiritual. "Into this song," Lovell wrote, "the slave poet poured his whole soul of desire for freedom, earthly freedom."[49] And finally, I offer this quote from Martin Luther King, Jr., in Montgomery before fifteen thousand listeners at Holt Street Baptist Church, just hours after Rosa Parks had been arrested for refusing to leave her seat on a city bus: "We are determined here in Montgomery to work and fight until justice runs down like water and righteousness in a mighty stream."[50]

Which brings me to the title of these two volumes, *Nothing But Love in God's Water*. I have been working with the Black Gospel Music Restoration Project (BGMRP) since 2005, digitizing the loaned and donated vinyl from gospel music's "golden age." One such loan came from gospel collector Bob Marovich of Chicago, who has generously loaned the BGMRP his massive 45 collection. The song is titled "The Old Ship of Zion" and is by the previously unknown Mighty Wonders of Aquasco, Maryland. The BGMRP's original audio engineer, Tony Tadey, called me after he had digitized it and together we listened to "The Old Ship of Zion" in the small studio with its state-of-the-art speakers. "The Old Ship of Zion" is an adaptation of an old spiritual, sung a cappella by a group of four or five men in a tiny, resonant church.[51] It is probably the first and only take. The lyrics are simple:

> *Tis the old ship of Zion*
> *Tis the old ship of Zion*
> *Tis the old ship of Zion*
> *Step on board if you want to see Jesus*
> *There's nothing but love in God's water*
> *There's nothing but love in God's water*
> *There's nothing but love in God's water*
> *Step on board if you want to see Jesus*
> *And follow me*[52]

I was speechless—and in tears. There is an extraordinary quality about the soloist's voice, a haunting, timeless evocation of a distant time. In that song, I heard forgiveness. There were Tidewater plantations along the Patuxent in Maryland in antebellum times and the area suffered its share of abuses during the modern civil rights movement. The singers were of an age to have suffered under the restrictive, abusive chains of segregation and blind prejudice. And yet they sang that there's *nothing* but love in God's water. Step on board—white or black or anyone else— if you want to see Jesus. And follow me. I'll take you there. We'll go together.

That song was always in the back of my mind as I began to listen to the civil rights–related songs on the "B" sides of the 45s that arrived at the BGMRP at Baylor, sometimes in bad condition, sometimes in pristine condition, sometimes having been played so often that their surface was shiny and nearly flat like glass. I thought of how brave those artists must have been in the early 1960s to record songs with titles like "Ain't No Segregation in Heaven." And how much these flip sides were like the coded messages of the spirituals, sung to be heard only by those with ears to hear.

That was the beginning of what became *Nothing but Love in God's Water.* I wanted to follow the continuation of the protest spirituals of the slaves right through the modern civil rights movement and through to the present day, where those same freedom songs are sung around the world. The image that I kept in the back of my mind as I read and researched and interviewed was that of a river—God's water—that flowed then and flows now in an unbroken stream.

Which brings me to this point: I began volume 1 by repeating Zora Neale Hurston's stories of the mythical, mystical High John the Conqueror, the unstoppable supernatural friend of slaves and former slaves. Hurston, who gathered her stories of High John long before the modern civil rights movement, said his "sign" was a "laugh, and his singing-symbol a drum-beat." She called him "our hope-bringer." He was able, she said, to appear instantaneously wherever he was needed most, wherever the oppression of slavery and the violence of Jim Crow was the greatest.[53] Perhaps it seems strange that Hurston would use a mythical figure to represent the indomitable will of the African-American instead of one of the heroes of the Christian Bible. High John, she writes, came from Africa and returned to Africa, though, like the legends of King Arthur in England, she says he remains eternally vigilant to return in the time of the African-American's greatest need.[54] During the 1950s and '60s, Guy and Candie Carawan, Pete Seeger, Bernice Johnson Reagon, and the other Freedom Singers, along with hundreds of mostly anonymous singers, took the spirituals and freedom songs across the South, like yeast leavening a loaf of bread, until the songs had permeated every movement action, no matter how small. In the twenty-first century, High John is aided by social media, where Twitter and Facebook instantaneously spread the messages and songs of the demonstrators and their supporters in Ferguson, Hong Kong, and the Arab Spring.

The freedom songs continue to be sung for the same reasons they have always been sung, they give the singers, and their causes, something that cannot be found elsewhere. Remembering always, as Reagon wisely adds, "the songs . . . ring truest when used for major and radical change." Those who sing them from a religious worldview believe there is divine power in them. Those who come from other worldviews and sing them may offer psychological or sociological reasons for their continued influence. Regardless, to repeat an earlier quote from Eyerman and Jamison: "Music enters into what we have called the collective memory, and songs can conjure up long-lost movements from extinction as well as reawakening forgotten structures of feeling." The reoccurring themes of water, of baptism, of immersion and rebirth, are intentional. They are at the core of the Christian faith. I love the image of the spirituals bubbling just below the surface, waiting. I love that the singers of these songs believed that once these always-ancient, always-new songs were retrieved and that if they were sung for the right reasons, for the right causes, they could wash away the sins of racism and intolerance.

> *Just like a tree planted by the water,*
> *We shall not be moved.*

This is where the journey has taken me. I have tried to follow this mighty river of song. What I have discovered is what the singers of these songs have always known—that the freedom songs and protest spirituals that have endured for centuries remain transformational today. In that time, only the most moving and memorable of melody lines have survived. Through the belief and the blood of the singers, these songs have been polished and honed and burnished to a glorious sheen. All excess has been burned away.

**What remains transcends time.**
**What remains is the power to change lives.**

**—ROBERT DARDEN, JANUARY 2015**

# Notes

## Introduction

The epigraph for the introduction is drawn from *Playboy* magazine (January 1965), cited in James Melvin Washington, ed., *A Testament of Hope: The Essential Writings of Martin Luther King, Jr.* (San Francisco: Harper & Row, 1986), 348.

1. See John D'Emilio, *Lost Prophet: The Life and Times of Bayard Rustin* (New York: Free Press, 2003).
2. Richard H. King, "Citizenship and Self-Respect: The Experience of Politics in the Civil Rights Movement," *Journal of American Studies* 22, no. 1 (April 1988): 11.
3. Dick Cluster, ed., *They Should Have Served That Cup of Coffee* (Boston: South End Press, 1979), 20.
4. Ellen C. Leichtman, "The Different Sounds of American Protest: From Freedom Songs to Punk Rock," *Popular Culture, Crime, and Social Control/ Sociology of Crime, Law, and Deviance* 14 (2010): 181. In his book, *They Knew Lincoln*, published in 1942, John E. Washington writes about "Old Aunt" Phoebe Bias, who told of a black church service on New Year's Eve in Washington, DC. The church was filled at sundown and the freed slaves sang until the 10 p.m. service began. After a sermon and more singing, the pastor read the entire Emancipation Proclamation. At midnight, the congregation sang, "Before I'd be a slave, I'll be carried to my grave" and "many other old songs of freedom and hope." James E. Washington, *They Knew Lincoln* (New York: E. P. Dutton, 1942), 90–91.
5. Louis-Charles Harvey, "Black Gospel Music and Black Theology," *Journal of Religious Thought* 43, no. 2 (Fall/Winter, 1986–87): 29–33.
6. Johnny E. Williams, "Linking Beliefs to Collective Action: Politicized Religious Beliefs and the Civil Rights Movement," *Sociological Forum* 17, no. 2 (June 2002): 215–18.
7. Sandra L. Barnes, "Black Church Culture and Community Action," *Social Forces* 84, no. 2 (December 2005): 985–86.
8. Peter Guralnick, *Dream Boogie: The Triumph of Sam Cooke* (New York: Back Bay Books, 2005), 139.
9. Joseph Williams, Jr., interview with the author, May 7, 2009, transcript of tape recording, Institute for Oral History, Baylor University, Waco, Texas, 25.
10. Robert Shelton, "Singing for Freedom: Music in the Integration Movement," *Sing Out!* 12 (December 1962): 12.
11. T. V. Reed, *The Art of Protest: Culture and Activism from the Civil Rights Movement to the Streets of Seattle* (Minneapolis: University of Minnesota Press, 2005), 29.
12. Keith D. Miller, "Epistemology of a Drum Major: Martin Luther King, Jr. and the Black Folk Pulpit," *Rhetoric Society Quarterly* 18, no. 2/4 (Summer–Autumn 1988): 225, 234.
13. James H. Cone, *The Cross and the Lynching Tree* (Maryknoll, NY: Orbis Books, 2011), 72.

14. Jonathan Rieder, *The Word of the Lord Is Upon Me: The Righteous Performance of Martin Luther King, Jr.* (Cambridge: Belknap Press of Harvard University Press, 2008), 130.

15. Pete Seeger and Bob Reiser, *Everybody Says Freedom* (New York: W. W. Norton, 1990), 82.

16. Rieder, *The Word of the Lord Is Upon Me*, 185.

17. Aldon Morris, *The Origins of the Civil Rights Movement: Black Communities Organizing for Change* (New York: The Free Press, 1984), 194.

18. Clayborne Carson, ed., *The Papers of Martin Luther King, Jr.,* vol. 3, *Birth of a New Age, December 1955–December 1956* (Berkeley: University of California Press, 1997), 437.

19. Clayborne Carson, ed., *The Papers of Martin Luther King, Jr.,* vol. 4, *Symbol of the Movement, January 1957–December 1958* (Berkeley: University of California Press, 1992), 19.

20. Burns, *To the Mountaintop: Martin Luther King Jr.'s Sacred Mission to Save America, 1955–1968* (San Francisco: HarperSanFrancisco, 2004), 146–54. Detailed information on King's life post-Montgomery can also be found in Taylor Branch, *Parting the Waters: America in the King Years, 1954–1963* (New York: Simon & Schuster Paperbacks, 1988); Clayborne Carson, ed., *The Autobiography of Martin Luther King, Jr.* (New York: Warner Books, 1998); David Levering Lewis, *King: A Biography,* 3rd ed. (Urbana: University of Illinois Press, 2013).

21. Pat Watters and Reese Cleghorn, *Climbing Jacob's Ladder: The Arrival of Negroes in Southern Politics* (New York: Harcourt, Brace, 1967), 27.

22. Lewis, *King,* 90–91.

23. Carson, *Papers of Martin Luther King, Jr.,* 4:13.

24. Ibid., 179.

25. Ibid., 13–15; "Pilgrimage Girds for Rights Cause," *New York Times,* May 4, 1957, 15; "Dr. King to Lead Anti-Bias Trek," *New York Times,* May 12, 1957, 50; "'Freedom Pilgrims' Gather in Capital," *New York Times,* May 17, 1957, 26.

26. James L. Hicks, "King Emerges as Top Negro Leader," *New York Amsterdam News,* June 1, 1957, 1, 25; Scott A. Sandage, "A Marble House Divided: The Lincoln Memorial, the Civil Rights Movement, and the Politics of Memory, 1939–1963," *Journal of American History* 80, no. 1 (June 1993): 154; Laurraine Goreau, *Just Mahalia, Baby* (Waco, TX: Word Books, 1975), 231.

27. "Attack on the Conscience," *Time Magazine* 69, no. 7 (February 2, 1957): 19; George Barrett, "'Jim Crow, He's Real Tired,'" *New York Times,* March 3, 1957, 11. Several books have been written on Little Rock, including Elizabeth Huckaby, *Crisis at Central High: Little Rock, 1957–1958* (Baton Rouge: Louisiana State University Press, 1980) and Elizabeth Jacoway, *Turn Away Thy Son: Little Rock, the Crisis That Shocked the Nation* (New York: Free Press, 2007).

28. Todd Gitlin, *The Sixties: Years of Hope, Days of Rage* (Toronto: Bantam Books, 1987), 75.

29. Lewis, *King,* 82.

30. Guy Carawan and Candie Carawan, "'Freedom in the Air': An Overview of the Songs of the Civil Rights Movement," *Black Music Research Bulletin* 12, no. 1 (Spring 1990): 2.

31. David J. Garrow, *Bearing the Cross: Martin Luther King, Jr., and the Southern Christian Leadership Conference* (New York: William Morrow, 1986), 98.

32. Josh Dunson, *Freedom in the Air: Song Movements of the '60s* (New York: Little New World Paperbacks, 1965), 38–39.

33. Frank Adams, with Myles Horton, *Unearthing Seeds of Fire: The Idea of Highlander* (Winston-Salem: John F. Blair, Publisher, 1975), 131–32.

34. Poinsette Clark, with LeGette Blythe, *Echo in My Soul* (New York: E. P. Dutton, 1962), 5–6.

35. "Highlander: Over 80 Years of Fighting for Justice," http://highlandercenter.org/media/timeline/.

36. http://www.newportjazzfest.net.

37. Goreau, *Just Mahalia, Baby,* 233, 255.

38. Martin Halliwell, *American Culture in the 1950s* (Edinburgh: Edinburgh University Press, 2007), 143–44.

39. "Presents Birthday Gift," *Jet,* October 29, 1959, 10.

40. Martin Luther King, Jr., "My Trip to the Land of Gandhi," *Ebony,* July 1959, 84–85.

41. Octavia Vivian, *Coretta: The Story of Coretta Scott King* (Minneapolis: Fortress Press, 2006), 25.

42. Guy Carawan and Candie Carawan, *Sing for Freedom: The Story of the Civil Rights Movement Through Its Songs* (Montgomery: NewSouth Books, 2007), xvii.

43. David K. Dunaway, "Folk Protest and Political Music in the United States," *Journal of American Folklore* 105, no. 417 (Summer 1992): 376.

44. John Blake, "Freedom Riders inspire new generation of Arab protest leaders," *CNN,* May 15, 2011, http://www.cnn.com/2011/US/05/15/freedom.riders.arab/index.html.

45. Seeger, *Everybody Says Freedom,* 82.

## Chapter 1

The epigraphs for this chapter are drawn from John Lewis, interview with the author, May 20, 2009, transcript of tape recording, Institute for Oral History, Baylor University, Waco, Texas, 6; and Jerry Zolten, *Great God A'Mighty! The Dixie Hummingbirds: Celebrating the Rise of Soul Gospel Music* (Oxford: Oxford University Press, 2003), 237.

1. Barbara Ann Posey, "Why I Sit-In," *Social Progress* 51 (February 1961): 8–9; Ingrid Monson, *Freedom Sounds: Civil Rights Call Out to Jazz and Africa* (New York: Oxford University Press, 2007), 161–62.

2. Raymond Gavins, "The NAACP in North Carolina During the Age of Segregation," in *New Directions in Civil Rights Studies,* ed. Armstead L. Robinson and Patricia Sullivan (Charlottesville: University Press of Viriginia, 1991), 105–7.

3. Trezzant W. Anderson, "They Decided to Do Something About Discrimination: 'We Just Get Tired,' Say Students," *Pittsburgh Courier,* March 5, 1960, 3. There are several fine studies on the sit-in phenomenon, including Miles Wolff, *How It All Began: The Greensboro Sit-Ins* (New York: Stein and Day, 1971); Carson Clayborne, *In Struggle: SNCC and the Black Awakening of the 1960s* (Cambridge, MA: Harvard University Press, 1981); Martin Oppenheimer, *The Sit-In Movement of 1960* (Brooklyn: Carlson Publishing, 1989); and the interviews with participants in Howell Raines, ed., *My Soul Is Rested: Movement Days in the Deep South Remembered* (New York: G. P. Putnam's Sons, 1997).

4. Clayborne Carson, ed., *The Papers of Martin Luther King, Jr., vol. 4, Symbol of the Movement, January 1957–December 1958* (Berkeley: University of California Press, 1992), 38.

5. *Courier* News Service, "They Don't Fear Arrest!: Over 200 Students Jailed in 'Sit-ins,'" *Pittsburgh Courier,* March 5, 1960, 3.

6. Susan Leigh Foster, "Choreographies of Protest," *Theatre Journal* 55, no. 3 (October 2003): 395–412.

7. William G. Roy, *Reds, Whites, and Blues: Social Movements, Folk Music, and Race in the United States* (Princeton: Princeton University Press, 2010), 196.

8. Jack Newfield, *A Prophetic Minority* (New York: New American Library 1966, 1970), 37–38.

9. David Halberstam, *The Children* (New York: Fawcett Books, 1998), 231–32.

10. Memo from Guy Carawan to Myles (Horton) and Connie (Conrad Brown) on work in the South since 1959, Highlander Folk School Papers, Social Action Collection, State Historical Society of Wisconsin, Madison,

Wisconsin, reel 7:347–353. Cited in Peter J. Ling, "Developing Freedom Songs: Guy Carawan and the African-American Tradition of the South Carolina Sea Islands," *History Workshop Journal* 44 (Autumn 1997): 205–6.

11. Halberstam, *The Children*, 231–32.

12. Raines, *My Soul Is Rested*, 98–99.

13. Bernice Johnson Reagon, "Let the Church Sing 'Freedom,'" *Black Music Research Journal* 7 (1987): 107–8.

14. Seth Cagin and Philip Dray, *We Are Not Afraid: The Story of Goodman, Schwerner, and Chaney and the Civil Rights Campaign for Mississippi* (New York: Macmillan, 1988), 77.

15. Emily Stopher, *The Student Nonviolent Coordinating Committee: The Growth of Radicalism in a Civil Rights Organization* (Brooklyn: Carlson Publishing, 1968, 1989), 6–7.

16. Guy Carawan and Candie Carawan: *A Personal Story Through Sight & Sound,* http://digitalstudio.ucr.edu/studio_projects/carawan/civilrights.html.

17. Aimee Isgrig Horton, *The Highlander Folk School: A History of Its Major Programs, 1932–1961* (Brooklyn: Carlson Publishing, 1989), 246.

18. Bernice Johnson Reagon, "The Civil Rights Movement," in Mellonee V. Burnim and Portia K. Maultsby, eds., *African American Music: An Introduction* (New York: Routledge/Taylor Francis, 2006), 609.

19. Julius Lester, "Freedom Songs in the South," *Broadside* 37 (February 7, 1964).

20. Irwin Silber, "He Sings for Integration," *Sing Out!* 10 (Summer 1960): 4–7.

21. Guy Carawan and Candie Carawan, *Sing for Freedom: The Story of the Civil Rights Movement Through Its Songs* (Montgomery: NewSouth Books, 2007), 17.

22. Ibid., 18.

23. Halberstam, *The Children*, 232.

24. Branch, *Parting the Waters*, 274–75.

25. Various artists, *Nashville Sit-In Story* (Folkways FH 5590), 1960. Reissued by the Smithsonian Folkways Archival, 2007.

26. Carawan, *Sing for Freedom*, 30.

27. Various artists, *The Sit-In Story: The Story of the Lunch Room Sit-Ins* (Folkways FH 5502), 1961. Reissued by the Smithsonian Folkways Archival, 2007.

28. Dunson, *Freedom in the Air*, 40–43.

29. Wilma Dykeman and James Stokely, "'Sit Down Chillun, Sit Down!'" *The Progressive* (June 1960): 10.

30. "Atlanta Negroes March in Protest," *New York Times*, December 12, 1960, 1, 32.

31. "Line of March," *Jet,* December 15, 1960, 37.

32. Virginia Delavan, "This Happened to Us: Experience in a Tallahassee Jail," *Social Progress,* February 1961, 6–8.

33. Martin Kuhlman, "Direct Action at the University of Texas During the Civil Rights Movement, 1960–1965," *The Southwestern Historical Quarterly* 98, no. 4 (April 1995): 563.

34. Gwendolyn Zoharah Simmons, in Faith S. Holsaert and others (eds.), *Hands on the Freedom Plow: Personal Accounts by Women in SNCC* (Urbana: University of Illinois Press, 2010), 17–18.

35. Jean Denton Thompson, interview with author, May 7, 2009, transcript of tape recording, Institute for Oral History, Baylor University, Waco, Texas, 2–5.

36. Willa Ward-Royster, as told to Toni Rose, *How I Got Over: Clara Ward and the World-Famous Ward Singers* (Philadelphia: Temple University Press, 1997), 139.

37. "Mahalia Jackson Believes in Kennedy," *Chicago Defender*, October 29, 1960, 12. Cited in Guido Van Rijn, *Kennedy's Blues: African-American Blues and Gospel Songs on JFK* (Jackson: University Press of Mississippi, 2010), 22. Mahalia Jackson, on meeting Kennedy at an inaugural ball, said, "I feel that I'm part of this man's hopes. He lifts my spirit and makes me feel a part of the land I live in." And at the inauguration itself: "Everybody felt excited and

proud about being there and it was a great moment for Americans. I haven't changed my mind about President Kennedy since then and I never will." Mahalia Jackson with Evan McLeod Wylie, *Movin' On Up* (New York: Hawthorn Books, 1966), 132–39.

38. Paul F. Boller, *Presidential Campaigns* (New York: Oxford University Press, 1984), 299–300.

39. "Sinatra's 'Clan' Raises Dems $1 1/2 Million at Gala," *Jet,* February 2, 1961, 60–62.

40. Van Rijn, *Kennedy's Blues,* 25. As one of the best-known African-American performers/actors throughout the 1950s and '60s, Belafonte's activism was particularly noteworthy. Among the many examples of his ongoing work on behalf of civil rights and social justice, Belafonte and Sidney Poiter headlined a New York rally sponsored by the City Central Labor Council of the AFL-CIO to mark the sixth anniversary of *Brown v. Board of Education.* The crowd, on Thirty-Eighth Street between Seventh and Eighth Avenues, was estimated to be more than fifteen thousand people. The size of the rally, along with the participation of numerous union leaders, serves also as a reminder of organized labor's support of the movement during these crucial early years. ("15,000 Attend Garment Center Civil Rights Rally," *New York Times,* May 18, 1960, 22.)

41. Goreau, *Just Mahalia, Baby,* 285–87.

42. Branch, *Parting the Waters,* 392.

43. Stopher, *The Student Nonviolent Coordinating Committee,* 6–7.

## Chapter 2

The epigraph for this chapter is drawn from Guy Carawan and Candie Carawan, *Sing for Freedom: The Story of the Civil Rights Movement Through Its Songs* (Montgomery: NewSouth Books, 2007), 33.

1. Excellent resources on the Freedom Rides include Raymond Arsenault, *Freedom Riders: 1961 and the Struggle for Racial Justice* (Oxford: Oxford University Press, 2006); Eric Etheridge, *Breach of Peace: Portraits of the 1961 Mississippi Freedom Riders* (New York: Atlas, 2008); Thomas M. Armstrong and Natalie R. Best, *Autobiography of a Freedom Rider: My Life as a Foot Soldier for Civil Rights* (Deerfield Beach, FL: Health Communications, 2011); and Derek C. Catsam, *"A Brave and Wonderful Thing": The Freedom Rides and Integration of Interstate Transport, 1941–1965* (PhD diss., Ohio University, 2003), among others.

2. Catsam, *"A Brave and Wonderful Thing,"* 167.

3. James Peck, *Freedom Ride* (New York: Simon & Schuster, 1962), 18–19, 26.

4. James Farmer, *Lay Bare the Heart: An Autobiography of the Civil Rights Movement* (Fort Worth: Texas Christian University Press, 1998), 196–98.

5. Arsenault, *Freedom Riders,* 101.

6. "10 Negroes Seized in Carolina Sit-In," *New York Times,* February 1, 1961, 39.

7. Claude Sitton, "4 Negroes Jailed in Carolina Sit-In," *New York Times,* February 7, 1961, 36.

8. Peck, *Freedom Ride,* 103–7.

9. Arsenault, *Freedom Riders,* 122–23.

10. Catsam, *"A Brave and Wonderful Thing,"* 167. See also James Forman, "Freedom Rides: Speech by James Foreman and Interview with Lucretia Collins," *Southern Exposure* 9, no. 1 (Spring 1981): 35–36.

11. "Bi-Racial Buses Attacked, Riders Beaten in Alabama," *New York Times,* May 15, 1961, 1, 22.

12. Bernice Johnson Reagon, "Songs That Moved the Movement," *Perspectives: The Civil Rights Quarterly* 15, no. 3 (Summer 1983): 30.

13. Farmer, *Lay Bare the Heart,* 199–204.

14. "Bi-Racial Group Cancels Bus Trip," *New York Times,* May 16, 1961, 1; "Crowd at Bus Station," *New York Times,* May 20, 1961, 18.

15. Ann Bausum, *Freedom Riders: John Lewis and Jim Zwerg on the Front Lines*

*of the Civil Rights Movement* (Washington, DC: National Geographic Society, 2006), 45.

16. Branch, *Parting the Waters*, 436.

17. Forman, "Freedom Rides," 35–37.

18. Simeon Booker, "*Jet* Team Braves Mob Action: Eyewitness Report on Dixie 'Freedom Ride,'" *Jet*, June 1, 1961, 14–21.

19. Stuart H. Loory, "Freedom Riders in Montgomery." *New York Herald Tribune*, May 21, 1961. Reprinted in *Black Protest: History, Documents, and Analyses*, ed. Joanne Grant (Greenwich: Fawcett, 1968), 320–21.

20. Etheridge, *Breach of Peace,* 21–22.

21. Branch, *Parting the Waters,* 454–55.

22. Farmer, in Raines, *My Soul Is Rested,* 122–23.

23. Andrew Manis, *A Fire You Can't Put Out: The Civil Rights Life of Birmingham's Reverend Fred Shuttlesworth* (Tuscaloosa: University of Alabama Press, 1999), 278.

24. Mahalia Jackson with Evan McLeod Wylie, *Movin' On Up* (New York: Hawthorn Books, 1966), 174–75.

25. Arsenault, *Freedom Riders,* 236–37.

26. Farmer, *Lay Bare the Heart,* 6–7.

27. William Sloane Coffin, Jr., *Once to Every Man: A Memoir* (New York: Atheneum, 1977), 161.

28. John Lewis, interviewed in Beardslee, William R., *The Way Out Must Lead In: Life Histories in the Civil Rights Movement* (Westport: Lawrence Hill, 1977, 1983), 168–69.

29. Farmer, *Lay Bare the Heart,* 10, 14.

30. Farmer, in Raines, 126–27.

31. Alphonso Petway, interview with author, June 2, 2009, transcript of tape recording, Institute for Oral History, Baylor University, Waco, 1–5.

32. Pete Seeger, *The Incompleat Folksinger* (New York: Simon & Schuster, 1972), 78.

33. Pauline Knight-Ofosu, interview with author, June 5, 2009, transcript of tape recording, Institute for Oral History, Baylor University, Waco, 3.

34. Howard Zinn, *SNCC: The New Abolitionists* (Boston: Beacon Press, 1964), 54.

35. Etheridge, *Breach of Peace,* 25, 28, 45.

36. Lewis, in Beardslee, *The Way Out Must Lead In,* 15.

37. Etheridge, *Breach of Peace,* 232.

38. John Lewis, interview with author, May 20, 2009, transcript of tape recording, Institute for Oral History, Baylor University, Waco, 1–6.

39. David Fankhauser, interview with author, May 13, 2009, transcript of tape recording, Institute for Oral History, Baylor University, Waco, 2–8.

40. Bob Filner, interview with author, May 22, 2009, transcript of tape recording, Institute for Oral History, Baylor University, Waco, 1–8.

41. Zinn, *SNCC,* 57.

42. Mary King, *Freedom Song: A Personal Story of the 1960s Civil Rights Movement* (New York: William Morrow, 1987), 226.

43. Zinn, *SNCC,* 55.

44. Carawan, *Sing for Freedom,* 47–51.

45. Jean Denton Thompson, interview with author, May 7, 2009, tape recording, Institute for Oral History, Baylor University, Waco, 1–13.

46. Reginald Green, interview with author, May 12, 2009, tape recording, Institute for Oral History, Baylor University, Waco, 6–7.

47. Bernard Lafayette, interviewed in *American Experience: Freedom Riders*, written and directed by Stanley Nelson (PBS/WGBH and Firelight Films, 2011), DVD.

48. Arsenault, *Freedom Riders,* 330.

49. Goreau, *Just Mahalia,* 314–16.

50. Ingrid Monson, *Freedom Sounds: Civil Rights Call Out to Jazz and Africa* (Oxford: Oxford University Press, 2007), 190–92.

51. Arsenault, *Freedom Riders,* 349–53.

52. Ibid., 353–55.

53. Lewis, in Beardslee, *The Way Out Must Lead In,* 173.

54. Zinn, *SNCC,* 57.

55. Matthew D. Lassiter and Joseph Crespino, eds., *The Myth of Southern Exceptionalism* (Oxford: Oxford University Press, 2010), 126–27.

56. Raines, *My Soul Is Rested,* 128.

57. Arsenault, *Freedom Riders,* 385–92.

58. Memo from Guy Carawan to Myles (Horton) and Connie (Conrad Brown) on work in the South since 1959, Highlander Folk School Papers, Social Action Collection, State Historical Society of Wisconsin, Madison, Wisconsin, reel 7:347–353. Cited in Peter J. Ling, "Developing Freedom Songs: Guy Carawan and the African-American Tradition of the South Carolina Sea Islands," *History Workshop Journal* 44 (Autumn 1997): 207.

59. Zinn, *SNCC,* 60. For instance, Belafonte co-hosted a concert with A. Philip Randolph on January 27, 1961. An ad for the event claimed that only 48 tickets remained for the event, a "Tribute of Martin Luther King." Among those mentioned as scheduled to perform were Frank Sinatra, Dan Martin, Sammy Davis, Jr., Peter Lawford, and Joey Bishop. "Only 48 Tickets Left," *New York Times,* January 19, 1961, 25.

60. Arsenault, *Freedom Riders,* 403.

61. Various artists, *We Shall Overcome: Songs of the Freedom Riders and the Sit-Ins* (Folkways FWO5591), 1961. Released on CD by Smithsonian Folkways Archival (FH 5591), 2007.

62. Julian Bond, interviewed in *American Experience: Freedom Riders,* written and directed by Stanley Nelson (PBS/WGBH and Firelight Films, 2011), DVD.

63. Various artists, *Sit-In Songs: Songs of the Freedom Riders* (Dauntless DS 4601); "Record Albums," *CORE-LATOR* (February 1964), and in multiple other issues.

64. Arsenault, *Freedom Riders,* 508. Arsenault is referring to Chuck Berry's "Promised Land," released in 1964, in which the lyrics name several stops by the Freedom Riders, including Charlotte, Rock Hill (which he "bypasses"), Birmingham, and New Orleans. Berry has not publicly (to my knowledge) confirmed nor denied the song's strong allusion to the Freedom Rides.

65. Martin Luther King, Jr., "Love, Law and Civil Disobedience." Address delivered November 16, 1961, to the annual meeting of the Fellowship of the Concerned in Atlanta. Reprinted in *New South* 16, no. 11 (December 1961): 10–11.

66. Jon Michael Spencer, *Protest & Praise: Sacred Music of Black Religion* (Minneapolis: Fortress Press, 1990), 94–95.

67. Guy Carawan and Candie Carawan, "'Freedom in the Air': An Overview of the Songs of the Civil Rights Movement," *Black Music Research Bulletin* 12, no. 1 (Spring 1990): 3.

68. Raines, *My Soul Is Rested,* 129.

69. David Halberstam, *The Children,* 347–48.

70. Trymaine Lee, "In the Valley of the Shadow of Freedom Riders," *Huffington Post,* May 30, 2011. See http://www.huffingtonpost.com/2011/05/09/in-the-valley-of-the-shadow-of-freedom-riders_n_859739.html.

**Chapter 3**

The epigraph to this chapter is drawn from Faith S. Holsaert, Martha Prescod Norman Noonan, Judy Richardson, Betty Garman Robinson, Jean Smith Young, and Dorothy M. Zellner, eds., *Hands on the Freedom Plow: Personal Accounts by Women in SNCC* (Urbana: University of Illinois Press, 2010), 99.

1. Aldon D. Morris, *The Origins of the Civil Rights Movement: Black Communities Organizing for Change* (New York: The Free Press, 1984), 239–41.

2. Paula Giddings, *When and Where I Enter: The Impact of Black Women on Race and Sex in America* (New York: William Morrow, 1984), 282.

3. Morris, *The Origins of the Civil Rights Movement,* 239–41.

4. Holsaert et al., *Hands on the Freedom Plow,* 106.

5. Howard Zinn, *SNCC: The New Abolitionists* (Boston: Beacon Press, 1964), 124–28.

6. Holsaert et al., *Hands on the Freedom Plow,* 108–9.

7. Zinn, *SNCC,* 128–30.

8. Pete Seeger and Bob Reiser, *Everybody Says Freedom* (New York: W. W. Norton, 1989), 72–73.

9. Josh Dunson, *Freedom in the Air: Song Movements of the '60s* (New York: Little New World Paperback, 1965), 62.

10. Zinn, *SNCC,* 128–30.

11. Holsaert et al., *Hands on the Freedom Plow,* 174.

12. Constance Curry, Joan C. Browning, et al., *Deep in Our Hearts: Nine White Women in the Freedom Movement* (Athens: University of Georgia Press, 2000), 142–43.

13. Margaret Long, "Let Freedom Sing," *The Progressive* (November 1965): 29–30.

14. Joe Street, *The Culture War in the Civil Rights Movement* (Gainesville: University Press of Georgia, 2007), 41.

15. Claude Sitton, "202 More Negroes Seized in Georgia," *New York Times,* December 14, 1961, 47.

16. "Albany, Ga. Jails 267 Negro Youths," *New York Times,* December 13, 1961, 51.

17. James Forman, *The Making of Black Revolutionaries* (Washington, DC: Open Hand Publishing, 1985), 253.

18. Bernice Johnson Reagon, "Songs That Moved the Movement," *Perspectives: The Civil Rights Quarterly* 15, no. 3 (Summer 1983): 28.

19. Seeger and Reiser, *Everybody Says Freedom,* 77.

20. Reagon, "Songs That Moved the Movement," 28.

21. Holsaert et al., *Hands on the Freedom Plow,* 122–23.

22. Juan Williams, *Eyes on the Prize: America's Civil Rights Years, 1954–1965* (Boston: Blackside, 1987), 163.

23. Taylor Branch, *Parting the Waters: America in the King Years, 1954–63* (New York: Simon & Schuster Paperbacks, 1988), 532.

24. Pat Watters, *Down to Now: Reflections on the Southern Civil Rights Movement* (New York: Pantheon Books, 1971), 12–13.

25. Jim Bishop, *The Days of Martin Luther King, Jr.* (New York: G. P. Putnam's Sons, 1971), 260–61.

26. Williams, 170–74.

27. Ibid.

28. "Harry Belafonte to Play Martin Luther King Fete," *Chicago Defender,* May 26–June 1, 1962, 16.

29. "Mahalia Jackson, Dick Gregory Join NAACP Fete," *Chicago Defender,* June 16–22, 1962, 36.

30. Howard Carroll, interview by the author, August 4, 2009, transcript of tape recording, Institute for Oral History, Baylor University, Waco, 2–3. Other artists participated in other ways. Bob Dylan composed "The Death of Emmett Till" and performed it at benefit for CORE in February 1962. Dylan performed it regularly during his concerts from 1962–63, but the song did not appear on an album until many years later. See Philip C. Kolin, "Haunting America: Emmett Till in Music and Song," *Southern Cultures* 15, no. 3 (Fall 2009): 119, 121.

31. "They're Marching Off to Jail—For Freedom and King," *Chicago Defender,* July 14–20, 1962, 3.

32. Bishop, *The Days of Martin Luther King, Jr.,* 272.

33. Williams, *Eyes on the Prize,* 170–74.

34. "We Held Our Staff Meetings Right There in Jail," *Jet,* August 23, 1962, 16.

35. Larry Still, "'Courts Take Time, We Want Freedom Now'—Albany Leaders." *Jet,* August 16, 1962, 16.

36. David Levering Lewis, *King: A Biography* (Urbana: University of Illinois Press, 2012), 161.

37. William M. Kunstler, *Deep in My Heart* (New York: William Morrow & Company, 1966), 104–5.

38. Claude Sitton, "Sheriff Harasses Negroes at Voting Rally in Georgia," *New York Times,* July 27, 1962, 1, 9.

39. Andrew Young, *An Easy Burden: The Civil Rights Movement and the*

*Transformation of America* (Waco: Baylor University Press, 2008), 183.

40. Branch, *Parting the Waters,* 620.

41. Pat Watters and Reese Cleghorn, *Climbing Jacob's Ladder: The Arrival of Negroes in Southern Politics* (New York: Harcourt, Brace & World, 1967), 168. After the burning of this and other churches in Georgia, African-American comic Dick Gregory mused, "Negroes are really in trouble. The Supreme Court fixed it so we can't pray in school and the bigots burned down the churches. If it weren't for jails, we wouldn't have any place to pray." "Words of the Week," *Jet,* October 4, 1962, 30.

42. E. W. Kenworthy, "Clergymen Seek Action in Georgia," *New York Times,* August 7, 1962, 18. The Kennedy administration did take other public steps that doubtless enraged segregationists. The Staple Singers, for instance, performed at one of the inauguration balls and again at the White House in 1962. See Greg Kot, *I'll Take You There: Mavis Staples, the Staple Singers, and the March Up Freedom's Highway* (New York: Scribner, 2014), 92. As for Belafonte, another African-American artist who would often be publicly tied to the Kennedys, the *New York Times* reported that on June 7, following an integrated concert before more than five thousand in Atlanta, Belafonte and his associates were twice refused admission to the King's Inn Restaurant just blocks away from the City Auditorium. The concert had been a benefit for King and the SCLC. As the manager, Charles Leb, said, "I'm a Jew myself. I know how it is to be discriminated against. I'm a great admirer of Belafonte. But I can't integrate my restaurant because the others won't." ("Belafonte Barred 2nd Time in Atlanta," *New York Times,* June 8, 1962, 64.)

43. Seeger, *Everybody Says Freedom,* 85.

44. Zinn, *SNCC,* 172–181.

45. "Integration Leader Wary of Being Tricked Out of Jail: Rev. M. L. King Diary in Jail," *Jet,* August 23, 1962, 14–21.

46. Hedrick Smith, "'Outsider' Issue Stirs Albany, Ga.," *New York Times,* August 12, 1962, 1, 13; Hedrick Smith, "Dr. King Speaks to 1,000 in Albany," *New York Times,* August 13, 1962, 16.

47. "Girls Jailed in Albany; NAACP Splits in N.J.," *Chicago Defender,* August 11–17, 1962, 1.

48. Holsaert et al., *Hands on the Freedom Plow,* 114.

49. Ralph Lord Roy, "In Summer of '62, Living King's Challenge," *New York Times,* January 18, 2009, L14.

50. Larry Still, "Courts Take Time," 16.

51. Robert Shelton, "Songs a Weapon in Rights Battle: Vital New Ballads Buoy Negro Spirits Across the South," *New York Times,* August 20, 1962, 1.

52. Ibid., 14.

53. Forman, cited in Street, *The Culture War in the Civil Rights Movement,* 164.

54. Watters, *Climbing Jacob's Ladder,* 169–70.

55. Guy Carawan and Candie Carawan, eds., *Sing for Freedom: The Story of the Civil Rights Movement Through Its Songs* (Montgomery: NewSouth Books, 2008), 56–57; Claude Sitton, "Negroes Defy Ban, March in Georgia," *New York Times,* July 20, 1962, 1, 32.

56. Williams, *Eyes on the Prize,* 169.

57. James Forman, *The Making of Black Revolutionaries,* 248.

58. Carawan and Carawan, *Sing for Freedom,* 58–59.

59. "Oh Pritchett, Oh, Kelley," "If You Miss Me at the Back of the Bus," "Oxford Town," and "Paths of Victory," *Broadside* 17 (December 1962).

60. Tom Dent, *Southern Journey: A Return to the Civil Rights Movement* (Athens: University of Georgia Press, 2001), 242–43.

61. Howard Zinn, *The Southern Mystique* (New York: Alfred A. Knopf, 1964), 163.

62. Zinn, *SNCC,* 131.

63. Bernice Reagon, "In Our Hands: Thoughts on Black Music," *Sing Out!* 24 (January–February 1976): 1.

64. Holsaert et al., *Hands on the Freedom Plow,* 146–47, 151.

65. Tom Hayden, *Reunion: A Memoir* (New York: Random House, 1988), 70.

66. T. V. Reed, *The Art of Protest: Culture and Activism from the Civil Rights Movement to the Streets of Seattle* (Minneapolis: University of Minnesota Press, 2005), 35–36.

67. Robert Sherman, "Sing a Song of Freedom," *Saturday Review,* September 28, 1963, 65.

68. Various artists, Guy Carawan and Alan Lomax, producers. *Freedom in the Air: A Documentary on Albany, Georgia, 1961–1962* (Vanguard SNCC-101).

69. Robert Shelton, "Folk Crusade on Disks," *New York Times,* December 2, 1962, 203. Shelton also reviewed *Sit-In Songs: Songs of the Freedom Riders* (Dauntless DM 4301), *We Shall Overcome: Songs of the "Freedom Riders" and the "Sit-Ins"* (Folkways FH 5591), and *The Nashville Sit-In Story* (Folkways FH 5590).

70. Watters, *Climbing Jacob's Ladder,* 160.

71. Lynne Olson, *Freedom's Daughters: The Unsung Heroes of the Civil Rights Movement from 1830 to 1970* (New York: Scribner, 2001), 233.

72. Jocelyn Arem, ed., *Caffé Lena: Inside America's Legendary Folk Music Coffeehouse* (Brooklyn: powerHouse Books, 2013), 63.

73. Pete Seeger, *The Incompleat Folksinger* (Lincoln: University of Nebraska Press, 1992), 234–35.

74. Mellonee V. Burnim and Portia K. Maultsby, eds., *African Amerian Music: An Introduction* (New York: Routledge/Taylor & Francis, 2005), 615–16.

75. Holsaert et al., *Hands on the Freedom Plow,* 145.

76. Reed, *The Art of Protest,* 23.

77. Robert Shelton, "Carnegie Is Still Going Strong: Capacity Crowd at Hootenanny," *New York Times,* September 24, 1962, 36.

78. "Gospel for Freedom," *Chicago Defender* (City Edition), October 6, 1962, 32.

79. Williams, *Eyes on the Prize,* 178.

80. Gary Steven Selby, "Scoffing at the Enemy: The Burlesque Frame in the Rhetoric of Ralph David Abernathy," *Southern Communication Journal* 70, no. 2 (2005): 138.

81. Watters, *Climbing Jacob's Ladder,* 209.

82. *Eyes on the Prize,* transcript, page 61, http://www.pbs.org/wgbh/amex/eyesontheprize/about/pt.html.

83. Barbara Deming, *Prisons That Could Not Hold* (Athens: University of Georgia Press, 1995), 1, 15, 69, 77, 95, 108.

84. Forman, *The Making of Black Revolutionaries,* 260.

85. Bob Zellner, with Constance Curry, *The Wrong Side of Murder Creek: A White Southerner in the Freedom Movement* (Montgomery: NewSouth Books, 2008), 148–49.

86. William G. Roy, *Reds, Whites, and Blues: Social Movements, Folk Music, and Race in the United States* (Princeton: Princeton University Press, 2010), 198–200.

87. Clayborne Carson, *In Struggle: SNCC and the Black Awakening of the 1960s* (Cambridge: Harvard University Press, 1981), 64.

88. *Eyes on the Prize,* transcript, 63.

89. Robert Shelton, "Singing for Freedom: Music in the Integration Movement," *Sing Out!* 12 (December–January 1962): 16.

90. Dent, *Southern Journey,* 242.

**First Interlude**

The epigraph to this chapter is taken from a biography of Charles Neblett found at http://www.jodisolomonspeakers.com/speaker/charles-neblett.

1. A good summary of the McComb project can be found in John Dittmer, *Local People: The Struggle for Civil Rights in Mississippi* (Urbana: University of Illinois Press, 1994), 102–10; see also Anthony Lewis, "Mississippi Cases Worry U.S. Aides." *New York Times,* October 11, 1961, 28.

2. Grace Elizabeth Hale, "Black as Folk: The Southern Civil Rights Movement and the Folk Music Revival" in Matthew D. Lassiter and Joseph Crespino, eds., *The Myth of Southern Exceptionalism: Class, Race, and Partisan Change in the Postwar South* (Oxford: Oxford University Press, 2010), 127.

3. Claude Sitton, "Negro Vote Drive in Mississippi Is Set Back as Violence Erupts," *New York Times*, October 24, 1961, 28.

4. Howard Zinn, *SNCC: The New Abolitionists* (Boston: Beacon Press, 1965), 66–67.

5. Robert P. Moses and Charles E. Cobb, *Radical Equations: Math Literacy and Civil Rights* (Boston: Beacon Press, 2001), 53.

6. Guy Carawan and Candie Carawan, *We Shall Overcome!: Songs of the Southern Freedom Movement* (Montgomery: NewSouth Books, 2007), 81.

7. Dittmer, *Local People*, 110.

8. Eric Burner, *And Gently He Shall Lead Them: Robert Parris Moses and Civil Rights in Mississippi* (New York: New York University Press, 1994), 61.

9. Carawan and Carawan, *We Shall Overcome!*, 71, 76.

10. Mellonnee V. Burnim and Portia K. Maultsby, eds., *African American Music: An Introduction* (New York: Routledge, 2005), 620.

11. Carawan and Carawan, *We Shall Overcome!*, 76.

12. Jabari Asim, "Charles Neblett, Fighting for Our Rights," *Washington Post*, May 17, 2004, http://www.washingtonpost.com/wp-dyn/articles/A33093-2004May17.html.

13. Tom Hayden, *Revolution in Mississippi: Special Report* (New York: Students for a Democratic Society, 1962), 5–27.

14. Carawan and Carawan, *We Shall Overcome!*, 71–74.

15. Clayborne Carson, *In Struggle: SNCC and the Black Awakening of the 1960s* (Cambridge: Harvard University Press, 1981), 50.

## Chapter 4

The epigraph for this chapter is taken from a speech by the Reverend Fred Shuttlesworth, "Eighth Annual Address by Rev. Shuttlesworth to the ACMHR," June 5, 1964, Apostolic Overcoming Holy Church of God, Fred Shuttlesworth Papers, Civil Rights Institute, Birmingham, Alabama.

1. "Sit-in Benefit Bill Headed by Monk, Mingus," *(Baltimore) Afro-American*, February 2, 1963, 11. See also, Program: Carnegie Hall, 1962–63 Season, "A Salute to Southern Students" and http://www.carnegiehall.org/BlogPost.aspx?id=4294987557.

2. Glenn T. Eskew, *But for Birmingham: The Local and National Movements in the Civil Rights Movement* (Chapel Hill: University of North Carolina Press, 1997) 215.

3. Andrew M. Manis, *A Fire You Can't Put Out: The Civil Rights Life of Birmingham's Reverend Fred Shuttlesworth* (Tuscaloosa: University of Alabama Press, 1999), 342.

4. Wilson Fallin, Jr., "Black Baptist Women and the Birmingham Civil Rights Movement, 1956–1963," *Baptist History and Heritage* (Summer/Fall 2005): 41–43.

5. The civil rights experiment in Birmingham has been wonderfully documented by a host of excellent histories, including Taylor Branch, *Parting the Waters: America in the King Years, 1954–1963* (New York: Simon and Schuster Paperbacks, 1988); Glenn T. Eskew, *But for Birmingham: The Local and National Movements in the Civil Rights Struggle* (Chapel Hill: University of North Carolina Press, 1997); Martin Luther King, Jr., *Why We Can't Wait* (New York: Signet Classics, 2000); David Garrow, *Bearing the Cross: Martin Luther King, Jr., and the Southern Leadership Conference* (New York: William Morrow, 1986); Cynthia Levinson, *We've Got a Job: The 1963 Birmingham Children's March* (Atlanta: Peachtree Publishers, 2012); Andrew M. Manis,

*A Fire You Can't Put Out: The Civil Rights Life of Birmingham's Reverend Fred Shuttlesworth* (Tuscaloosa: University of Alabama Press, 1999); and Diane McWhorter, *Carry Me Home: Birmingham, Alabama: The Climactic Battle of the Civil Rights Revolution* (New York: Simon & Schuster, 2001).

6. Aldon D. Morris, *The Origins of the Civil Rights Movement: Black Communities Organizing for Change* (New York: Free Press, 1984), 257.

7. Eskew, *But for Birmingham,* 91, 95.

8. King, *Why We Can't Wait,* 46–47.

9. Eskew, *But for Birmingham,* 219–21. See also Howell Raines, *My Soul Is Rested: Movement Days in the Deep South Remembered* (New York: G. P. Putnam's Sons, 1977), 122–23, 148–47.

10. Eskew, *But for Birmingham,* 125, 139.

11. King, *Why We Can't Wait,* 48.

12. Robert Darden, *Nothing But Love in God's Water: Black Sacred Music from the Civil War to the Civil Rights Movement,* vol. 1 (University Park, PA: Pennsylvania State University Press, 2014), 59–85.

13. Mamie Brown-Mason, Interview with the author, July 6, 2009, Birmingham, transcript of tape recording, Institute for Oral History, Baylor University, Waco, 5–6.

14. Eskew, *But for Birmingham,* 138–39.

15. Wilson Fallin, Jr., *Uplifting the People: Three Centuries of Black Baptists in Alabama* (Tuscaloosa: University of Alabama Press, 2007), 228.

16. Brown-Mason interview, 7–9.

17. Pete Seeger and Bob Reiser, *Everybody Says Freedom* (New York: W. W. Norton, 2009), 104–8.

18. Dennis Chong, *Collective Action and the Civil Rights Movement* (Chicago: University of Chicago Press, 1991), 183.

19. Carlton Reese, tape recording, Birmingham Civil Rights Institute, Oral History Project, Birmingham, vol. 16, 5.

20. Lee Trymaine, "Take It to Church: The Music of the Movement." *Huffington Post,* May 15, 2011, http://www ington Post, May 15, 2011, http://www

.huffingtonpost.com/2011/05/30/gospel-and-the-freedom-ri_n_868299.html.

21. Eloise Ford Gaffney, interview with the author, July 3, 2009, Birmingham, transcript of tape recording, Institute for Oral History, Baylor University, Waco, 4–9.

22. Cynthia Levinson, *We've Got a Job: The 1963 Birmingham Children's March* (Atlanta: Peachtree Publishers, 2012), 39. In 1963, the Alabama Christian Movement Choir self-released an LP titled *We've Got a Job* (CM1001 10828). This rare recording featured photographs of Shuttlesworth, Gardner, King, Abernathy, and Reese on the album jacket, along with a photograph of the choir itself. Various soloists accompanied the choir on a set of songs that included "Demand It Now," "Yes, We Want Our Freedom," "Come Down Lord, Want My Freedom," "I Want to Be Free," "Freedom's Going to Reign," "Freedom Is Just Ahead," "Freedom Shall Be Mine," and others.

23. Horace Huntley and John W. McKerley, eds., *Foot Soldiers for Democracy: The Men, Women, and Children of the Birmingham Civil Rights Movement* (Urbana: University of Illinois Press, 2009), 97.

24. Manis, *A Fire You Can't Put Out,* 342–45.

25. Foster Hailey, "4 Negroes Jailed in Birmingham as the Integration Drive Slows," *New York Times,* April 5, 1963, 16.

26. Eskew, *But for Birmingham,* 225.

27. Ibid., 225–26.

28. B. A. Allison and R. A. Watkins, Surveillance of the mass meetings in Birmingham, April 10, 1963, report of April 8, 1963, box 3.2, pages 1–5, Papers of Eugene "Bull" Connor, Birmingham Public Library, Birmingham.

29. Foster Hailey, "Alabama Police Jail Blind Singer," *New York Times,* April 10, 1963, 29.

30. Eskew, *But for Birmingham,* 231.

31. Foster Hailey, "Negroes United in Birmingham," *New York Times,* April 11, 1963, 21.

32. Eskew, *But for Birmingham*, 235.

33. Foster Hailey, "Negroes Defying Birmingham Writ," *New York Times,* April 12, 1963, 1, 13.

34. King, *Why We Can't Wait,* 58–60.

35. Ralph David Abernathy, *And the Walls Came Tumbling Down: An Autobiography* (New York: Harper & Row, 1989), 246–47.

36. Eliot Wigginton, ed., *Refuse to Stand Silently By: An Oral History of Grass Roots Social Activism in America, 1921–64* (New York: Doubleday Religious Publishing Group, 1999), 292–93.

37. McWhorter, *Carry Me Home,* 344.

38. King, *Why We Can't Wait,* 72.

39. Foster Hailey, "Dr. King Arrested in Birmingham," *New York Times,* April 13, 1963, 1, 13.

40. "Dr. King vs. Bull Connor: Eyes of the World on Bitter Birmingham Struggle," *(Baltimore) Afro-American,* April 20, 1963, 2.

41. Jonathan Rieder, *Gospel of Freedom: Martin Luther King, Jr.'s Letter from Birmingham Jail and the Struggle That Changed a Nation* (New York: Bloomsbury Press, 2013), 38–39.

42. Cliff Mackay, "I'll Stay in Prison the Rest of My Days . . . ," *(Baltimore) Afro-American,* May 4, 1963, 12.

43. King, *Why We Can't Wait,* 77–78. The complete letter is reprinted in *Why We Can't Wait*; and in New York, Harry Belafonte made public a letter urging the administration to respond to the brutal treatment of protesters. The letter was signed by Belafonte, actor Marlon Brando, Reverend Dr. Harry Emerson Fosdick, and Jacob S. Ptofsky, president of the Amalgamated Clothing Works of America. See "Belafonte Answers King's Urgent S-O-S; Sends $60,000 to Ala.," *(Baltimore) Afro-American,* May 4, 1963, 1.

44. "Dr. King Leaves Birmingham Jail," *New York Times,* April 21, 1963, 70.

45. Foster Hailey, "8 Negroes Seized in Alabama Walk," *New York Times,* May 2, 1963, 18.

46. King, *Why We Can't Wait,* 101–2; Garrow, *Bearing the Cross,* 247–48.

47. Rieder, *Gospel of Freedom,* 114.

48. Levinson, *We've Got a Job,* 71.

49. Erskine R. Faush, Sr., interview with the author, November 11, 2009, transcript of tape recording, Institute for Oral History, Baylor University, Waco, 9.

50. Nettie L. Flemmon, Birmingham Civil Rights Institute, *Oral History Project,* vol. 16, 13.

51. Manis, *A Fire You Can't Put Out,* 369.

52. Levinson, *We've Got a Job,* 71–72.

53. Bob Marovich, private correspondence with the author, December 18, 2013.

54. Faush, 11.

55. Foster Hailey, "500 Are Arrested in Negro Protest at Birmingham," *New York Times,* May 3, 1963, 1, 15.

56. McWhorter, *Carry Me Home,* 367.

57. Levinson, *We've Got a Job,* 71–75.

58. Eskew, *But for Birmingham,* 265–66.

59. R. A. Watkins, R. S. Whitehouse, and T. H. Cook, Surveillance reports, May 3, 1963, meeting of May 2, 1963, box 13.4, pages 1–5, Papers of Eugene "Bull" Connor, Birmingham Public Library, Birmingham. Parenthetical in the original notes.

60. Rieder, *Gospel of Freedom,* 115.

61. Manis, *A Fire You Can't Put Out,* 371.

62. Levinson, *We've Got a Job,* 82.

63. Eskew, *But for Birmingham,* 267–68.

64. McWhorter, *Carry Me Home,* 371.

65. *Mighty Times: The Children's March,* directed by Robert Houston and Bobby Hudson (Montgomery, AL: HBO Family and the Southern Poverty Law Center, 2004), DVD. Author's transcription of a description by Gwen Webb.

66. Foster Hailey, "Dogs and Hoses Repulse Negroes at Birmingham," *New York Times,* May 4, 1963, 1, 8.

67. McWhorter, *Carry Me Home,* 372.

68. Steve Taylor, interview with the author, June 30, 2009, Birmingham, transcript of tape recording, Institute for Oral History, Baylor University, Waco, 3.

69. Levinson, *We've Got a Job,* 103–4.

70. Manis, *A Fire You Can't Put Out,* 373.

71. Levinson, *We've Got a Job*, 108.
72. Andrew Young, *An Easy Burden: The Civil Rights Movement and the Transformation of America* (Waco: Baylor University Press, 2008), 232–33.
73. McWhorter, *Carry Me Home*, 386. In an indication of the esteem in which the Carawans were held by movement activists, after their arrest, Andrew Young interrupted that evening's mass meeting to tell those assembled what had happened and that the Carawans "are the ones who taught us many of the songs we sing in the movement." See Branch, *Parting the Waters*, 766.
74. Tom Brokaw, *Boom! Voices of the Sixties* (New York: Random House, 2007), 579.
75. McWhorter, *Carry Me Home*, 386.
76. King, *Why We Can't Wait*, 107.
77. McWhorter, *Carry Me Home*, 387.
78. Young, *An Easy Burden*, 223.
79. Surveillance Reports, May 7, 1963, report on meeting of May 5, 1963, box 13.4, Papers of Eugene "Bull" Connor, Birmingham Public Library, Birmingham.
80. Foster Hailey, "Birmingham Talks Pushed; Negroes March Peacefully," *New York Times*, May 6, 1963, 1, 59.
81. Joan Baez, *And a Voice to Sing With: A Memoir* (New York: Summit Books, 1987), 105.
82. McWhorter, *Carry Me Home*, 391.
83. Seeger and Reisner, *Everybody Says Freedom*, 112.
84. Len Holt, "Eyewitness: The Police Terror in Birmingham," *National Guardian*, May 16, 1963. Reprinted in Joanne Grant, *Black Protest: History, Documents, and Analyses* (Greenwich: Fawcett Publications, 1968), 344–46.
85. Levinson, *We've Got a Job*, 112–13.
86. Dick Gregory with Robert Lipsyte, *Nigger: An Autobiography by Dick Gregory* (New York: E. P. Dutton, 1964), 194.
87. Claude Sitton, "Birmingham Jails 1,000 More Negroes," *New York Times*, May 7, 1963, 1, 33.
88. Baez, *And a Voice to Sing With*, 105.
89. McWhorter, *Carry Me Home*, 392–93.
90. Seeger and Reiser, *Everybody Says Freedom*, 116.
91. Cleopatra Kennedy, interview with the author, July 10, 2009, Birmingham, transcript of tape recording, Institute for Oral History, Baylor University, Waco, 12–16.
92. ACMHR Choir, Rev. Ralph Abernathy, and Rev. Martin Luther King, Jr., *Birmingham, Alabama, 1963: Mass Meeting*, produced by Candie Carawan and Guy Carawan (Washington, DC: Smithsonian Folkways Archival, 1990), CD.
93. Baez, *And a Voice to Sing With*, 106.
94. Holt, "Eyewitness: The Police Terror in Birmingham," 347–48.
95. Ellen Levine, *Freedom's Children: Young Civil Rights Activists Tell Their Own Stories* (Thorndike, ME: Thorndike Press, 1993), 146–47.
96. Henry Burton, interview with the author, July 7, 2009, Birmingham, transcript of tape recording, Institute for Oral History, Baylor University, Waco, 15.
97. Levinson, *We've Got a Job*, 118.
98. Eskew, *But for Birmingham*, 278.
99. Brown-Mason interview, 30–37.
100. Holt, "Eyewitness: The Police Terror in Birmingham," 347–48.
101. Claude Sitton, "Rioting Negroes Routed by Police at Birmingham," *New York Times*, May 8, 1963, 1, 28.
102. Barry Taylor, interview with the author, June 30, 2009, Birmingham, transcript of tape recording, Institute for Oral History, Baylor University, Waco, 8–11.
103. Gaffney interview, 9–11.
104. Eskew, *But for Birmingham*, 284–90.
105. John D. Pomfret, "Kennedy Reacts: Early Report of Peace Leads Him to Hail Racial Conferees," *New York Times*, May 9, 1963, 1, 27.
106. Eskew, *But for Birmingham*, 290–91.
107. B. A. Allison and R. A. Watkins, Surveillance reports of mass meetings, May 10, 1963, on the May 9, 1963, meeting at Sixth Avenue Baptist Church, box 13.4, Papers of Eugene "Bull"

Connor, Birmingham Public Library, Birmingham.

108. Taylor interview, 4–5.

109. N. B. Wooding, interview with the author July 8, 2009, Birmingham, transcript of tape recording, Institute for Oral History, Baylor University, Waco, 6–13.

110. Huntley and McKerley, *Foot Soldiers for Democracy*, 102.

111. Larry Still, "Gregory, Hibbler Gave Punch to Dixie Freedom Movement: Should Negro Stars Join Freedom Fight?" *Jet*, May 9, 1963, 21–23; Laurraine Goreau, *Just Mahalia, Baby* (Waco: Word Books, 1975), 350–52.

112. Claude Sitton, "Hurdles Remain: Negroes Warn of New Protest Today If Parleys Fail," *New York Times,* May 9, 1963, 1, 17.

113. Claude Sitton, "Birmingham Talks Reach an Accord on Ending Crisis," *New York Times,* May 10, 1963, 1, 14.

114. "Dick Gregory Accuses Police of Brutality in Alabama Jail," *New York Times,* May 10, 1963, 14.

115. Claude Sitton, "Birmingham Pact Sets Timetable for Integration," *New York Times,* May 11, 1963, 1, 8.

116. Philip Benjamin, "Negroes' Boycott in Birmingham Cuts Heavily into Retail Sales," *New York Times,* May 11, 1963, 9.

117. Garrow, *Bearing the Cross*, 182.

118. Harry Belafonte with Michael Shnayerson, *My Song: A Memoir* (New York: Alfred A. Knopf, 2011), 262–65.

119. Eskew, *But for Birmingham*, 300; Claude Sitton, "50 Hurt in Negro Rioting After Birmingham Blasts," *New York Times,* May 13, 1963, 1, 24.

120. Hedrick Smith, "Bombs Touch Off Widespread Riot at Birmingham," *New York Times,* May 12, 1963, 1, 53.

121. Bob Friedman, interview by author, November 11, 2009, transcript of tape recording, Institute for Oral History, Baylor University, Waco, 16.

122. Levine, *Freedom's Children*, 150–51.

123. Eskew, *But for Birmingham*, 300; Claude Sitton, "50 Hurt in Negro Rioting After Birmingham Blasts," *New York Times,* May 13, 1963, 1, 24.

124. McWhorter, *Carry Me Home,* 433.

125. Anthony Lewis, "U.S. Sends Troops into Alabama after Riots Sweep Birmingham; Kennedy Alerts State's Guard," *New York Times,* May 13, 1963, 1, 55.

126. King, *Why We Can't Wait*, 114.

127. Levinson, *We've Got a Job*, 132.

128. "Taking Collection," *Jet,* May 20, 1963, 32.

129. Claude Sitton, "Birmingham Still Quiet; Security Measures Lifted," *New York Times,* May 14, 1963, 1, 26; Claude Sitton, "Whites Cautious on Alabama Pact," *New York Times,* May 15, 1963, 1, 26.

130. Claude Sitton, "Birmingham Pact Picks Up Support," *New York Times,* May 6, 1963, 1, 22.

131. Claude Sitton, "Negroes Ask Scope of Birmingham Pact," *New York Times,* May 17, 1963, 1, 14; Henrick Smith, "Birmingham Pact Faces Major Test," *New York Times,* May 18, 1963, 12.

132. Claude Sitton, "Whites Cautious on Alabama Pact," *New York Times,* May 15, 1963, 1, 26.

133. Anthony Lewis, "Supreme Court Legalizes Sit-Ins in Cities Enforcing Segregation; Birmingham's Schools Drop 1,100," *New York Times,* May 21, 1963, 1, 19.

134. Claude Sitton, "Negro Students Ousted for Birmingham Protests," *New York Times,* May 21, 1963, 1, 18; "Pupils Take Case to Federal Court," *New York Times,* May 22, 1963, 27; Claude Sitton, "U.S. Appeals Judge Orders Birmingham to Reinstate Pupils," *New York Times,* May 23, 1963, 1, 19; Claude Sitton, "Boutwell Seated in Birmingham; Peace Hopes Rise," *New York Times,* May 24, 1963, 1, 37.

135. "Greatest Freedom Rally Here Nets Heroes Over $75,000," *Los Angeles Sentinel,* May 30, 1963, 1, 4; Louie Robinson, "50,000 Jam L.A. Ball Park for Biggest Rights Rally," *Jet,* June 13, 1963, 54–60.

136. Goreau, *Just Mahalia, Baby*, 349–52.

137. Shelley Stewart, with Nathan Hale Turner, Jr., *The Road South: A Memoir* (New York: Warner Books, 2002), 186–89, 245–49.

138. Brian Ward, *Radio and the Struggle for Civil Rights in the South* (Gainesville: University of Florida Press, 2004), 202.

139. Martin Luther King, Jr., "Remembrance: January 15, 1929–April 4, 1968," *Jack the Rapper* 13, no. 666 (January 11, 1989): 1. King would also cite the work of DJs Purvis Spann for the Mississippi Summer Project of 1964 and the Magnificent Montague during the Watts riots, and the fund-raising efforts on behalf of the SCLC of Georgie Woods in Philadelphia.

140. Anthony Heilbut, *The Gospel Sound: Good News and Bad Time*, rev. ed. (New York: Limelight Editions, 1989), 71, 297.

141. James Alex Taylor, interview with the author, June 30, 2009, Birmingham, transcript of tape recording, Institute for Oral History, Baylor University, Waco, 2–3.

142. Wayne Williams, interview with the author, June 30, 2009, Birmingham, transcript of tape recording, Institute for Oral History, Baylor University, Waco, 2.

143. "King of the Gospel Writers: Thomas A. Dorsey Gave up Blues to Write World's Best Known Gospel Songs," *Ebony*, November 1962, 126.

144. All articles from the *(Baltimore) Afro-American*, June 1, 1963, 1–2, 12–13: "U.S. Taking a Terrific Beating Because of Racial Outbursts," "Governor Wallace: In a Squeeze," "Police Dogs in Ala. Spur N.C. Unrest," and "$300,000 Spent for Freedom Fight."

145. Len Holt, *An Act of Conscience* (Boston: Beacon Press, 1965), 84–95.

146. McWhorter, *Carry Me Home*, 469.

147. "Integration: Worried Leaders," *Newsweek*, July 15, 1963, 20; McWhorter, *Carry Me Home*, 464.

148. B. T. Gillespie, "'Like a Slaughterhouse': Wounded Fill Wards of Hospitals," *(Baltimore) Afro-American*, June 22, 1963, 1–2.

149. Robert Shelton, "Negro Songs Here Aid Rights Drive," *New York Times*, June 22, 1963, 15.

150. "Fund Raisers for Freedom," *Ebony*, October 1963, 122.

151. Ingrid Monson, *Freedom Sounds: Civil Rights Call Out to Jazz and Africa* (Oxford: Oxford University Press, 2007), 202.

152. Allan Blanchard and Earl B. Dowdy, "125,000 March on Woodward; Detroit Officials Praise Rally," *Detroit News*, June 24, 1963, 1, 2A; Anthony Ripley, "City 'Walk' Is Triumph for Dr. King," *Detroit News*, June 24, 1963, 1, 20A; "Mayor Proud of Big Turnout," *Detroit News*, June 24, 1, 19A; Nick Salvatore, *Singing in a Strange Land: C. L. Franklin, the Black Church, and the Transformation of America* (Urbana: University of Illinois Press, 2006), 252–54.

153. Albert Anderson, "The Week in Records: Dr. King Speaks," *(Baltimore) Afro-American*, September 14, 1963, 9; and Martin Luther, King, Jr., *The Great March to Freedom: Detroit June 23, 1963*, Gordy Records GLP 906, 1963. Also released that summer was the Staple Singers' *This Land*, Riverside 3524, which included renditions of "Blowin' in the Wind" and "This Land Is Your Land," in addition to several remade spirituals. See Greg Kot, *I'll Take You There: Mavis Staples, the Staple Singers, and the March up Freedom's Highway* (New York: Scribner, 2014), 83.

154. Robert Shelton, "Rights Song Has Own History of Integration," *New York Times*, July 23, 1963, 21.

155. Milton Esterow, "Birmingham Hall to Be Painted on Date Set for Integrated Show," *New York Times*, July 16, 1963, 25; Tim Trainor, "What's New," *New York Times*, August 5, 1963, 40; "Artists Integrate Birmingham Stage," *(Baltimore) Afro-American*, August 17, 1963, 19.

156. Art Sears, "13,000 Bring Own Chairs, Raise $10,000 in B'ham's Star-Packed

Show," *Jet,* August 22, 1963, 58–62. In addition to performing at fund-raisers and benefits, Ray Charles gave generously to the SCLC and other civil rights organizations. He was once asked why he was not on the marches, along with certain other celebrities. "First," he wrote in his autobiography, "I wouldn't have known when to duck when they started throwing broken beer bottles at my head. And secondly, I'd defeat Martin's purpose. My temperament just wouldn't stand certain treatment." See Ray Charles and David Ritz, *Brother Ray: Ray Charles' Own Story* (Cambridge: Da Capo Press, 1978), 2004.

157. Margaret Long, "Let Freedom Sing," *The Progressive* (November 1965): 30.

158. Garrow, *Bearing the Cross,* 239.

159. Howard Sitkoff, *King: Pilgrimage to the Mountaintop* (New York: Hill and Wang, 2008), 92.

160. Charles Euchner, *Nobody Turn Me Around: A People's History of the 1963 March on Washington* (Boston: Beacon Press, 2010), 107.

161. Paul Hemphill, *Leaving Birmingham: Notes of a Native Son* (Tuscaloosa: The University of Alabama Press, 2000), 10.

## Chapter 5

The epigraphs for this chapter are drawn from Lerone Bennett, "Masses Were March Heroes," *Ebony,* November, 1963, 35; and Denise Sullivan, *Keep on Pushing: Black Power Music from Blues to Hip Hop* (Chicago: Lawrence Hill Books, 2011), 23–24.

1. Robert L. Zangrando, "The Direction of the March," *Negro History Bulletin* 27, no. 3 (December 1, 1963): 62.

2. Robert Darden, *Nothing But Love in God's Water: Black Sacred Music from the Civil War to the Civil Rights Movement,* vol. 1 (University Park: Pennsylvania State University Press, 2014), 94–95.

3. The most detailed books on the March on Washington are Thomas Gentile, *March on Washington: August 28, 1963* (Washington, DC: New Day Publications, 1983); Charles Euchner, *Nobody Turn Me Around: A People's History of the 1963 March on Washington* (Boston: Beacon Press, 2010); and William Powell Jones, *The March on Washington: Jobs, Freedom and the Forgotten History of Civil Rights* (New York: W.W. Norton, 2013).

4. For more information on Bayard Rustin see John D'Emilio, *Lost Prophet: The Life and Times of Bayard Rustin* (New York: Free Press, 2010); Jerald Podair, *Bayard Rustin: American Dreamer* (Lanham: Rowman & Littlefield, 2009); and *Brother Outsider: The Life of Bayard Rustin* produced and directed by Nancy D. Kates and Bennett Singer (PBS/P.O.V. documentary: Independent Television Service, 2002), DVD.

5. Brian Ward, *Just My Soul Responding: Rhythm and Blues, Black Consciousness and Race Relations* (London: UCL Press, 1998), 133.

6. Richard Carlin and Kinshasha Holman Conwill, eds., *Ain't Nothing Like the Real Thing: How the Apollo Theater Shaped American Entertainment* (Washington, DC: National Museum of African American History and Culture/ Smithsonian Books, 2010), 171.

7. Ingrid Monson, *Freedom Sounds: Civil Rights Call Out to Jazz and Africa* (Oxford: Oxford University Press, 2007), 209–10.

8. Arthur Hatfield, "200,000 Marchers D.C. Bound," *(Baltimore) Afro-American,* August 24, 1963, 1–2; "Lancaster, Judy Garland Join 'March on D.C.' Backers," *(Baltimore) Afro-American,* August 24, 1963, 8.

9. "Jazz for Freedom," *Ebony,* November 1963, 40.

10. Kitty Kelley, *Let Freedom Ring: Stanley Tretick's Iconic Images of the March on Washington* (New York: A Thomas Dunne Book/St. Martin's Press, 2013), 4.

11. "Civil Rights: The March's Meaning," *Time* 82, no. 10 (September 6, 1963): 14.

12. Les Ledbetter, "Trains Rolled in Every 11½ Minutes," *(Baltimore) Afro-American,* September 7, 1963, 6.

13. "Freedom March Sidelights," *Michigan Chronicle,* September 23, 1963, 2.

14. Jack A. Smith, "This Was Washington August 28: The Day Itself," *National Guardian* 15, no. 48 (September 5, 1963): 4.

15. D'Emilio, *Lost Prophet,* 354.

16. Smith, "This Was Washington August 28," 4.

17. Euchner, *Nobody Turn Me Around,* 8–9.

18. Gentile, *March on Washington,* 147–48.

19. Euchner, *Nobody Turn Me Around,* 8–9.

20. David Levering Lewis, *King: A Biography* (Urbana: University of Illinois Press, 1970), 224.

21. Mary Stratford, "241,000 Join in Fervent Appeal to the Congress," *(Baltimore) Afro-American,* September 7, 1963, 2.

22. Martin Weil and Adam Bernstein, "Odetta; Matriarch for Generation of Folk Singers," *Washington Post,* December 4, 2008, B6.

23. E. W. Kenworthy, "200,000 March for Civil Rights in Orderly Washington Rally; President Sees Gain for Negro," *New York Times,* August 29, 1993, 16. Odetta was much revered in the African-American community. Rosa Parks was once asked which of the songs of the movement meant the most to her. "All of the songs Odetta sings," she said. See Tim Weiner, "Odetta, Civil Rights Voice, Dies at 77," *New York Times,* December 4, 2008, B12.

24. Sullivan, *Keep on Pushing,* 30–31.

25. David Hajdu, *Positively 4th Street: The Lives and Times of Joan Baez, Bob Dylan, Mimi Baez Farina and Richard Farina* (New York: Picador/Farrar, Straus and Giroux, 2001), 181–82.

26. Joe Smith, *Off the Record: An Oral History of Popular Music* (New York: Warner Books, 1988), 161.

27. Baruch Whitehead, "We Shall Overcome: The Roles of Music in the U.S. Civil Rights Movement" from Olivier Urbain, ed., *Music and Conflict Transformation: Harmonies and Dissonances in Geopolitics* (London: I.B. Thauris, 2008), 86.

28. Euchner, *Nobody Turn Me Around,* 132–33.

29. Ronald D. Cohen, *Rainbow Quest: The Folk Music Revival and American Society, 1940–1970* (Amherst: University of Massachusetts Press, 2002), 205.

30. Ann Moody, *Coming of Age in Mississippi* (New York: A Dell Book, 1976), 334.

31. David Levering Lewis, *King: A Biography,* 224.

32. D'Emilio, *Lost Prophet,* 355.

33. Kelley, *Let Freedom Ring,* 103.

34. Nan Robertson, "For 200,000 Who Were There It Was a Date to Live Forever," *New York Times,* August 29, 1963, 20.

35. Smith, "This Was Washington August 28," 4.

36. Euchner, *Nobody Turn Me Around,* 143–45.

37. Jervis Anderson, *A. Philip Randolph: A Biographical Portrait* (New York: Harcourt Brace Jovanovich, 1973), 328.

38. Kelley, *Let Freedom Ring,* 117.

39. Gentile, *March on Washington,* 217.

40. Euchner, *Nobody Turn Me Around,* 163.

41. Gentile, *March on Washington,* 224–25.

42. Laurraine Goreau, *Just Mahalia, Baby: The Mahalia Jackson Story* (Waco: Word Books, 1975), 358.

43. John Lewis, interview with the author, May 20, 2009, transcript of tape recording, Institute for Oral History, Baylor University, Waco, 4.

44. "Freedom March Sidelights," *Michigan Chronicle,* September 23, 1963, 2.

45. Mortimer Zuckerman, "March on Washington: A Day of Valor and I Was There," *New York Daily News,* August 28, 2003, 45.

46. Bennett, "Masses Were March Heroes," 119–22.

47. Rachelle Horowitz, quoted in Michael A. Fletcher, "A Change Is Gonna Come," *Smithsonian* 44, no. 4 (July–August 2013): 46.

48. Lewis, *King: A Critical Biography*, 227.

49. Michiko Kakutani, "The Lasting Power of Dr. King's Dream Speech," http://www.nytimes.com/2013/08/28/us/the-lasting-power-of-dr-kings-dream-speech.html?pagewanted=all.

50. Leonard Freed, *This Is the Day: The March on Washington* (Los Angeles: J. Paul Getty Museum, 2013), 4–5. From the Preface by Michael Eric Dyson. There is some debate whether it was Jackson or someone else who spontaneously called to King to incorporate elements from the earlier speech into his prepared text. More of the contemporary accounts cite Jackson than anyone else.

51. Jim Bishop, *The Days of Martin Luther King* (New York: G. P. Putnam's Sons, 1971), 327.

52. "Freedom March Sidelights," *Michigan Chronicle*, September 23, 1963, 2.

53. Bruce Feiler, *America's Prophet: Moses and the American Story* (New York: William Morrow, 2009), 251–52.

54. Harvard Sitkoff, *King: Pilgrimage to the Mountaintop* (New York: Hill and Wang, 2009), 125.

55. Euchner, *Nobody Turn Me Around*, 206.

56. Anderson, *A. Philip Randolph*, 329. However, "We Shall Overcome" was never on the official program, according to Danny Lyon. Those in attendance, led by SNCC members, family, and friends, instead sang it spontaneously at the end. The program organizers had intentionally left it off, fearing a demonstration since "the powers that be thought the song would be provocative." Lyons, the SNCC photographer, said it was sung anyway as a "brief moment of defiance." Danny Lyon, *Memories of the Civil Rights Movement* (Chapel Hill: University of North Carolina Press, 1992), 84.

57. Jonathan Rieder, *Gospel of Freedom: Martin Luther King, Jr.'s Letter from Birmingham Jail and the Struggle That Changed a Nation* (New York: Bloomsbury Press, 2013), 143.

58. Ralph Abernathy, interviewed in *Eyes on the Prize: America's Civil Rights Years, 1954–1965,* directed by Callie Crossley and James A. DeVinney, narrated by Julian Bond. From Episode Four: "No Easy Walk." (American Experience, PBS, 1987), DVD. Transcript by author.

59. Bishop, *The Days of Martin Luther King*, 322.

60. Hajdu, *Positively 4th Street*, 183.

61. "Civil Rights: The March's Meaning," *Time* 82, no. 10 (September 6, 1963), 14.

62. Dorothy I. Height, "'We Wanted the Voice of a Woman to Be Heard': Black Women and the 1963 March on Washington," in Bettye Collier-Thomas and V. P. Franklin, eds., *Sisters in the Struggle: African American Women in the Civil Rights-Black Power Movement* (New York: New York University Press, 2001), 83–91.

63. Gentile, *March on Washington*, 140–42, 225; "March on Washington for Jobs and Freedom, August 28, 1963: Lincoln Memorial Program," http://www.ourdocuments.gov.

64. Allan Morrison, "Josephine Baker Flies from Paris for D.C. March," *Jet*, September 12, 1963, 60.

65. "3 Rights Buses Are Stoned," *New York Times*, August 29, 1963, 17.

66. "Shots, Rocks Hit 'Freedom' Buses," *(Baltimore) Afro-American*, September 7, 1963, 6.

67. Euchner, *Nobody Turn Me Around*, 210–11.

68. David Levering Lewis, *W. E. B. Du Bois: Biography of a Race, 1868–1919* (New York: Henry Holt, 1993), 1–5. Sidney Poitier and writers James Baldwin and John Killens were told of Du Bois's passing early that morning while waiting in the lobby of Washington's Willard Hotel. Killens remembered that someone had said, "'The Old Man died.' Just that. And not one of us asked, 'What old man?'" (ibid., 3).

69. Russell Baker, "Capital Is Occupied by a Gentle Army," *New York Times*, August 29, 1963, 1, 17.

70. N. B. Wooding, interview with the author, July 8, 2009, Birmingham, transcript of tape recording, Institute for Oral History, Baylor University, Waco, 11.

71. Warren Weaver, "Congress Cordial But Not Swayed," *New York Times*, August 29, 1963, 1, 16–17; Kenworthy, "200,000 March for Civil Rights in Orderly Washington Rally; President Sees Gain for Negro," 1, 6.

72. Jack Langguth, "Marchers Aware 'Today is History,'" *New York Times*, August 29, 1963, 20.

73. Bayard Rustin, "The Washington March . . . a Ten Year Perspective," *The Crisis* (August/September 1973): 224.

74. Bennett, "Masses Were March Heroes," 124. With the success and publicity generated by the March on Washington, various record labels rush released LPs related to King and the civil rights movement: The small Dooto label in Los Angeles released *Martin Luther King at Zion Hill* (Dooto PICA-DTL 831), an amateurish, unauthorized recording of one of King's earlier sermons. The SCLC went to court to have Dooto withdraw the LP, which had grossed nearly $5,000 in a few months. Motown Records, which had recorded King's Cobo Hall speech in Detroit, finally released *The Great March to Freedom: Dr. Martin Luther King Speaks, June 23, 1963* (Gordy GLP 906) after the March on Washington, just in time to capitalize on the March on Washington and cut into sales for the authorized *We Shall Overcome!: Documentary of the March on Washington*. The authorized LP was produced by the Council for United Civil Rights Leadership, overseen by WRVR, the radio station of Riverside Church in New York (Folkways Records FD 5592). All proceeds were earmarked for the SCLC. However, two more unauthorized recordings of the March, one from Twentieth Century Fox (*Freedom March on Washington:* *August 29, 1963,* recorded live by Fox Movietone News, TFM 3110) and the Mr. Maestro label's *Emancipation March on Washington* (Mayco Associates), were also released and were withdrawn once legal proceedings began. Brian Ward, "Recording the Dream," *History Today* 38, no. 4 (April 1998): 23–24.

## Second Interlude

The epigraph for this chapter is drawn from Unita Blackwell, with JoAnne Prichard Morris, *Barefootin': Life Lessons from the Road to Freedom* (New York: Crown, 2006), 91.

1. Good sources on the bombing of the Sixteenth Street Baptist Church include Frank Sikora, *Until Justice Rolls Down: The Birmingham Church Bombing Case* (Tuscaloosa: University of Alabama Press, 1991) and *4 Little Girls,* directed by Spike Lee (New York: HBO Home Video, 1997), DVD.

2. Diane McWhorter, *Carry Me Home: Birmingham, Alabama: The Climactic Battle of the Civil Rights Revolution* (New York: Simon & Schuster, 2001), 525–26. In the Birmingham Police Surveillance Files from the Birmingham Public Library, a copy of the church bulletin from Sunday September 15 reveals the hymns scheduled to be sung that morning: "On Jordan's Stormy Banks," "Into My Heart," "Come Thou Fount," "I'm a Pilgrim," and "Pass Me Not O Blessed Savior." The scheduled sermon was titled "The Rock That Will Not Roll." Bulletin copy courtesy of Jenna DeWitt.

3. Claude Sitton, "Birmingham Bomb Kills 4 Negro Girls in Church; Riots Flare; 2 Boys Slain," *New York Times,* September 16, 1963, 1, 26; "Bombing Is 21st at Birmingham," *New York Times,* September 16, 1963, 26; "Dr. King Goes to Birmingham; Appeals to President for Action," *New York Times,* September 16, 1963, 26; "Wilkins Accuses Wallace of Encouraging 'Murder,'" *New York Times,* September 16, 1963, 26.

4. Julian Williams, "Black Radio and Civil Rights: Birmingham, 1956–1963, *Journal of Radio Studies* 12, no. 1 (May 2005): 58.

5. Kevin Phinney, *Souled America: How Black Music Transformed White Culture* (New York: Billboard Books, 2005), 175.

6. Stanley Keeble, interview with the author, August 8, 2009, Chicago, transcript of tape recording, Institute for Oral History, Baylor University, Waco, 20–21.

7. Claude Sitton, "Birmingham Gets a Negro Warning," *New York Times*, September 18, 1963, 1, 26.

8. "Shuttlesworth Speaks at Rites for Carole Rosamond Robertson," *Birmingham World*, September 21, 1963, 3.

9. John Herbers, "Funeral Is Held for Bomb Victims," *New York Times*, September 19, 1963, 17.

10. Andrew M. Manis, *A Fire You Can't Put Out: The Civil Rights Life of Birmingham's Reverend Fred Shuttlesworth* (Tuscaloosa: University of Alabama Press, 1999), 406.

11. "Thousands Attend Rites for 3 'Bombing' Victims," *Birmingham World*, September 21, 1963, 1.

12. "6,000 Mourners Jam Rites for Three Victims of Bombing," *Birmingham News*, September 19, 1963, 10.

13. James D. Williams, "State Troopers Waited, But Orders Never Came," *(Baltimore) Afro-American*, September 28, 1963, 6.

14. Lillian Foscue, "Big Crowd Attends 3 Negroes' Funeral," *Birmingham Post-Herald*, September 19, 1963, 1, 4.

15. McWhorter, *Carry Me Home*, 536–37.

16. "Birmingham Pays Homage to Slain Teen-Age Boys," *Birmingham World*, September 25, 1963, 1.

17. Eloise Ford Gaffney, interview with the author, July 3, 2009, Birmingham, transcript of tape recording, Institute for Oral History, Baylor University, Waco, 18–21.

18. Henry Burton, interview with the author, July 7, 2009, Birmingham, tape recording, Institute for Oral History, Baylor University, Waco, 23–25.

19. "Dorothy Love Coates, Singer of Gospel Music, Dies at 74," *New York Times*, April 12, 2002, B7.

20. Anthony Heilbut, *The Gospel Sound: Good News and Bad Times* (New York: Limelight Editions, 1989), 160–65.

21. "Dorothy Love Coates, Singer of Gospel Music, Dies at 77," B7. Anita Bernadette McAllister once heard a sermon by Coates in which she cited the old protest spiritual "Just as God delivered Daniel, why not every man" and said she immediately thought of Harriet Tubman, giving listeners the "Codes from the Underground." Anita Bernadette McAllister, "The Musical Legacy of Dorothy Love Coates: African American Female Gospel Singer with Implications for Education and Theater Education" (PhD diss., Kansas State University, 1995), 74.

22. Dr. Bobby Jones, with Lesley Sussman, *Make a Joyful Noise: My 25 Years in Gospel Music* (New York: St. Martin's Press, 2000), 44–45.

23. Linwood Heath, interview with the author, May 26, 2009, transcript of tape recording, Institute for Oral History, Baylor University, Waco, 2.

24. Robert M. Marovich, *A City Called Heaven: The Birth of Gospel Music in Chicago* (Urbana: University of Illinois Press, 2015), 302–4.

25. Tom Glazer, *Songs of Peace, Freedom, and Protest* (New York: David McKay, 1970), 24–25. Spike Lee chose Baez's version of "Birmingham Sunday" as the opening and theme music of his Oscar-nominated documentary *Four Little Girls*.

26. Nina Simone, with Stephen Cleary, *The Autobiography of Nina Simone* (Cambridge: Da Capo Press, 1991), 90–91.

27. J. C. Thomas, *Chasin' the Trane: The Music and Mystique of John Coltrane* (Garden City: Doubleday, 1975), 167–68.

28. Anne Moody, *Coming of Age in Mississippi* (New York: Dell Books, 1976), 320.

29. John Herbers, "Birmingham Bombs Rock Negro Homes," *New York Times*, September 26, 1963, 1, 29.

30. "At the Height of His Powers," *(Baltimore) Afro-American,* November 30, 1963, 1.

31. "President Kennedy Set Many Racial Precedents," *(Baltimore) Afro-American,* November 30, 1963, 1.

32. Laurraine Goreau, *Just Mahalia, Baby* (Waco: Word Books, 1975), 363–68.

33. Guido van Rijn, *Kennedy's Blues: African-American Blues and Gospel Songs on JFK* (Jackson: University Press of Mississippi, 2010), 113–65.

34. Jerry Zolten, *Great God A'mighty! The Dixie Hummingbirds: Celebrating the Rise of Soul Gospel Music* (Oxford: Oxford University Press, 2003), 271–74.

35. "New York Beat," *Jet,* December 12, 1963, 64–65.

36. "Entertainment," *Jet,* December 26, 1963, 56.

37. "Kennedy's Death Causes Tour and Concert Cancellations," *downbeat* (January 2, 1963): 11. One interesting side note: According to *downbeat,* jazz artist Thelonious Monk cancelled his Philharmonic Hall concert shortly after the assassination as well. The weekly newsmagazine *Time* reportedly scrapped more than three million copies of the cover of the magazine that week, replacing the planned cover, which featured a picture of Monk and a story on jazz, with a cover photograph of new president Lyndon Johnson.

38. Van Rijn, *Kennedy's Blues,* 123.

## Chapter 6

The epigraphs for this chapter are drawn from Bruce Watson, *Freedom Summer* (New York: Viking Penguin, 2010), 71–72; L. C. Dorsey, *Freedom Came to Mississippi* (New York: Field Foundation, 1977), 24.

1. Some of the excellent books on the movement's work in Mississippi in the 1960s include: Charles M. Payne, *I've Got the Light of Freedom: The Organizing Tradition and the Mississippi Freedom Struggle* (Berkeley: University of California Press, 1995); Anne Moody, *Coming of Age in Mississippi* (New York: Bantam Dell, 1968); Mary King, *Freedom Song: A Personal Story of the 1960s Civil Rights Movement* (New York: William Morrow, 1987); Sally Belfrage, *Freedom Summer* (New York: Viking, 1965); Elizabeth Sutherland, ed., *Letters from Mississippi* (New York: McGraw-Hill, 1965); Clayborne Carson, *In Struggle: SNCC and the Black Awakening of the 1960s* (Cambridge: Harvard University Press, 1981); Howard Zinn, *SNCC: The New Abolitionists* (Boston: Beacon Press, 1964); Doug McAdam, *Freedom Summer* (Oxford: Oxford University Press, 1988); Bruce Watson, *Freedom Summer* (New York: Viking Penguin, 2010); John Dittmer, *Local People: The Struggle for Civil Rights in Mississippi* (Urbana: University of Illinois Press, 1994).

2. *Sing for Freedom: The Story of the Civil Rights Movement Through Its Songs,* Smithsonian Folkways Recordings, 1992. From the liner notes/booklet, written by Guy Carawan and Candie Carawan, page 7.

3. Payne, *I've Got the Light of Freedom,* 110–12.

4. Jeff Place and Ronald D. Cohen, *The Best of Broadside, 1962–1988: Anthems of the American Underground from the Pages of Broadside Magazine* (Washington, DC: Smithsonian Folkways Recordings, SFW CD 40130), 2000. Produced, compiled, and annotated by Jeff Place and Ronald D. Cohen, page 8. There were other fronts in the antisegregation war, of course. In February 1962, SNCC field secretaries Bob Zellner and Chuck McDrew drove to Louisiana to visit another field secretary, Dion Diamond, who was being held in the East Baton Rouge Parish Jail for his registration efforts. The two were almost immediately charged with

vagrancy and criminal anarchy and tossed in the prison, where other prisoners beat them. Eventually, Zellner and McDew were placed in "the hole," two adjacent five-foot by seven-foot cells. Once they discovered the other's presence, Zellner said they sang freedom songs. "As the police pounded on the door threatening to whip us, we sang, 'Woke Up This Morning with My Mind [Stayed] on Freedom,'" Zellner said. "Even after they turned the heaters on and blasted us with unbearable heat for seven days, we continue to sing, 'We'll walk hand in hand.'" See Guy Carawan and Candie Carawan, *Sing for Freedom: The Story of the Civil Rights Movement Through Its Songs* (Montgomery: New-South Books, 2007), 82.

5. Payne, *I've Got the Light of Freedom,* 141–46.

6. Pete Seeger and Bob Reisner, *Everybody Says Freedom* (New York: W. W. Norton, 1989), 165–66.

7. Joe Sinsheimer, "'Never Turn Back': The Movement in Greenwood, Mississippi," *Southern Exposure* 15, no. 2 (Summer 1987): 43.

8. Andrew Young, *An Easy Burden: The Civil Rights Movement and the Transformation of America* (Waco: Baylor University Press, 2008), 150–51.

9. Seeger and Reisner, *Everybody Says Freedom,* 179.

10. Bob Moses, "Mississippi: 1961–1962," *Liberation* 14, no. 9 (January 1970): 16–17.

11. Fannie Lou Hamer, quoted in Howell Raines, *My Soul Is Rested: Movement Days in the Deep South Remembered* (New York: G. P. Putnam's Sons, 1977), 249–50.

12. Charles Marsh, *God's Long Summer: Stories of Faith and Civil Rights* (Princeton: Princeton University Press, 1997), 15.

13. Payne, *I've Got the Light of Freedom,* 150–56.

14. Charles C. Euchner, *Nobody Turn Me Around: A People's History of the 1963*

*March on Washington* (Boston: Beacon Press, 2010), 106.

15. Bernice Johnson Reagon, cited in Vicki L. Crawford, Jacqueline Anne Rouse, and Barbara Woods, eds., *Women in the Civil Rights Movement: Trailblazers and Torchbearers, 1941–1965* (Bloomington: Indiana University Press, 1993), 204.

16. Young, *An Easy Burden,* 150–51.

17. Mark Stern, *Calculating Visions: Kennedy, Johnson, and Civil Rights* (New Brunswick: Rutgers University Press, 1992), 67.

18. Peter B. Levy, "The New Left and Labor: The Early Years (1960–1963)," *Labor History* 31, no. 3 (1990): 300–1.

19. Payne, *I've Got the Light of Freedom,* 156–59. The NAACP committed to selling ten thousand copies of comic Dick Gregory's live recording *My Brother's Keeper,* with proceeds earmarked to support sharecroppers in LaFlore County, Mississippi. NAACP officials termed Gregory's project "an extension" of their work in Mississippi. On February 11, Gregory, at his own expense, had airlifted fourteen thousand pounds of food to impoverished Greenwood, Mississippi. "N.A.A.C.P. to Sell 10,000 'My Brothers Keeper,'" *(Baltimore) Afro-American,* March 23, 1963, 11; "4 Religious Groups Join Gregory in Food Program," *(Baltimore) Afro-American,* March 30, 1963, 11; "Miss. Bows to Pressure: 22,000 to Eat Again as U.S. Intervenes," *(Baltimore) Afro-American,* March 30, 1963, 1.

20. Carson, *In Struggle,* 80–81.

21. "Congressman's Shocking Report on Miss.: Tells Sordid Words of Terror to Members of U.S. Congress," *Jet,* May 2, 1963, 20–21; "Uses 'Nigger,' Miss. Mayor Goofs 'All's Well' Talk," *Jet,* May 2, 1963, 60–61.

22. "Fight for Voting Rights," *(Baltimore) Afro-American,* April 13, 1963, 12.

23. Moses J. Newson, "'We're in for Long, Hard Fight,' Say Vote Crusaders," *(Baltimore) Afro-American,* April 13,

1963, 1. There were other civil rights hot spots around the nation. The events in St. Augustine that summer drew national attention for the level of violence against protesters. See Taylor Branch, *Pillar of Fire: America in the King Years, 1963–65* (New York: Simon & Schuster Paperbacks, 1998), 328–33, 375–80, 395–96. Clyde Appleton writes vividly of the movement in Raleigh in Spring 1963 and compares his memories of a number of protest songs, such as "We Are Soldiers, "Woke Up This Morning with My Mind Stayed on Freedom," "Go Down, Moses," "Pressin' On," "I'm Gonna Tell God How You Treat Me" (called "I'm Gonna Sit at the Welcome Table" in other cities), and "We Shall Overcome" and how differently they sounded in Raleigh than on the various Carawan collections for Folkways. According to Appleton, "We Shall Overcome" "did not enjoy the special status of a song of more influence or deeper meaning to the freedom-movement activists than many other freedom songs." Like the spirituals, the few collections of protest spirituals and freedom songs are only a snapshot of how these ever-evolving pieces of music sounded in a particular location at a particular time. Clyde Appleton, "Singing in the Streets of Raleigh, 1963: Some Recollections," *Black Perspective in Music* 3, no. 3 (Autumn 1975): 243–52.

24. James Forman, *The Making of Black Revolutionaries* (Washington, DC: Open Hand Publishing, 1972), 299–303.

25. Kay Mills, *This Little Light of Mine: The Life of Fannie Lou Hamer* (New York: Dutton Books, 1993), 53–61, 66.

26. Endesha Ida Mae Holland, *From the Mississippi Delta: A Memoir* (Chicago: Lawrence Hill Books, 1997), 208–23.

27. Moody, *Coming of Age in Mississippi*, 294–98.

28. Robert Schlesinger, "The Story Behind JFK's Landmark Civil Rights Speech," *U.S. News and World Report*, June 11, 2013, http://www.usnews.com/opinion /blogs/robert-schlesinger/2013/06/11 /the-story-behind-jfks-1963-landmark -civil-rights-speech.

29. Diane McWhorter, *Carry Me Home: Birmingham, Alabama: The Climactic Battle of the Civil Rights Revolution* (New York: Simon & Schuster, 2001), 464.

30. Unattributed articles from *(Baltimore) Afro-American*, June 8, 1963: "JFK's Proposed Law Would Open Eating Places All Over," "Garbage Trucks Haul Kids," "Walls of Jim Crow Seen Crumbling," 1–3.

31. Juan Williams, *Eyes on the Prize: America's Civil Rights Years, 1954–1965* (New York: Viking, 2002), 220–21.

32. Adolph J. Slaughter, "Widow Visits JFK," *(Baltimore) Afro-American,* June 29, 1963, 1–2.

33. Gail Lumet Buckley, *The Hornes: An American Family* (New York: Alfred A. Knopf), 248.

34. Ray Abrams, "Mrs. Evers Prays: Husband's Death 'Was Not in Vain,'" *(Baltimore) Afro-American,* June 22, 1963, 6.

35. Aaron Henry, with Constance Curry, *Aaron Henry: The Fire Ever Burning* (Jackson: University Press of Mississippi, 2000),150.

36. Michael Vinson Williams, *Nobody Turn Me Around: Mississippi Martyr* (Fayetteville: University of Arkansas Press), 289, 291; Branch, *Pillar of Fire*, 826–27.

37. Euchner, *Nobody Turn Me Around,* 106.

38. Abrams, Ray, "Violence Follows Funeral: U.S. Aide Blocks Cops in Jackson," *(Baltimore) Afro-American*, June 22, 1963, 1–2.

39. Theodore H. White, *The Making of the President 1964* (New York: Atheneum, 1965), 181, 186.

40. Williams, *Nobody Turn Me Around*, 3.

41. Guido van Rijn, *Kennedy's Blues: African-American Blues and Gospel Songs on JFK* (Jackson: University Press of Mississippi, 2010), 101–2, 184.

42. Holland, *From the Mississippi Delta*, 238–41.

43. Pete Seeger, "The Integration Battle: A 'Singing Movement,'" *Broadside* 30

(August 1963): page number not listed. One of the more intriguing moments came after the concert. On the rickety porch behind the Freedom House in Greenwood, movement photographer Danny Lyon took a picture of a smiling Bob Dylan, playing his guitar and singing for a handful of people. Closest to Dylan and leaning in to better hear is Bernice Johnson Reagon. Steven Kasher, *The Civil Rights Movement in America: A Photographic History* (New York: Abbeville Press, 1996), 146–47.

44. Bernice Johnson Reagon, quoted in Mellonee V. Burnim and Portia K. Maultsby, eds., *African American Music: An Introduction* (New York: Routledge, 2005), 614–15.

45. Eric Burner, *And Gently He Shall Lead Them: Robert Parris Moses and Civil Rights in Mississippi* (New York: New York University Press, 1994), 16, 109.

46. Robert Shelton, "'Freedom Songs' Sweep North," *New York Times*, July 6, 1963, 7. For more on the Hutchinson Family Singers, see Darden, *Nothing But Love in God's Water,* vol. 1, 11–12.

47. "Northern Folk Singers Help Out at Negro Festival in Mississippi," *New York Times*, July 7, 1963, 43.

48. Howard Zinn, "The Battle-Scarred Youngsters," *The Nation* (October 5, 1963): 193–95.

49. Bernice Johnson Reagon, "Let the Church Sing 'Freedom,'" *Black Music Research Journal* 7 (1987): 105–18.

50. *The Story of Greenwood, Mississippi* (Smithsonian Folkways FD 5593), produced by Guy Carawan for the Student Nonviolent Coordinating Committee.

51. *Voices of the Civil Rights Movement: Black American Freedom Songs, 1960–1966.* Two-disk CD set. Smithsonian Folkways Records CD SF40084, 1997. Liner notes and annotations by Bernice Johnson Reagon and Doris Evans McGinty.

52. John Phillips, with Jim Jerome, *Papa John: An Autobiography by John Phillips* (New York: Dolphin Books, 1986), 116–18.

53. Dick Weissman, *Which Side Are You On? An Inside History of the Folk Music Revival in America* (New York: Continuum, 2005), 143. While few of the mostly African-American jazz artists toured the South during this period, there were a number of benefits for the SNCC featuring Mahalia Jackson, Thelonious Monk, Herbie Man, Charles Mingus, Miles Davis, Max Roach, Abbey Lincoln, Count Basie, Duke Ellington, Dizzy Gillespie, Sarah Vaughan, Clark Terry, and others. The Friends of the SNCC concerts raised more than $359,000, which enabled the perpetually cash-strapped SNCC to establish additional voter registration projects in the South. See Ingrid Monson, "Monk Meets SNCC," *Black Music Research Journal* 19, no. 2 (Autumn 1999): 187–99; "All Star Troupe on the Road for NAACP and CORE," *downbeat,* April 9, 1964, 13.

54. Clarice T. Campbell, *Civil Rights Chronicle: Letters from the South* (Jackson: University of Mississippi Press, 1997), 197–98. African-Americans in Mississippi and the rest of the Deep South could receive cutting-edge jazz, R & B, soul, freedom songs, and gospel music from Robert F. Williams, an expatriated American living in Cuba and broadcasting over a 50,000-watt station provided by the Cuban government. Williams, later identified with the Black Panther Party, provided commentary and news reports unavailable to black Mississippians throughout 1963 and 1964 via Radio Free Dixie. Timothy B. Tyson, *Radio Free Dixie: Robert F. Williams & the Roots of Black Power* (Chapel Hill: University of North Carolina Press, 1999); personal correspondence with Timothy B. Tyson, January 3, 2011.

55. Seeger and Reisner, *Everybody Says Freedom*, 180.

56. William M. Kunstler, *Deep in My Heart* (New York: William Morrow, 1966), 250–52.

57. Mills, *This Little Light of Mine*, 82–85.

58. Zinn, *SNCC,* 186–89.

59. George Breitman, ed., *Malcolm X Speaks: Selected Speeches and Statements Edited with Prefatory Notes* (New York: Grove Weidenfeld, 1965), 105–12.

60. Kristen Meyers Turner, "Guy and Candie Carawan: Mediating the Music of the Civil Rights Movement" (master's thesis, University of North Carolina, 2011), 45–47. The Carawans hosted another folk festival on the Georgia Sea Islands (where they lived) in December 1964. Among the attendees was Bob Moses, who invited them to present a workshop for Freedom Corps volunteers, May 6–9, 1965, in Edwards, Mississippi. Bernice Johnson Reagon organized "The Conference for Southern Community Cultural Revival" October 1–3, 1965, at the Highlander Folk School. This workshop was directed more toward folk studies and folk music performers. Turner, "Guy and Candie Carawan: Mediating the Music of the Civil Rights Movement," 52–56.

61. Josh Dunson, "Slave Songs at the 'Sing for Freedom,'" *Broadside*, 46 (May 30, 1964). For more information on the music and to hear selections, see *Lest We Forget*, vol. 3, *Sing for Freedom.* Workshop 1964 with the Freedom Singers, Birmingham Movement Choir, Georgia Sea Island Singers, Doc Reese, Phil Ochs, Len Chandler. Produced by Guy and Candie Carawan, Highlander Center, 1965 Folkways Records and Service Corp. Re-released as a CD in 2007 by Smithsonian Folkways Records, FH 5488. Also featuring music from Mississippi is *Lest We Forget*, vol. 1, *Movement Soul: Sounds of the Freedom Movement in the South, 1963–1964: Songs, Sermons, Shouts, Prayers, Testimony* (Smithsonian Folkways Records, FD 5486, 2006). First released by Folkways Recordings and Service Corp. in 1980. Originally recorded and edited by Alan Ribback and David Baker and released in 1965 as *Live Recordings of Songs and Sayings from the Freedom Movement in the Deep South* (ESP 1056), this is both a fascinating and frustrating record of numerous movement actions. The two twenty-minute sides from the LP are presented in rapid-fire, montage format, with snippets from, as the title states, songs, sermons, shouts, prayers, and testimony. Attribution is listed in the accompanying booklet. For instance, three short segments are featured from a voter registration rally in Jackson, November 1963: Willie Peacock leading a few bars of "Oh, Freedom," two sentences from a speech by Dave Dennis, and a portion of a prayer from Sam Block. From a mass meeting in Indianola in August 1964, the producers present three different short statements by Fannie Lou Hamer. More than half of the selections are drawn from movement actions and music in Selma, Alabama, in 1963.

62. Zinn, *SNCC*, 102–6.

63. Belfrage, *Freedom Summer*, 1–9; Watson, *Freedom Summer,* 15–19.

64. Sutherland, *Letters from Mississippi*, 3, 13.

65. Ron Ridenour, "Freedom Summer Orientation," Veterans of the Civil Rights Movement, 1–4. Used by permission. See http://www.crmvet.org/info/ridenou1.htm.

66. Seth Cagin and Philip Dray, *We Are Not Afraid: The Story of Goodman, Schwerner, and Chaney and the Civil Rights Campaign for Mississippi* (New York: Macmillan, 1988), 33–35.

67. Len Holt, *The Summer That Didn't End* (New York: William Morrow, 1965), 51.

68. Cagin and Dray, *We Are Not Afraid*, 33–35.

69. R. W. Apple, "2 of Missing Men Feared for Lives," *New York Times,* June 25, 1964, 18; Claude Sitton, "Hope for 3 Wanes as Dulles Opens Mississippi Talks," *New York Times,* June 25, 1964, 1, 18.

70. Belfrage, *Freedom Summer*, 12.

71. Sutherland, *Letters from Mississippi*, 31–33.

72. Jean Smith Young, quoted in Faith S. Holsaert, Martha Prescod Norman Noonan, Judy Richardson, et al., eds., *Hands on the Freedom Plow: Personal Accounts by Women in SNCC* (Urbana: University of Illinois Press, 2010), 246.

73. McAdam, *Freedom Summer*, 67–72.

74. Harry Belafonte, with Michael Shnayerson, *My Song: A Memoir* (New York: Alfred A. Knopf, 2011), 4–9.

75. Belfrage, *Freedom Summer*, 52–55.

76. Tracy Sugarman, *We Had Sneakers, They Had Guns: The Kids Who Fought for Civil Rights in Mississippi* (Syracuse: Syracuse University Press, 2009), 36–38.

77. Chana Kai Lee, *For Freedom's Sake: The Life of Fannie Lou Hamer* (Urbana: University of Illinois Press, 1999), 67–72.

78. Mills, *This Little Light of Mine*, 105–8.

79. Sutherland, *Letters from Mississippi*, 212–14.

80. Robert A. Caro, *The Years of Lyndon Johnson: The Passage of Power* (New York: Alfred A. Knopf, 2012), 565–69. Among Johnson's most ardent supporters was Mahalia Jackson, who wrote a gospel song based on "Onward Christian Soldiers" for the president during the 1964 campaign, "Onward President Lyndon," which she subtitled "A Song Written by Mahalia Jackson Especially for Lyndon Baines Johnson." Laurraine Goreau, *Just Mahalia, Baby* (Waco: Word Books, 1975), 395.

81. Watson, *Freedom Summer*, 121, 132. Also present for the signing that day were Jim Forman, A. Philip Randolph, Whitney Young, Roy Wilkins, Dorothy Height, Robert Kennedy, Burke Marshall, and others. See Mary King, *Freedom Song*, 407.

82. King, 409–11.

83. Susie Erenrich, ed., *Freedom Is a Constant Struggle: An Anthology of the Mississippi Civil Rights Movement* (Montgomery: Black Belt Press, 1999), 215.

84. Chana Kai Lee, 85–89.

85. Mills, *This Little Light of Mine*, 115–16.

86. Unita Blackwell, with JoAnne Prichard Morris, *Barefootin': Life Lessons from the Road to Freedom* (New York: Crown, 2006), 110.

87. Mills, *This Little Light of Mine*, 111–32.

88. Blackwell, *Barefootin'*, 115.

89. Belfrage, *Freedom Summer*, 244–46.

90. Liz Carpenter, *Ruffles and Flourishes* (Garden City: Doubleday, 1970), 208–9. Clara Ward and the Ward Singers toured in support of Kennedy and Johnson during the 1960 campaign, serving as "crowd-warmers" before the speakers took the stage. At a Madison Square Garden rally for Johnson in 1964, "the crowd had to be calmed down after we sang," remembered Willa Ward. "They were so fired up, it took a while before the people on the platform could make themselves heard over the din." Willa Ward-Royster, as told to Toni Rose, *How I Got Over: Clara Ward and the World-Famous Ward Singers* (Philadelphia: Temple University Press, 2000), 139.

91. Sutherland, *Letters from Mississippi*, 45, 50.

92. David Levering Lewis. *King: A Biography* (Urbana: University of Illinois Press, 1970), 247.

93. Erenrich, *Freedom Is a Constant Struggle*, 208–11.

94. Belfrage, *Freedom Summer*, 137–61.

95. Watson, *Freedom Summer*, 154–63.

96. Holland, *From the Mississippi Delta*, 254–62.

97. Todd Gitlin, *The Sixties: Years of Hope, Days of Rage* (Toronto: Bantam Books, 1987), 136, 151.

98. Claude Sitton, "Chaney Was Given Brutal Beating," *New York Times*, August 8, 1964, 7.

99. Watson, *Freedom Summer*, 211–13.

100. Cagin and Dray, *We Are Not Afraid*, 410–11. Also singing at Andrew Goodman's funeral were Peter, Paul & Mary, who performed "Blowin' in the Wind" "with tears running down our faces." Erenrich, *Freedom Is a Constant Struggle*, 236.

101. Sutherland, *Letters from Mississippi,* 189.

102. Ibid., 120–21.

103. Bob Cohen, "The Mississippi Caravan of Music," *Broadside* 51 (October 20, 1964). Cohen's article ends with Cohen printing the home telephone numbers of various people associated with the Caravan, including Julius Lester, soliciting more folk artists to join the project: "The struggle in Mississippi is what this great country of the United States of America is all about. It's what the songs we sing are about. If people are jailed, beaten, murdered, and their houses and churches bombed and burned, just because they wish to sing their life's song with a straight back and a strong voice, then as long as this is happening, none of us are truly free to sing out, be it in nightclubs, concert halls or even our own homes." Gil Turner and the New World Singers and Carolyn Hester both recorded Turner's tribute to the Reverend George W. Lee, who was killed in Belzoni, Mississippi in 1955: "There's a man by my side a walkin' / There's a voice inside me a talkin' / There's a word needs sayin' / Carry it on, carry it on, carry it on, carry it on." Erenrich, *Freedom Is a Constant Struggle,* 12.

104. Erenrich, *Freedom Is a Constant Struggle,* 201–7.

105. Tracy Sugarman, *Stranger at the Gates: A Summer in Mississippi* (New York: Hill and Wang, 1966), 92–95.

106. Erenrich, *Freedom Is a Constant Struggle,* 201–7, 225.

107. Alan Young, *The Pilgrim Jubilees* (Jackson: University Press of Mississippi, 2001), 110–11.

108. Robert Dixon, interview with the author, August 7, 2009, Chicago, transcript of tape recording, Institute for Oral History, Baylor University, Waco, 5–6.

109. Bernice Johnson Reagon and Sweet Honey in the Rock, *We Who Believe in Freedom: Sweet Honey in the Rock . . .*

*Still on the Journey* (New York: Anchor Books, 1993), 162.

110. Sugarman, *Strangers at the Gate,* 116–17.

111. "Without These Songs . . ." *Newsweek,* August 31, 1964, 74.

112. Sugarman, *Strangers at the Gate,* 146–54.

113. Payne, *I've Got the Light of Freedom,* 261–62.

114. *Sing for Freedom: The Story of the Civil Rights Movement Through Its Songs.* Smithsonian Folkways Recordings, 1992. From the enclosed booklet, written by Guy Carawan and Candie Carawan, 7.

115. C. Eric Lincoln and Lawrence H. Mamiya, *The Black Church in the African American Experience* (Durham: Duke University Press, 1990), 370–71.

116. Reagon and Sweet Honey in the Rock, *We Who Believe in Freedom,* 160–61.

117. Tammy L. Kernodle, "'I Wish I Knew How It Would Feel to Be Free': Nina Simone and the Redefining of the Freedom Song of the 1960s," *Journal of the Society for American Music,* 2, no. 3 (2008): 306.

118. "Special Merit Picks," Freedom Singers, *We Shall Overcome, Billboard,* December 1963, 12.

119. Freedom Singers, *We Shall Overcome.* Mercury Records MG 20879, released November/December 1963, no producer listed. Freedom Singers, *The Freedom Singers Sing of Freedom Now!* Mercury Records MG 20924 and SP 60924, circa August 1964, produced by Franklin Fried and Chad Mitchell. The Smothers Brothers, then one of most popular folk music/comedy acts in the nation, assisted in the production of both albums for their record label, Mercury. Mellonee V. Burnim and Portia K. Maultsby, eds., *African American Music: An Introduction* (New York: Routledge, 2005), 618. In 1963, the Freedom Singers' nonstop touring and appearances, along with the various benefits on the SNCC's behalf, raised more than a third of the SNCC's funds for that year. Not

everyone was pleased with their efforts. The radio station manager at the all-white, fundamentalist Christian college Bob Jones University returned a box of *The Freedom Singers Sing Freedom Now!* LPs with disparaging notes attached. Matthew D. Lassiter and Joseph Crespino, eds., *The Myth of Southern Exceptionalism* (Oxford: Oxford University Press, 2010), 136–37. Two other significant civil rights–related albums were released in 1963. The Alabama Christian Movement Choir's *We've Got a Job,* directed by Carlton Reese (who also played the organ), was recorded during a concert on August 30, 1963, at L. R. Hall Auditorium in Birmingham. The LP includes splendid renditions of "Ave Maria," various spirituals and hymns, and closes with "We Shall Overcome." On the jacket is printed, "We are singing for freedom. Through our songs, we are acknowledging the presence of God as we struggle in this fight." Also released in 1963 was the two-disk set, *A Jazz Salute to Freedom,* featuring more than thirty top jazz artists. The set, produced by CORE, was first advertised in *Billboard* magazine on September 21, 1963, and includes performances by Cannonball Adderley, Steve Allen, Louis Armstrong, Count Basie, Harry Belafonte, Tony Bennett, Miles Davis, Duke Ellington, Maynard Ferguson, Stan Getz, Dizzy Gillespie, Woody Herman, Lambert, Hendricks and Ross, Charlie Parker, Bud Powell, Max Roach, Horace Silver, Art Tatum, Sarah Vaughan, Dina Washington, and others. Perhaps no name appears on the rosters of movement benefits more than Cannonball Adderley. According to Val Coleman, Adderley was essential: "Let me tell you who was the first and most important supporter of CORE, long before anybody else in the jazz community . . . Cannonball Adderley. Cannonball did stuff for us when people didn't know who the hell we were." Ingrid Monson, *Freedom Sounds: Civil Rights*

*Call Out to Jazz and Africa* (Oxford: Oxford University Press, 2007), 222.
120. Sutherland, *Letters from Mississippi,* 150–51.

## Chapter 7

The epigraph for this chapter is drawn from a quote by Bruce Hartford in Pete Seeger and Bob Reiser, *Everybody Says Freedom* (New York: W. W. Norton, 1989), 207.

1. As with other civil rights actions, the Selma campaign is well-chronicled by a number of excellent accounts, including: Charles E. Fager, *Selma, 1965: The March That Changed the South* (Boston: Beacon Press, 1985); David J. Garrow, *Protest at Selma: Martin Luther King, Jr., and the Voting Rights Act of 1965* (New Haven: Yale University Press, 1978); Sheyann Webb and Rachel West Nelson, as told to Frank Sikora, *Selma, Lord, Selma: Girlhood Memories of the Civil-Rights Days* (Tuscaloosa: University of Alabama Press, 1980), and others.
2. Michael B. Friedland, *Lift Up Your Voice Like a Trumpet: White Clergy and the Civil Rights and Antiwar Movements, 1954–1973* (Chapel Hill: University of North Carolina Press, 1998), 116–17.
3. Howard Zinn, *SNNC: The New Abolitionists* (Boston: Beacon Press, 1965), 148.
4. John Herbers, "Whites in Selma, Ala., Disturbed over Determined Negro Drive," *New York Times,* October 13, 1963, 77.
5. Pat Watters and Reese Cleghorn, *Climbing Jacob's Ladder: The Arrival of Negroes in Southern Politics* (New York: A Harbinger Book, 1967), 249–50.
6. Zinn, *SNCC,* 149–50.
7. "Selma, Ala., Jails 156 in 2 Marches," *New York Times,* September 25, 1963, 32; John Herbers, "Selma, Ala., Balks Negro Marchers," *New York Times,* September 27, 1963, 30.
8. Bernice Johnson Reagon, *Songs of the Civil Rights Movement, 1955–1965:*

*A Study in Culture History* (PhD diss., Howard University, 1975), 167–70.

9. The original LP (ESP-Disk, Ltd., ESP 1056), recorded and edited by Alan Ribback, has been re-released as *Lest We Forget*, vol. 1, *Movement Soul: Sounds of the Freedom Movement in the South, 1963–1964* (Smithsonian Folkways Records, FD 5486, 2006). Descriptions from the liner notes by Ribback.

10. Zinn, *SNCC*, 150–51.

11. Ibid.,152–66.

12. William R. Beardslee, *The Way Out Must Lead In: Life Histories in the Civil Rights Movement* (Westport: Lawrence Hill, 1983), 22–23.

13. James Feron, "Dr. King Accepts Nobel Peace Prize as 'Trustee,'" *New York Times,* December 11, 1964, 1, 22; James Feron, "Dr. King Stresses Nonviolence Role," *New York Times,* December 12, 1964, 1, 18.

14. Coretta Scott King, *My Life with Martin Luther King, Jr.* (London: Hodder & Stoughton, 1970), 23–29.

15. "King Will Give the $54,600 Cash to Rights Fight," *Jet,* October 29, 1964, 14–28.

16. "Dr. King Will Lead Selma Rights Test," *New York Times,* January 15, 1965, 14.

17. Webb, Nelson, and Sikora, *Selma, Lord, Selma,* 17–19.

18. Howell Raines, *My Soul Is Rested: Movement Days in the Deep South Remembered* (New York: G. P. Putnam's Sons, 1977), 204. The first church in Selma to open its doors for mass meetings was Tabernacle Baptist Church, followed by the First Baptist Church. Brown Chapel AME (sometimes referred to as Brown's Chapel in some stories) on Sylvan Street, however, was most frequently used as the home church by the movement because of its location in the middle of "projects." Bettie Mae Fikes, interviewed in Faith S. Holsaert, Martha Prescod Norman Noonan, et al., eds., *Hands on the Freedom Plow: Personal Accounts by Women in SNCC* (Urbana: University of Illinois Press, 2010), 465.

19. "Dr. King Will Lead Selma Rights Test," *New York Times,* January 15, 1965, 14; "Selma Police Arrest," *New York Times,* January 22, 1965, 16; John Herbers, "Negro Teachers Protest in Selma," *New York Times,* January 23, 1965, 18; "U.S. Court Backs Negroes in Selma," *New York Times,* January 24, 1965, 40; "34 Negroes Seized in Selma Voter Line," *New York Times,* January 27, 1965, 16; "24 More Are Arrested in Negro Voter Line in Selma," *New York Times,* January 28, 1965, 15; "Dr. King in Selma, Urges Voter March," *New York Times,* January 31, 1965, 16.

20. Webb, Nelson, and Sikora, *Selma, Lord, Selma,* 38–39.

21. Ibid., 48–51.

22. Bernard LaFayette, Jr., and Kathryn Lee Johnson, *In Peace and Freedom: My Journey in Selma* (Lexington: University Press of Kentucky, 2013), 48.

23. John Herbers, "Dr. King and 770 Others Seized in Alabama Protest," *New York Times,* February 2, 1965, 1, 21; John Herbers, "Negroes Step Up Drive in Alabama; 1,000 More Seized," *New York Times,* February 4, 1965, 1, 22.

24. John Herbers, "Speed Negro Vote, Alabama Is Told." *New York Times,* February 5, 1965, 1, 17; "A Letter from Martin Luther King from a Selma, Alabama Jail," *New York Times,* February 5, 1965, 15; John Herbers, "Negro Goals in Selma," *New York Times,* February 6, 1965, 10; Roy Reed, "Negroes Suspend Selma Protests," *New York Times,* February 7, 1965, 44; and Fager, *Selma, 1965,* 54.

25. Roy Reed, "165 Selma Negro Youths Taken on Forced March," *New York Times*, February 11, 1965, 1, 19; John Herbers, "600 Negroes Hold Protest in Selma," *New York Times,* February 12, 1965, 58; John Herbers, "Negroes in Selma Offer Their Prayers for Stricken Sheriff Clark," *New York Times,* February 13, 1965, 1, 17; "Selma Negroes Set Vote March Today," *New York Times*, February 15, 1965, 15.

26. Beardslee, *The Way Out Must Lead In,* 114–15.

27. John Herbers, "Dr. King Urges Selma Negroes to Wage a More Militant Drive," *New York Times,* February 18, 1965, 26; and John Herbers, "Selma Negroes Tell of Attack," *New York Times,* February 22, 1965, 12; and Fager, *Selma, 1965,* 74.

28. *Eyes on the Prize,* transcript, page 4. See http://www.pbs.org/wgbh/amex /eyesontheprize.

29. Fager, *Selma, 1965,* 76–77.

30. Roy Reed, "A Twilight March Stopped in Selma," *New York Times,* February 24, 1965, 1, 28; Roy Reed, "Selma Reported to Seek Harmony," *New York Times,* February 26, 1965, 14; Roy Reed, "266 Apply to Vote as Selma Speeds Negro Registration," *New York Times,* March 2, 1965, 1, 19.

31. Roy Reed, "Hero's Burial Set for Slain Negro," *New York Times,* February 28, 1965, 55; Roy Reed, "Alabama Victim Called a Martyr," *New York Times,* March 3, 1965, 23.

32. Fager, *Selma, 1965,* 85–86.

33. Richie Jean Sherrod Jackson, *The House by the Side of the Road: The Selma Civil Rights Movement* (Tuscaloosa: University of Alabama Press, 2001), 90.

34. Garrow, *Protest at Selma,* 72.

35. Friedland, *Lift Up Your Voice Like a Trumpet,* 121; Roy Reed, "White Alabamians Stage Selma March to Support Negroes," *New York Times,* March 7, 1965, 1, 46; Joseph W. Ellwanger, *Strength for the Struggle: Insights from the Civil Rights Movement and Urban Ministry* (Milwaukee: MavinMark Books, 2014), 100–110.

36. David R. Goldfield, *Black, White, and Southern: Race Relations and Southern Culture, 1940 to Present* (Baton Rouge: Louisiana State University Press, 1990), 163; Charles Mohr, "Johnson, Dr. King Confer on Rights," *New York Times,* March 6, 1965, 9.

37. Goldfield, *Black, White and Southern,* 163–64.

38. Fager, *Selma, 1965,* 93.

39. Beardslee, *The Way Out Must Lead In,* 25–26; Roy Reed, "Alabama Police Use Gas and Clubs to Rout Negroes," *New York Times,* March 8, 1965, 1, 20; Fager, *Selma, 1965,* 94.

40. Beardslee, *The Way Out Must Lead In,* 25–26; Roy Reed, "Alabama Police Use Gas and Clubs to Rout Negroes," *New York Times,* March 8, 1965, 1, 20; "Dr. King Announces Plan for New Walk and Assails Attack," *New York Times,* March 8, 1965, 20; Gay Talese, "New York Doctors Barred at Scene," *New York Times,* March 8, 1965, 20; *Eyes on the Prize,* transcript, pages 5–6. See http://www.pbs.org/wgbh/amex /eyesontheprize.

41. Garrow, *Protest at Selma,* 78.

42. Webb, Nelson, and Sikora, *Selma, Lord, Selma,* 105–6.

43. David R. Jones, "10,000 March in Detroit," *New York Times,* March 10, 1965, 1, 23; "The Text of Judge's Order Banning Alabama March," *New York Times,* March 10, 1965, 23.

44. Laurraine Goreau, *Just Mahalia, Baby* (Waco: Word Books, 1975), 406.

45. "Armstrong Speaks Out on Racial Injustice," *downbeat* 12, no. 9 (April 22, 1965): 14.

46. George B. Leonard, "Midnight Plane to Selma," *Nation* 200, no. 19 (May 10, 1965): 502–5.

47. Andrew Kopkind, "Selma: Ain't Gonna Let Nobody Turn Me 'Round,'" *New Republic* 152 (March 20, 1965): 7–9; John Herbers, "U.S. Mediated Peaceful Confrontation," *New York Times,* March 10, 1965, 22; Gay Talese, "The Walk through Selma," *New York Times,* March 10, 1965, 1, 22; Fager, *Selma, 1965,* 101; Garrow, *Protest at Selma,* 83–87; Jack Mendelsohn, *The Martyrs: Sixteen Who Gave Their Lives for Racial Justice* (New York: Harper & Row, 1966), 166. For a discussion of what kinds of "deals," if any, King and the SCLC, the federal government, Wallace, and his law enforcement officers may have made

regarding the short Tuesday march, see Garrow, *Protest at Selma,* 273–74.

48. Simeon Booker, "Ambulance Stalled, but Troopers Refused to Give Aid," *Jet,* March 25, 1965, 26–28.

49. Fager, *Selma, 1965,* 108–9.

50. John Herbers, "Mayor and Police Block 3 New Marches in Selma," *New York Times,* March 11, 1965, 1, 21.

51. Fager, *Selma, 1965,* 112–16.

52. John Herbers, "Clergyman Dies of Selma Beating," *New York Times,* March 12, 1965, 1, 18.

53. John Herbers, "Boston Minister Dies as Result of Beating in Selma After Civil Rights March," *New York Times,* March 12, 1965, 1, 18; Tom Wicker, "Johnson Reveals Alert to Troops in Selma Crisis," *New York Times,* March 12, 1965, 1, 12; Fager, *Selma, 1965,* 123.

54. Fager, *Selma, 1965,* 126–29.

55. Al Kuettner, *March to a Promised Land: The Civil Rights Files of a White Reporter, 1952–1968* (Sterling, VA: Capital Books, 2006), 139.

56. John Herbers, "Police Blockades Stormed in Selma," *New York Times,* March 13, 1965, 1, 63; John Herbers, "Selma Stiffens Ban on Marches," *New York Times,* March 14, 1965, 1, 22; Gay Talese, "Kinship Grows Between Negroes and White Volunteers in Selma," *New York Times,* March 14, 1965, 22; Fager, *Selma, 1965,* 121–22, 133–34.

57. Tom Wicker, "Johnson Urges Congress at Joint Session to Pass Law Insuring Negro Vote," *New York Times,* March 16, 1965, 1, 31; Richard N. Goodwin, *Remembering America: A Voice from the Sixties* (Boston: Little, Brown, 1988), 310; Webb, West, and Sikora, *Selma, Lord, Selma,* 121; Garrow, *Protest at Selma,* 105–7; Beardslee, *The Way Out Must Lead In,* 27.

58. "Montgomery Crowd Dispersed by Police," *New York Times*, March 15, 1965, 31; Ben A. Franklin, "March to Montgomery Hazardous, Troopers Say," *New York Times,* March 15, 1965, 31; Roy Reed, "Police Rout 600 in Montgomery; 8 Marchers Hurt," *New York Times,* March 16, 1965, 1, 26; Ben A. Franklin, "5-Day March Plan Is Given to Court," *New York Times,* March 17, 1965, 36; Fager, *Selma, 1965,* 141–42; David Halberstam, *The Children* (New York: Fawcett Books, 1998), 516.

59. Ben A. Franklin, "U.S. Court Allows Alabama March; Enjoins Wallace," *New York Times,* March 17, 1965, 1, 20; Roy Reed, "Accord Reached in Montgomery," *New York Times,* March 18, 1965, 1, 21; Garrow, *Protest at Selma,* 111–12.

60. Thomas R. Kendrick, "Selma Rights Activity Includes New Marches," *Washington Post,* March 20, 1965, A10; Roy Reed, "Hundreds Pour into Selma for March to Montgomery," *New York Times,* March 21, 1965, 1, 76; Roy Reed, "Freedom March Begins at Selma; Troops on Guard," *New York Times*, March 22, 1965, 1, 26; Fager, *Selma, 1965,* 145–49; Reverend John B. Morris, cassette tapes, "The Saga of Selma," Episcopalian Seminary and Archives, Austin, Texas, 84-4-5, March 1965, tape 1, side 1.

61. Roy Reed, "Hundreds Pour into Selma for March to Montgomery," *New York Times,* March 21, 1965, 1, 76; Paul L. Montgomery, "The Marchers on Highway 80 Are of All Sorts and One Belief," *New York Times,* March 22, 1965, 27; LaFayette, *In Peace and Freedom,* 131–32; William G. Roy, *Reds, Whites, and Blues: Social Movements, Folk Music, and Race in the United States* (Princeton: Princeton University Press, 2010), 204; Renata Adler, "Letter from Selma," *The New Yorker* (April 10, 1965): 126; Fager, *Selma, 1965,* 150–52; Andrew Young, *An Easy Burden: The Civil Rights Movement and the Transformation of America* (Waco: Baylor University Press, 2008), 364.

62. "Broadway Answers Selma!" *New York Times*, March 22, 1965, 39; Roy Reed, "Rights Marchers Push into Region Called Hostile," *New York Times,*

March 23, 1965, 1, 28; Paul Gardner, "N.B.C. Will Show March Live on TV," *New York Times,* March 23, 1965, 78; Fager, *Selma, 1965,* 153–56.

63. Roy Reed, "Alabama March Passes Midpoint," *New York Times,* March 24, 1965, 1, 33; Ben A. Franklin, "Top Entertainers in Alabama Tonight," *New York Times,* March 24, 1965, 33; Paul L. Montgomery, "Marchers Reply to Jeers with Music," *New York Times,* March 24, 1965, 33; John Lewis, with Michael D'Orso, *Walking with the Wind: A Memoir of the Movement* (New York: A Harvest Book, 1998), 359.

64. Gladys McFadden, interview with the author, June 9, 2009, transcript of tape recording, Institute for Oral History, Baylor University, Waco, 7; Richard Harrington, "The Gospel According to Mavis," *Washington Post,* October 31, 2004, Arts No1; Jeff Brown, interview with the author, July 2, 2009, transcript of tape recording, Institute for Oral History, Baylor University, Waco, 7–8; Bryan McKenzie, "Civil Rights Leader Silva Dead at 83," *Charlottesville (Virginia) Daily Progress,* March 7, 2008; David King Dunaway, *How Can I Keep from Singing? The Ballad of Pete Seeger* (New York: Villard Books, 2008), 293–96; John Lewis, interview with the author, May 20, 2009, transcript of tape recording, Institute for Oral History, Baylor University, Waco, 3, 6.

65. Roy Reed, "Alabama Marchers Reach Outskirts of Montgomery," *New York Times,* March 25, 1965, 1, 27; Paul L. Montgomery, "Band in Vanguard All the Way from Selma to Montgomery," *New York Times,* March 25, 1965, 27; Adler, "Letter from Selma,"150; Morris, cassette tapes, 84-4-5, tape 3; Fager, *Selma, 1965,* 157–58.

66. Donald Janson, "Stars Give Show for Rights March," *New York Times,* March 25, 1965, 27.

67. Gary Fishgall, *Gonna Do Great Things: The Life of Sammy Davis, Jr.* (New York: Scribner, 2003), 202–3.

68. David Evanier, *All the Things You Are: The Life of Tony Bennett* (New York: John Wiley & Sons, 2011), 150–55.

69. David Crosby and David Bender, *Stand and Be Counted: Making Music, Making History* (San Francisco: Harper San Francisco, 2000), 20–21.

70. Nadine Cohodas, *Princess Noire: The Tumultuous Reign of Nina Simone* (New York: Pantheon Books, 2010), 171–73.

71. Alan Levine, "Sound and Fury," Letter to the Editor, *New York Times Book Review,* March 21, 2010, 7.

72. Coretta Scott King, *My Life with Martin Luther King, Jr.* (London: Hoddard & Stoughton, 1970), 279.

73. *Eyes on the Prize,* transcript, 12. See http://www.pbs.org/wgbh/amex /eyesontheprize.

74. Pete Seeger, "You Can't Write Down Freedom Songs," *Sing Out!* 15 (July 1965): 11.

75. Dunaway, *How Can I Keep from Singing?,* 296–97.

76. Roy Reed, "24,000 Go to Alabama's Capitol; Wallace Rebuffs Petitioners; Rights Worker Is Slain," *New York Times,* March 26, 1965, 1, 22; "Weary Freedom Marchers Begin the Return Trip," *New York Times,* March 26, 1965, 23.

77. Ralph David Abernathy, *And the Walls Came Tumbling Down: Ralph David Abernathy, an Autobiography* (New York: Harper & Row, 1989), 358.

78. Keith D. Miller, "Epistemology of a Drum Major: Martin Luther King, Jr. and the Black Folk Pulpit," *Rhetoric Society Quarterly* 18, no. 3/4 (Summer–Autumn 1988): 230.

79. Young, *An Easy Burden,* 367.

80. Margaret Long, "Let Freedom Sing," *The Progressive* (November 1965): 27–29.

81. Paul L. Montgomery, "Woman Is Shot to Death on Lowndes County Road," *New York Times,* March 26, 1965, 1, 23; David R. Jones, "Mrs. Liuzzo's Body Is Returned to Detroit in Teamster's Plane," *New York Times,* March 27, 1965, 10; Charles Mohr, "Bids Congress Act,"

*New York Times,* March 27, 1965, 1, 11; Roy Reed, "Witness to Slaying Cites Harassment on Road Earlier," *New York Times,* March 27, 1965, 1, 10; Roy Reed, "Dr. King to Step Up Drive for Alabama Civil Rights," *New York Times,* March 28, 1965, 1, 58; David R. Jones, "4 Rights Leaders Attend Funeral," *New York Times,* March 31, 1965, 22; "Tony Bennett Tells Why He Marched with Dr. King in Selma," *Jet,* April 6, 1992, 16; Bernice Johnson Reagon, *Songs of the Civil Rights Movement, 1955–1965: A Study in Culture History* (PhD diss., Howard University, 1975), 174. Liuzzo was said to have sung "We Shall Overcome" as she lay dying from her wounds. See Caryle Murphy, "The Rise of the Rights Anthem; 'We Shall Overcome': The Song, the History," *Washington Post,* January 17, 1988, G1.

82. Fager, *Selma, 1965,* 188–91.

83. E. W. Kenworthy, "Johnson Signs Voting Rights Bill, Orders Immediate Enforcement; 4 Suits Will Challenge Poll Tax," *New York Times,* August 7, 1965, 1, 8; John Herbers, "U.S. Acts Quickly to Enforce Law on Voting Right," *New York Times,* August 8, 1965, 1 58; Lewis, *Walking with the Wind,* 361–62.

84. "Notes from Mississippi," *The Student Voice, 1960–1965,* July 1965 edition, 2. Periodical of the Student Nonviolent Coordinating Committee, compiled by the staff of the Martin Luther King, Jr., Papers Project, Clayborne Carson, senior editor and director (Westport: Meckler, 1990).

85. Seeger and Reiser, *Everybody Says Freedom,* 208.

86. Peter Bart, "New Negro Riots Erupt on Coast; 3 Reported Shot," *New York Times,* August 13, 1965, 1, 26; Peter Bart, "2,000 Troops Enter Los Angeles on Third Day of Negro Rioting; 4 Die as Fires and Looting Grow," *New York Times,* August 14, 1965, 1, 8.

87. Roy Reed, "White Seminarian Slain in Alabama; Deputy Is Charged,"

*New York Times,* August 21, 1965, 1, 9; Roy Reed, "Voter Drive Is Spurred in Alabama," *New York Times,* August 23, 1963, 19; John Fenton, "Slain Seminarian Honored at Rites," *New York Times,* August 25, 1965, 24.

88. Charles W. Eagles, *Outside Agitator: Jon Daniels and the Civil Rights Movement in Alabama* (Chapel Hill: University of North Carolina Press, 1993), 182–84.

89. Ellen Levine, *Freedom's Children: Young Civil Rights Activists Tell Their Own Stories* (Thorndike, ME: Thorndike Press, 1993), 206; Fager, *Selma, 1965,* 210–11.

90. Various artists, *Freedom Songs: Selma, Alabama* (Folkways Records, FH 5594), 1965, recorded and produced by Carl Benkert. Re-released on CD by Smithsonian Folkways Recordings (FH 5594), 2006.

91. Len Chandler, Pete Seeger, and the Freedom Voices, *WNEW's Story of Selma* (Folkways Records FH 5595), 1965, produced by Mike Stein and Jerry Graham. Re-released on CD by Smithsonian Folkways Records (FH 5595), 2007. One particularly rare recording from the campaign is *Highway into History: The Selma to Montgomery March* ("A Live Recording of the 5 Days in March the World Will Long Remember"), Vee-Jay Records, program notes by Joe Greene, "Recording events of March 21, 1965." One song from the Selma campaign is also included on *Voices of the Civil Rights Movement: Black American Freedom Songs, 1960–1966* (Smithsonian Folkways Records, CD FD 40084), 1997: "Governor Wallace" by the SNCC Freedom Singers.

## Third Interlude

The epigraphs for this chapter are drawn from Mary King, *Freedom Song: A Personal Story of the 1960s Civil Rights Movement* (New York: William Morrow, 1987), 23–24; and Stokely Carmichael, quoted in Guy Carawan and Candie Carawan, *Sing* for Freedom: The Story of the Civil Rights Movement through Its Songs (Montgomery: NewSouth Books, 2008), 103.

1. Pat Watters, "St. Augustine," *New South* 19, no. 9 (September 1964): 3–5.

2. Dorothy Cotton, quoted in Carawan and Carawan, *Sing for Freedom,* 115.

3. Andrew Young, *A Way Out of No Way: The Spiritual Memoirs of Andrew Young* (Nashville: Thomas Nelson, 1994), 89–93.

4. Watters, "St. Augustine," 3–4.

5. Fred Powledge, "88 More Seized in St. Augustine," *New York Times,* April 2, 1965, 18; Fred Powledge, "Protesters Fail in St. Augustine," *New York Times,* April 4, 1964, 1, 13; John Herbers, "Martin Luther King and 17 Others Jailed Trying to Integrate St. Augustine Restaurant," *New York Times,* June 12, 1964, 17; John Herbers, "16 Rabbis Arrested as Pool Dive-In Sets off St. Augustine Rights Clash," *New York Times,* June 19, 1964, 1, 16; Pat Watters, *Down to Now: Reflections on the Southern Civil Rights Movement* (New York: Pantheon Books, 1971); 287; Taylor Branch, *Pillar of Fire: American in the King Years, 1963–65* (New York: Simon & Schuster, 1998), 340.

6. Watters, *Down to Now*, 282–83, 286.

7. Cotton in Carawan and Carawan, *Sing for Freedom*, 117–19.

8. Robert Shelton, "Newport Folk-Music Festival Opens 3-Day Run Before 13,000," *New York Times*, July 27, 1963, 9; Robert Shelton, "Folk-Music Fete Called a Success," *New York Times,* July 29, 1963, 15; Leroy F. Aarons, "Fresh Voice Rising in Folk Wilderness," *Washington Post*, August 18, 1963, G1; Robert Shelton, "Cream of Newport Folk Festival," *New York Times,* July 19, 1964, X11; Sean Wilentz, *Bob Dylan in America* (New York: Doubleday, 2010), 276–77.

9. Robert Shelton, "Newport Begins Its Folk Festival," *New York Times*, July 24, 1964, 16; Robert Shelton, "'64 Folk Festival Ends in Newport," *New York Times,* July 27, 1964, 21; Robert Shelton, "Symbolic Finale: Folk Music Winds up with Songs of the Negro Integration Movement," *New York Times,* August 2, 1964, 89; Robert Shelton, text, and David Gahr, photography, *The Face of Folk Music* (New York: Citadel Press, 1968), 130–31.

10. Robert Shelton, "Folk Music Fills Newport Coffers," *New York Times*, July 26, 1965, 16; Robert Shelton, "Beneath the Festival's Razzle Dazzle," *New York Times*, August 1, 195, X11; Ronald D. Cohen, *Rainbow Quest: The Folk Music Revival and American Society, 1940–1970* (Amherst: University of Massachusetts Press, 2002), 208–30; Jerry Zolten, *Great God A'mighty! The Dixie Hummingbirds, Celebrating the Rise of Soul Gospel Music* (Oxford: Oxford University Press, 2003), 276–80; Robert Shelton, "A Fare-Thee-Well for Newport Sing," *New York Times*, July 25, 1966, 23.

11. Trent Dalton, "Sweet Harmony," *Brisbane (Australia) News,* August 21, 2002, E1.

12. Edward C. Burks, "Meredith Begins Vote March Today," *New York Times*, June 5, 1966, 78; Roy Reed, "Meredith Is Shot in Back on Walk into Mississippi," *New York Times,* June 7, 1966, 1, 29; Heinz-Dietrich Fischer, *Press Photography Awards, 1942–1988* (Munich: K. G. Saur Books, 2000), 12.

13. John Kifner, "Rights Leaders Plan to Take up Meredith's March in Mississippi," *New York Times*, June 7, 1966, 28; Gene Roberts, "Troopers Shove Group Resuming Meredith March," *New York Times,* June 8, 1966, 1, 26; Douglas E. Kneeland, "Meredith to Resume March June 16 in Mississippi," *New York Times,* June 10, 1966, 34.

14. Martin Luther King Jr., *Where Do We Go from Here: Chaos or Community?* (New York: Harper & Row, 1967), 25–26.

15. David R. Underhill, "March Doubles Vote Registration Along Route Through

Mississippi," *The Southern Courier* 2, no. 25 (June 18--19, 1966): 1; Gene Roberts, "Negroes Win Voting Gains on Stop in Grenada, Miss.," *New York Times,* June 15, 1966, 1, 26.

16. Roy Reed, "Dr. King Bids U.S. Guard New March," *New York Times,* June 23, 1966, 23; Homer Bigart, "Accord by King Angers Marchers," *New York Times*, June 25, 1966, 15; Paul Good, "The Meredith March," *New South* (Summer 1966): 11–14.

17. Good, "The Meredith March," 2–4.

18. King, *Where Do We Go from Here,* 29–30.

19. Good, "The Meredith March," 4–11.

20. Gene Roberts, "Meredith Leads the March on Eve of Rally in Jackson," *New York Times*, June 26, 1966, 1, 40; Gary Fishgall, *Gonna Do Great Things: The Life of Sammy Davis, Jr.* (New York: Scribner, 2011), 224–25; James Sullivan, *The Hardest Working Man: How James Brown Saved the Soul of America* (Gotham Books, 2008), 111–13.

21. Roberts, "Meredith Leads the March on Eve of Rally in Jackson," 1, 40.

22. Reed, "Dr. King Bids U.S. Guard New March," 23; Bigart, "Accord by King Angers Marchers," 15; Good, "The Meredith March," 14–16.

23. Julius Lester, "The Angry Children of Malcolm X," in August Meier, Elliott Rudwick, and Francis L. Broderick, eds., *Black Protest Thought in the Twentieth Century* (Indianapolis: Bobbs-Merrill Educational Publishing, 1971), 482. On August 9, black demonstrators in Grenada protested the use of tear gas, bricks, firecrackers, lead pipes and bottles by whites during a civil rights demonstration the previous evening. As law enforcement officers watched, a white mob attacked the nonviolent protest, leaving dozens injured. "You're going to see a show tonight," Sheriff Suggs Ingram told reporters prior to the attack. A number of reporters were injured as well. The original demonstration had been

called to protest renewed difficulties in voter registration that re-emerged in the days following the Meredith march. See Gene Roberts, "White Mob Routs Grenada Negroes," *New York Times,* August 10, 1966, 1, 28.

24. Peter Guralnick, *Dream Boogie: The Triumph of Sam Cooke* (New York: Back Bay Books, 2005), 370–71, 512–13, 552, 588.

25. Dave Marsh and John Swenson, eds., *New Rolling Stone Record Guide* (New York: Random House, 1983), 112–13.

26. Greg Kot, *I'll Take You There: Mavis Staples, the Staple Singers, and the March up Freedom's Highway* (New York: Scribner, 2014), 92–109.

27. Bob Gulla, *Icons of R&B and Soul: An Encyclopedia of Artists Who Revolutionized Rhythm,* 2 vols. (Westport: Greenwood Press, 2008), 239.

28. "People Get Ready: Song Inspired by March on Washington Carries Enduring Message," http://www.npr.org/news /specials/march40th/people.html.

29. Craig Werner, *Higher Ground: Stevie Wonder, Aretha Franklin, Curtis Mayfield, and the Rise and Fall of American Soul* (New York: Crown, 2004), 125.

30. Dick Weissman, *Which Side Are You On? An Inside History of the Folk Music Revival in America* (New York: Continuum, 2005), 139–40; Werner, *Higher Ground,* 65; Brian Ward, *Just My Soul Responding: Rhythm and Blues, Black Consciousness, and Race Relations* (Berkeley: University of California Press, 1998), 76; Werner, *Higher Ground,* 125; The Impressions, "People Get Ready," *The 500 Greatest Songs of All Time* http://www.rollingstone.com /music/lists/the-500-greatest-songs-of -all-time-20110407 ; "People Get Ready: Song Inspired by March on Washington Carries Enduring Message," http:// www.npr.org/news/specials/march40th /people.html. In 1967, the Impressions released the Curtis Mayfield–penned "We're a Winner," which was also seen as a civil rights–related song. The

lyrics, "And we're movin' on up / Lord have mercy / We're movin' on up," reflect directly an earlier song of black empowerment made famous by another Chicago resident, Mahalia Jackson, and her rendition of Brewster's "Movin' on Up (A Little Bit Higher"). See also Michael A. Gonzales, "The Legend of Soul: Long Live Curtis Mayfield!," in Monique Guillory and Richard C. Green, eds., *Soul: Black Power, Politics, and Pleasure* (New York: New York University Press, 1998), 232–33; and "We're a Winner," The Impressions, ABC-Records, 45-11022, released 1967.

31. Margaret Long, "Let Freedom Ring," *The Progressive* (November 1965): 29.

## Chapter 8

The epigraphs for this chapter are drawn from a quote by Harry Belafonte, interviewed in *Soundtrack for a Revolution*, directed by Bill Guttentag and Dan Sturman, Spark Media/WGBH, 2011; and a song parody by Len Chandler, quoted in Guy Carawan and Candie Carawan, *Freedom Is a Constant Struggle: Songs of the Freedom Movement* (New York: Oak Publishers, 1968), 223.

1. As with most of the major campaigns of the civil rights movement, there are a number of excellent, in-depth accounts of the events in Chicago, including Alan B. Anderson and George W. Pickering, *Confronting the Color Line: The Broken Promise of the Civil Rights Movement in Chicago* (Athens: University of Georgia Press, 1986); Taylor Branch, *At Canaan's Edge: America in the King Years, 1965–68* (New York: Simon & Schuster, 2006); David J. Garrow, *Bearing the Cross: Martin Luther King, Jr., and the Southern Christian Leadership Conference* (New York: William Morrow, 1986); David J. Garrow, ed., *Chicago 1966: Open Housing Marches, Summit Negotiations, and Operation Breadbasket* (Brooklyn: Carlson Publishing, 1989); and James R. Ralph, Jr., *Northern Protest: Martin Luther King, Jr., Chicago, and the Civil Rights Movement* (Cambridge: Harvard University Press, 1993), among others.

2. Ralph, *Northern Protest*, 7–21.

3. Austin C. Wehrwein, "Dr. King Starts Drive in Chicago," *New York Times*, July 25, 1965, 39; Austin C. Wehrwein, "Dr. King Attends Winnetka Rally," *New York Times*, July 26, 1965, 12; Austin C. Wehrwein, "Dr. King's Drive Ends in Chicago," *New York Times*, July 27, 1965, 18; Austin C. Wehrwein, "Dr. King Puts Life in Chicago's Drive," *New York Times*, July 30, 1965, 59; Alvin Adams, "King Campaign Heads North; 'Skip Harlem' Advises Powell," *Jet*, August 12, 1965, 6–7.

4. Ralph, *Northern Protest*, 35–45.

5. Mary Lou Finley, interview with the author, February 22, 2010, transcript of tape recording, Institute for Oral History, Baylor University, Waco, 1–10.

6. Branch, *At Canaan's Edge*, 321.

7. Laurraine Goreau, *Just Mahalia, Baby* (Waco: Word Books, 1975), 420–21.

8. Garrow, *Bearing the Cross*, 455.

9. Ibid., 448–49.

10. "Dr. King Focuses Drive on Chicago," *New York Times*, October 11, 1965, 44; Ralph, *Northern Protest*, 53.

11. John H. Britton, "Showdown Looms: Moral Power Against Poverty Profiteers," *Jet*, February 10, 1966, 17; Ralph, *Northern Protest*, 50–52, 94.

12. Britton, "Showdown Looms," 15–20.

13. Donald Janson, "Dr. King to Rent Slum Apartment," *New York Times*, January 21, 1966; 51; Austin C. Wehrwein, "Dr. King Occupies a Flat in Slums," *New York Times*, January 27, 1966, 37; "Dr. King Seizes a Slum Building," *New York Times*, February 24, 1966, 75; "Dr. King Assailed for Slum Tactic," *New York Times*, February 25, 1966, 18.

14. Marshall Frady, *Jesse: The Life and Pilgrimage of Jesse Jackson* (New York: Random House, 1996), 196–98; Ralph, *Northern Protest*, 62–71. King later

repaid Evans's faith in the movement by appearing at a fund-raiser for Fellowship Church at Chicago's Aire Crown Theatre of McCormick Place in late 1966. The church was eventually completed on April 15, 1973. See Dorothy June Rose, *From Plough Handle to Pulpit: The Life Story of Rev. Clay Evans* (Warminster, PA: Neibauer Press, 1981, 1997), 44–47. "Many ministers who were with us had to back off because they didn't want their buildings to be condemned or given citations for electrical work, faulty plumbing, or fire code violations," Evan once said. See Adam Cohen and Elizabeth Taylor, *American Pharaoh: Mayor Richard Daley: His Battle for Chicago and the Nation* (Boston: Little, Brown, 2000), 359.

15. Anderson and Pickering, *Confronting the Color Line,* 190; Goreau, *Just Mahalia, Baby*, 422.

16. Jules Schwerin, *Got to Tell It: Mahalia Jackson, Queen of Gospel* (New York: Oxford University Press, 1992), 151; Dempsey J. Travis, *An Autobiography of Black Politics* (Chicago: Urban Research Press, 1987), 357.

17. Gene Roberts, "New Leaders and New Course for 'Snick,'" *New York Times,* May 22, 1966, 208; Branch, *At Canaan's Edge,* 492–93; Austin C. Wehrwein, "Dr. King and CORE Chief Act to Heal Breach," *New York Times,* July 11, 1966, 1, 19.

18. "Dr. King to Stage Big Rally Today," *New York Times*, July 10, 1966, 54; Austin C. Wehrwein, "Dr. King and CORE Chief Act to Heal Breach," *New York Times,* July 11, 1966, 1, 19; Austin Wehrwein, "Dr. King Declares Daley Balks Him," *New York Times*, July 12, 1966, 26; Craig Werner, *Higher Ground: Stevie Wonder, Aretha Franklin, Curtis Mayfield, and the Rise and Fall of American Soul* (New York: Crown, 2004), 4–5; Goreau, *Just Mahalia, Baby*, 427; Anderson and Pickering, *Confronting the Color Line,* 203; Branch, *At Canaan's Edge,* 501; Cohen, *American Pharaoh*, 384; Philip S. Foner, *Organized Labor and the Black Worker, 1619–1973* (New York: Praeger, 1974), 363; Liam T. A. Ford, *Soldier Field: A Stadium and Its City* (Chicago: University of Chicago Press, 2009), 206–8; Finley interview, 11.

19. Anderson and Pickering, *Confronting the Color Line,* 210–11; Ralph, *Northern Protest,* 109–11; Branch, *At Canaan's Edge,* 502–3; Coretta Scott King, *My Life with Martin Luther King, Jr.* (London: Hodder & Stoughton, 1970), 296–97.

20. Goreau, *Just Mahalia, Baby*, 427–28; Anderson and Pickering, *Confronting the Color Line,* 220–24; "Dr. King Presses Drive in Chicago," *New York Times,* July 30, 1966, 11.

21. "54 Hurt as Whites in Chicago Hurl Bricks at Rights Marchers," *New York Times,* August 1, 1966, 1, 15; "Dr. King Calls Chicago Police Lax in March Duty," *New York Times,* August 2, 1966, 12; Anderson and Pickering, *Confronting the Color Line,* 224–25; Andrew Young, *An Easy Burden: The Civil Rights Movement and the Transformation of America* (Waco: Baylor University Press, 2008), 413; Chester Higgins, "May Sue Chicago in Vicious Destruction of Rights' Property," *Jet,* August 18, 1966, 52–55; Ralph, *Northern Protest,* 120–21.

22. Gene Roberts, "Rock Hits Dr. King as Whites Attack March in Chicago," *New York Times,* August 6, 1966, 1, 52; Karen Koko, "Chicago's Race March— A Walk on the Wild Side," *National Catholic Reporter* 2, no. 40 (August 10, 1966): 1, 12; Ralph, *Northern Protest,* 122–31.

23. David Wallace, interview with the author, January 22, 2009, transcript of tape recording, Institute for Oral History, Baylor University, Waco, 21–25.

24. David L. Lewis, *King: A Biography* (New York: Praeger, 1970), 333.

25. Henry P. Leiferman, "Profession: Concert Singer, Freedom Movement

Lecturer," *New York Times,* November 26, 1972, SM52.

26. Finley interview, 16–17.

27. Garrow, *Bearing the Cross,* 500–524; Chester Higgins, "Rights Marches in Lily-White Areas Trigger Hate, Violence," *Jet,* August 25, 1966, 14–22; Gene Roberts, "Whites in Chicago Mob Negro March," *New York Times,* August 8, 1966, 1, 55; Douglas Robinson, "Daley Calls upon Rights Groups to 'Reconsider' 2 New Protests," *New York Times,* August 10, 1966, 28; Donald Janson, "Dr. King Planning to March Today," *New York Times*, August 21, 1966, 47; Jacques Nevard, "Marchers Pelted in Chicago Suburb," *New York Times*, August 24, 1966, 34; Jacques Nevard, "Guard to Protect Cicero Marchers," *New York Times,* August 25, 1966, 24; Jacques Nevard, "An Accord May Cancel March Through Cicero," *New York Times,* August 26, 1966, 16; Jacques Nevard, "Housing Pact Set, Dr. King Calls Off Chicago Marches," *New York Times,* August 27, 1966, 1, 17.

28. Paul Good, "Bossism, Racism and Dr. King," *Nation* 23, no. 8 (September 19, 1966): 238–39.

29. Mike Royko, *Boss: Richard J. Daley of Chicago* (New York: E. P. Dutton, 1971), 154.

30. Frederick C. Harris, "Black Churches and Machine Politics in Chicago," in R. Drew Smith and Frederick C. Harris, eds., *Black Churches and Local Politics: Clergy Influence, Organizational Partnerships, and Civic Empowerment* (Lanham: Rowman & Littlefield, 2005), 124.

31. Ralph, *Northern Protest*, 173.

32. Adrian Dove, "Soul Story," *New York Times,* December 8, 1968, 361; Ralph, *Northern Protest,* 200; Rose, *Plough Handle to Pulpit,* 51; Greg Kot, *I'll Take You There: Mavis Staples, the Staple Singers, and the March Up Freedom's Highway* (New York: Scribner, 2014); Robert Dixon, interview with the author, August 7, 2009, Chicago,

transcript of tape recording, Institute for Oral History, Baylor University, Waco, 7; Wallace interview, 21–35. Information on the earliest days of Operation Breadbasket was provided by Betty Magness via personal correspondence with the author.

33. Gregory Donald Gay, interview with the author, August 11, 2009, Chicago, transcript of tape recording, Institute for Oral History, Baylor University, Waco, 11–14; Maceo Woods, interview with the author, August 11, 2009, Chicago, transcript of tape recording, Institute for Oral History, Baylor University, Waco, 11–12, 17, 19–21; Reuben Burton, interview with the author, August 8, 2009, Chicago, transcript of tape recording, Institute for Oral History, Baylor University, Waco, 4–5; Inez Andrews, interview with the author, September 2, 2009, transcript of tape recording, Institute for Oral History, Baylor University, Waco, 5–6.

34. Ben Branch interview, conducted by Joan Beifuss, Tom Buckner, and Bill Thomas, August 15, 1968, at SCLC Headquarters at the CME Church at 531 South Parkway in Chicago, tape recording transcript. Ben Branch #178, Mississippi Valley Collection, University of Memphis, #1, CTN 20 Sanitation Strike Collection, Box 20, Folder 27.

35. Hermene Hartman, interview with the author, September 19, 2009, transcript of tape recording, Institute for Oral History, Baylor University, Waco, 2–5, 10.

36. Viv Broughton, *Too Close to Heaven: The Illustrated History of Gospel Music* (London: Midnight Books, 1996), 95–96.

37. Gay interview, 24–30.

38. Dempsey, *An Autobiography of Black Politics*, 389.

39. Guy Carawan and Candie Carawan, *Sing for Freedom: The Story of the Civil Rights Movement Through Its Songs* (Montgomery: NewSouth Books, 1968), 229.

40. Tammy Kernodle, "'I Wish I Knew How It Would Feel to Be Free': Nina Simone and the Redefining of the Freedom Song of the 1960s," *Journal of the Society for American Music* 2, no. 3 (2008), 308.

41. Jimmy Collier, interview with the author, October 14, 2009, transcript of tape recording, Institute for Oral History, Baylor University, Waco, 15, 21, 23.

42. Jimmy Collier, "Burn, Baby, Burn," *Sing Out!* (June/July 1966), 8.

43. Kernodle, "'I Wish I Knew How It Would Feel to Be Free,'" 308.

## Chapter 9

The epigraph for this chapter is an old African-American spiritual, collected by John Lovell, Jr., *Black Song: The Forge and the Flame: The Story of How the Afro-American Spiritual Was Hammered Out* (New York: Paragon House, 1986), 192.

1. Detailed accounts of the events of 1967 and early 1968 can be found in several excellent biographies of King and the movement during this period, including David J. Garrow, *Bearing the Cross: Martin Luther King, Jr. and the Southern Leadership Conference* (New York: William Morrow, 1986); Taylor Branch, *At Canaan's Edge: America in the King Years, 1965–68* (New York: Simon & Schuster, 2006).

2. Garrow, *Bearing the Cross*, 529–32.

3. "Dr. King Leads Chicago Peace Rally," *New York Times*, March 26, 1967, 44; Douglas Robinson, "Dr. King Proposes a Boycott of War," *New York Times*, April 5, 1967, 1, 2; Douglas Robinson, "Jewish Veterans Attack Dr. King's Stand on War," *New York Times*, April 6, 1967, 10; "Dr. King's Error," *New York Times*, April 7, 1967, 36; "N.A.A.C.P. Decries Stand of Dr. King on Vietnam," April 11, 1967, 1, 17; Charles DeBenedetti, *An American Ordeal: The Antiwar Movement of the Vietnam Era* (Syracuse: Syracuse University Press, 1990), 173–74.

4. See Malcolm McLaughlin, *The Long Hot Summer of 1967: Urban Rebellion in America* (London: Palgrave Macmillan, 2014) for a detailed account of that summer. Robert Dallek, *Flawed Giant: Lyndon Johnson and His Times, 1961–1973* (Oxford: Oxford University Press, 1999), 411–15; DeBenedetti, *An American Ordeal*, 191; James H. Cone, *God of the Oppressed* (Maryknoll: Orbis Books, 1997), 5; William Beecher, "Goal Now 525,000," *New York Times*, August 4, 1967, 1, 2; R. W. Apple, "Vietnam: The Signs of Stalemate," *New York Times*, August 7, 1967, 1, 14.

5. Gene Roberts, "Dr. King Planning Protests to 'Dislocate' Large Cities,'" *New York Times*, August 16, 1967, 1, 29; Gene Roberts, "Dr. King Stresses Pride in His Race," *New York Times*, August 19, 1967, 12; Barbara H. Flowers, "A New Man in an Old World," *Southern Courier*, August 19–20, 1967, 1, 7.

6. Robert T. Chase, "Class Resurrection: The Poor People's Campaign of 1968 and Resurrection City," *Essays in History: The Annual Journal Produced by the Corcoran Department of History at the University of Virginia*, 1998, http://www.essaysinhistory.com/articles/2012/116; Walter Rugaber, "Dr. King Planning to Disrupt Capital in Drive for Jobs," *New York Times*, December 5, 1967, 1, 32; "The Responsibility of Dissent," *New York Times*, December 6, 1967, 46.

7. Laurraine Goreau, *Just Mahalia, Baby* (Waco: Word Books, 1975), 473.

8. Garrow, *Bearing the Cross*, 591–94.

9. For more information on the Memphis campaign, see Michael K. Honey, *Going Down Jericho Road: The Memphis Strike, Martin Luther King's Last Campaign* (New York: W. W. Norton, 2007; David J. Garrow, *The FBI and Martin Luther King, Jr.: From "Solo" to Memphis* (New York: W. W. Norton, 1981); Michael Eric Dyson, *April 4,*

*1968: Martin Luther King's Death and How It Changed America* (New York: Basic Civitas Books, 2008); Joan Turner Beifuss, *At the River I Stand: Memphis, the 1968 Strike, and Martin Luther King* (Brooklyn: Carlson Publishing, 1989); Garrow, *Bearing the Cross: Martin Luther King, Jr., and the Southern Leadership Conference* (New York: William Morrow, 1986); Taylor Branch, *At Canaan's Edge: America in the King Years, 1965–68* (New York: Simon & Schuster, 2006); Rebecca Burns, *Burial for a King: Martin Luther King Jr.'s Funeral and the Week That Transformed Atlanta and Rocked the Nation* (New York: Scribner, 2011), 28.

10. Steve Estes, " 'I Am a Man!': Race, Masculinity, and the 1968 Memphis Sanitation Strike," *Labor History* 41, no. 2 (2000), 153–58, doi:10.1080/0023656005009914.

11. "'Striker' Protests Quelled in Memphis," *New York Times*, February 24, 1968, 26; "Leaders of Strike Curbed in Memphis," *New York Times*, February 25, 1968; 42; Douglas E. Kneeland, "Memphis Facing a Negro Boycott," *New York Times*, February 26, 1968, 27.

12. Bil Carpenter, *Uncloudy Days: The Gospel Music Encyclopedia* (San Francisco: Backbeat Books, 2005), 258.

13. James H. Cone, "Martin Luther King, Jr., and the Third World," *Journal of American History* 74, no. 2 (September 1987): 467.

14. Estes, "'I Am a Man!'," 158.

15. Anthony Heilbut, *The Gospel Sound: Good News and Hard Times* (New York: Limelight Editions, 1989), 97–105.

16. Sylvan Fox, "Memphis Is Beset by Racial Tension," *New York Times*, March 18, 1968, 28; Garrow, *Bearing the Cross*, 604–6; Beifuss, *At the River I Stand*, 137, 191–96; David Levering Lewis, *King: A Critical Biography* (Urbana: University of Illinois Press, 1970), 379; Garrow, *King and the FBI*, 189; Honey, *Going Down Jericho Road*, 281–83.

17. Philip S. Foner, *Organized Labor and the Black Worker, 1619–1973* (New York: Praeger, 1974), 382.

18. "Dr. King Reschedules March for Strikers in Memphis," *New York Times*, March 25, 1968, 46; C. Gerald Fraser, "Dr. King Takes 'Poor People's Campaign' to Groups in Harlem and Queens," *New York Times*, March 27, 1968, 24; Beifuss, *At the River I Stand*, 204.

19. Walter Rugaber, "A Negro Is Killed in Memphis March," *New York Times*, March 29, 1968, 1, 29; Garrow, *Bearing the Cross*, 610–13; Beifuss, *At the River I Stand*, 222–24, 244–45; Dyson, *April 4, 1968*, 31–32; Honey, *Going Down Jericho Road*, 337–38.

20. Walter Rugaber, "Dr. King to March in Memphis Again," *New York Times*, March 30, 1969, 31; Max Frankel, "President Offers U.S. Aid to Cities in Curbing Riots," *New York Times*, March 30, 1969 1, 30; "Mini-Riot in Memphis . . . ," *New York Times*, March 30, 1968, 32; Ben A. Franklin, "Dr. King Hints He'd Cancel March If Aid Is Offered," *New York Times*, April 1, 1968, 20; Dallek, *Flawed Giant*, 527–29.

21. Garrow, *King and the FBI*, 198.

22. "Hundreds of Negroes View Body of Youth in Memphis," *New York Times*, April 2, 1968, 14.

23. Beifuss, *At the River I Stand*, 267.

24. Earl Caldwell, "Court Bars March in Memphis; Dr. King Calls Order 'Illegal,'" *New York Times*, April 4, 1968, 30; Beifuss, 276–77;

25. "I've Been to the Mountain Top." See complete audio of speech at http://archives.ubalt.edu/bsr/articles/king%20speech.pdf.

26. Deuteronomy 34:1–8; Beifuss, *At the River I Stand*, 278–80.

27. Honey, *Going Down Jericho Road*, 416, 424.

28. Beifuss, *At the River I Stand*, 283–91.

29. Ben Branch, interview by Joan Beifuss, Tom Buckner, and Bill Thomas., August 15, 1968 in Memphis, #178,

Mississippi Valley Collection, University of Memphis, #41, CTN 20 Sanitation Strike Collection, Box 20, Folder 27; Gerold Frank, *An American Death: The True Story of the Assassination of Dr. Martin Luther King, Jr., and the Greatest Manhunt of Our Time* (Garden City: Doubleday, 1972), 67–71.

30. Earl Caldwell, "Guard Called Out," *New York Times,* April 5, 1968, 1, 24; Walter Rugaber, "Mrs. King Is Planning to Fly to Memphis Today," *New York Times,* April 5, 1968, 24; "Widespread Disorders," *New York Times,* April 5, 1968, 1, 26; "President's Plea," *New York Times,* April 5, 1968, 1, 24; Jack Gould, "TV: Networks React Quickly to King Murder," *New York Times,* April 5, 1968, 95.

31. Reverend James M. Lawson, Jr., interview by Joan Beifuss and David Yellin, Series 11, May 25, 1972 in Memphis, #317, Mississippi Valley Collection, University of Memphis, #41, Sanitation Strike Collection, Box 22, Folder 142, CTN 22, #178.

32. Burns, *Burial for a King,* 28.

33. Douglas Brinkley, *Rosa Parks* (New York: Lipper/Viking, 2000), 205.

34. Greg Kot, *I'll Take You There: Mavis Staples, the Staple Singers, and the March Up Freedom's Highway* (New York: Scribner, 2014), 124–25.

35. Robert Dixon, interview with the author, August 7, 2009, Chicago, transcript of tape recording, Institute for Oral History, Baylor University, Waco, 8.

36. Coretta King, *My Life with Martin Luther King, Jr.* (London: Hodder & Stoughton, 1970), 334–48; Honey, *Going Down Jericho Road,* 452–53; Beifuss, *At the River I Stand,* 116.

37. Coretta King, *My Life with Martin Luther King, Jr.*, 334–38.

38. Honey, *Going Down Jericho Road*, 465–69; Floyd McKissick, *Three-Fifths of a Man* (New York: Macmillan, 1969), 133–34.

39. R. W. Apple, "Kennedy Appeals for Nonviolence," *New York Times*, April 5,

1968, 33; Thurston Clarke, *The Last Campaign: Robert F. Kennedy and 82 Days That Inspired America* (Henry Holt, 2008), 96–98.

40. James Sullivan, *The Hardest Working Man: How James Brown Saved the Soul of America* (New York: Gotham Books, 2008), 85–103.

41. Burns, *Burial for a King,* 35.

42. Gladys McFadden, interview with the author, June 9, 2009, transcript of tape recording, Institute for Oral History, Baylor University, Waco, 10.

43. Max Frankel, "President Grave: Sets Day of Mourning for Dr. King—Meets Rights Leaders," *New York Times,* April 6, 1968, 1, 23; Ben A. Franklin, "Many Fires Set: White House Guard by G.I.'s—14 Dead in U.S. Outbreaks," *New York Times,* April 6, 1968, 1, 22; Nan Robertson, "Johnson Leads U.S. in Mourning," *New York Times,* April 6, 1968, 25; Walter Rugaber, "Dr. King's Funeral to Be Held Tuesday in Church Where He Was Co-Pastor," *New York Times,* April 6, 1968, 24.

44. Coretta King, *My Life with Martin Luther King, Jr.,* 338–39; Burns, *Burial for a King,* 89, 97, 103–5.

45. Michael Stern, "10,000 Here Join Tribute to King," *New York Times,* April 8, 1968, 1, 32; Earl Caldwell, "Mrs. King to March in Husband's Place in Memphis Today," *New York Times,* April 8, 1968, 1, 33; Goreau, *Just Mahalia, Baby,* 486–87; Beifuss, *At the River I Stand,* 338–39.

46. Beifuss, *At the River I Stand,* 339–43; Coretta King, *My Life with Martin Luther King, Jr.,* 340; J. Anthony Lukas, "Mrs. King Asks 'Peaceful Society' after Orderly Memphis March; Troops in Baltimore Reinforced," *New York Times,* April 9, 1968, 1, 34; Leon Dash and Paul Valentine, "A March for 'All People,'" *Washington Post,* April 9, 1968, 1, A10; Anthony Ripley, "50,000 Expected for Funeral of Dr. King in Atlanta Today," *New York Times,* April 9, 1968, 1, 34.

47. Ripley, "50,000 Expected for Funeral of Dr. King in Atlanta Today," 1, 34; Burns,

*Burial for a King,* 136–47; Coretta King, *My Life with Martin Luther King, Jr.,* 341–42.

48. Homer Bigart, "Leaders at Rites," *New York Times,* April 10, 1968, 1, 33; J. Anthony Lukas, "Atlanta Is Peaceful During the Funeral," *New York Times,* April 10, 1968, 1, 34; Burns, *Burial for a King,* 153–55; Nikhil Pal Singh, *Climbin' Jacob's Ladder: The Black Freedom Movement Writings of Jack O'Dell* (Berkeley: University of California Press, 2010), 164; Clarke, *The Last Campaign,* 131–33; John Kifner, "Followers Sing on Final March," *New York Times,* April 10, 1968, 33; Wayne Hampton, *Guerilla Minstrels: John Lennon, Joe Hill, Woody Guthrie, Bob Dylan* (Knoxville: University of Tennessee Press, 1986), 58; Coretta King, *My Life with Martin Luther King, Jr.,* 343.

49. Goreau, *Just Mahalia, Baby,* 488; Burns, *Burial for a King,* 157; Coretta King, *My Life with Martin Luther King, Jr.,* 343.

50. Beifuss, *At the River I Stand,* 343–44; Burns, *Burial for a King,* 158; Jack Gould, "TV: Memorable Viewing Experience," *New York Times,* April 10, 1968, 95.

51. Robert Dallek, *Flawed Giant: Lyndon Johnson and His Times, 1961–1973* (New York: Oxford University Press, 1998), 534; Burns, *Burial for a King,* 161, 181; Honey, *Going Down Jericho Road,* 489–93.

52. Vron Ware and Les Black, *Out of Whiteness: Color, Politics, and Culture* (Chicago: University of Chicago Press, 2002), 248.

53. Eileen Southern, *The Music of Black Americans* (New York: W. W. Norton, 1997), 491.

## Epilogue

1. For more on the Poor People's Campaign, see Charles Fager, *Uncertain Resurrection: The Poor People's Washington Campaign* (Grand Rapids: William B. Eerdmans Publishing, 1969); Gerald D. McKnight, *The Last Crusade: Martin Luther King, Jr., the FBI, and the Poor People's Campaig.* (New York: Westview Press, 1998); David King Dunaway, *How Can I Keep from Singing: The Ballad of Pete Seeger* (New York: Villard Books, 2008), 341–43.

2. Rabbi Everett Gendler and Rabbi Joshua Heschel, "Conversation with Martin Luther King," *Conservative Judaism* 22, no. 3 (Spring 1968): 1, 17–18; Burns, *Burial for a King,* 188; Fager, *Uncertain Resurrection,* 20, 39, 70–85, 116–17; McKnight, *The Last Crusade,* 84–85; Dunaway, *How Can I Keep from Singing,* 341–43.

3. Brenda Bretz, "The Poor People's Campaign: An Evolution of the Civil Rights Movement," *Sociological Viewpoints* (Spring 2010): 23–24.

4. Dunaway, *How Can I Keep from Singing,* 341–43; Bernice Johnson Reagon, "Songs That Moved the Movement," *Perspectives: The Civil Rights Quarterly* 15, no. 3 (Summer 1983): 35; Robert T. Chase, "Class Resurrection: The Poor People's Campaign of 1968 and Resurrection City," *Essays in History: The Annual Journal Produced by the Corcoran Department of History at the University of Virginia* (1998): 17–18; John Szwed, *Alan Lomax: The Man Who Recorded the World* (New York: Penguin Books, 2010), 362–63; Jimmy Collier, telephone interview with the author, October 14, 2009, transcript of tape recording, Institute for Oral History, Baylor University, Waco, 28–29.

5. Gladys McFadden, telephone interview with the author, June 9, 2009, transcript of tape recording, Institute for Oral History, Baylor University, Waco, 3–5.

6. Joe Ligon, interview with the author, May 26, 2009, transcript of tape recording, Institute for Oral History, Baylor University, Waco, 5–6.

7. Warren Weaver, Jr., "Kennedy Shot and Gravely Wounded After Winning California Primary; Suspect Seized in Los

Angeles Hotel," *New York Times,* June 5, 1968, 1, 32; Fred P. Graham, "Suspect in Assassination of Dr. King Is Seized in London," *New York Times,* June 9, 1968, 1, 74; Joseph Novitski, "Harlem's Anguish Eased by Arrest," *New York Times,* June 9, 1968, 1, 78; *Eyes on the Prize: America's Civil Rights Movement, 1954–1968.* From the episode "The Promised Land (1967–1968), directed by Callie Crossley and James A. DeVinney. *American Experience,* PBS, DVD, produced by Blackside, transcript page 186.

8. Ben A. Franklin, "Over 50,000 March in Capital in Support of the Poor," *New York Times,* June 20, 1968, 1, 30; Robert B. Semple, Jr., "Mood of the Marchers: Patience Worn Then and a Feeling This Is the Last Chance," *New York Times,* June 20, 1968, 31.

9. Earl Caldwell, "87 Poor in Capital Held in Protests," *New York Times,* June 21, 1968, 1, 24; "Tear Gas Is Used by Capital Police at Marcher's City," *New York Times,* June 23, 1968, 25; "Abernathy Firm as Permit Expires," *New York Times,* June 24, 1968, 1, 22; Ben A. Franklin, "Troops Ordered into Washington to Curb Outbreak," *New York Times,* June 25, 1968, 1, 29; Joseph A. Loftus, "City of the Poor Shuts Peacefully," *New York Times,* June 25, 1968, 29; Fager, *Uncertain Resurrection,* 116–17; McLaughlin, *The Long, Hot Summer of 1968,* 156–58; Ben A. Franklin, "Abernathy Gets 20-Day Jail Term; Capital Calmer," *New York Times,* June 26, 1968, 1, 30.

## Afterword

The epigraph for this chapter is drawn from David W. Stowe, *How Sweet the Sound: Music in the Spiritual Lives of Americans* (Cambridge: Harvard University Press, 2004), 264.

1. Caryle Murphy, "The Rise of the Rights Anthem; 'We Shall Overcome': The Song, the History," *Washington Post,* January 17, 1988, G1.

2. Freedom songs and protest spirituals are still sung both in the United States and abroad. I have drawn from a variety of sources for that information (with the location where the singing took place), a sampling of which are listed here: Branch, "Myths and Miracles from the King Years," (Gdansk, Poland, and Prague); Vincent Harding, *Hope and History: Why We Must Share the Story of the Movement* (Maryknoll: Orbis Books, 1999), 3–4, (Tiananmen Square, Beijing, and Leipzig, East Germany); Jon Platt, "'Ferguson October' Utilizes Social Media to Promote Action," *The Baylor Lariat,* October 11, 2014, 1 (Ferguson, Missouri); Noah Adams, "The Inspiring Force of 'We Shall Overcome,'" NPR, August 28, 2013, http://www.npr.org/2013/08/28/216482943/the-inspiring-force-of-we-shall-overcome (North Korea, Beirut, China, Soweto, South Africa); John Blake, "Freedom Riders Inspire New Generation of Arab Protest Leaders," CNN, May 15, 2011, http://www.cnn.com/2011/US/05/15/freedom.riders.arab, (Egypt); Monica Davey, "Amid Mourning for Michael Brown, Call for Change," *New York Times,* August 25, 2014, 1 (Ferguson); Lisa Leff, "Recent Police Demonstrations Inspire New Protest Songs," TwinCities.com, December 12, 2014, http://www.twincities.com/music/ci_27126100/recent-police-demonstrations-inspire-new-protest-songs (Ferguson and New York City); Jonathan Gatehouse, "Upstaging Hong Kong's Umbrella Revolution," *Macleans,* October 5, 2014, http://www.macleans.ca/news/world/upstaging-hong-kongs-umbrella-revolutionaries (Hong Kong). Additionally, Jim Forman writes that during the Vietnam War, Johnny Wilson, a member of the SNCC, was a guest at a conference in Prague attended by representatives of the National

Liberation Front and the government of the Democratic Republic of North Vietnam. According to Wilson, the representatives asked the Americans present to sing "We Shall Overcome," and said that they often sang it, for the song "gave them inspiration and hope." Cited in James Forman, *The Making of Black Revolutionaries* (Washington, DC: Open Hand Publishing, 1972), 513.

3. Taylor Branch, "Myths and Miracles from the King Years," Beall-Russell Lecture Series, Baylor University, October 29, 2007. Transcription by Noelle Davies, 8–9.

4. Ron Eyerman and Andrew Jamison, "Movement and Cultural Change," in *The Social Movements Reader: Cases and Concepts,* ed. Jeff Goodwin and James M. Jasper (Malden, MA: Blackwell, 2003), 368.

5. Donald Solomon, interview with the author, June 28, 2009, Birmingham, transcript of tape recording, Institute for Oral History, Baylor University, Waco, 24.

6. Jon Michael Spencer, *Protest & Praise: Sacred Music of Black Religion* (Minneapolis: Fortress Press, 1990), 104.

7. C. Eric Lincoln and Lawrence H. Mamiya, *The Black Church in the African American Experience* (Durham: Duke University Press, 1990), 372–73.

8. Kerran L. Sanger, *"When the Spirit Says Sing!" The Role of Freedom Songs in the Civil Rights Movement* (New York: Garland Publishing, 1995), 99.

9. Clay Evans, interview with Patty Nolan-Fitzgerald and Mary Pendergast, March 19, 2014, Chicago, tape recording. Transcription courtesy of Patty Nolan-Fitzgerald and the Reverend Clay Evans.

10. Wyatt T. Walker, *Somebody's Calling My Name!: Black Sacred Music and Social Change* (Valley Forge: Judson Press, 1979), 181.

11. Wyatt T. Walker, "Freedom's Song: The Soulful Journey of the Negro Spiritual," *Negro Digest* (July 1963): 86.

12. James 5:16 (AV). The more modern NRSV renders the same verse as "The prayer of the righteous is powerful and effective."

13. Dave Marsh and Daniel Wolff, "No Hiding Place," in *Da Capo Best Music Writing 2000*, guest editor Peter Guralnick; series editor Douglas Wolk (New York: Da Capo Press, 2000), 413–15.

14. J. Jefferson Cleveland and William B. McClain, "Preface," *Songs of Zion* (Nashville: Abingdon Press, 1981), ix.

15. Spencer, *Protest & Praise,* 103. One of the most frequently cited verses related to Jesus's views on violence is Matthew 26:51–53: "Suddenly, one of those with Jesus put his hand on his sword, drew it, and struck the slave of the high priest, cutting off his ear. Then Jesus said to him, 'put your sword back into its place; for all who take the sword will perish by the sword.'" See also John 18:10–11 and Luke 22:50–51, *The New Interpreter's Study Bible, New Revised Standard Version with the Apocrypha* (Nashville: Abingdon Press, 2003), 1795.

16. John Wesley Work, *Folk Song of the American Negro* (New York: Negro Universities Press, 1915), 37.

17. James Alex Taylor, interview with the author, June 30, 2009, Birmingham, transcript of tape recording, Institute for Oral History, Baylor University, Waco, 6. That said, as W. J. Hodge told Shuttlesworth biographer Andrew M. Manis: "When Martin marched, they weren't singing no Indian songs. They were singing black spirituals and it was out of that context that he preached." Andrew M. Manis, "A Fire You Can't Put Out: The Meanings of Fred Shuttlesworth and His Movement," in *Birmingham Revolutionaries: The Reverend Fred Shuttlesworth and the Alabama Christian Movement for Human Rights,* ed. Marjorie L. White and Andrew M. Manis (Macon: Mercer University Press, 2000), 55–56. But King, as the focal point of the

movement, *was* immersed in Gandhian nonviolence and, as his various biographers have shown, this concept shaped his worldview.

18. Henry Burton, Jr., interview with the author, July 7, 2009, Birmingham, transcript of tape recording, Institute for Oral History, Baylor University, Waco, 18–20.

19. Candi Staton, interview with the author, May 21, 2009, transcript of tape recording, Institute for Oral History, Baylor University, Waco, 6–7.

20. T. V. Reed, *The Art of Protest: Culture and Activism from the Civil Rights Movement to the Streets of Seattle* (Minneapolis: University of Minnesota Press, 2005), 14.

21. Eloise Ford Gaffney, interview with the author, July 3, 2009, Birmingham, transcript of tape recording, Institute for Oral History, Baylor University, Waco, 22.

22. George Lipsitz, *Midnight at the Barrelhouse: The Johnny Otis Story* (Minneapolis: University of Minnesota Press, 2010), 105.

23. Richard L. Madden, "New York Leads Songs of Protest," *New York Times,* April 29, 1968, 22.

24. Alex Dobkin, "Pages from Mississippi," cited in *Freedom Is a Constant Struggle: An Anthology of the Mississippi Civil Rights Movement*, ed. Susie Erenrich (Washington, DC: Cultural Center for Social Change, 1999), 195–99.

25. Ron Eyerman and Andrew Jamison, *Music and Social Movement: Mobilizing Traditions in the Twentieth Century* (Cambridge: Cambridge University Press, 1998), 35–36.

26. Julius Lester, "Freedom Songs in the North," *Broadside* 43 (March 30, 1964): 12.

27. Kerran L. Sanger, "Slave Resistance and Rhetorical Self-Definition: Spirituals as Strategy," *Western Journal of Communication* 59 (Summer 1995): 179–92. John Lovell, Jr., whose *Black Song: The Forge and the Flame* is the greatest single resource on the spirituals, suggested seven purposes for the spirituals: "1. To give the community a true, valid, use of song. 2. To keep the community invigorated. 3. To inspire the uninspired individual. 4. To enable the group to face its problems. 5. To comment on the slave situation. 6. To stir each member to personal solutions and to a sense of belonging in the midst of a confusing and terrifying world. 7. To provide a code of language for emergency use." Clearly, save for the seventh purpose, this list matches the stated uses of the freedom songs, many of which are based on the spirituals. John Lovell, Jr., *Black Song: The Forge and the Flame,* 2nd ed. (New York: Paragon House, 1986), 198. In his essay "Songs of Persuasion and Their Entrepreneurs," Serge Denisoff breaks down all protest songs into even more categories. See Serge Denisoff, *Sing a Song of Social Significance* (Bowling Green: Bowling Green University Press, 1972), 2–3.

28. Gaffney interview, 16.

29. Vincent Harding, "Community as a Liberating Theme in Civil Rights History," in *New Directions in Civil Rights Studies,* ed. Armstead L. Robinson and Patricia Sullivan (Charlottesville: University Press of Virginia, 1991), 21.

30. J. E. Johnson, "The Gospel of Bessie Griffin," *Wavelength* (January 1982): 27.

31. Jimmy Collier, interview with the author, October 14, 2009, transcript of tape recording, Institute for Oral History, Baylor University, Waco, 28–29.

32. Reuben Burton, interview with the author, August 8, 2009, Chicago, transcript of tape recording, Institute for Oral History, Baylor University, Waco, 16.

33. Cleopatra Kennedy, interview with the author, July 10, 2009, Birmingham, transcript of tape recording, Institute for Oral History, Baylor University, Waco, 28–29.

34. John Lawrence, interview with the author, June 20, 2009, Birmingham,

transcript of tape recording, Institute for Oral History, Baylor University, Waco, 8, 11.

35. Roscoe Robinson, interview with the author, June 30, 2009, Birmingham, transcript of tape recording, Institute for Oral History, Baylor University, Waco, 38.

36. Eddie Jackson, interview with the author, June 26, 2009, Shreveport, transcript of tape recording, Institute for Oral History, Baylor University, Waco, 10.

37. Maceo Woods, interview with the author, August 11, 2009, Chicago, transcript of tape recording, Institute for Oral History, Baylor University, Waco, 25.

38. Dick W. Simpson, interview with the author, November 24, 2009, transcript of tape recording, Institute for Oral History, Baylor University, Waco, 4.

39. Robinson and Sullivan, *New Directions in Civil Rights Studies*, 22.

40. Rachel Harding and Vincent Harding, "Singing to Freedom," *Sojourners* 33, no. 8 (August 2004): 34.

41. Barry Leon Taylor, interview with the author, June 30, 2009, Birmingham, transcript of tape recording, Institute for Oral History, Baylor University, Waco, 14.

42. William R. Beardslee, *The Way Out Must Lead In: Life Histories in the Civil Rights Movement* (Wesport: Lawrence Hill, 1983), 60.

43. Ann Lee, interview with the author, February 22, 2010, transcript of tape recording, Institute for Oral History, Baylor University, Waco, 7, 17.

44. Hermene Hartman, interview with the author, September 19, 2009, transcript of tape recording, Institute for Oral History, Baylor University, Waco, 9.

45. Rosephanye Powell, interview with the author, July 22, 2009, transcript of tape recording, Institute for Oral History, Baylor University, Waco, 18.

46. Jacques Attali, *Noise: The Political Economy of Music* (Minneapolis: University of Minnesota Press, 1985), 11. Translated by Brian Massumi from the 1977 French edition of *Bruits: essai sur l'economie politique de la musique* by Jacques Attali.

47. Courtney Pace Lyons, *"Freedom Faith": The Civil Rights Journey of Dr. Prathia Hall* (PhD diss., Baylor University, 2014), 73. Excerpted from an interview by Meredith Woods, October 4, 1999, Film and Media Archive, Washington University, St. Louis, Missouri.

48. Bernice Johnson Reagon, "The Lined Hymn as a Song of Freedom," *Black Music Research Bulletin* 12, no. 1 (Spring 1990): 7.

49. Lovell, *Black Song,* 330.

50. Clarence B. Jones and Joe Engel, *What Would Martin Say?* (New York: Harper-Collins, 2008), 40–43.

51. Robert Darden, "Gospel's Got the Blues," *New York Times,* February 15, 2005, A19. I had just completed *People Get Ready: A New History of Black Gospel Music* (Continuum, 2004) and was frustrated that much of the music I was writing about was unavailable and had not been available for a long, long time. I wrote an editorial bemoaning the loss of this music—the foundation of most American popular music—and said that future generations would judge us harshly if we allowed it to disappear. The *New York Times* published the piece as an op-ed column on February 15, 2005. That morning, Charles Royce, a New York investor, offered to fund any effort to "save" the fast-vanishing vinyl legacy from gospel's "golden age" (roughly 1945 to 1970). I met with the Baylor University Libraries and we laid the groundwork for what became the world's largest initiative to identify, acquire, digitize, catalog, and—someday—make accessible this irreplaceable music. As loans and donations began arriving at the offices of what we had dubbed the Black Gospel Music Restoration Project, we were fascinated to notice how many of the

"B" or flip sides of gospel 45s contained messages related to the civil rights movement. "The Old Ship of Zion" was one of those 45s. Aquasco is barely a hamlet on the Patuxent River. The disk itself appears to be self-pressed, recorded circa 1970–72 at a studio in Arlington, Virginia. Only three copies have surfaced thus far. "The Old Ship of Zion" is both an adaptation of an old gospel hymn and a still older spiritual and was "associated with the culture of the 19th-century Underground Railroad." Bernice Johnson Reagon, *Give Your Hands to the Struggle,* Smithsonian Folkways, SFW 40049, 1997. From

liner notes by Bernice Johnson Reagon, 17. Originally released on Paredon Records (P-1028), 1975.

52. Mighty Wonders of Aquasco, Maryland, "Old Ship of Zion." John Stewart, Jr., soloist. Mark Custom Records, Box 3671, Arlington, Virginia 22203, MC-8991 A.

53. Zora Neale Hurston, "High John de Conquer," in *The Book of Negro Folklore,* ed. Langston Hughes and Arna Bontemps (New York: Dodd, Mead & Company, 1958), 93.

54. "High John de Conquer," Zora Neale Hurston, *American Mercury* (October 1943): 450–58.

# Index